Employment Outlook

June 1998

ORGANISATION FOR ECONOMIC CO-OPERATION AND DEVELOPMENT

The OECD Employment Outlook

provides an annual assessment of labour market developments and prospects in Member countries. Each issue contains an overall analysis of the latest market trends and short-term forecasts, and examines key labour market developments. Reference statistics are included.

The **OECD Employment Outlook** *is the joint work of members of the Directorate for Education, Employment, Labour and Social Affairs, and is published on the responsibility of the Secretary-General. The assessments of countries' labour market prospects do not necessarily correspond to those of the national authorities concerned.*

The Organisation for Economic Co-operation and Development (OECD)

was set up under a Convention signed in Paris on 14 December 1960, which provides that the OECD shall promote policies designed:

- *to achieve the highest sustainable economic growth and employment and a rising standard of living in Member countries while maintaining financial stability, and thus to contribute to the development of the world economy;*
- *to contribute to sound economic expansion in Member as well as non-member countries in the process of economic development; and*
- *to contribute to the expansion of world trade on a multilateral, non-discriminatory basis in accordance with international obligations.*

The original Member countries of the OECD are: Austria, Belgium, Canada, Denmark, France, Germany, Greece, Iceland, Ireland, Italy, Luxembourg, the Netherlands, Norway, Portugal, Spain, Sweden, Switzerland, Turkey, the United Kingdom and the United States. The following countries became Members subsequently through accession at the dates indicated hereafter: Japan (28 April 1964), Finland (28 January 1969), Australia (7 June 1971), New Zealand (29 May 1973), Mexico (18 May 1994), the Czech Republic (21 December 1995), Hungary (7 May 1996), Poland (22 November 1996) and Korea (12th December 1996). The Commission of the European Communities takes part in the work of the OECD (Article 13 of the OECD Convention).

Publié en français sous le titre :

PERSPECTIVES DE L'EMPLOI

Juin 1998

TABLE OF CONTENTS

Editorial

Chapter 1

RECENT LABOUR MARKET DEVELOPMENTS AND PROSPECTS

Chapter 2

MAKING THE MOST OF THE MINIMUM: STATUTORY MINIMUM WAGES, EMPLOYMENT AND POVERTY

Chapter 3

GETTING STARTED, SETTLING IN: THE TRANSITION FROM EDUCATION TO THE LABOUR MARKET

STATISTICAL ANNEX

LIST OF TABLES

LIST OF CHARTS

Towards an employment-centred social policy

Economic growth is not likely to produce big falls in OECD unemployment in the near future...

OECD area GDP grew by just over 3 per cent in 1997, its best performance since 1989, in spite of the Asian financial crisis. Growth is projected to average about 2½ per cent in 1998-1999, though prospects are very different across the regions. As a result, the unemployment rate is likely to fall only very slowly through 1999 to about 7 per cent, or more than 35 million job-seekers.

... so governments still assign a high priority to policies to increase employment...

Progress in tackling high unemployment has been quite mixed across countries. Over the 1990s, structural unemployment has declined in just six countries – Australia, Denmark, Ireland, the Netherlands, New Zealand and the United Kingdom. It has remained stable at a low level only in Norway, the United States and Japan, although in the latter, the unemployment rate has risen sharply recently and is of concern. Therefore, reducing unemployment and expanding job opportunities remain a high priority and will require a range of measures, including sound macro-economic policies – a message reinforced at the October 1997 meeting of OECD Labour Ministers. They, in particular, requested the OECD to assign a high priority to monitoring and evaluating alternative approaches to an employment-centred social policy to increase employment, and reduce welfare dependency and poverty. This topic is also being debated by OECD Social Policy Ministers on 23-24 June 1998.

... and want social protection measures, such as minimum wages and in-work benefits, to be part of the strategy to promote employment.

This editorial addresses the potential roles that minimum wages and employment-conditional benefits can play as part of an employment-centred social policy. The underlying premise is that social protection systems can alleviate family poverty, but they are insufficient for promoting wider participation in society unless they are closely tied to measures to promote labour market integration.

The benefits and costs of minimum wages need to be looked at objectively...

As shown in Chapter 2, statutory minimum wages currently exist in 17 Member countries and are slated to be introduced soon in two others (Ireland and the United Kingdom). In other countries, minimum wages are established by collective agreement and, hence, tend to vary by sector. Analysis of statutory minimum wages arouses strong passions on the part of both proponents and opponents and there is a wide range of theoretical and empirical results on their effects. In order to assess their potential contribution to an employment-oriented social policy, a dispassionate and ongoing assessment of their benefits and costs is required.

... including their effects on earnings inequality, poverty, incentives and employment levels...

In the context of concerns about growing earnings inequality and in-work poverty in a number of OECD countries, statutory minimum wages can play a role in preventing earnings from falling below socially acceptable levels. Indeed, their basic purpose is often presented as ensuring fair pay in the labour market and helping reduce in-work poverty. They may also increase incentives to enter the labour market and find work ("making work pay"). On the cost side of the ledger, they may give rise to disemployment effects.

... so we need to know which workers gain, the effect on inequality and poverty and whether jobs are lost.

Following a brief look at the level and coverage of minimum wages in OECD countries, three questions are addressed: Who are the workers most likely to be affected by a minimum wage? What is the impact of minimum wages on earnings inequality and family poverty? What is the evidence on the employment effects of minimum wages?

Minimum wages are set at very different levels across countries.

The level of statutory minimum wages varies greatly across countries, ranging from 20-33 per cent of the median earnings of full-time workers in the Czech Republic, Japan and Spain, to around 60 per cent in Belgium and France. Not surprisingly, the higher the level of the minimum wage relative to average or median earnings, the lower is the proportion of low-paid jobs in total employment (Chapter 2). In addition, higher minimum wages are also associated with less inequality in earnings between men and women, and younger workers compared with adults.

The main beneficiaries are young workers and women...

The beneficiaries of a minimum wage are low-wage workers. Youth and women are the groups most likely to be in minimum-wage jobs. And, as shown in the 1997 *Outlook*, it is particularly women and the less skilled who are most likely to be trapped in low-paying jobs, whereas for many youths they are often a stepping stone to better paying jobs.

... and lower-paid workers in higher-income families may also gain...

However, a criticism of a minimum wage is that it fails to "target" efficiently those workers in families who really need help. Instead, it also helps many workers in households with median incomes and above because many low-paid workers live in such households, while it fails to help households with no workers at all.

... indeed most full-time, low-paid workers are not in poor households...

There are large differences across countries in the *overlap* between low pay and low family incomes when all families, regardless of their work status, are considered. Around 20 per cent of full-time/full-year low-paid workers live in poor households in European Union countries, rising to almost 40 per cent in the United States. Thus, many poor people live in households with nobody in paid work: on average for the OECD as a whole, roughly 40 per cent of low-income individuals live in such households.

... so rises in minimum wages have low impact on overall poverty.

The fact that low-paid workers are not highly concentrated in poor households suggests that increases in statutory minimum wages, in most cases, are likely to have a limited impact in cutting overall family poverty rates. This distributional case for minimum wages is, therefore, weak. However, it should also be emphasized that weakening or reducing the generosity of the welfare system, especially in tandem with declines in minimum wages, could risk increasing the extent of in-work poverty.

On the cost side, minimum wages seem to have destroyed some teenagers' jobs, though accounting for only a fraction of all those lost, with no discernible impact for adults...

One of the strongest criticisms of minimum wages is that, to the extent they are set at above market-clearing levels, they will price some people with low productivity out of jobs. The large number of country-specific studies have yielded a range of empirical estimates. A few recent American studies suggest no employment impact, although the balance of the evidence suggests some adverse effects on youth unemployment. The evidence for nine countries provided in Chapter 2 suggests that higher minima adversely affect teenage employment: a 10 per cent increase in the minimum is associated with a 1½ to 3 per cent decline in teenage employment, the effects being essentially the same across countries regardless of whether they have high or low minimum wages. The evidence also shows that hikes in the minimum, on their own, can explain only a small fraction of the large observed falls in teenage employment rates over the past two decades in almost all countries. The cross-country evidence suggests that the minimum has no significant impact on overall adult employment.

... so a lower rate for young workers may be desirable.

Employment losses for young people lead naturally to the question of whether there should be flexibility in setting a separate minimum for young people. This is important because of the widespread desire to facilitate a better transition from education to the world of work. Indeed, as shown in Chapter 3, there are large cross-country differences in the proportion of new school leavers who find jobs quickly, with the highest likelihood in those countries where many youths go through apprenticeship programmes (*e.g.* Austria, Germany and Luxembourg). Young people undergoing apprenticeship training are usually paid a relatively low wage or allowance. Hence, it seems desirable in countries which have a minimum wage to apply a lower rate to young people, and a number of countries already do this.

Minimum wages are neither the solution to overall family poverty nor the general scourge on jobs that opposite sides proclaim...

The bottom line on statutory minimum wages is that both opponents and proponents have overstated their respective cases. If minimum wages are set carefully, they can improve the material well-being of some low-wage workers, have some positive impact on work incentives and limit the extent of earnings inequality which has widened significantly in some Member countries. But minimum wages are not *the* solution for family poverty and low family incomes, and they can give rise to job losses, especially for young people.

... and effects vary in different countries, some of which set higher minimum wages, coupled with cuts in payroll taxes and/or wage subsidies to help low-productivity workers find jobs, while others top up lower wages with in-work benefits.

The overall effectiveness of statutory minimum wages as part of an employment-centred social policy depends crucially on their interactions with tax/benefit systems and the size of any disemployment effects. The policy debate on the role of statutory minimum wages as part of an employment-centred social policy encompasses a range of views. Some continental European countries have opted for fairly high minimum wages coupled with payroll tax cuts and/or wage subsidies targeted on low-wage workers. Others support somewhat more modest minimum wages with employment-conditional benefits to top-up the incomes of families with low incomes, and view these two instruments as complementary. Finally, some doubt the complementarity of minimum wages and employment-conditional benefits on the basis that minimum wages may reduce employment and that employment-conditional benefits can more effectively achieve redistributional goals.

In-work benefits have the advantages of being targeted to needy families and protecting against temporary income falls...

There are two important positive features of a judiciously implemented policy of employment-conditional benefits. First, they are better targeted than a minimum wage to deal with in-work poverty among families. Second, in an era of high perceived job and earnings insecurity, they can act as a form of temporary earnings "insurance". One estimate of eligibility for the US earned income tax credit (EITC) suggested that, while in any single year only about 1 in 6 families are eligible for the EITC, over a ten-year period 2 in 5 families will have one or more years in which their wage income declines so much that they would become eligible.

... but they are costly, potentially allow employers to capture the benefit, and create poverty traps...

However, on their own, employment-conditional benefits are not a panacea. They can be quite costly to the public purse, much more so than a minimum wage which is "paid" for by firms and consumers rather than taxpayers. They have also been criticised on grounds of "moral hazard", *i.e.* the possibility that merely offering such "insurance" can change behaviour in undesirable ways. While they are intended to subsidise workers, they may end up subsidising employers. In the absence of an effective wage floor, this could come about either through the benefits having such a large supply effect that wages are driven down or through collusion between firms and workers to keep wages low knowing that the government will make up the difference. There is, however, little evidence that current schemes have had this effect. Means-tested benefits also create high effective marginal tax rates (poverty traps) where individuals have little incentive to work more hours or expend more effort.

... so minimum wages and in-work benefits need to be jointly set in order to produce the best results...

In short, policies on minimum wages or employment-conditional benefits should not be considered in isolation. Their strengths and weaknesses on distributional and efficiency criteria can be complementary. For this beneficial effect to occur, however, both have to be set jointly and be seen as part of an overall package for alleviating some work disincentives, and the unemployment and poverty traps which face many low-earning workers. The fact that complementarity of these two measures is dependent on setting them jointly, highlights the fact that their respective levels are crucial.

... taking into account the complex interaction between taxes, benefits and the wage distribution distinctive to each country.

While specifying "optimum" levels is difficult, as a rule the higher the minimum wage and the lower the earnings thresholds for entitlement to employment-conditional benefits, the less likely these two measures are to be complements. The difficulties facing countries in this domain are also mirrored in current policy stances. To simplify, the lower are minimum wages relative to average or median earnings and the more unequal the earnings distribution, the more likely are employment-conditional benefits to be used. The more compressed the earnings distribution, the more likely countries have been to use tax abatements or employer subsidies to stimulate hiring of less qualified workers, often also at a high budgetary cost. The bottom line is that the interactions between tax/benefit systems and minimum wages are complex, and designing the appropriate policy mix will depend greatly on individual country circumstances.

These social measures can be designed to help employment, but the long-term aim should be to enhance workers' market value rather than rely solely on social protection.

A well-designed policy package of economic measures, with an appropriately set minimum wage in tandem with in-work benefits, is likely, on balance, to be beneficial in moving towards an employment-centred social policy. Empirical work is scanty, but urgently needed on how to design such a package. Ideally, the objective must be to improve labour market conditions so that the "earnings insurance" implicit in statutory minimum wages and in-work benefits is less and less needed by unskilled workers. However, even a well-designed policy package would leave no room for complacency. First, it is not clear how effective the change in work incentives from such measures will be. Second, not all people will be able to take full advantage of such incentives and they must not be left out in the cold if social cohesion is to be more than a slogan. It is important that everyone who is able, be given the appropriate help to participate in the labour market through the provision of social and labour market services, help with child-care costs and the like.

Thus, the surest support to the well-being of the least advantaged is to invest in their productive potential.

The long-run well-being of individuals on the bottom rung of the economic ladder depends both on increasing their employment opportunities and raising their productivity. It is only by directing attention to the additional need to develop long-run policies to increase the skills and competences of the less skilled, and to encourage the businesses where they work to invest in this human capital, that further sustained progress on improving the standards of living of disadvantaged groups in OECD countries will be possible. The policy package outlined above should help to focus the debate on this crucial issue.

6 May 1998

CHAPTER I

Recent labour market developments and prospects

Special focus on patterns of employment and joblessness from a household perspective

A. INTRODUCTION

Several favourable forces have been operating on the global economy. Growth in the OECD area averaged 3.1 per cent in 1997, the best outcome since 1989, inflation continued to be subdued, and fiscal consolidation is on track nearly everywhere. Developments in the labour market partly reflect the improved macroeconomic conditions: unemployment in the OECD area as a whole declined slightly, from 7.5 per cent of the labour force in 1996 to 7.2 per cent this year, or some 35.4 million people. But the fall in unemployment was not universal: unemployment rates rose in 10 OECD countries. The outlook for 1998 and 1999 partly depends on the impact of the recent financial crisis in East Asia on the wider economy. The growth rate of OECD GDP is projected to moderate to around 2.4 per cent in both years. Unemployment in the OECD area is expected to stabilise at around 7 per cent of the labour force.

Section B provides an overview of these recent developments and prospects. Section C analyses the labour market and its developments over the past decade from the perspective of households. Although patterns and trends of employment, unemployment and inactivity are normally analysed at the individual level, it is also very helpful to analyse them from a household perspective. Many labour supply decisions are best understood within a framework that treats households, rather than individuals, as the basic decision unit. Furthermore, a focus on households is probably more appropriate for making judgements about welfare, as the economic well-being of individuals may depend largely on the degree of support they receive from other members of their households.

Special attention is paid in Section C to patterns of non-employment, *i.e.* the proportion of the working-age household population with nobody in paid work. Non-employment is important for the following reasons: first, it is often regarded as a broader indicator of labour market slack than the unemployment rate, as the latter does not take account of differences in participation that are only

partly voluntary; second, when considered at the level of households, non-employment is an indication of potential welfare problems, since there is no income from paid employment to support that household's living standards. After taking account of trends in household population structures, the analysis shows how employment and non-employment are distributed across households, highlighting how many households have nobody in employment. The analysis also looks at the relationship between an individual's position in the income distribution and the labour market status of his or her household, again with a particular focus on joblessness. The final section summarises the main findings of the chapter.

B. RECENT DEVELOPMENTS AND PROSPECTS

1. Economic activity

Economic conditions improved in 1997. In the OECD area GDP is estimated to have risen by 3.1 per cent (Table 1.1), the best outcome since 1989. At close to 4 per cent, growth was particularly buoyant in the United States and Canada, reflecting strong domestic demand. Economic growth also strengthened in the European Union, where real GDP grew by 2.6 per cent compared with 1.7 per cent in 1996. Activity picked up in Spain and started to gather pace in France and Germany; there was continued strong growth in the United Kingdom and some other smaller countries (Denmark, Finland, Ireland, the Netherlands and Portugal). Most emerging market economies in Europe also enjoyed a good year: growth continued to be strong in Poland and accelerated in Hungary following the slowdown in 1995-1996. In the Czech Republic, on the other hand, growth slowed sharply, as financial market pressures forced an exchange rate depreciation. Mexico continued its strong recovery following the recent crisis.

Japan and Korea are the two major exceptions to this picture of stronger output growth in 1997. Growth slowed in Japan, with domestic demand

Table 1.1. **Growth of real GDP in OECD countries**[a, b]

Annual percentage change

	Share in total OECD GDP 1991	Average 1985-1995	1996	1997	Projections	
					1998	1999
Australia	1.7	3.0	3.7	2.7	3.2	3.2
Austria	0.8	2.6	1.6	2.1	2.7	2.9
Belgium	1.0	2.1	1.5	2.7	2.7	2.8
Canada	3.2	2.2	1.2	3.8	3.3	3.0
Czech Republic	0.6	..	3.9	1.0	0.9	1.2
Denmark	0.6	1.7	3.5	3.4	3.0	2.8
Finland	0.5	1.4	3.6	5.9	4.2	3.0
France	6.2	2.1	1.5	2.4	2.9	2.8
Germany[c]	8.1	1.4	1.4	2.2	2.7	2.9
Greece	0.6	1.6	2.7	3.5	3.0	3.4
Hungary	0.4	..	1.3	3.8	4.3	4.6
Iceland	0.0	1.9	5.5	5.0	4.6	3.4
Ireland	0.3	5.0	7.7	10.5	8.6	6.6
Italy	5.8	2.0	0.7	1.5	2.4	2.7
Japan	14.1	3.0	3.9	0.9	−0.3	1.3
Korea	2.4	8.7	7.1	5.5	−0.2	4.0
Luxembourg	0.1	5.9	3.0	3.7	3.4	3.5
Mexico	3.0	1.2	5.2	7.0	5.3	4.9
Netherlands	1.5	2.6	3.3	3.3	3.7	3.2
New Zealand	0.3	1.6	2.7	2.8	3.1	3.4
Norway	0.5	2.6	5.3	3.5	4.1	3.0
Poland	1.0	..	6.1	6.9	5.8	5.6
Portugal	0.6	3.2	3.0	3.5	3.8	3.2
Spain	3.0	2.9	2.3	3.4	3.5	3.3
Sweden	0.9	1.4	1.3	1.8	2.6	2.4
Switzerland	0.9	1.3	−0.2	0.7	1.5	1.8
Turkey	1.6	4.4	7.2	6.3	5.5	5.0
United Kingdom	5.4	2.3	2.2	3.3	1.7	1.8
United States	35.2	2.4	2.8	3.8	2.7	2.1
OECD Europe[d]	**40.2**	**2.1**	**2.1**	**2.8**	**2.9**	**2.9**
EU	**35.2**	**2.0**	**1.7**	**2.6**	**2.7**	**2.7**
Total OECD[d]	**100.0**	**2.5**	**2.8**	**3.1**	**2.4**	**2.5**

.. Data not available.

a) The OECD Secretariat's projection methods and underlying statistical concepts and sources are described in detail in "Sources and Methods: OECD Economic Outlook" which can be downloaded from the OECD Internet site (http://www.oecd.org/eco/out/source.htm).
b) Aggregates are computed on the basis of 1991 GDP weights expressed in 1991 purchasing power parities.
c) The average growth rate has been calculated by chaining on data for the whole of Germany to the corresponding data for western Germany prior to 1992.
d) Average for 1985-1995 excludes the Czech Republic, Hungary and Poland.
Source: OECD Economic Outlook, No. 63, May 1998.

being unexpectedly weak in the aftermath of moves to tighten fiscal policy. The emergence of financial turbulence in Southeast Asia during the middle of the year exacerbated the weakness of the Japanese economy and seriously affected the capacity of the Korean economy to grow in line with its potential.

A number of favourable factors lie behind the gradual improvement of the macroeconomic situation in the OECD area. Government budget deficits fell for the fourth year running, to reach an average level around 1.4 per cent of GDP. Favourable inflation trends almost everywhere have allowed monetary policy to provide an offset to the restraining effect on economic activity exercised by fiscal retrenchment in most countries. The broadly favour-

able movements in exchange rates between OECD countries which, since early 1995, have tended to support economies where activity has been weak and to restrain demand and activity in countries which appear to be close to capacity limits, have largely been maintained. In particular, the continued strength of the dollar and sterling has probably helped offset any emerging wage pressures in the United Kingdom and the United States, whilst the weakness of currencies in continental Europe has provided some stimulus to external demand.

These favourable forces are expected to persist over the 1998-1999 projection period. Inflation is likely to remain subdued across nearly all of the

OECD area, although it may show a modest upward trend in the United States and some European countries. An easing in the speed of fiscal retrenchment is expected for 1998 which should reduce the restraining effect on demand. However, in Japan, despite some easing, fiscal policy remains oriented towards deficit reduction, and in Korea new spending obligations, especially linked to the restructuring of banks, are likely to be offset by a tightening of fiscal policy. The Asian crisis is projected to have little overall macroeconomic impact in most OECD countries, although a slowdown in world trade growth is expected. Mature expansions should proceed at sustainable non-inflationary rates, but more slowly than in 1997 in countries where growth has been running at above-trend rates and spare capacity has largely been eliminated, notably the United States, the United Kingdom, Canada and some smaller European countries. In the prospective Euro area, recoveries that are in relatively early stages should be strong enough to absorb spare capacity: growth should rise to close to 3 per cent in Germany and France, and pick up gradually in Italy to 2.7 per cent by 1999. Growth is also expected to remain strong in Hungary, Mexico, Poland and Turkey, while remaining sluggish in the Czech Republic. Australia and New Zealand are expected to record somewhat stronger growth at around 3 per cent, despite their exposure to the Asian crisis. The short-term outlook for Japan and Korea, on the other hand, is poor. Output is likely to fall slightly in 1998, and the two economies may only return to a modest growth path in 1999. Against this background, average growth in the OECD area as a whole is expected to slow down at around 2½ per cent over the projection period.

2. Employment and unemployment

Employment increased by 1.7 per cent in 1997 for the OECD as a whole, the best result since 1993 (Table 1.2). Above-average employment gains were recorded in Canada, Mexico, Spain, Turkey, the United States and some smaller European countries. Germany and Sweden recorded losses of 1 per cent or over.

The growth of the OECD labour force, on average, was slightly slower than that of employment (Table 1.2). As a result, OECD area unemployment declined slightly in 1997 to 7.2 per cent of the labour force, or some 35.4 million persons (Table 1.3). Unemployment rates fell in some high-unemployment countries, including Finland, Ireland, Poland and Spain. Denmark, Hungary, Mexico, the Netherlands, Norway and the United Kingdom also experienced sizeable declines. By contrast, unemployment increased by more than one point in

Germany, and substantial increases were also recorded in the Czech Republic, Korea, New Zealand and Switzerland.

Unemployment in the OECD area is expected to stabilise over the projection period, remaining around 7 per cent of the labour force. Further declines are projected for the European Union, as employment should rise more strongly than at any time since 1990. Nonetheless, unemployment in the European Union, at over 10 per cent of the labour force in 1999, will remain a serious economic and social problem. Sizeable reductions in the unemployment rate are also anticipated in Australia, Canada, Hungary, Norway, Poland, and Switzerland. In the United Kingdom and the United States, the projected slowdown in economic activity may lead to a mild reversal of the downward trend in the unemployment rate. Larger rises in unemployment are expected in those countries where the growth outlook is poor, notably the Czech Republic, Korea and, to a lesser extent, Japan.

3. Wages and unit labour costs

Wage growth, as measured by growth in compensation per employee in the business sector, picked up slightly in 1997 (Table 1.4), in spite of a further deceleration in inflation. When "high-inflation countries" (i.e. the Czech Republic, Greece, Hungary and Poland) are excluded, the growth rate for employee compensation was 3.6 per cent in 1997, up from 2.9 per cent in 1996. Despite the slight pick-up, the growth rate of wages in 1997 was still below the average annual rate of 4.1 per cent for the period 1985-1995.

Reflecting modest wage increases and a slowdown in productivity, unit labour costs grew at a somewhat faster pace in 1997 than in 1996 (Table 1.4). Excluding the high-inflation countries, area-wide unit labour costs grew by 1.8 per cent, as against 1.2 per cent in 1996. There are signs that the labour market is beginning to tighten in Denmark, the Netherlands, Norway, the United Kingdom and the United States, as growth of both compensation per employee and unit labour costs picked up in these countries.

In the OECD area as a whole, growth in compensation per employee in the business sector is expected to fall back slightly to around 3 per cent over the projection period. A slight acceleration in wage inflation in some countries – Denmark, Finland, Ireland, the Netherlands and the United Kingdom – should be more than offset by wage moderation in the other countries. As the slowdown in productivity growth is projected to continue throughout 1998 and 1999, the deceleration in unit

Table 1.2. **Employment and labour force growth in OECD countries**[a]

Annual percentage change

	Employment						Labour force					
	Level 1996 (000s)	Average 1985-1995	1996	1997	Projections 1998	Projections 1999	Level 1996 (000s)	Average 1985-1995	1996	1997	Projections 1998	Projections 1999
Australia	8 385	2.0	1.3	0.8	1.7	1.8	9 166	2.1	1.3	0.9	1.1	1.4
Austria	3 416	0.7	-0.7	0.3	0.5	0.8	3 646	0.9	-0.2	0.2	0.4	0.6
Belgium	3 710	0.4	0.4	0.3	1.0	0.9	4 255	0.4	0.1	0.2	0.6	0.4
Canada	13 676	1.4	1.3	1.9	2.2	1.8	15 149	1.3	1.5	1.3	1.5	1.5
Czech Republic	5 110	..	0.4	-0.7	-1.1	-0.9	5 294	..	0.8	0.3	0.3	-0.1
Denmark	2 598	0.1	1.3	2.3	1.9	1.7	2 844	0.2	-0.4	1.2	0.8	1.1
Finland	2 096	-1.6	1.4	3.2	2.6	1.9	2 503	-0.3	0.2	1.0	0.2	0.2
France	22 448	0.3	0.0	0.3	1.1	1.3	25 594	0.5	0.8	0.4	0.5	0.5
Germany[b]	34 460	0.5	-1.2	-1.3	0.1	0.8	38 425	0.5	-0.2	-0.1	0.2	0.3
Greece	3 872	0.6	1.3	1.2	1.0	1.2	4 318	0.9	1.6	1.3	1.2	1.2
Hungary	3 605	..	-0.5	-0.1	0.8	1.1	4 006	..	-0.8	-1.5	-0.2	0.6
Iceland	127	0.3	2.1	2.1	1.8	1.3	133	0.7	1.5	1.6	1.4	1.2
Ireland	1 317	1.5	3.4	4.2	3.6	3.5	1 494	0.9	3.1	2.3	2.6	2.2
Italy	20 088	-0.3	0.4	0.0	0.3	0.5	22 851	0.1	0.5	0.2	0.0	0.2
Japan	64 863	1.1	0.5	1.1	-0.1	0.2	67 111	1.1	0.7	1.1	0.0	0.3
Korea	20 763	3.1	1.9	1.5	-3.2	-0.6	21 188	2.9	1.9	2.0	0.1	0.0
Luxembourg	168	1.0	0.8	1.6	1.6	1.5	174	1.1	1.2	2.0	1.6	1.4
Mexico	15 491	..	5.0	13.3	3.2	2.8	16 392	..	4.1	11.3	2.8	2.8
Netherlands	6 187	1.8	2.0	2.5	1.9	1.9	6 628	1.6	1.5	1.4	1.4	1.5
New Zealand	1 688	0.5	3.4	0.5	0.7	1.5	1 798	0.8	3.2	1.2	0.8	1.2
Norway	2 137	0.3	2.8	2.9	1.8	1.0	2 246	0.6	2.7	2.1	1.0	0.7
Poland	14 969	..	1.2	1.4	1.5	1.6	17 076	..	0.0	0.1	0.3	0.7
Portugal	4 217	0.3	0.5	1.9	1.6	1.2	4 550	0.2	0.6	1.3	1.1	0.9
Spain	12 408	0.9	1.5	2.9	2.6	2.4	15 950	1.2	0.9	1.1	1.0	1.0
Sweden	3 956	-0.6	-0.9	-1.0	0.6	0.7	4 302	-0.1	-0.5	-1.1	-0.8	0.2
Switzerland	3 807	1.2	0.3	-0.2	0.2	0.7	3 978	1.6	0.8	0.3	-0.4	0.3
Turkey	20 895	2.0	2.4	2.4	2.1	2.0	22 236	1.9	1.5	2.0	2.0	2.0
United Kingdom	26 455	0.6	1.1	1.7	0.5	0.0	28 753	0.3	0.4	0.5	0.4	0.4
United States	126 708	1.5	1.4	2.2	1.5	0.8	133 938	1.4	1.2	1.8	1.4	1.1
OECD Europe[c]	**20 895**	**0.6**	**0.6**	**0.8**	**1.0**	**1.1**	**221 255**	**0.6**	**0.5**	**0.5**	**0.6**	**0.7**
EU	**26 455**	**0.4**	**0.3**	**0.6**	**0.9**	**0.9**	**166 286**	**0.5**	**0.5**	**0.4**	**0.5**	**0.5**
Total OECD[d]	**126 708**	**1.1**	**1.1**	**1.7**	**0.9**	**0.9**	**485 997**	**1.1**	**1.0**	**1.4**	**0.8**	**0.8**

.. Data not available.

a) See note a) to Table 1.1.
b) The average growth rate has been calculated by chaining on data for the whole of Germany to the corresponding data for western Germany prior to 1992.
c) Averages for 1985-1995 exclude the Czech Republic, Hungary and Poland.
d) Averages for 1985-1995 exclude the Czech Republic, Hungary, Mexico and Poland.
Source: OECD Economic Outlook, No. 63, May 1998.

Table 1.3. **Unemployment in OECD countries**[a]

	Percentage of labour force			Projections		Millions			Projections	
	Average 1985-1995	1996	1997	1998	1999	Average 1985-1995	1996	1997	1998	1999
Australia	8.5	8.5	8.6	8.1	7.7	0.7	0.8	0.8	0.8	0.7
Austria	5.1	6.3	6.2	6.1	5.9	0.2	0.2	0.2	0.2	0.2
Belgium	11.1	12.8	12.7	12.3	11.9	0.5	0.5	0.5	0.5	0.5
Canada	9.6	9.7	9.2	8.6	8.3	1.4	1.5	1.4	1.3	1.3
Czech Republic	..	3.5	4.4	5.8	6.6	..	0.2	0.2	0.3	0.3
Denmark	9.7	8.6	7.6	6.7	6.2	0.3	0.2	0.2	0.2	0.2
Finland	9.2	16.3	14.5	12.4	11.0	0.2	0.4	0.4	0.3	0.3
France	10.4	12.3	12.4	11.9	11.3	2.6	3.1	3.2	3.1	2.9
Germany[b]	7.8	10.3	11.4	11.5	11.1	2.7	4.0	4.4	4.4	4.3
Greece	8.2	10.3	10.4	10.6	10.6	0.3	0.4	0.5	0.5	0.5
Hungary	..	10.0	8.7	7.8	7.3	..	0.4	0.3	0.3	0.3
Iceland	2.3	4.4	3.9	3.5	3.4	0.0	0.0	0.0	0.0	0.0
Ireland	15.2	11.9	10.2	9.3	8.2	0.2	0.2	0.2	0.1	0.1
Italy	10.0	12.1	12.3	12.0	11.8	2.3	2.8	2.8	2.7	2.7
Japan	2.5	3.4	3.4	3.5	3.6	1.6	2.2	2.3	2.4	2.4
Korea	2.8	2.0	2.6	5.7	6.3	0.5	0.4	0.6	1.2	1.4
Luxembourg	1.8	3.3	3.6	3.6	3.5	0.0	0.0	0.0	0.0	0.0
Mexico	..	5.5	3.7	3.4	3.4	..	0.9	0.7	0.6	0.6
Netherlands	7.1	6.7	5.6	5.1	4.8	0.4	0.4	0.4	0.3	0.3
New Zealand	7.0	6.1	6.7	6.7	6.4	0.1	0.1	0.1	0.1	0.1
Norway	4.3	4.9	4.1	3.3	3.0	0.1	0.1	0.1	0.1	0.1
Poland	..	12.3	11.2	10.1	9.3	..	2.1	1.9	1.7	1.6
Portugal	6.2	7.3	6.7	6.3	6.0	0.3	0.3	0.3	0.3	0.3
Spain	19.5	22.2	20.8	19.6	18.4	3.0	3.5	3.4	3.2	3.0
Sweden	4.0	8.1	8.0	6.7	6.2	0.2	0.3	0.3	0.3	0.3
Switzerland	1.9	4.7	5.2	4.5	4.1	0.1	0.2	0.2	0.2	0.1
Turkey	7.9	6.0	5.7	5.6	5.6	1.6	1.3	1.3	1.3	1.3
United Kingdom	9.1	8.0	6.9	6.8	7.2	2.6	2.3	2.0	2.0	2.1
United States	6.3	5.4	4.9	4.8	5.0	7.9	7.2	6.7	6.7	7.0
OECD Europe[c]	**9.4**	**10.5**	**10.2**	**9.9**	**9.5**	**17.4**	**23.2**	**22.8**	**22.1**	**21.5**
EU	**9.9**	**11.4**	**11.2**	**10.9**	**10.5**	**15.6**	**18.9**	**18.7**	**18.2**	**17.7**
Total OECD[d]	**7.1**	**7.5**	**7.2**	**7.1**	**7.0**	**29.6**	**36.4**	**35.4**	**35.2**	**35.1**

.. Data not available.
Notes and source: See Table 1.2.

Table 1.4. **Business sector labour costs in OECD countries**[a, b]

Percentage changes from previous period

	Compensation per employee			Projections		Unit labour costs			Projections	
	Average 1985-1995	1996	1997	1998	1999	Average 1985-1995	1996	1997	1998	1999
Australia	4.8	5.2	4.3	4.4	4.4	3.8	2.8	1.7	2.8	3.0
Austria	4.8	2.0	2.0	2.2	2.7	2.4	-0.6	0.0	-0.2	0.5
Belgium	4.3	1.0	2.7	2.5	2.6	2.6	0.1	0.1	0.8	0.6
Canada	3.9	3.6	4.4	1.9	3.1	3.1	3.8	2.5	0.8	1.8
Czech Republic	..	17.0	12.2	11.9	10.2	..	12.8	10.2	9.4	7.7
Denmark	5.0	3.6	4.0	4.3	4.7	3.2	0.8	2.5	2.8	3.2
Finland	6.7	2.9	1.7	3.4	2.8	2.6	-0.2	-2.2	1.5	1.3
France	3.7	2.8	3.3	2.3	2.4	1.5	0.9	0.8	0.4	0.8
Germany[c]	0.0	2.4	2.2	1.8	1.9	0.0	-0.4	-1.5	-1.0	-0.3
Greece	14.4	10.9	9.5	6.7	5.5	13.3	9.1	6.7	4.4	3.1
Hungary	..	19.0	20.0	18.3	16.0	..	16.8	15.4	14.3	12.0
Ireland	4.8	3.5	4.9	6.0	5.9	0.9	-0.8	-1.3	0.9	2.8
Italy	6.8	4.3	4.4	3.2	2.8	4.1	3.8	2.5	0.8	0.2
Japan	2.5	0.5	1.8	0.2	0.7	0.5	-2.9	1.9	0.5	-0.4
Korea	13.3	9.9	8.2	-1.1	2.0	7.0	4.3	3.8	-4.3	-2.7
Netherlands	2.5	2.1	2.5	2.7	3.6	1.3	0.8	1.4	1.1	2.3
New Zealand	6.0	2.4	2.9	3.1	2.9	4.7	3.0	0.9	0.5	0.9
Norway	5.4	3.0	4.8	5.0	5.8	3.6	2.4	3.9	3.4	5.0
Poland	..	26.7	20.5	14.6	13.3	..	20.2	14.3	10.0	9.1
Portugal	12.6	5.5	6.0	4.1	4.0	8.9	2.4	4.1	1.6	1.7
Spain	6.6	3.6	3.1	3.0	3.5	4.2	2.6	2.7	2.0	2.6
Sweden	6.8	6.2	3.6	4.1	4.0	4.4	4.0	0.5	1.7	2.1
Switzerland	3.6	0.7	0.5	0.7	1.2	3.5	1.3	-0.4	-0.7	0.0
United Kingdom	6.1	3.3	4.9	5.4	4.8	4.6	2.5	3.4	4.0	2.8
United States	3.8	3.0	4.2	3.8	3.9	3.1	2.0	2.3	3.0	2.7
OECD Europe[d, e]	**4.2**	**4.2**	**4.2**	**3.6**	**3.5**	**2.7**	**2.4**	**1.8**	**1.5**	**1.5**
EU[e]	**4.4**	**3.3**	**3.5**	**3.1**	**3.1**	**2.8**	**1.6**	**1.2**	**1.0**	**1.1**
Total OECD *less* high inflation countries[e, f]	**4.1**	**2.9**	**3.6**	**2.8**	**3.0**	**2.6**	**1.2**	**1.8**	**1.6**	**1.4**
Total OECD[d, e]	**4.0**	**3.3**	**3.9**	**3.0**	**3.2**	**2.7**	**1.6**	**2.1**	**1.8**	**1.6**

.. Data not available.
a) See note a) to Table 1.1.
b) Aggregates are computed on the basis of 1991 GDP weights expressed in 1991 purchasing power parities.
c) The average growth rate has been calculated by chaining on data for the whole of Germany to the corresponding data for western Germany prior to 1992.
d) Averages for 1985-1995 exclude the Czech Republic, Hungary and Poland.
e) Countries shown.
f) High inflation countries are defined as countries which have had, on average, 10 per cent or more inflation in terms of the GDP deflator during the 1990s. Consequently, the Czech Republic, Greece, Hungary and Poland are excluded from the aggregate.

Source: OECD *Economic Outlook,* No. 63, May 1998.

labour costs is expected to be less pronounced, at 1.6 per cent in 1998 and 1.4 per cent in 1999.

C. PATTERNS OF EMPLOYMENT AND JOBLESSNESS: A HOUSEHOLD PERSPECTIVE

1. Introduction

Patterns and trends of employment, unemployment and inactivity are normally analysed only at the individual level, aggregated up to the whole economy, and used as measures of overall labour market performance. Clearly, however, labour supply decisions of individuals are not made independently of their household situation, and, from a social welfare perspective, the analysis of the labour force status of individuals only offers a partial picture, as the economic well-being of individuals may depend largely on the degree of support they receive from other members in their households. As a consequence, there has been growing interest recently in analysing how labour market activity affects households and families [Gregg and Wadsworth (1994, 1996); OECD (1995a)].[1] This section takes up the household perspective, with special attention paid to jobless households, *i.e.* those with nobody in work [see Annex 1.A for definitions and data sources].

The analysis focuses on non-employment for two main reasons. First, the non-employment rate, which is calculated as the sum of the unemployed and the inactive divided by the population of working age, can be considered as a broader indicator of under-utilisation of labour resources than the unemployment rate, as it takes account of differences in participation that are only partly voluntary. In particular, it takes account of those who may have been discouraged from searching for work and are thus not counted as unemployed under the standard definition, but instead, as being out of the labour force. However, many of them also state that they would like a job if one were available. But not all non-employment reflects under-utilisation of labour resources. Women who are not in paid employment may be producing valuable services in the form of household work and the caring of children or elderly relatives. Young people may be investing in their own human capital in the form of education and training. Many older people may have chosen voluntarily to retire from the labour market.

The examination of non-employment patterns becomes even more important from the household perspective. The absence of any income from paid work coming into a household is an indicator of potential welfare problems for the household in

question. It often implies the need for income support from the social protection system.[2] Different labour market and social policies come into play if a substantial proportion of the unemployed and the inactive are living in households with no other adults in employment. However, just as with non-employment at the individual level, so-called "jobless" households must not always be considered as a policy problem. Some households consist only of students, or of persons aged between 55 and 64 years who may enjoy a reasonable standard of living due to retirement benefits and other non-work income.

At the same time, the presence of some work in the household is not always sufficient to protect its members from the risk of low income. The number of adults working in the household, the total amount of hours worked and the level of earnings are important factors in accounting for the economic well being of household members. The final sub-section of this chapter offers a brief overview of these factors, by looking at the relationship between the position of individuals in the income distribution and the labour market status of their households. A distinction is drawn between jobless households, households with some work, and households with someone in full-time work throughout the year (also see Chapter 2).

Due to the complex links between the factors determining the economic well-being of households and their members, a detailed examination of the policy implications of joblessness at the household level is well beyond the scope of this chapter. The analysis is descriptive in nature and addresses the following questions: How are employment and non-employment distributed across working-age households? Has this distribution changed over the past decade? What are the characteristics of those working-age households where nobody is employed? To what extent do demographic and social factors explain the labour force status of household members? Finally, to what extent is joblessness at the household level a cause of concern for the economic well-being of household members?

To best answer these questions, the unit of observation should be the economic unit within which resources are held in common, and decision-making is done. For practical reasons, it is assumed here that, with few exceptions, the economic unit is the household, generally defined by two criteria: the sharing of the same dwelling; and common domestic arrangements. In terms of resource-pooling, however, the household may not always be the most appropriate unit of observation. Reality spans a range of possible levels of economic integration, from all resources being held in common to every individual in the household constituting a separate economic unit. Indeed, there remains much to learn about decision-making and allocation processes within the household: in general, economic integration is more likely to occur within a family unit whose members are linked by close kinship relations but, even then, particular groups, such as spouses or children not in the labour force, may have little control over the use of the household budget.

The employment profile of households is described on the basis of the number of adults in the household who are in employment, irrespective of their hours worked. The analysis is confined to the working-age population. Working-age households are defined as those that contain at least one person of working age (15 to 64 years old). The exceptions are Australia, the Czech Republic, Japan, Mexico, New Zealand and Switzerland where, due to data constraints, working-age households are defined as all households with a working-age head.

2. Non-employment at the individual and household level

The non-employment rate at the *individual* level is the sum of the inactive and the unemployed divided by the population of working age. Chart 1.1 provides background information on patterns and trends of non-employment disaggregated by gender, and between unemployment and inactivity. Non-employment rates differ considerably across countries: they are highest in Greece, Ireland, Italy, and Spain, and lowest in Japan, New Zealand, Switzerland and the United States. Within countries, non-employment rates for women are always higher than for men. The right-hand side of the chart shows that one common trend across all OECD countries has been the continued rise in participation, and usually employment, rates for women that, in many cases, more than "compensated" for the decline in participation rates for men and/or a rise in the aggregate unemployment/population ratio. As a consequence, the employment rate for the working-age population increased or remained stable in many countries. The largest declines in non-employment and rises in employment over the period 1985-1996 were recorded in the Netherlands and Ireland, where gains in female participation were combined with substantial falls in the unemployment/population ratio. In France, Greece, Italy, New Zealand and Portugal, the rise in female participation rates did not fully offset the increase in the unemployment/population ratio, and the share of jobless persons in the working-age population increased.

The picture changes when taking a *household* perspective. Chart 1.2, Panel A, plots non-employment rates at the individual level against the household non-employment rate. Two features are striking. First, there is much less variation between countries if non-employment is measured across households rather than across individuals: 16 of the 22 countries shown are concentrated in a narrow band of household jobless rates between about 13 and 22 per cent, while individual non-employment rates range between 28 and 53 per cent. Below this band, the Czech Republic, Japan, Mexico and Switzerland have the lowest household jobless rates. Above it, Belgium and Finland record the highest rates. Second, although there is a positive correlation between non-employment rates for individuals and for households, the countries with the highest non-employment rates do not have the highest proportion of households without any work. For example, Greece, Ireland, Italy and Spain have the highest proportion of individuals in the working-age population not in work, but their household jobless rate is the same as in Germany, the Netherlands and New Zealand, and lower than in the United Kingdom, all countries where individual non-employment rates are lower.

These two features are explained by the fact that the risk for non-employed persons of living in jobless households varies across countries, and in general is lowest (highest) in countries where individual non-employment rates are highest (lowest), as shown more clearly in Chart 1.3. In southern European countries, Ireland, Luxembourg and Mexico, a relatively low proportion of the inactive population live in households without a person in employment, while in Finland and the United Kingdom, over 50 per cent of them do not share their dwelling with somebody in employment. The pattern is similar for those who are unemployed, except for Ireland, where the share of unemployed persons living in households with no other persons in employment is relatively high.

The results outlined above suggest that the phenomenon of non-employment requires careful interpretation when drawing conclusions about economic welfare. In Greece, Ireland, Italy and Spain, high non-employment rates for persons can probably be sustained because they have a lower impact on households, as many unemployed and inactive individuals share a dwelling with somebody in employment. However, it is likely that household formation and the composition of households are not exogenous to the economic environment and are, themselves, affected by individual risks of joblessness. Where extended families tend to live together, the family/household can play a crucial role in providing protection for all its members against adverse overall economic and labour market conditions.

Chart 1.1.

Non-employment rates for working-age individuals[a]

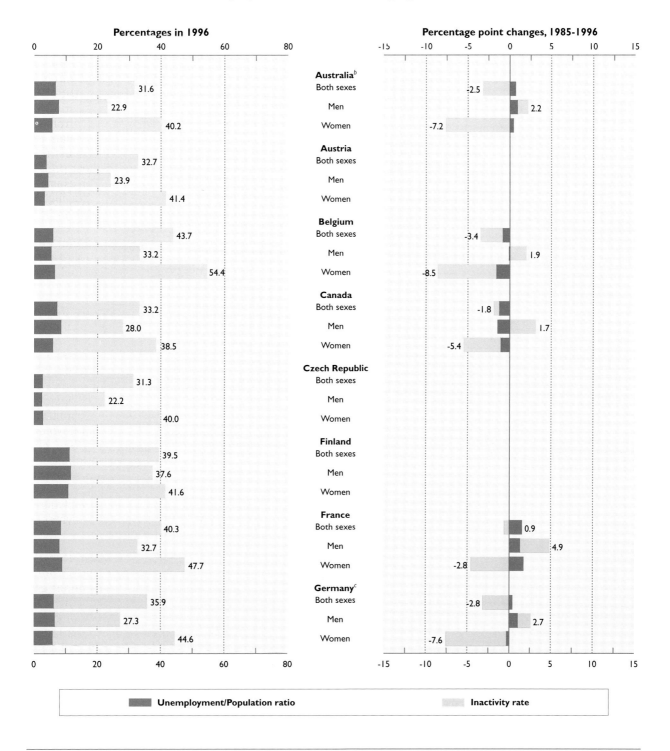

Percentages in 1996

Percentage point changes, 1985-1996

| | Unemployment/Population ratio | Inactivity rate |

a) Persons aged 15 to 64 years.
b) 1986 instead of 1985.
c) Data for Germany relate to the former western Germany for comparisons between 1985 and 1996, but refer to the whole of Germany for 1996 levels.
Source: See Annex 1.A.

Chart 1.1. *(cont.)*

Non-employment rates for working-age individuals[a]

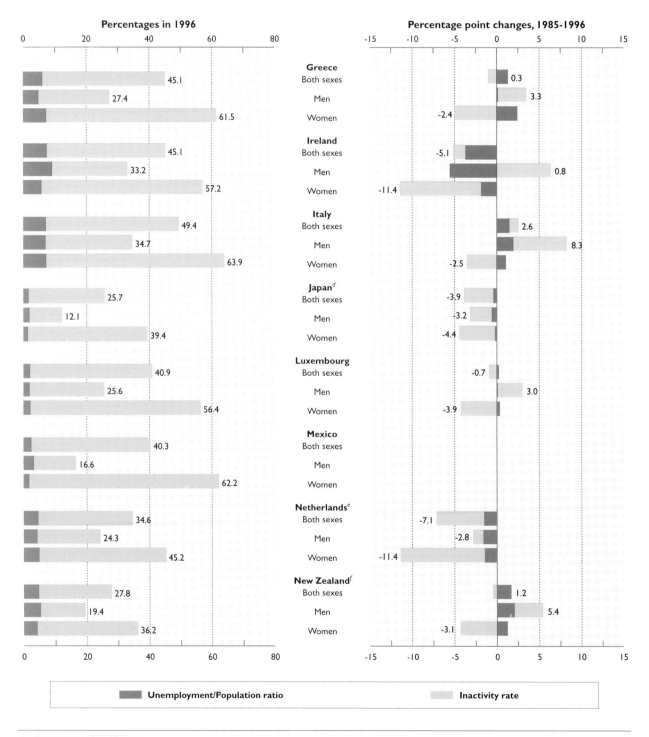

Percentages in 1996

Greece Both sexes	45.1
Men	27.4
Women	61.5
Ireland Both sexes	45.1
Men	33.2
Women	57.2
Italy Both sexes	49.4
Men	34.7
Women	63.9
Japan[d] Both sexes	25.7
Men	12.1
Women	39.4
Luxembourg Both sexes	40.9
Men	25.6
Women	56.4
Mexico Both sexes	40.3
Men	16.6
Women	62.2
Netherlands[e] Both sexes	34.6
Men	24.3
Women	45.2
New Zealand[f] Both sexes	27.8
Men	19.4
Women	36.2

Percentage point changes, 1985-1996

Greece Both sexes	0.3
Men	3.3
Women	-2.4
Ireland Both sexes	-5.1
Men	0.8
Women	-11.4
Italy Both sexes	2.6
Men	8.3
Women	-2.5
Japan[d] Both sexes	-3.9
Men	-3.2
Women	-4.4
Luxembourg Both sexes	-0.7
Men	3.0
Women	-3.9
Mexico Both sexes	
Men	
Women	
Netherlands[e] Both sexes	-7.1
Men	-2.8
Women	-11.4
New Zealand[f] Both sexes	1.2
Men	5.4
Women	-3.1

■ **Unemployment/Population ratio**   □ **Inactivity rate**

a)   Persons aged 15 to 64 years.
d)   1992 instead of 1996 and 1987 instead of 1985.
e)   1988 instead of 1985.
f)   1986 instead of 1985.
Source: See Annex 1.A.

Chart 1.1. *(cont.)*

Non-employment rates for working-age individuals[a]

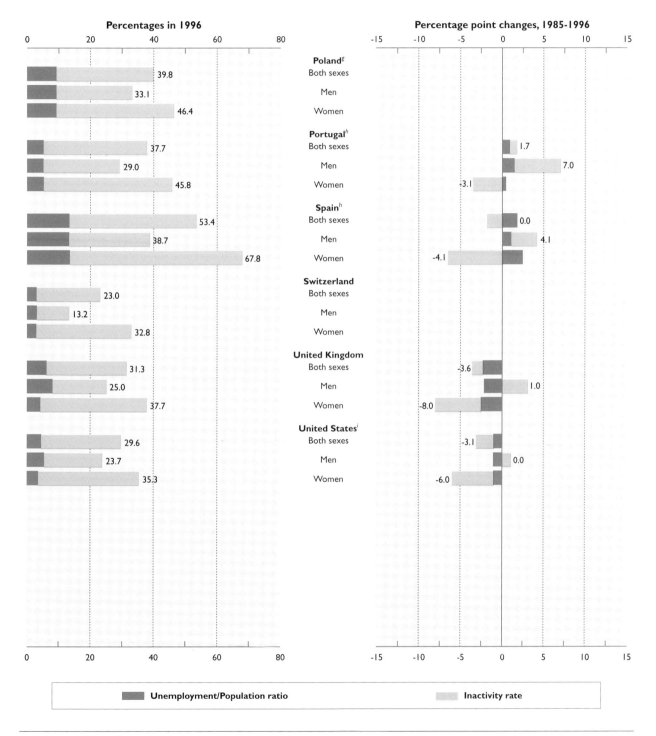

| | Unemployment/Population ratio | | Inactivity rate |

a) Persons aged 15 to 64 years.
g) 1995 instead of 1996.
h) 1988 instead of 1985.
i) 1986 instead of 1985.
Source: See Annex 1.A.

Chart 1.2.

Non-employment rates for working-age individuals and households[a]

Panel A.   Percentages in 1996[b]

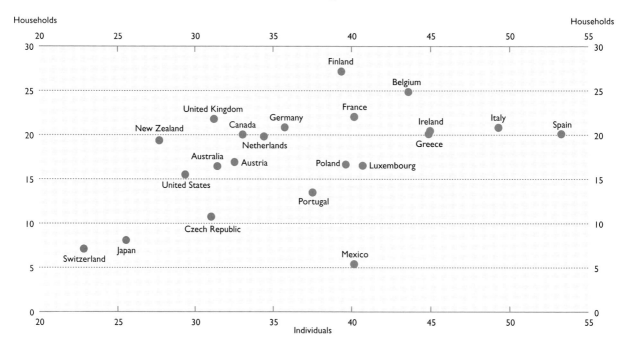

Panel B.   Percentage point changes, 1985-1996[c]

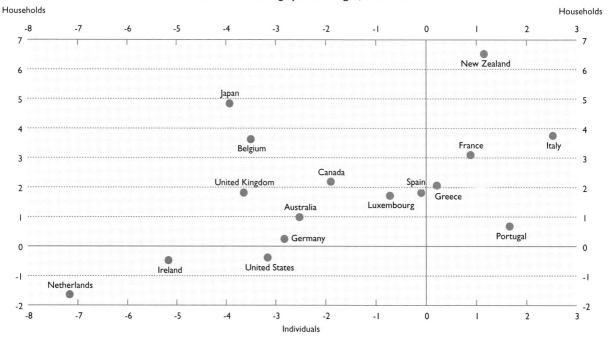

a)   Working-age households are defined as households where there is at least one adult member of working age, except for Australia, the Czech Republic, Japan, Mexico, New Zealand and Switzerland, where they are defined as households with a head of working age.

b)   Japan: 1992; Poland: 1995 for individuals.

c)   Australia, New Zealand and the United States: 1986-1996; Japan: 1987-1992; the Netherlands, Portugal and Spain: 1988-1996. Data for Germany relate to the former West Germany.

Source: See Annex 1.A.

Chart 1.3.

Risk of living in households with no other persons in employment for unemployed and inactive persons

As a percentage of all persons of working age[a] who are unemployed or inactive in 1996

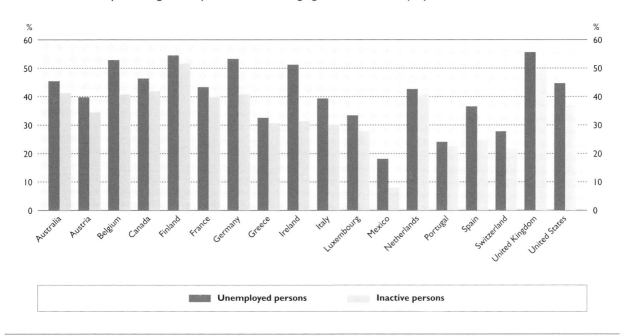

a) Persons aged 15 to 64 years.
Source: See Annex I.A.

Although the risk of living in jobless households for the non-employed population varies across countries, all show a similar variation between different groups (Table 1.5). Non-employed prime-age men and older persons are more likely to live in jobless households than are youth or prime-age women. In general, well over one-half of unemployed or inactive prime-age men live in households where nobody has work. Seen in a family context, this is consistent with previous findings that unemployed men are more likely to have non-employed spouses [for a summary discussion of empirical studies in this area, see OECD (1997a)]. For older persons, retirement is likely the main reason for non-employment. Their propensity to live in jobless households is partly due to the fact that they either live alone or they share their dwelling with other persons of their age, who are also likely to be retired. In all countries, unemployed youth and prime-age women are more likely to live in jobless households, compared with youth and women not in the labour force. For the latter, inactivity is likely dominated by attending education or caring for family responsibilities and may be contingent upon others in the household having paid work. It is worth

noting that the share of unemployed youth who live in workless households is, at over 40 per cent, highest in Finland, Ireland and the United Kingdom, and lowest in the southern European countries, Austria, Luxembourg, Mexico and Switzerland. In these latter countries, it is also true that a smaller proportion of unemployed and inactive prime-age women live in non-employed households.

How have individual and household jobless rates changed over time? As is evident in Chart 1.2, Panel B, there is a positive correlation between changes at the individual and changes at the household level.[3] Over the past decade, only in Ireland, the Netherlands and the United States has the rise in employment been strong enough to lead to a reduction in the incidence of non-employment at the household level. In other countries where employment rose, the jobs created were not sufficient to increase the number of households with someone in work and, in many cases, were not evenly distributed across households. In Belgium, Japan and the United Kingdom, the individual-based non-employment rate decreased more than in the United States, yet the household jobless rate increased. The largest increase in the household-

Table 1.5. **Risk of living in households with no other persons in employment for different groups of the non-employed population**[a]

As a percentage of the non-employed population in each age group in 1996, and percentage point changes between 1985 and 1996[b]

	All non-employed persons				Unemployed persons				Persons not in the labour force			
	Youth[c]	Prime-age men[c]	Prime-age women[c]	Older persons[c]	Youth[c]	Prime-age men[c]	Prime-age women[c]	Older persons[c]	Youth[c]	Prime-age men[c]	Prime-age women[c]	Older persons[c]
Australia												
Levels	25.9	60.2	34.1	63.6	29.4	60.8	44.9	60.1	24.5	59.6	32.4	63.8
Changes	4.5	0.9	9.8	0.8	-2.1	-1.5	9.1	-5.0	7.1	3.5	9.3	1.2
Austria												
Levels	14.2	47.4	22.3	58.4	20.5	45.9	41.5	50.6	13.5	48.5	19.5	58.6
Changes	..	..	..	..	..	..	..	..	..	..	..	..
Belgium												
Levels	18.0	70.0	32.3	70.8	38.2	71.4	44.3	74.2	16.0	68.9	29.2	70.7
Changes	3.5	8.0	13.5	3.9	11.9	6.0	21.5	11.4	3.5	10.1	11.3	3.8
Canada												
Levels	25.0	59.1	37.6	63.2	31.3	57.3	41.0	51.6	23.7	60.7	36.4	64.0
Changes	1.0	1.4	12.5	5.6	0.7	0.4	3.7	-7.1	1.8	2.0	13.2	6.6
Finland												
Levels	35.0	59.6	45.8	76.4	46.5	63.0	51.1	66.3	30.7	56.9	42.6	77.4
Changes	..	..	..	..	..	..	..	..	..	..	..	..
France												
Levels	21.8	58.1	28.4	72.7	29.1	58.1	37.2	61.5	20.7	58.1	24.3	73.1
Changes	4.1	1.1	8.8	2.4	4.3	1.5	6.6	-1.8	5.0	0.4	6.9	2.6
Germany												
Levels	18.5	60.0	26.1	68.9	43.3	62.9	41.6	63.2	16.0	57.2	22.1	69.4
Changes	3.1	0.2	9.1	-1.0	15.4	-1.3	9.6	-4.2	2.6	2.2	8.4	-0.7
Greece												
Levels	19.3	53.5	18.6	58.3	21.3	53.4	29.5	55.4	19.0	53.6	16.8	58.4
Changes	0.3	-5.2	0.5	1.9	-1.8	-4.7	0.9	-7.9	0.6	-5.7	-0.5	2.1
Ireland												
Levels	26.9	61.0	26.9	50.6	42.4	61.2	42.9	61.9	24.7	60.7	24.6	50.0
Changes	4.8	-6.1	5.2	4.2	10.7	-8.3	2.7	5.4	5.9	0.3	4.8	4.5
Italy												
Levels	15.9	51.8	22.1	55.9	25.7	61.4	34.9	61.6	13.9	45.9	20.1	55.8
Changes	5.4	1.8	10.1	-1.5	8.1	9.2	11.5	3.6	5.4	-2.7	9.0	-1.6
Luxembourg												
Levels	7.9	44.0	14.4	62.1	—	—		—	—	44.8	13.3	62.1
Changes	1.8	5.9	5.8	2.9	—	—		—	—	8.1	5.1	2.8
Mexico												
Levels	5.9	29.1	7.2	19.6	8.5	34.6	15.5	30.5	5.7	24.8	7.0	19.3
Changes	..	..	..	..	..	..	..	..	..	..	..	..

Table 1.5. **Risk of living in households with no other persons in employment for different groups of the non-employed population**[a] (cont.)

As a percentage of the non-employed population in each age group in 1996, and percentage point changes between 1985 and 1996[b]

	All non-employed persons				Unemployed persons				Persons not in the labour force			
	Youth[c]	Prime-age men[c]	Prime-age women[c]	Older persons[c]	Youth[c]	Prime-age men[c]	Prime-age women[c]	Older persons[c]	Youth[c]	Prime-age men[c]	Prime-age women[c]	Older persons[c]
Netherlands												
Levels	23.2	64.1	23.8	70.3	30.7	65.2	31.3	64.3	21.8	63.6	22.6	70.4
Changes	*-0.5*	*-0.8*	*3.3*	*3.7*	*-6.7*	*-9.1*	*-2.8*	*-10.1*	*0.7*	*6.6*	*4.2*	*4.0*
Portugal												
Levels	10.3	32.2	17.7	46.5	16.0	31.0	22.1	43.5	9.6	33.1	16.7	46.6
Changes	*1.0*	*-5.7*	*3.7*	*1.5*	*3.7*	*-3.1*	*5.0*	*-0.6*	*1.0*	*-6.5*	*3.1*	*1.6*
Spain												
Levels	15.5	51.2	19.9	49.5	25.2	52.5	30.6	50.1	12.8	48.5	16.2	49.4
Changes	*0.9*	*-1.3*	*4.8*	*2.0*	*2.6*	*-2.9*	*1.1*	*-1.2*	*1.5*	*1.5*	*3.4*	*2.2*
Switzerland												
Levels	6.6	33.7	11.5	56.4	16.1	33.0	22.1	50.8	5.7	34.5	10.1	56.8
Changes	..	..	..	..	..	..	..	..	..	..	..	..
United Kingdom												
Levels	33.1	66.1	45.4	66.9	41.6	67.1	51.7	61.1	30.8	65.1	44.4	67.4
Changes	*4.6*	*1.6*	*19.3*	*4.5*	*5.4*	*0.9*	*20.3*	*3.7*	*5.6*	*4.2*	*19.4*	*4.5*
United States												
Levels	21.9	58.9	34.0	59.9	29.4	54.8	48.0	58.3	20.6	61.2	32.2	60.0
Changes	*0.0*	*4.6*	*6.2*	*1.2*	*-1.5*	*3.6*	*4.0*	*0.3*	*0.7*	*4.0*	*6.7*	*1.3*
EU[d]												
Levels	**20.0**	**55.3**	**26.4**	**62.1**	**31.7**	**57.8**	**38.2**	**59.5**	**19.1**	**54.2**	**24.0**	**62.3**
Changes	***2.6***	***0.0***	***7.6***	***2.2***	***5.4***	***-1.2***	***7.6***	***-0.2***	***3.2***	***1.7***	***6.8***	***2.4***
OECD[d]												
Levels	**18.2**	**50.5**	**24.6**	**56.3**	**27.5**	**51.9**	**35.0**	**53.6**	**17.2**	**49.8**	**22.7**	**56.5**
Changes	***2.5***	***0.5***	***8.0***	***2.3***	***3.9***	***-0.7***	***7.2***	***-1.0***	***3.2***	***2.0***	***7.5***	***2.5***

.. Data not available.
— Data are not shown because they may be associated with relatively large sampling errors.
a) Persons aged 15 to 64 years old
b) Australia and the United States: 1986-1996; and the Netherlands, Portugal and Spain: 1988-1996. Data for Germany relate to the former West Germany for comparisons between 1985 and 1996, but refer to the whole of Germany for 1996 levels.
c) Youth: 15 to 24 years of age; prime-age persons: 25 to 54 years of age; older persons: 55 to 64 years of age.
d) Unweighted average for above countries and years only.
Source: See Annex 1.A.

based jobless rate was recorded in New Zealand, where the individual non-employment rate also increased.

Although non-employment (employment) rates for women declined (increased) most everywhere, the burden of increases in joblessness at the household level has fallen mainly on prime-age women in most countries. In the United Kingdom, for example, the risk for prime-age women to live in households with no adults in employment increased by more than 19 percentage points (Table 1.5).

3. Trends and patterns of joblessness across households

The overall household jobless rate, and its changes, are the combined result of the mix of household types, the non-employment rate within each household type, and changes in both.

Table 1.6 shows the household population structure in 1996 and its changes over the past decade. Six types of households are distinguished, on the basis of the number of adults living in the household (one, two, three or more), and the presence, or not, of children aged less than 15 years. In Canada, Finland and the United States, more than one-third of all working-age households contain only one adult, while in southern European countries, Ireland and Mexico, households with two or more adults represent more than 80 per cent of all working-age households. Children are more likely to be found in households with two adult members. The share of single-adult households in total households with children is highest in the United Kingdom and the United States.[4] Presence of children is less common when there are at least three adult members in the household.[5]

The proportion of households comprised of single adults has increased everywhere: on average, such households accounted for over 20 per cent of all OECD households of working age in 1996, an increase of 4.5 percentage points over their share in 1985. Two-adult households without children have generally seen their share in the total number of households increase, although by little. By contrast, the share of childless households with three or more adults increased only in southern European countries and Ireland. In general, single-adult households with children have increased, while the opposite pattern was recorded for two-adult households with children. The highest increase in the share of single-adult households with children was recorded in the United Kingdom.

Not surprisingly, the risk of joblessness in a household decreases with the number of adults present. As shown in Table 1.7, the *incidence* of non-

employment is highest among single-adult households, either with or without children,[6] except in Austria and Luxembourg, where it is highest in childless households with two adult members. More than one-half of single-adult households with children are without employment in Australia, Belgium, Ireland, the Netherlands, and the United Kingdom. Over time, the incidence of non-employment among adults living alone has declined everywhere except in Canada, France, Ireland and the United States. When there are children present, single-adult households have become more vulnerable to non-employment in Belgium, Canada, France, Luxembourg, Portugal and Spain.

Within multi-adult households, the presence of children is generally associated with a low incidence of joblessness. Over the past decade, non-employment rates for these households have been fairly stable, as the presence of more than one adult provides a buffer against adverse changes in the labour market. That said, in Italy, non-employment rates for two-adult households recorded a large increase, especially when there are children, while they declined substantially in Ireland.

The presence of young children is a critical element in the decisions of household members over the allocation of their time between market work and the nurturing and rearing of children. The decision will be influenced by the level of income available to households, either from work if another household member is in employment, or from social benefits and other sources, and by the quality and access to child-care facilities.[7] However, there is no simple causal relationship between the presence of children and the labour supply of household members, as the labour force status and earning capacity of the household certainly has a bearing on the decision to have children.

Considering Tables 1.6 and 1.7 together, the trends recorded in the United Kingdom stand out: the risk of non-employment within the two dominant household types has declined, but a sharp rise in the proportion of households with a high incidence of joblessness, *i.e.* single-adult households, caused the aggregate workless household rate to grow. This appears more clearly from Chart 1.4, showing the decomposition of changes in aggregate household non-employment rates into changes in the mix of household types and changes in non-employment rates within each. The results show that over the period 1985-1996, increases in joblessness at the household level are largely due to a shift towards household types with a relatively high incidence of joblessness, *i.e.* single-adult households. In Ireland, the Netherlands and the United States, however, this shift was more than offset by a reduction of the jobless rate *within* household types. In France and

Table 1.6. Working-age households[a] by type

Distribution in 1996, and percentage point changes between 1985 and 1996[b]

	Single-adult households without children	Single-adult households with children	Two-adult households without children	Two-adult households with children	Three or more-adult households without children	Three or more-adult households with children
Australia						
Levels	17.3	4.2	27.7	25.3	16.2	9.4
Changes	3.0	1.0	2.2	-3.2	-1.1	-1.9
Austria						
Levels	21.0	3.0	26.1	20.7	21.4	7.8
Changes	..	..	..	..	..	..
Belgium						
Levels	18.2	2.9	27.7	23.2	21.3	6.7
Changes	7.9	1.3	0.5	-5.4	-1.9	-2.3
Canada						
Levels	27.7	4.3	25.4	20.7	15.5	6.4
Changes	2.6	0.9	1.5	-2.5	-0.9	-1.6
Finland						
Levels	34.6	3.6	27.9	18.8	11.6	3.4
Changes	4.4	..	..	..	..	..
France						
Levels	22.2	3.3	27.8	23.5	15.6	7.6
Changes	4.4	0.7	0.4	-3.8	-0.9	-0.8
Germany						
Levels	26.9	2.8	30.3	19.5	15.0	5.5
Changes	4.4	0.6	0.6	0.8	-5.0	-1.4
Greece						
Levels	12.4	1.0	25.7	21.0	30.7	9.4
Changes	2.5	-0.1	3.4	-6.0	3.7	-3.5
Ireland						
Levels	14.0	3.1	21.0	24.0	23.0	14.8
Changes	3.2	1.6	2.5	-7.1	2.1	-2.3
Italy						
Levels	12.7	1.4	21.4	22.9	33.0	8.5
Changes	1.6	0.1	1.0	-5.7	5.8	-2.7
Luxembourg						
Levels	21.6	2.2	23.9	24.2	20.6	7.6
Changes	7.5	0.6	-2.3	0.3	-4.2	-1.8
Mexico						
Levels	4.3	3.0	8.6	37.6	13.3	33.3
Changes	..	..	..	..	..	..
Netherlands						
Levels	23.8	2.2	32.2	21.9	14.4	5.4
Changes	2.7	0.0	4.2	-2.1	-3.5	-1.3
Portugal						
Levels	7.5	1.6	21.8	20.1	37.2	11.8
Changes	1.4	-0.1	0.3	-4.1	6.3	-3.7
Spain						
Levels	5.3	1.0	17.6	21.9	40.5	13.7
Changes	1.1	0.3	0.0	-3.1	6.1	-4.4
Switzerland						
Levels	25.5	2.0	27.6	23.2	15.9	5.8
Changes	..	..	..	..	..	..
United Kingdom						
Levels	20.0	6.4	30.1	22.5	14.9	6.1
Changes	6.9	3.5	-0.4	-2.9	-4.4	-2.6
United States						
Levels	31.3	6.8	22.1	20.3	10.9	8.6
Changes	3.6	1.1	-0.4	-1.4	-2.7	-0.3
EU[c]						
Levels	**18.5**	**2.7**	**25.7**	**21.9**	**23.0**	**8.3**
Changes	*4.0*	*0.8*	*0.9*	*-3.6*	*0.4*	*-2.4*
OECD[c]						
Levels	**19.2**	**3.0**	**24.7**	**22.9**	**20.6**	**9.5**
Changes	*3.8*	*0.8*	*1.0*	*-3.3*	*0.0*	*-2.2*

.. Data not available.

a) Working-age households are defined as households where there is at least one adult member of working age (15 to 64 years old), except for Australia, Mexico and Switzerland, where they are defined as households with a working-age head.

b) Australia and the United States: 1986-1996; and the Netherlands: 1988-1996. Data for Germany relate to the former West Germany for comparisons between 1985 and 1996, but refer to the whole of Germany for 1996 levels.

c) Unweighted average for above countries and years only.

Source: See Annex 1.A.

Table 1.7. Risk of non-employment for working-age households[a] by type and presence of children

As a percentage of households in each type in 1996, and percentage point changes between 1985 and 1996[b]

		Single-adult households without children	Single-adult households with children	Two-adult households without children	Two-adult households with children	Three or more-adult households without children	Three or more-adult households with children	All working-age households
Australia	Levels	32.6	57.1	15.8	9.4	5.5	6.6	16.3
	Changes	-0.9	-5.3	-2.3	1.6	0.2	-0.5	0.9
Austria	Levels	29.4	23.5	29.8	3.3	6.3	2.0	16.8
	Changes	:	:	:	:	:	:	:
Belgium	Levels	44.0	51.1	39.1	6.3	11.0	10.0	24.8
	Changes	-4.6	16.1	-0.4	0.9	-0.3	2.2	3.6
Canada	Levels	30.9	48.9	22.4	8.2	9.1	6.5	19.9
	Changes	1.0	2.9	1.5	0.2	1.0	0.7	2.2
Finland	Levels	42.1	41.8	28.9	7.2	11.8	5.6	27.1
	Changes	:	:	:	:	:	:	:
France	Levels	37.1	34.0	31.9	5.9	11.5	6.7	21.9
	Changes	3.4	5.2	0.2	1.6	1.0	0.6	3.1
Germany	Levels	31.8	38.0	28.1	5.5	8.0	4.6	20.7
	Changes	-5.6	-5.7	-1.6	1.3	2.3	2.5	0.2
Greece	Levels	46.9	35.4	35.9	3.1	11.9	4.2	20.1
	Changes	-1.9	-7.4	2.5	-2.1	-0.1	-1.2	2.0
Ireland	Levels	38.3	61.2	25.9	12.0	13.4	11.2	20.4
	Changes	0.6	-18.6	-3.6	-5.5	0.2	0.1	-0.5
Italy	Levels	41.4	28.9	38.9	6.6	13.9	6.7	20.7
	Changes	-3.0	-1.6	1.5	4.3	3.2	3.4	3.7
Luxembourg	Levels	25.5	29.7	31.4	2.1	10.1	1.8	16.4
	Changes	-1.2	7.7	-1.0	0.5	3.6	0.5	1.7
Mexico	Levels	20.6	33.6	10.0	2.8	3.6	1.5	5.2
	Changes	:	:	:	:	:	:	:
Netherlands	Levels	35.6	55.1	23.7	5.7	5.7	5.3	19.7
	Changes	-4.7	-13.7	-4.5	-1.4	-1.8	-1.1	-1.7
Portugal	Levels	42.0	25.2	29.2	2.5	7.2	1.8	13.3
	Changes	-1.3	1.8	-0.4	-0.7	0.4	-0.7	0.6
Spain	Levels	46.6	39.4	39.0	9.0	17.1	9.7	20.0
	Changes	-1.1	1.6	-1.5	0.8	1.5	2.3	1.8
Switzerland	Levels	15.5	17.1	6.9	1.7	2.0	1.1	7.0
	Changes	:	:	:	:	:	:	:
United Kingdom	Levels	35.8	60.8	21.5	10.7	7.9	8.5	21.6
	Changes	-6.4	-3.9	-2.3	-1.4	0.4	1.5	1.8
United States	Levels	22.4	34.1	16.4	5.7	7.1	5.7	15.4
	Changes	0.5	-7.5	-2.9	-1.1	0.3	-1.4	-0.4
EU[c]	Levels	38.2	40.3	31.0	6.2	10.5	6.0	20.3
	Changes	-2.3	-1.7	-1.0	-0.2	0.9	0.9	1.5
OECD[c]	Levels	34.4	39.7	26.4	6.0	9.1	5.5	18.2
	Changes	-1.8	-2.0	-1.1	-0.1	0.8	0.6	1.3

.. Data not available.
Notes and source: See Table 1.6.

Chart 1.4.

Decomposition of changes in household^a non-employment rates into changes in the mix of household types and changes in non-employment rates by household type^b
Percentage point changes

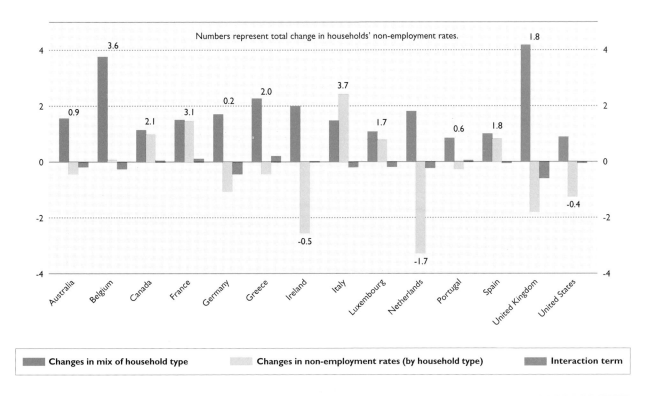

Changes in mix of household type   **Changes in non-employment rates (by household type)**   **Interaction term**

a)   Working-age households are defined as households where there is at least one adult member of working age, except for Australia, where they are defined as households with a working-age head.

b)   Changes between 1985 and 1996, except for Australia and the United States: 1986-1996; the Netherlands, Portugal and Spain: 1988-1996. Data for Germany relate to the former West Germany.

Changes in households' non-employment rates are decomposed using the following calculation:

$$\Delta N = \underset{j=1,6}{\Sigma(\Delta s_j)\, n_{jo}} + \underset{j=1,6}{\Sigma(\Delta n_j)\, s_{jo}} + \underset{j=1,6}{\Sigma\,(\Delta n_j)\,\Delta s_j}$$

where n_{jo} are households' non-employment rates by household type in the base year and s_{jo} the shares of each household type in total households in the base year. The first term, $\Sigma\,(\Delta\, s_j)\, n_{jo}$, represents the contribution of changes in the mix of household types in total changes of households' non-employment rates; the second term, $\Sigma\,(\Delta n_j)\, s_{jo}$, represents the contribution of changes in non-employment rates within each household type; and the third term, $\Sigma\,(\Delta n_j)\,\Delta s_j$, is the interaction between those two effects.

Source: See Annex 1.A.

Italy, the deterioration of employment patterns within each household type accounts for a large part of the rise in aggregate worklessness across households.

Table 1.8 outlines the *distribution*, rather than the incidence as in Table 1.7, of workless households by type and by the presence, or not, of children. In this case, workless households consist mainly of those without children, except in Mexico. In general, single adults dominate the non-employed household population in those countries where individual non-employment rates are lowest. In contrast, in the remaining countries, worklessness is largely concentrated in childless households with two adults. In all countries except Germany and Italy, the share of single-adult households in total jobless households increased.

4. Polarisation or dispersion of work across households?

So far, the analysis has concentrated exclusively on joblessness. As was noted in the introduction to

Table 1.8. **Non-employed households[a] by type and presence of children**

Distribution in 1996, and percentage point changes between 1985 and 1996[b]

		Single-adult households without children	Single-adult households with children	Two-adult households without children	Two-adult households with children	Three or more-adult households without children	Three or more-adult households with children
Australia	Levels	34.6	14.7	26.8	14.7	5.5	3.8
	Changes	3.5	1.6	-3.3	0.1	-0.5	-1.4
Austria	Levels	36.7	4.1	46.2	4.0	8.0	0.9
	Changes	..	..	..	..	..	..
Belgium	Levels	32.2	6.0	43.7	5.9	9.5	2.7
	Changes	8.7	3.3	-7.0	-1.4	-2.9	-0.6
Canada	Levels	43.1	10.5	28.6	8.5	7.1	2.1
	Changes	0.8	1.7	0.5	-2.0	-0.4	-0.5
Finland	Levels	53.8	5.6	29.9	5.0	5.0	0.7
	Changes	..	..	..	..	..	..
France	Levels	37.6	5.0	40.5	6.3	8.2	2.3
	Changes	5.8	1.2	-5.7	0.2	-1.0	-0.4
Germany	Levels	41.4	5.2	41.2	5.2	5.8	1.2
	Changes	-0.6	0.5	-2.0	1.4	0.2	0.5
Greece	Levels	28.9	1.7	46.0	3.3	18.2	2.0
	Changes	2.2	-0.8	4.7	-4.5	0.3	-1.9
Ireland	Levels	26.3	9.5	26.8	14.1	15.2	8.1
	Changes	6.8	3.6	0.5	-12.0	2.0	-1.0
Italy	Levels	25.4	2.0	40.3	7.4	22.2	2.8
	Changes	-3.7	-0.4	-4.8	3.3	5.0	0.5
Luxembourg	Levels	33.6	4.0	45.8	3.2	12.7	0.8
	Changes	8.0	1.6	-11.9	0.5	1.8	0.0
Mexico	Levels	18.4	21.2	17.9	21.9	10.0	10.6
	Changes	..	..	..	..	..	..
Netherlands	Levels	43.1	6.3	38.7	6.3	4.2	1.4
	Changes	3.3	-0.8	1.8	-1.7	-2.1	-0.6
Portugal	Levels	23.6	3.0	47.9	3.8	20.2	1.6
	Changes	2.7	-0.1	-2.4	-2.3	3.5	-1.4
Spain	Levels	12.4	1.9	34.5	9.9	34.7	6.6
	Changes	1.5	0.4	-4.8	-1.4	5.1	-0.7
Switzerland	Levels	56.7	5.0	27.2	5.5	4.7	0.9
	Changes	..	..	..	..	..	..
United Kingdom	Levels	33.1	18.1	29.8	11.1	5.4	2.4
	Changes	5.2	8.4	-6.7	-4.3	-1.9	-0.7
United States	Levels	45.6	15.1	23.6	7.5	5.1	3.2
	Changes	7.2	0.1	-3.8	-1.8	-0.8	-0.8
EU[c]	**Levels**	**32.9**	**5.6**	**39.3**	**6.6**	**13.0**	**2.6**
	Changes	**3.6**	**1.5**	**-3.5**	**-2.0**	**0.9**	**-0.6**
OECD[c]	**Levels**	**34.8**	**7.7**	**35.3**	**8.0**	**11.2**	**3.0**
	Changes	**3.7**	**1.4**	**-3.2**	**-1.8**	**0.6**	**-0.6**

.. Data not available
Notes and source: See Table 1.6

this section, the number of adults working in the household is one important determinant of the economic well-being of its members. The analysis that follows examines the distribution of work across multi-adult households and how it has changed over the past decade. In order to avoid the problem arising from cross-country differences in the demographic patterns and trends of the population aged 65 and over, the data presented in Table 1.9 only relate to those households where there are no persons of this age.

In all the countries for which data are available, households with at least two adults in employment dominate the household population. Only in Greece, Italy, Luxembourg and Spain, is the largest share of two-adult households represented by those where there is only one employed person.

Since 1985, the proportion of two-adult households where both adults work increased in all countries, and this increase is mainly accounted for by a decline in the share of households where only one adult is in work, although in Ireland, Luxembourg, the Netherlands, Spain and the United Kingdom, the share of two-adult households where nobody is in work also declined. Within households with at least three adult members, the share of those with at least two adults in employment increased everywhere except in Germany, Italy, Luxembourg and Portugal. With few exceptions, the share of households with only one adult employed decreased, while that of jobless households increased.

Looking at multi-adult households taken together, the picture shows a growing concentration of employment in the same households. In 9 of the 11 countries, there is some evidence of *polarisation of employment, i.e.* of a simultaneous increase in the proportion of both workless households and households with at least two adults in employment, coupled with a decline in the share of households with only one adult member in employment. In Greece, Luxembourg, Portugal, Spain and the United Kingdom, however, the growth of jobless households was negligible. Ireland and the Netherlands are the exceptions: the share of households with at least two members employed increased by more than 10 percentage points, while the share of jobless households decreased by more than one percentage point.[8]

Concentration of employment within the same households may be due to many factors. There may be common characteristics between household members (either observable or unobservable) which make it likely that they will be either all employed or non-employed. A correlation between the labour force status of household members may, therefore, reflect a tendency for individuals sharing common characteristics to live together in the same household. For example, household members are usually searching for jobs in the same local labour market and a depressed labour market will have some impact on all of them. Another potential common characteristic is educational attainment, as people with similar educational background may be more likely to form a household. Since persons with fewer educational qualifications typically experience higher unemployment and non-employment rates compared with more educated persons, households whose members all have a low level of educational attainment could be over-represented among workless households.[9] As the employment probabilities of the low skilled have deteriorated in many countries, the number of workless households may have increased as a consequence.[10]

Another force that could partly account for polarisation of the population into "work-rich" and "work-poor" households are the disincentive effects arising from the interactions of the tax and benefit systems, which may give rise to situations where, if one member of the household is on benefit, the other household members may have little incentive to work. To get out of this trap, all members of the household must find a job simultaneously. This problem is more likely to occur in countries with extensive means-testing of welfare benefits based on family resources.[11, 12]

5. Household joblessness and individual economic well-being

The risk and extent of economic distress for individuals without work depend on many factors. One is the degree of income sharing with other household members. This subsection looks at the relationship between an individual's position in the household income distribution and the labour market status of his or her household.

As the income data refer to annual amounts (except in Australia), the labour force status of households is redefined accordingly. Workless households are now defined as those where no adult member was in *paid* employment at any time during the year, whereas a working household is defined as one that had at least one adult member in paid employment at some time during the reference period. Also, a distinction is drawn between full-time/full-year employment and employment involving any number of hours at any time of the year. Comparisons are made across countries and, within countries, across different groups of households, for one point in time (mid-1990s).[13]

Table 1.9. **Labour force status of households with at least two adults of working age and nobody aged 65 and over**

Distribution by type in 1996, and percentage point changes between 1985 and 1996[a]

	All multi-adult households			Two-adult households			Three or more- adult households		
	Nobody employed	One adult employed	Two or more adults employed	Nobody employed	One adult employed	Both adults employed	Nobody employed	One adult employed	Two or more adults employed
Austria									
Levels	9.0	28.7	62.3	12.0	33.7	54.4	3.3	19.5	77.2
Changes	..	..	..	..	..	..	..	..	..
Belgium									
Levels	15.0	32.1	52.9	18.3	32.0	49.7	8.5	32.2	59.3
Changes	1.2	−9.3	8.1	1.5	−10.0	8.4	0.4	−8.1	7.7
Finland									
Levels	13.7	33.9	52.5	15.5	36.8	47.7	7.9	24.3	67.9
Changes	..	..	..	..	..	..	..	..	..
France									
Levels	12.1	33.6	54.3	14.3	35.5	50.2	7.0	29.4	63.6
Changes	1.0	−2.6	1.6	1.4	−2.8	1.4	0.1	−1.9	1.8
Germany									
Levels	11.5	33.1	55.4	14.0	36.8	49.2	5.1	23.7	71.2
Changes	1.7	−4.6	2.9	0.7	−7.7	7.0	2.1	−1.3	−0.7
Greece									
Levels	10.4	41.8	47.7	12.6	46.4	41.0	7.5	35.9	56.6
Changes	0.3	−5.8	5.5	1.2	−8.7	7.5	−0.5	0.1	0.4
Ireland									
Levels	13.4	35.2	51.3	14.6	39.5	45.9	11.9	29.7	58.3
Changes	−1.8	−13.0	14.8	−3.7	−18.8	22.5	1.5	−2.8	1.3
Italy									
Levels	12.5	43.5	44.0	14.9	46.2	38.9	9.8	40.3	49.9
Changes	3.7	−5.4	1.7	4.3	−8.2	3.8	3.5	−1.0	−2.4
Luxembourg									
Levels	8.8	44.4	46.9	11.1	46.9	42.0	4.2	39.2	56.6
Changes	0.3	−2.1	1.7	−0.6	−6.1	6.7	1.3	4.0	−5.3
Netherlands									
Levels	10.3	30.6	59.0	12.3	33.8	53.9	4.9	21.9	73.3
Changes	−1.2	−9.6	10.9	−1.7	−11.2	12.9	−1.4	−8.3	9.8
Portugal									
Levels	7.1	28.1	64.8	10.7	33.5	55.9	3.7	22.9	73.3
Changes	0.2	−2.7	2.5	0.8	−5.3	4.4	0.1	1.5	−1.6
Spain									
Levels	12.8	46.2	41.1	14.8	52.1	33.0	11.0	40.9	48.1
Changes	0.5	−5.4	4.8	−0.1	−8.1	8.2	1.5	−1.7	0.2
United Kingdom									
Levels	10.9	23.8	65.3	12.6	27.3	60.1	6.5	14.5	78.9
Changes	0.0	−7.1	7.1	−0.8	−11.1	12.0	0.8	−0.8	0.0
EU[b]									
Levels	**11.3**	**35.0**	**53.7**	**13.7**	**38.5**	**47.8**	**7.0**	**28.8**	**64.2**
Changes	**0.5**	**−6.1**	**5.6**	**0.3**	**−8.9**	**8.6**	**0.8**	**−1.9**	**1.0**

..   Data not avalaible.

a)   The Netherlands, Portugal and Spain: 1988-1996. Data for Germany relate to the former West Germany for comparisons between 1985 and 1996, but refer to the whole of Germany for 1996 levels.

b)   Unweighted average for above countries and years only.

Source: See Annex 1.A.

Table 1.10. **Risk of low income[a] for members of different types of households[b]**

As a percentage of working-age individuals belonging to households in each group

Individuals living in the following types of households	Australia 1995	Belgium 1993	Denmark 1993	Finland 1995	France 1993	Germany 1993	Greece 1993	Ireland 1993	Italy 1993	Luxembourg 1993	Netherlands 1993	Portugal 1993	Spain 1993	United Kingdom 1993	United States 1995	EU[f]	OECD[f]
Single-adult households, without work[c]	87.6	43.7	52.4	70.0	56.0	59.9	30.4	76.9	31.9	44.6	52.2	45.9	47.1	55.4	77.0	**49.7**	**55.4**
of which: without children	..	38.5	53.0	..	53.6	57.5	29.1	70.7	32.2	42.1	47.9	46.6	45.8	45.1	68.5	**46.8**	**42.0**
of which: with children	..	72.1	44.5	..	76.8	78.3	47.9	86.8	28.1	67.8	78.6	37.0	58.0	74.7	93.8	**62.6**	**56.3**
Single-adult households, some work during the year[d]	11.5	14.0	21.6	17.4	19.6	19.4	15.2	10.2	9.0	25.2	18.3	26.1	16.8	14.0	18.4	**17.4**	**17.1**
of which: single adult households in full-time, full year work[e]	..	7.3	10.1	..	9.0	11.7	7.9	7.4	4.9	21.3	8.8	18.4	9.1	5.9	8.5	**10.2**	**8.7**
Two or more- adult households, without work[c]	61.2	41.8	31.8	25.7	30.6	31.2	27.9	43.4	31.6	22.2	28.0	40.3	36.9	41.2	63.6	**33.9**	**37.2**
of which: without children	..	33.8	29.9	..	28.2	26.8	27.5	21.9	29.3	16.5	19.3	36.7	31.8	28.8	54.1	**27.5**	**25.6**
of which: with children	..	62.4	40.1	..	40.6	58.7	30.1	55.9	38.3	82.3	59.6	53.6	54.8	62.4	87.8	**53.2**	**48.4**
Two or more- adult households, some work during the year[d]	7.4	7.9	6.9	6.5	12.6	11.4	14.3	6.4	15.2	14.3	10.1	12.6	14.8	8.3	12.4	**11.2**	**10.7**
of which: at least two in full-time, full-year work[e]	..	3.3	2.8	..	3.5	3.9	3.4	0.6	5.2	6.3	1.4	7.2	3.3	4.0	3.3	**3.7**	**3.2**
All workless households[c]	71.1	42.2	43.8	45.0	36.8	40.4	28.3	48.9	31.6	26.6	35.1	41.0	37.6	45.5	67.9	**38.2**	**42.8**
of which: without children	..	34.9	44.1	..	34.9	36.8	27.8	33.9	29.8	21.5	28.2	38.2	32.9	33.8	53.4	**33.1**	**30.4**
of which: with children	..	63.7	41.7	..	45.8	64.2	31.6	59.2	37.8	79.2	63.6	52.8	54.9	65.9	89.9	**55.0**	**50.0**
All households with some work[d]	7.8	8.4	9.5	7.7	13.2	12.4	14.4	6.6	14.9	15.2	10.9	12.9	14.8	8.7	13.0	**11.8**	**11.4**
All households with at least one adult in full-time, full-year work[e]	..	6.2	5.8	..	9.8	9.4	12.8	4.5	12.6	14.1	8.6	11.6	11.1	6.2	8.6	**9.4**	**8.1**

.. Data not available.

a) Low income refers to the bottom quintile of household annual income distribution. Adjusted income per equivalent household member is derived by dividing total income of the household by the number of adult equivalents. In particular, the adjusted income of an individual *i* who is a member of household *j*, is defined to be:

(1) $W_i = Y_j / S_j^{0.5}$

Y_j is the value of total household income. S_j is the number of members in household *j* and 0.5 is the equivalence elasticity. It follows from (1) that all members of the same household have the same level of "adjusted" household income (W_i). The measure of scale used – $S^{0.5}$ – incorporates diminishing weights for each additional person in the household. For the definition of the income concept used in each country, see Annex 1.A.

b) Household members of working age (15 to 64 years old). In *Australia*: individuals aged 15 and over who are members of households with a working-age head. For *Finland*: household members aged 15 and over.

c) EU countries (except Finland): no adult member (aged 16 or more) in the household was in wage and salary employment or self-employed for one month or more during the year. *Australia*: no adult member (aged 18 or more) in the household was in wage and salary employment or self-employed for at least 6 months during the year. *Finland*: no adult member (aged 16 or more) in the household was in wage and salary employment or self-employed for more than 3 weeks during the year. *United States*: no adult member (aged 15 or more) in the household was in wage and salary employment or self-employment during the year.

d) EU countries (except Finland): at least one adult member (aged 16 or more) in the household was in wage and salary employment or self-employed for one month or more during the year. *Australia*: at least one adult member (aged 18 or more) in the household was in wage and salary employment or in self-employment during the reference week. *Finland*: at least one adult member (aged 15 or more) in the household was in wage and salary employment or self-employed for at least 6 months during the year. *United States*: at least one adult member (aged 15 or more) in the household was in wage and salary employment or self-employed for more than 3 weeks during the year.

e) EU countries (except Finland): a full-time, full-year worker is a wage and salary earner or a self-employed on a full-time basis (30 hours or more per week) for at least 10 months during the year. *Australia* and *Finland*: this category is not available. *United States*: a full-time, full-year worker is a wage and salary earner or a self-employed on a full-time basis (35 hours or more per week) for at least 40 weeks during the year.

f) Unweighted average for above countries and years only. For EU, unweighted average for EU-12 (excluding Finland).

Source: See Annex 1.A.

Income includes all sources of monetary incomes received by the household (wages, dividends, etc.), and monetary social transfers, such as pensions and private transfers. In order to reflect households' living standards as accurately as possible, income is expressed as adjusted income per equivalent household member, where the varying size of households and economies of scale in consumption are taken into account using an equivalence scale.[14]

Individuals in jobless households have a much higher risk of being in the bottom quintile of the income distribution compared with individuals in households with someone in paid employment (Table 1.10). This is particularly the case when there are children in the household. Working-age members of non-employed households are particularly exposed to the risk of low household income in Australia, Finland, Ireland and the United Kingdom. In all countries, the risk of low income is highest for single adult-households not in work, though this varies a lot across countries, ranging from less than one-third in Greece and Italy to over 80 per cent in Australia.

When the household has access to some earned income, it is important to distinguish between different degrees of "employment intensity", as individuals living in households with two adults in full-time jobs will likely be materially better off than members of households where there is only some part-time employment. In 7 of the 12 countries for which this type of data are available, the presence of some full-time/full-year work in the household is sufficient to lift more than nine out of ten working-age individuals above the income limit of the bottom quintile of households. With the exception of Italy, full-time/full-year employed heads of single-adult households fare worse than members of households with at least two members in full-time/full-year work.

Although the risk of low income is higher among households with nobody in paid employment, it does not follow that low-income individuals live mainly in workless households. Table 1.11 shows that members of workless households make up more than one-half of the bottom income quintile distribution only in Australia, Belgium, Finland and Ireland. More than one-half of all low-income individuals of working age in the other ten countries live in working households, with the largest shares in southern European countries and Luxembourg. In these countries, the presence of at least one adult in a full-time job throughout the year is not sufficient for the household to escape the bottom quintile of the income distribution. The distribution of low-income individuals by the labour force status of their households obviously reflects the distribution of the overall population by the employment patterns of their households. Countries where a relatively high proportion of the population live in households without any paid employment are more likely to have a high share of all low-income individuals also living in these households.

Table 1.11. **Distribution of low-income[a] working-age individuals[b] by the labour force status of their households**

	Non-employed households[c]	Households with some work[d]	of which: households with at least one member in full-time, full-year work[e]
Australia 1995	56.7	43.3	..
Belgium 1993	61.0	39.0	25.8
Denmark 1993	41.9	58.1	30.0
Finland 1995	74.0	26.0	..
France 1993	41.9	57.6	36.8
Germany 1993	36.8	63.2	43.3
Greece 1993	24.4	75.6	59.5
Ireland 1993	65.3	34.7	20.3
Italy 1993	28.7	71.3	53.4
Luxembourg 1993	20.7	79.3	68.7
Netherlands 1993	44.0	56.0	39.8
Portugal 1993	22.9	77.1	64.9
Spain 1993	29.2	70.8	44.7
United Kingdom 1993	49.8	50.1	31.5
United States 1995	27.0	73.0	43.3
EU[f]	**38.9**	**61.1**	**39.9**
OECD[f]	**41.6**	**58.3**	**37.5**

Notes and source: See Table 1.10.

D. CONCLUSIONS

Patterns of non-employment ("joblessness") differ depending on whether the perspective adopted is that of the individual or the household. Belgium and Finland have the highest rates of jobless households, whereas the jobless rate for individuals is highest in Greece, Ireland, Italy and Spain. Variation across countries is much lower if non-employment is measured over households rather than individuals. Furthermore, although there is a positive cross-country correlation between individual- and household-based non-employment (or employment) rates, the countries with the highest non-employment rates do not have the highest proportions of households without any work, as unemployed and inactive individuals tend to live in households with someone who has a job.

Joblessness in the household has an important bearing on the income situation of its members: non-employed people of working age living with no other person in employment have a far higher risk of low income, compared with those who live in households with some work, especially in Australia, Finland, Ireland and the United Kingdom. In these countries, the incidence of low income is greatly reduced if there is some employment in the household. Members of jobless households with children are particularly exposed to the risk of low income. Nonetheless, the majority of people in the bottom of the income distribution are, in most countries, living in households with someone in paid work, and often with a full-time job throughout the year.

Over the past decade, the overall share of households with no adult members in employment increased, except in Ireland, the Netherlands and the United States. In many cases, the increase in the incidence of household joblessness occurred even as non-employment rates at the individual level fell.

Changes in the structure of the household population are very important in accounting for this. The increasing number of single-adult households, for which the incidence of joblessness is highest, accounts for a large part of the growth in household non-employment rates, especially in Belgium and the United Kingdom. By contrast, in Italy, the increased incidence of non-employment within multi-adult households accounts for the largest share of the total increase in household joblessness. Within the generally dominant type of household (with at least two adult members), there is some evidence of so-called "polarisation" of employment, i.e. the simultaneous increase of both workless households and households with at least two adults in work.

The results outlined in this section shed new light on labour market-related issues. In countries like Greece, Ireland, Italy and Spain, high non-employment rates for persons can probably be sustained because they have a lower impact on households, as many unemployed and inactive individuals share a dwelling with somebody in employment. However, it is likely that household formation and the composition of households are not exogenous to the economic environment and are, themselves, affected by individual risks of joblessness. Many factors intervene in the explanation of the causes and consequences of joblessness at the household level, and a detailed examination of its policy implications is well beyond the scope of this chapter.

The examination undertaken provides a first example of analysis that could be carried out with household- (or family-) based data. There is still much scope for analysis of households' labour force patterns. In particular, the next step could analyse in detail the reasons for both inactivity and unemployment in a household framework.

Notes

1. Economic theory has attempted to provide insights into some of the forces that shape the labour supply decisions of households. The theoretical models that underlie the empirical analysis of joint labour supply decisions within a (two-adult) household can be classified into two broad categories: in a more traditional model, the household is considered as the basic decision unit and is characterised by a unique utility function that is maximised under a budget constraint. In practice, these models extend the assumption of a single decision-maker to the household members, either by assuming they all have exactly the same preferences or by assuming that one household member makes all the decisions affecting all members. One drawback of this approach is that it treats the household as a black box: while it characterises its relationships with the outside economy, it says nothing about its internal decision processes. A second type of model, developed more recently, assumes that household members engage in a bargaining process, thus taking account of the infrahousehold decision processes. Examples of the latter approach are provided by Lundberg and Pollak (1994) and Chiapporri (1992).

2. Data for European Union countries from the European Community Household Panel (ECHP, see Annex 1.A) show that between 60 and 90 per cent of working-age adults in workless households rely upon social transfers as their largest source of household income.

3. The correlation between percentage point changes in the two rates between 1985 and 1996 is 0.52.

4. It is interesting to observe that, on a cross-country basis, the proportion of single-adult households with children is strongly correlated with the individual non-employment rates (the correlation when Mexico and Switzerland are excluded is –0.75 and statistically significant). This finding supports the idea that household formation and the composition of households are endogenous to the economic environment, as both are affected by individual risks of joblessness.

5. It is quite likely that a large proportion of these households are composed of two parents and youth aged between 15 and 24 years. In the definition adopted for this analysis, these youth are counted as adult household members. In fact, between 20 and 50 per cent of members of this type of household are in this age band. Most of them are inactive and, most likely, attending school, although in Australia, Italy and Spain, a large share are unemployed.

6. The population of single-adult households (with or without children) is rather heterogeneous: Finland, followed by Belgium, Canada and France, record the highest share of unemployed persons in such households, whereas in Austria, Greece, Luxembourg and Portugal more than 80 per cent of the adults are out of the labour force. When looking at the distribution of single-adult households by age of the adult, Finland and Greece have the highest share of youth, whereas in Italy, Luxembourg and Spain, a relatively large share are aged 55 to 64 years.

7. Families with children that face the prospect of finding low-paid or part-time work normally have lower work incentives than families without, due to higher replacement rates and marginal effective tax rates. In particular, lone parents are usually affected by high marginal effective tax rates [OECD (1997a)].

8. These results differ from those in Gregg and Wadsworth (1996), who found evidence of employment polarisation also in Ireland, but not for France, Luxembourg and Portugal. Apart from differences in the household population analysed, this possibly indicates the sensitivity of the results to the period chosen, 1983-1994 for them, and 1985-1996 here.

9. The available data for Canada, the European Union countries and the United States seem to confirm this pattern. In all countries, the share of households whose members have completed less than upper secondary education is one and a half to over twice as high in workless households than in households with some work. Furthermore, the proportion of low-educated households decreases with the number of household members who are in employment.

10. Gregg and Wadsworth (1994) try to identify the factors that explain the growing differential between work-poor and work-rich households in the United Kingdom between the late 1970s and 1990, and find that the changing composition of employment (part-time versus full-time) accounts for about one-fifth to one-quarter of this phenomenon.

11. This was recognised as a problem in Australia, and the reform of income support arrangements of July 1995 addressed this problem to some extent by giving each partner in a household where neither has a high level of earnings an individual benefit entitlement [OECD (1997a)].

12. All the factors determining concentration of joblessness within households that are described here are forces that work against "the added worker effect", according to which, in the face of falling income due to the unemployment (or non-employment) of a household member, the number of family members seeking market work may increase. This "added worker effect" has been developed within the frame of the conventional models of labour supply, described in footnote 1. Some empirical studies show that the added-worker effect does exist, although it is rather small. It

tends to be confined to families whose sole breadwinner loses a job [Lundberg (1985)].

13. For an examination of changes in the overall income distribution in relation to work attachment of household members, see Burniaux *et al.* (1998). The main findings of this study were: individuals in households with no wage earners have lower than average incomes; changes over time in the relative incomes of various population groups tend to be small, compared with differences in levels. Such changes are, however, closely linked to changes in patterns of earnings and employment; and increases in the number of individuals living in households with no member at work appear likely to have been an important factor underlying increased income inequality.

14. Adjusted income per equivalent household member is derived by dividing total income of the household by the number of adult equivalents. In particular, the adjusted income of an individual i who is a member of household j (W$_i$), is defined to be:

$$W_i = Y_j / S_j^{0.5} \qquad (1)$$

where Y$_j$ is the value of total net household income, S$_j$ is the number of members in household j and 0.5 is the assumed value of the so-called "equivalence elasticity". It follows from (1) that all members of the same household have the same level of "adjusted" household income (W$_i$). The measure of scale used – S$^{0.5}$ – incorporates diminishing weights for each additional person in the household and is flatter than the usual OECD and modified OECD scales. Like these two latter equivalence scales, it takes an intermediate position between the measure of per capita household income (where total household income is simply divided by the number of household members) and the case of no adjustment for need. See OECD (1995*b*).

ANNEX I.A

Sources and definitions of data in Section C

This study uses data from labour force surveys, as well as other household surveys. While labour force surveys are normally used to produce information about individuals, data collection is also made for complete households. However, the accuracy of data at the household level may not be as high as for data at the individual level. One problem is that smaller households are often under-represented in the total number of households. Another problem is that most national labour force surveys base their grossing up procedure (where sample data are weighted to provide estimates of the population) on the individual person. Tate (1997) discusses this issue.

Working-age households are defined as all households that contain at least one person aged 15-64 years. In Australia, the Czech Republic, Japan, Mexico, New Zealand and Switzerland, however, working-age households are those with a working-age head. Both definitions have the disadvantage of including households containing adults aged 65 and over when they share the household with working-age adults or heads. However, as interest centres on household joblessness, this does not represent a problem. The definition based on the "presence of one adult of working age" is preferred over the "head of household" definition, since the latter excludes from the analysis some working-age persons, and because the definition of head of household may have changed between the two years of observation. For a discussion on this issue, see Hastings (1997). Depending on the country, the adopted definition of working-age households excludes from the analysis between one-eighth and one-quarter of all households. The share of households with all members aged 65 years and over in the total number of households is highest in Switzerland (more than 22 per cent), followed by Australia, Belgium, France, Germany, Greece, Italy and the United Kingdom (over 20 per cent of all households). In Canada, Ireland and Mexico, households with only adult members aged 65 and over represent less than 16 per cent of all households.

Households are characterised by the number of adults (aged between 15 and 64) in the household (one, two, three or more); the presence, or not, of children; and the number of adults employed (none, one, two or more).

Australia

Labour Force Survey. For Tables 1.6-1.9 and Charts 1.2 and 1.4, data refer to February 1986 and May 1996. For Table 1.5, and Charts 1.1 and 1.3, the data refer to September 1986 and 1996.

A household is a group of one or more persons in a private dwelling who consider themselves to be separate from other persons (if any) in the dwelling, and who make regular provision to take meals separately from other persons, i.e. at different times or in different rooms. A household may consist of any number of family and non-family members.

For Tables 1.10 and 1.11, data are from the Survey of Income and Housing Costs: 1995-96. This is a continuous survey, started in July 1994, that collects information on the amount and sources of income, and the characteristics of income units and persons resident in private dwellings throughout Australia.

The reference period for income and employment data is a week during the survey reference period between July 1995 to June 1996. Current weekly income data is calculated as the latest pay pro-rated to weekly amount. The definition of households corresponds to that in the Labour Force Survey.

Canada

Labour Force Survey for April 1985 and 1996. The statistical unit is the "economic family", defined as a group of two or more persons who live in the same dwelling and who are related by blood, marriage (including common-law) or adoption. Unattached individuals are treated as separate "economic families".

The Czech Republic

Labour Force Sample Survey, Spring 1996. A household includes persons sharing a dwelling for more than 3 months without letup, irrespective of the kind of stay.

European Union Countries (Austria, Belgium, France, Finland, Germany, Greece, Ireland, Italy, Luxembourg, the Netherlands, Portugal, Spain and United Kingdom)

Data for Tables 1.5-1.9 and Charts 1.1-1.4 were provided by EUROSTAT, based on results from the Spring Labour Force Sample Survey.

A household is defined in terms of two criteria: the sharing of the same dwelling and common living arrangements. The latter can include meals taken together or a shared room, and/or a joint budget, and/or the use of common equipment. Italy and Portugal add the requirement of kinship relations, while in Spain and France the condition of common housekeeping is waived.

Austrian data before 1995 were based on the "main source of income" concept, and, therefore, are not comparable with 1996 data, which are based on the labour force concept (in accordance with EUROSTAT definitions). In the Netherlands, an important series break occurred when the continuous labour force survey was introduced in 1987. Thus, the data used refer to 1988 instead of 1985. In Denmark and Sweden, the sample unit is the individual instead of the household: data on the composition of households are, therefore, not available. In Finland, they have been available only since 1995.

Data for Tables 1.10 and 1.11 were also provided by EUROSTAT, based on results from the first wave of the *European Community Household Panel* (ECHP). The ECHP is a standardised household survey that involves annual interviewing of a representative panel of households and individuals in each country, covering a wide range of topics on living conditions. The first wave was conducted in 1994, for the then 12 EU Member states, *i.e.* excluding Austria, Finland and Sweden. For a detailed description of the ECHP methodology, see EUROSTAT (1996).

Total net monetary income covers all market incomes (wages, self-employment income, investment income, rent received) plus social and private transfers received, minus income taxes and social insurance contributions. Imputed rent (*i.e.* the rent owner-occupiers would have to pay if they did not own the dwelling they live in), as well as personal income taxes are not taken into account. The definition of households corresponds to that given above.

Since income statistics refer to receipts during the year preceding the interview, the labour force characteristics of households also refer to that period, except for the Netherlands. In this country, information on the labour force situation of households in the year preceding the interview was not available, and the characteristics of persons and households refer to the time of the survey.

Finland

For Tables 1.5-1.9 and Charts 1.1-1.4, see above. For Tables 1.10 and 1.11: *Income Distribution Survey*, Statistics Finland. A household is a group of persons living together and having wholly or partly common household arrangements.

Japan

The Employment Status Survey, 1987 and 1992. A "household" consists of a group of two or more persons sharing living quarters and living expenses or one person living alone in an independent dwelling or in a rented room, a dormitory, boarding house, or similar facilities.

Mexico

National Employment Survey, 1996. "Households" are defined as persons who share the same dwelling, have common living arrangements, and share some income.

New Zealand

Census of Population and Dwellings, 1986 and 1996. A "household" is a group of persons who live in the same (private) dwelling. Households may be made up of one or more families, unrelated persons (*e.g.* flatmates, boarders) or single-person households.

Poland

Labour Force Survey, May 1996. A household is a group of relatives or persons related by marriage living together and sharing domestic arrangements.

Switzerland

Active Population Survey (since 1991), second quarter of 1996. The criterion applied to identify a household is the sharing of the same dwelling and the same phone number.

United States

Monthly Current Population Survey, March 1986 and 1996. Data are based on the concept of "family", defined as a group of two or more persons residing together and related by birth, marriage or adoption. Those living outside a family or with non-relatives only (*e.g.* a group of students living together) are considered as single adults. Therefore, for this country, the number of single adults will be slightly overestimated.

Income data in Tables 1.10 and 1.11 cover money income received before payments for personal income taxes, Social Security, Medicare deductions, etc. Non-money transfers, such as food stamps and health benefits, are not taken into account. Although income statistics refer to receipts during the year preceding the interview, the characteristics of the persons, such as age, labour force status, etc., and of their families, refer to the time of the survey. The definition of "family" corresponds to that given above.

Bibliography

BURNIAUX, J. M., DANG T. T., FORE, D., FORSTER, M., MIRA D'ERCOLE, M., OXLEY, H. (1998), "Income Distribution and Poverty in Selected OECD Countries", OECD Economics Department Working Papers, No. 189.

CHIAPPORRI, P. (1992), "Collective Labour Supply and Welfare", *Journal of Political Economy*, June, pp. 437-467.

EUROSTAT (1996), "The European Community Household Panel: Vol. 1 – Survey Methodology and Implementation", Theme 3, Series E, OPOCE, Luxembourg.

GREGG, P. and WADSWORTH, J. (1994), "More Work in Fewer Households?", *National Institute of Economic and Social Research*, Discussion Paper No. 72, London.

GREGG, P. and WADSWORTH, J. (1996), "It Takes Two: Employment Polarisation in the OECD", Centre for Economic Performance, Discussion Paper No. 304.

HASTINGS, D. (1997), "Economic Activity of Working-age Households", *Labour Market Trends*, September, pp. 333-338.

LUNDBERG, S. (1985), "The Added Worker Effect", *Journal of Labor Economics*, January, pp. 11-37.

LUNDBERG, S. and POLLAK, R. A. (1994), "Non-Co-operative Bargaining Models of Marriage", *American Economic Review*, May, pp. 132-137.

OECD (1995a), *Employment Outlook*, Paris, July.

OECD (1995b), "Income Distribution in OECD Countries", Social Policy Studies, No. 18, Paris.

OECD (1997a), *The OECD Jobs Strategy. Making Work Pay: Taxation, Benefits, Employment and Unemployment*, Paris.

TATE, P. (1997), "Data on Households and Families from the Labour Force Survey", *Labour Market Trends*, March, pp. 89-98.

CHAPTER 2

Making the most of the minimum: statutory minimum wages, employment and poverty

A. INTRODUCTION AND MAIN FINDINGS

1. Introduction

Several OECD countries have experienced a rise in earnings inequality and/or a widening of the gap in income between rich and poor over the past decade or so. This has led to a resurgence of interest in the links between employment growth, low pay and poverty. In particular, the impact of statutory minimum wages on employment and the distribution of earnings and income has been subject to intense scrutiny.

Analysis of minimum wages inevitably raises contentious theoretical, empirical and policy issues. On the one hand, statutory minimum wages are seen as playing an important role in ensuring that "fair" wages are paid and in bolstering the incomes of families with low-wage workers. On the other hand, it is argued that high minimum wages can destroy jobs and have a limited impact on poverty because many poor families have no working members. New life has been injected into this debate by the findings of Card and Krueger (1995, 1998) that minimum wage increases can, in some circumstances, result in net job gains rather than the losses predicted by conventional wisdom. However, while many reassessments of minimum wages have been carried out on a national basis, there have been few from an international perspective [for one of the few, see Dolado *et al.* (1996)]. The need for a reconsideration of the costs and benefits of statutory minimum wages is further reinforced by the fact that two Member countries, Ireland and the United Kingdom, are committed to introducing a national minimum wage for the first time in their histories.

Accordingly, this chapter covers the following issues: *i)* the setting and operation of statutory or national minimum wages (Section B); *ii)* their impact on employment (Section C); *iii)* their impact on the earnings of low-paid workers and household incomes (Section D); and *iv)* their interaction with tax/benefit systems (Section E). Statutory minimum wages are defined fairly broadly to include countries such as Belgium and Greece where the minimum wage, while determined through collective negotiation, is fairly universal in coverage.[1] Minimum wages are also effectively set through collective agreements in a number of other countries and, in some cases, such agreements are administratively extended to cover whole sectors of activities. However, these minima can vary substantially across sectors and according to a worker's age, experience and qualifications. Their impact on employment and the distribution of earnings and income is likely to be quite different than in the case of a uniform national minimum wage. For this reason, such collectively-set minima are excluded from the scope of this chapter.

2. Main findings

National or statutory minimum wages exist in 17 OECD countries, but there are substantial differences in the way they are set and operate. The main differences concern the level of the minimum relative to average wages; the extent of differentiation by age or region; mechanisms for indexation; and the roles of governments and the social partners in setting them.

There is little agreement, at either the theoretical or empirical level, about the precise employment effects of minimum wages, at least over moderate levels relative to average wages. However, there is general agreement that a statutory minimum wage is likely to reduce employment if set above a certain, usually unspecified, level. While sometimes conflicting, the weight of evidence suggests that young workers may be most vulnerable to job losses at a high level of the minimum wage. There is less evidence available on the employment effects, if any, for other groups such as women and part-time workers, who represent a large and growing proportion of the workforce.

Standard economic theory predicts that the imposition of a minimum wage will simply truncate the earnings distribution at that wage, but the empirical evidence points to much more complicated effects. Spikes tend to appear at the new minimum wage, indicating that many of those previously earning below the new minimum now earn exactly that amount. This suggests that minimum wages can be effective in achieving one of its equity goals of ensuring that "fair" wages are paid to workers. There is also some evidence of spillover effects that lead to an increase in wages for those previously at or just above the new minimum. Partly as a result of these effects, those countries with higher minimum wage rates relative to the median have less earnings dispersion and a lower incidence of low pay. In addition, minimum wages narrow earnings differentials across demographic groups, particularly between the young and old and between men and women.

Minimum wages can reduce poverty rates and income inequality among working families. However, their impact on family (household) poverty and income distribution is limited, because many poor families have no one working and many minimum-wage workers live in households with above-average incomes.

Minimum wages are not as well targeted at reducing in-work poverty as other measures such as in-work benefits which are means tested. However, means-tested benefits face other drawbacks: they may give rise to poverty traps; they may lead to a fall in the wages of low-paid workers; and they can be very expensive. This suggests that there may be some scope to complement in-work benefits with a national minimum wage. The overall net benefit of such a policy mix will depend upon the specific economic and institutional context of the labour market in each country.

B. MINIMUM-WAGE SYSTEMS IN OECD COUNTRIES

1. Coverage, operation and setting of minimum wages

Nearly all OECD countries have some form of minimum wage-setting arrangements in place in accordance with one or several of the relevant ILO conventions [ILO (1992)]. Currently, 17 countries have a statutory or national minimum wage which cuts across almost all sectors of the economy. An overview of their coverage, operation and setting is provided in Table 2.1.

Most countries opt to set a single national minimum rate, although there may be a reduced or "sub-minimum" rate for some groups such as youth and apprentices. Minimum wages are set at both the federal and regional levels in Canada and the United States, and at the regional level only in Japan and Mexico.[2] In the United States, just seven states and the District of Columbia set minimum wages

above the Federal rate, the lowest rate that can be set. In Canada, each province and territory sets its own hourly minimum. In 1997, it ranged from C$ 5 in Alberta to C$ 7 in British Columbia, compared with a national average of just under C$ 6.50. This range is wider than in Japan, where the spread of prefectural rates in 1997 around the national average of ¥ 635 per hour ranged from ¥ 578 in a number of prefectures to ¥ 671 for Tokyo.[3] In Mexico, basic rates are set for three broad regions as well as higher rates for 88 specific occupations in each region.[4] Premia also exist related to a worker's experience (Belgium and Greece), qualifications (Czech Republic), and marital and family status (Greece and Luxembourg).

There is substantial variation across countries in terms of coverage. Disabled workers are often excluded or come under separate regulations. Apprentices and trainees are often exempted or only qualify for a reduced rate. In some cases, public servants are also not covered (France, Greece and Luxembourg). In Canada and the United States, supervisory and managerial employees are typically excluded.

Sub-minimum rates for young workers are very common: over one-half of the countries in Table 2.1 apply a reduced rate for them, though the differential varies a lot. In the Netherlands, Belgium and Luxembourg, the adult rate is reduced successively for each year below 23, 21 and 18 years of age, respectively. Reduced rates for 17-year-olds and those under 17 are also set in France, but they are incorporated into relatively few collective agreements. In the other countries with a youth minimum, there is only a single rate. In some countries, such as France, there are also *de facto* sub-minimum wages for youths as a result of special employment programmes which allow employers either to pay lower wages than the SMIC or lower their social security charges.

The setting of statutory minima wages for younger workers has changed over recent years in several countries. In Spain, the separate rate for under 17-years-olds was abolished in 1990 with the rate for 17-year-olds applying to all workers less than 18. A further change in Spain was introduced at the beginning of 1998 when a single statutory minimum wage was established with no distinction by age. In 1994, New Zealand introduced a separate youth rate (60 per cent of the adult minimum) for workers aged less than 20. In Canada, while youth rates still exist in some provinces, there has been a marked tendency over recent years for these rates to be repealed. In contrast, a youth rate was introduced in the United States at the Federal level as recently as 1996, but it only applies to the first 90 consecutive calendar days of employment.

Table 2.1. **Summary of minimum wage systems in OECD countries with a national minimum**

Country and year of introduction[a]	Name and type of determination	Employees excluded	Rates for younger employees (age and % of adult rate)	Indexation or "uprating" procedures	Other remarks
Belgium (1975)	The minimum monthly wage – *Revenu minimum mensuel moyen garanti* (RMMMG) – is set by a national collective agreement.	Public sector workers, apprentices, trainees and workers in sheltered workshops.	20, 94%; 19, 88%; 18, 82%; 17, 76%; and under 17, 70%.	RMMMG is indexed to consumer prices on a branch-by-branch basis. The RMMMG is also increased when the central agreement is renegotiated, usually every two years.	Since 1991, additional steps to the RMMMG have been added for adult workers with more than 6 or 12 months tenure.
Canada (Women: 1918-1930; Men: 1930s-1950s)	Minimum hourly wages are set by statute at the Federal and Provincial levels.	Apprentices, farm workers, and supervisory and managerial workers are often excluded under provincial regulations.	Reduced rates for youth have generally been abolished.	No automatic indexation for general price or wage inflation.	Since July 1996, the Federal rate has been aligned with the rate in each province and territory.
Czech Republic (1991)	A basic minimum wage and Minimum Wage Tariffs (MWTs), on an hourly and monthly basis, are set by statute.	MWTs only apply to employees not covered by collective agreements. Public sector pay is set separately.	No reduced rates for young adults, but lower rates for minors.	No automatic indexation for general price or wage inflation.	Lower rates for disabled employees. MWTs vary according to complexity, responsibility and physical difficulty of job performed.
France (1950; 1970 in current form)	The minimum hourly wage – *Salaire minimum interprofessionnel de croissance* (SMIC) – is set by statute.	General government workers and disabled workers (who are covered by separate rules).	For workers with less than 6 months of tenure: 17, 90%; and under 17, 80%.	The SMIC is indexed to consumer prices (for rises of 2% or more) and must rise by at least half the increase in the hourly wage rate of workers. The SMIC can be raised by more than these prescribed increases by decree.	Apprentices and trainees entitled to 25% to 78% of the SMIC, depending on age and stage of training.
Greece (1953; 1990 in current form)	Minimum wages are set as a daily (manual workers) and monthly (non-manual workers) rate by the National General Employment Collective Agreement.	Applies to employees in the private sector only. Public sector pay levels are set separately by the government.	No reduced rates.	While there is no automatic indexation, the rate has been adjusted twice to three times a year.	Higher rates apply according to job tenure and marital status.
Hungary (1977; 1992 in current form)	The minimum (hourly and monthly) wage is set by statute.	All employees covered. Apprentices must receive at least 10% of the minimum wage.	No reduced rates.	There is no automatic indexation but the rate is normally adjusted annually with the agreement of the tripartite Interest Reconciliation Council.	Lower minimum wages can be granted in certain cases but this has not occurred in practice.

Table 2.1. **Summary of minimum wage systems in OECD countries with a national minimum** *(cont.)*

Country and year of introduction[a]	Name and type of determination	Employees excluded	Rates for younger employees (age and % of adult rate)	Indexation or "uprating" procedures	Other remarks
Japan (1959; 1968 in current form)	A statutory minimum (hourly and daily) wage is set for each of the 47 prefectures.	Some civil servants; apprentices and trainees; disabled and intermittent workers; newly hired workers on probation; and workers with very short working hours.	No reduced rates.	In consultation with local tripartite Minimum Wages Councils, minimum wages are revised every year, taking into account increases in wages and the cost of living.	Minimum wages are also set by prefecture for selected industries and at the national level for the coal and metal mining industries.
Korea (1988; 1990 in current form)	The minimum (hourly and daily) wage is set by statute.	Only business with more than 10 workers must observe the minimum wage. Exceptions also apply to: apprentices and trainees; newly hired workers on probation; and disabled and intermittent workers.	For workers with less than 6 months of job experience: under 18, 90%.	While there is no automatic indexation, the minimum wage is adjusted annually by the Minister of Labour after consulting the tripartite Minimum Wage Council.	Minimum wages were initially fixed for manufacturing only and then extended to all businesses in 1990.
Luxembourg (1944)	The minimum monthly wage – *Salaire social minimum* (SSM) – is set by statute.	Only covers private sector employees.	17, 80%; 16, 70%; and 15, 60%.	The SSM is indexed to consumer prices. Also reviewed biennially in line with economic and pay growth.	Rates are 20% higher for skilled and experienced workers. The minimum rate also varies according to marital and family status.
Mexico (1917; 1962 in current form)	Statutory daily minimum wages for three broad geographical zones are fixed by the tripartite National Minimum Wage Commission.	No exemptions.	No reduced rates.	While there is no automatic indexation, the minimum wage has been adjusted regularly.	Higher minimum rates are also set for 88 occupations in each region.
Netherlands (1968)	The minimum (daily, weekly and monthly) wage – *Minimumloon* – is set by statute.	Covers all employees with a labour contract. In 1992, coverage was extended to employees working less than 13 hours a week.	22, 85%; 21, 72.5%; 20, 61.5%; 19, 52.5%; 18, 45.5%; 17, 39.5%; 16, 34.5%; and 15, 30%.	Since 1992, the minimum wage is linked to average wage growth but indexation can be suspended if the ratio of welfare recipients to employment (in benefit and work years, respectively) rises above a given level.	The minimum wage was cut by 3% in 1984 and frozen in nominal terms until 1990 when indexation was restored.
New Zealand (1945; 1983 in current form)	The minimum (hourly, daily and weekly) wage s set by statute.	Apprentices and trainees; and disabled workers.	16 to 19, 60%.	No automatic indexation, but the Minister of Labour must undertake an annual review of the level.	

Table 2.1. **Summary of minimum wage systems in OECD countries with a national minimum** (cont.)

Country and year of introduction[a]	Name and type of determination	Employees excluded	Rates for younger employees (age and % of adult rate)	Indexation or "uprating" procedures	Other remarks
Poland (1990)	The minimum monthly wage is set by statute.	No exemptions.	No reduced rates.	Updated 3 to 4 times each year according to a formula, taking into account expenditures of low-income "working" households, price inflation and other economic factors.	
Portugal (1974)	The national minimum monthly wage – *Remuneracao minima nacional* (RMN) – is set by statute.	Armed forces.	Under 18, 75%.	Updated annually by law after tripartite consultation, taking into account inflation and economic performance.	Lower rates are set for apprentices trainees, domestic staff and disabled workers.
Spain (1963; 1976 in current form)	The minimum monthly wage – *Salario minimo interprofesional* (SMI) – is set by statute.	No exemptions.	Under 18, 89%.	Updated annually by law after tripartite consultation, taking into account inflation and economic performance.	As of 1 January 1998, there is no longer a reduced rate for younger workers.
Turkey (1971)	The minimum daily wage is set by statute.	Apprentices.	Under 16, 85%.	Usually updated annually through a tripartite Minimum Wage Board, taking account of the cost of purchasing a minimum basket of food and non-food items, as well as other economic developments.	Separate regional minima were discontinued in 1974. Prior to August 1989, a separate (lower) rate was set for agricultural workers.
United States (1938)	Federal and State minimum hourly wages are set by statute.	Executive, administrative and professional employees and other specific, but small, groups of workers.	From October 1996, a reduced Federal rate of $4.25 per hour may be paid to workers under 20 during their first 90 consecutive calendar days on the job.	No automatic indexation for price or wage inflation.	Subject to certain conditions, employers may pay trainees 85% of the Federal rate as well as lower rates for full-time students and disabled workers.

a) For many countries, there have been a substantial number of changes in the laws and regulations governing minimum wages. The year of introduction is simply meant to indicate when the central features of the current system were put into place.

Sources: National submissions to the Secretariat.

Countries also differ in how the minimum is initially set, its subsequent "uprating" and in whether it is automatically indexed for inflation. In most cases, minimum wages are set by the government unilaterally or following consultations with, or recommendations by, a tripartite body (France, Japan, Korea, Portugal and Spain). Belgium and Greece have hybrid systems: the minimum is set through a national agreement between the social partners, but is legally binding in all sectors (the private sector only in Greece). Only Belgium and Luxembourg appear to automatically index for price inflation, while in France, Greece, Japan, Portugal and Spain, both price and wage movements are either explicitly or implicitly taken into consideration in annual reviews of the minimum rate. In the Netherlands, minimum wages are linked to the average, collectively bargained, wage increase, but this link is conditional: indexing can be suspended if the ratio of the inactive to active population (expressed in benefit and work years, respectively) rises above a certain specified level.[5] In a few countries, criteria, such as the "expected" impact on employment, unemployment and competitiveness, are explicitly taken into account in annual or biennial reviews of the minimum wage (Luxembourg, New Zealand, Portugal and Spain).

2. Minimum-wage levels

Minimum wages can be set on either an hourly, daily, weekly or monthly basis which complicates cross-country comparisons of their levels. Therefore, the hourly equivalent of the adult minimum wage in each country at the end of 1997 is provided in Table 2.2, both in national currencies and in US$. In terms of US$ measured at current exchange rates, minimum hourly wages range from under 50 cents per hour in the Czech Republic, Hungary and Mexico to over $7 in Luxembourg. When converted into US$ using purchasing power parities (PPPs), the dispersion in rates is reduced somewhat, but remains substantial.

Another way to compare minimum wages across countries is to measure their value relative to some measure of average wages. In addition to taking cross-country productivity differences into account, such a ratio also provides an indication of how many workers are likely to be affected by the minimum. However, this ratio can vary substantially depending on how both the numerator (minimum wage) and denominator (average wage) are measured. As discussed in Box 1, using median rather than mean wages in the denominator provides a better basis for international comparisons because of differences across countries in the dispersion of earnings. Ideally, minimum wages should also be measured rela-

Table 2.2. **Minimum wage per hour, end-1997**[a]

| | In national currency[b] | | In US$, using[c] | |
			Exchange rates	PPPs
Belgium	250	(43 343/month)	6.77	6.40
Canada	6.47		4.53	5.33
Czech Republic	13.50		0.39	0.92
France	39.43		6.58	5.56
Greece	774	(6 195/day)	2.74	3.06
Hungary	98		0.48	1.05
Japan	635		4.88	3.38
Korea	1 485		1.05	2.15
Luxembourg	267	(46 275/month)	7.23	6.91
Mexico	3.04	(24.30/day)	0.38	0.59
Netherlands	12.95	(517.8/week)	6.42	6.00
New Zealand	7.00		4.07	4.46
Poland	2.60	(450/month)	0.74	1.57
Portugal	327	(56 700/month)	1.78	2.32
Spain	384	(66 630/month)	2.53	2.94
Turkey[d]	147.66	(1 181/month)	0.72	1.38
United States	5.15		5.15	5.15

a) In all cases, the minimum wage refers to the basic rate for adults.
b) For countries where the minimum wage is not usually expressed as an hourly rate, the given rate (shown in parentheses) has been converted to an hourly basis assuming a working time of 8 hours per day, 40 hours per week and 173.3 hours per month.
c) Exchange rates refer to the end of December 1997. The PPPs refer to provisional estimates of Purchasing Power Parities for final private consumption expenditure for December 1997.
d) The minimum wage rates in national currency refer to thousands of Turkish Lira.
Sources: OECD Minimum Wage Database; and for exchange rates and PPPs, OECD, *Main Economic Indicators.*

tive to the median value of basic earnings, *i.e.* excluding overtime and bonus payments, but such data are only available for a few countries. Finally, the gap between minimum and average wages varies considerably for different groups of workers and this may affect international comparisons of the overall ratio because of differences in the age, gender and skill composition of each country's workforce. For these reasons, the ratio of minimum to average wages is presented in Table 2.3 according to a range of earnings measures and for different groups of workers.

The ratio of minimum to average wages is higher when the denominator refers to median rather than mean earnings because earnings distributions are typically left-skewed. Similarly, the ratio is higher when measured in terms of basic rather than total earnings. Country rankings, however, are fairly stable whichever ratio is compared. In relative terms, minimum wages appear to be highest in Belgium and France, and lowest in the Czech Republic and Korea. On the basis of more partial information, they also appear to be quite low in Mexico and Turkey.

Table 2.3. **Adult minimum wage relative to a range of average earnings measures, mid-1997[a]**

Percentages

	Full-time median earnings						Full-time mean earnings			Mean hourly pay in manufacturing[d]
	Basic	Including overtime pay and bonuses					Basic	Including overtime pay and bonuses		
	All	All	Men	Women	Youth[b]	Low paid[c]	All	All	Youth[b]	
Belgium	61.1	50.4	49.2	55.2	65.5	71.6	52.6	43.4	63.3	59.9
Canada	..	39.6	35.1	46.8	..	90.1	..	35.7	58.4	38.2
Czech Republic	..	21.2	19.4	24.6	..	34.6	..	18.7	23.0	..
France	68.5	57.4	55.2	63.3	..	86.2	55.3	46.3	71.7	68.7
Greece	..	37.4	..	..	..	71.9	..	32.6	..	51.4
Hungary	39.7	30.8	26.5	42.1	44.9	64.7	34.9	27.1	43.9	40.7
Japan	..	..	..	..	..	..	..	..	..	46.8
Korea	30.6	24.4	21.2	36.0	35.0	47.4	27.4	21.5	33.5	30.7
Luxembourg	..	..	..	..	..	..	..	..	..	53.9
Mexico	..	..	..	..	..	..	..	..	..	27.6
Netherlands	55.9	49.4	47.2	61.0	..	77.6	51.1	45.2	76.1	58.1
New Zealand	47.4	45.6	41.9	51.4	59.2	81.4	41.0	39.4	..	52.8
Poland	..	44.6	39.6	49.6	..	78.3	..	40.8	..	..
Portugal	..	..	..	..	..	..	49.6	..	..	64.1
Spain	36.4	32.4	30.1	42.3	..	66.6	28.8	25.6	..	40.6
Turkey	..	..	..	..	..	..	..	..	..	27.7
United States	43.3	38.1	33.2	44.4	59.7	79.5	34.9	30.6	52.5	36.1

.. Data not available.

a) In all cases, the minimum wage refers to the basic rate for adults. The average earnings data for 1997 for the different groups of full-time workers and for manual workers in manufacturing are estimates based on extrapolating data for earlier years in line with other indicators of average earnings growth. All earnings data are gross of employee social security contributions.

b) Youth are defined as employees aged 20-24. For the Netherlands, the mean ratio is around 65 per cent in terms of the average minimum rate for youths (weighted by the youth labour force by single year of age). In other countries with reduced rates for youths, these generally apply below the age of 20.

c) The low paid are defined as employees in the bottom 20 per cent of the earnings distribution. By construction, median earnings for this group correspond to the upper earnings limit for the bottom decile of employees.

d) Hourly pay for manual workers for time worked, i.e. excluding sick pay, holiday pay and other annual or non-regular bonuses and supplements. For Korea, Mexico, Portugal and Spain, hourly pay for time worked has been partly estimated based on data on total direct pay.

Sources: Minimum wages: OECD Minimum Wage Database. Mean and median earnings for full-time workers: OECD estimates and OECD Earnings Database (for more details, see OECD. Employment Outlook, July 1996, Chapter 3); Mean hourly pay in manufacturing: US Bureau of Labor Statistics, International Comparisons of Hourly Compensation Costs for Production Workers in Manufacturing, 1975-1996.

Box 1.   **International comparisons of the ratio of minimum to average wages**

Minimum wages are often reported relative to mean earnings, but, for the purpose of international comparisons, it may be better to report them relative to median earnings. For example, a large rise in the earnings of a few highly-paid workers may be sufficient to raise the mean relative to the minimum wage, but it would be mistaken to regard this as a sign of a decline in the potential number of workers affected by the minimum. Moreover, countries with the lowest relative value of minimum wages also tend to have the greatest dispersion of earnings. This implies that the variation across countries in their minimum wages will be somewhat overstated when measured relative to mean rather than median earnings.

Across countries, the composition of total earnings varies substantially. For example, in 1995, overtime payments and annual bonuses boosted basic rates of pay by almost 30 per cent in Japan, but by less than 13 per cent in Spain. International comparisons may be sensitive to whether these supplementary payments are included. Given that it is not generally possible with available data to establish the average amount of these supplementary payments for minimum-wage workers, the denominator should, ideally, refer to average earnings measured on a consistent basis, *i.e.* in terms of basic rates of pay.* However, for many countries, it is difficult to obtain this type of measure and the available earnings data include some or all supplementary payments received by workers. In these cases, the relative importance of the minimum wage will be understated.

For workers, the value of the minimum relative to average wages in *net* terms is probably the most relevant measure. Given that overall income taxes on earnings are typically progressive, the minimum wage ratio on a gross basis will understate the ratio on a net basis. This understatement will vary across countries according to the degree of progressivity of each country's tax system. Similarly, for employers, the value of minimum wages relative to the average in terms of total labour costs is probably a more relevant measure. Employers' social security contributions, which make up the bulk of non-wage labour costs, are generally levied at a flat rate (at least up until mean or median earnings), so that the ratio of minimum to average wages is unlikely to be very different, whether measured in terms of gross earnings or labour costs. In Belgium, France and the Netherlands, however, there have been a number of reductions over recent years in employer social security contributions for low-wage workers and their minimum-wage ratio is now lower in terms of labour costs than in terms of gross earnings.

Finally, comparisons across countries may also be affected by differences in the composition of the workforce. For example, the aggregate ratio of minimum to average wages may be similar across countries, but differ greatly across groups. Thus, when possible, it is important to also look at these ratios for different groups of workers.** It is also important to take account of differences in the universe of workers covered by their earnings statistics. For example, in some countries the average wage received by all workers may be understated because government workers are excluded while, in others, it may be somewhat overstated because workers in small establishments are excluded.

---

*   In all cases in Table 2.3, the minimum wage has been calculated assuming a standard number of working hours and no supplementary payments.
**   Earnings statistics for many countries are not readily available for part-time workers. Therefore, most of the comparisons in Table 2.3 refer to full-time workers.

Women and youth have lower average wages than men and older workers and are, thus, more likely to be affected by the minimum wage. The gap between men and women's wages is particularly large in Korea: whereas the minimum wage amounts to 21 per cent of median earnings for men, it is 36 per cent for women. In all countries, the ratio is much higher still for low-paid workers. In Canada, in particular, whereas the weighted average of the provincial minima is quite modest in terms of median earnings for all workers, it amounts to some 90 per cent of median earnings of low-paid workers.

3.   Incidence and distribution of employment at statutory minima

Relatively few countries are able to provide information on the incidence and distribution of employment at minimum wages (Table 2.4). It is also difficult to make direct international comparisons because of differences in the way the incidence of minimum-wage work is measured and in the groups of workers covered by the statutory minimum. Nevertheless, it appears to be the case that the lower value of the minimum relative to average wages in

Table 2.4. **Minimum-wage employment according to various worker characteristics**[a]

Percentages

	A. Incidence[d]							B. Distribution[e]						
	France[b] 1996	Hungary 1997	Mexico 1996	Netherlands 1994	Poland 1996	Portugal[c] 1997	United States 1996	France[b] 1996	Hungary 1997	Mexico 1996	Netherlands 1994	Poland 1996	Portugal[c] 1997	United States 1996
Total	11.0	3.8	17.6	3.7	4.5	4.7	5.1	100.0	100.0	100.0	100.0	100.0	100.0	100.0
Sex														
Men	7.5	4.0	15.2	2.6	3.9	3.7	3.8	..	52.9	56.6	41.4	45.4	47.7	39.3
Women	16.5	3.6	22.1	5.5	5.1	6.3	6.5	..	47.1	43.4	58.6	54.6	52.3	60.7
Age														
Under 25	31.6	7.7	..	11.1	..	..	13.7	33.5	22.2	..	46.5	..	..	44.5
Under 20	..	11.9	..	14.0	..	..	22.5	..	3.7	..	14.1	..	12.6	26.6
20-24	..	7.2	..	10.2	..	..	8.7	..	18.5	..	32.4	..	..	17.9
25-54	..	3.4	..	2.4	..	..	3.1	..	75.4	..	53.5	..	..	44.0
55 and over	..	1.9	..	..	..	..	5.5	..	2.4	..	..	..	..	11.5
Education														
Basic education	..	5.1	..	..	..	..	14.7	..	68.8	..	..	..	..	38.7
Upper secondary	..	3.3	..	..	..	..	4.4	..	26.3	..	..	..	..	28.1
Higher education	..	1.0	..	..	..	..	3.1	..	4.9	..	..	..	..	33.2
Part-time/full-time status														
Full-time	..	3.8	..	2.1	..	..	2.8	..	..	..	37.9	..	..	45.0
Part-time	..	..	..	7.0	..	..	14.9	..	..	..	62.1	..	..	55.0
Selected industries														
Manufacturing	7.3	2.5	..	1.7	..	4.6	2.0	..	17.6	..	7.5	..	..	6.9
Wholesale/Retail trade	15.3	11.7	..	7.7	..	6.8	10.6	..	29.1	..	39.8	..	..	44.6
Public administration	..	0.3	..	..	..	..	1.8	..	0.7	..	..	..	..	1.8
Personal services	..	1.2	..	1.6	..	5.3	5.1	..	7.2	..	13.6	..	..	34.9
Selected occupations														
Sales workers	..	..	..	..	..	..	5.9	..	27.0	..	..	..	..	13.2
Service workers	..	11.3	..	..	..	..	16.5	..	..	..	..	..	..	46.6
Labourers	..	4.0	..	..	..	..	4.5	..	23.9	..	..	..	..	13.9

.. Data not available.

a) Data refer to all employees for France, Mexico, the Netherlands and the United States and to full-time employees only for Hungary, Poland and Portugal.

b) Data exclude employees in general government sector, domestic workers and workers on temporary contracts.

c) Data exclude employees in the general government sector. The age group "under 20" refers to persons under 18 years of age.

d) Percentage of all workers in each category who are paid minimum wages or less.

e) Percentage share of all minimum-wage workers in each category. The sub-categories may not cover all workers and hence may not add up to 100.

Sources: For Poland and the United States, Secretariat estimates derived from, respectively, the Survey of Earnings Distribution in the National Economy conducted by the Polish Central Statistical Office, and the Current Population Survey, by the US Bureau of Labor Statistics. The Polish data were derived from published tabulations of the monthly earnings distribution for full-time employees. The US data were derived from microdata on usual hourly earnings which were constructed by taking reported hourly earnings for workers paid by the hour and computing hourly earnings for other workers by dividing their usual weekly earnings by usual weekly hours of work. For all other countries, the data were provided by the national statistical authorities.

Chart 2.1.

Real minimum wages, 1970-1997[a]
Indices: 1975 or 1991 = 100

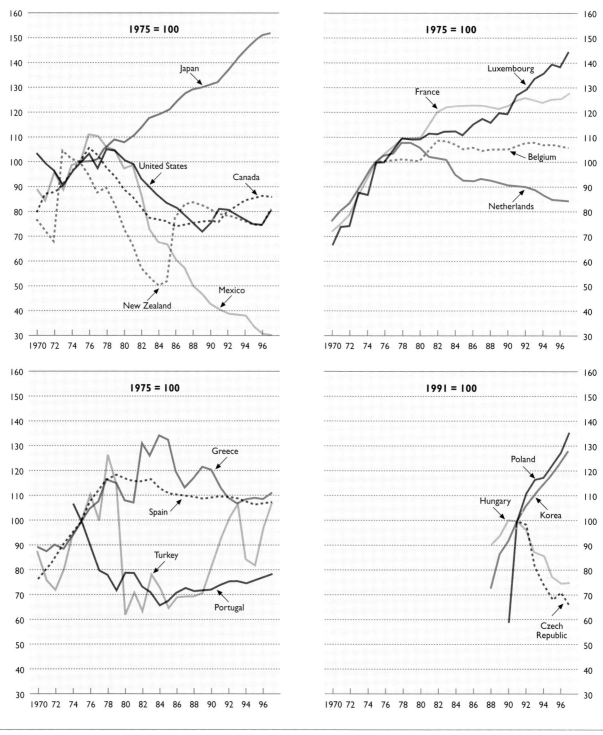

a)   For each country, annual average of the nominal value of the minimum wage deflated by the Consumer Price Index.
Source: OECD Minimum Wage Database.

Chart 2.2.

Ratio of minimum wages to average wages, 1970-1997[a]

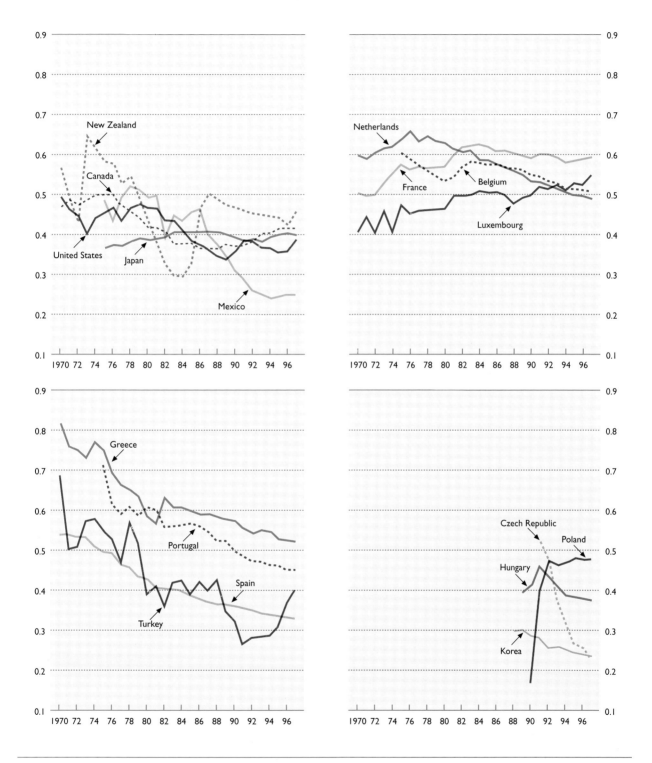

a)   Average wages refer to median earnings for full-time workers except as follows: for Greece, Luxembourg, Mexico and Turkey, they refer to mean earnings of manufacturing workers; and, for Portugal, they refer to mean earnings in the business sector. See Annex 2.A for more details.

Source: OECD Minimum Wage Database.

the United States than in France is also reflected in a much lower proportion of all employees paid at the minimum or less. In the United States, just over 5 per cent of all employees received hourly earnings at, or less than, the Federal minimum in 1996, whereas in France more than 10 per cent of all employees are currently paid the SMIC or less. At around 17 per cent, Mexico stands out for its high incidence of minimum-wage work. This reflects both a high degree of earnings inequality and extensive employment in the informal sector.

The profile of minimum-wage workers corresponds closely to that for low-paid workers reported in the 1996 *Employment Outlook* (Chapter 3, Table 3.5). The incidence of minimum-wage work tends to be highest amongst youth, women and part-time workers. It also tends to be much higher than average in retailing, hotels and restaurants, and in smaller firms. In terms of the distribution of minimum-wage workers, Table 2.4 suggests that, while younger workers are disproportionately affected, there are substantial numbers of older workers who are also affected.

4. Developments over time

In several countries, there has been a substantial erosion of the real value of the minimum wage since the mid to late-1970s (Chart 2.1). This is particularly apparent in the case of Mexico. Since their introduction, minimum wages have also fallen in real terms in the Czech Republic and Hungary, but have risen substantially in Poland. France and Luxembourg are the only other European countries to have recorded almost continuous rises, although the most substantial increases have occurred in Japan and Korea.

These trends could merely reflect developments in overall wage growth. However, as shown in Chart 2.2, minimum wages have also fallen relative to average wages in many countries over the past 25 years. The decline has been most pronounced in Mexico. The ratio has risen somewhat from a low level in Canada in recent years, but is still well below the level of the mid-1970s. In the United States, the trend decline reflects the fact that the Federal minimum is fixed in nominal terms and adjusted irregularly.

Among the European countries, there has been a trend decline in minimum wages in relative terms everywhere except France, Luxembourg and, more recently, Poland. In France, where the SMIC has been boosted by the occasional 'coup de pouce' over and above the rise in inflation, the ratio has remained stable since the early 1980s. However, in terms of labour costs, there has been a significant fall over the past five years. Since 1992, employer

social security contributions for low-wage workers have been reduced substantially and the cost of hiring a minimum-wage worker relative to one at median earnings has declined from nearly 60 per cent in 1992 to just over 50 per cent in 1996. Similarly, in Belgium and the Netherlands, there have also been reductions over recent years in employer social security charges for low-paid workers and the decline in the relative value of minimum wages in terms of labour costs is more pronounced than shown in Chart 2.2.

Information on how these changes in the relative value of minimum wages have affected the number of minimum-wage workers is very scanty. In both the Netherlands and the United States, the fall in the relative and real value of the minimum has been accompanied by a decline in the incidence of minimum-wage employment from over 10 per cent in the mid to late 1970s to around 5 per cent or less in 1996 and 1997. In France, the opposite has occurred: a higher proportion of workers is currently working at the level of the SMIC than at any time over the past 25 years.

C. EMPLOYMENT EFFECTS OF THE MINIMUM WAGE

One argument against a statutory minimum wage is that, if set above the market-clearing level, it will result in job losses and so the very workers that it is intended to benefit may lose out. However, some recent studies have questioned both the earlier empirical work as well as the theoretical basis for predicting job losses. There has been a resurgence of interest in alternative models of the labour market, and this section begins with a brief survey of them. The recent empirical literature is then reviewed, followed by an international analysis of minimum-wage effects on employment.

1. Theoretical considerations

Under the assumption of a perfectly competitive labour market, a minimum wage which is set above the market clearing-wage will result in a decline in labour demand and a lower equilibrium level of employment. Alternative economic models have been put forward that predict insignificant or positive employment effects of minimum wages. The simplest such model is a labour market with a monopsonistic employer. Others include efficiency-wage, human-capital models and search-theoretic models (see Box 2).

There has been much debate about which model best represents the way labour markets operate.[6] Generally, negative employment effects are more likely the higher the level of the minimum

Box 2. **Theoretical models of the employment effects of minimum wages**

As shown in Figure A, according to standard *neo-classical theory*, a minimum wage, W*m*, which is fixed above the market-clearing wage, W*e*, will lower labour demand to N*m* and lead to employment losses of N*e*–N*m*. This unambiguous prediction stems from a number of restrictive assumptions such as homogenous labour, perfectly competitive labour markets and perfect information. In practice, labour markets are characterised by heterogeneous firms and workers, and wage differentials for seemingly similar workers.

Figure A

Minimum wages and employment in a competitive labour market

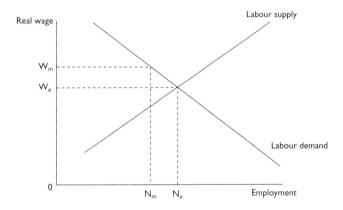

The simplest model where positive employment effects of the minimum wage may arise is a labour market with a *monopsonistic employer* or, more broadly, where firms have some discretion in wage-setting (see Figure B). In such a model, workers are assumed to have little negotiating power since they cannot easily obtain employment

Figure B

Minimum wages and employment in a monopsonistic labour market

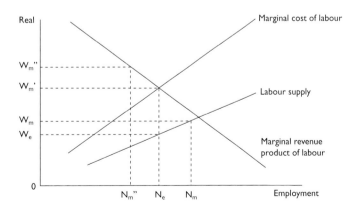

(continued on next page)

(continued)

with other employers. A monopsonistic labour market may arise because workers are not very mobile geographically. In this case, the employer is able to set wages, We, below the marginal product of labour. Imposing a minimum wage, say at Wm, may raise employment. The positive employment effect of the minimum wage will be maximised at the wage level corresponding to the market-clearing wage in a competitive labour market. For levels of the minimum wage above the competitive labour market wage, these job gains will be reversed with employment falling below its original level, Ne, for wages above Wm', say at Wm''. A higher elasticity of labour supply and/or a lower elasticity of labour demand imply a larger range in which minimum wages can be increased without generating job losses.

In *eciency-wage* models, employers are assumed to set wages for their employees above the market equilibrium level in order to increase workers' productivity and reduce shirking and job turnover. In this context, higher minimum wages may result in increased employment. As in the monopsony case, beyond a certain level, a rise in the minimum wage will produce negative employment effects. Rebitzer and Taylor (1995) show that, within an efficiency-wage framework, minimum wages will increase employment in the short-run. However, in the long-run, the gains may be lost, depending on the position of firms along the profit curve and on subsequent changes in product prices and the number of firms operating in the market.

Other models that allow for the possibility of positive employment effects of the minimum wage build on endogenous-growth considerations linked to *human capital investment* decisions. The key assumption is that minimum wages provide incentives for low-productivity workers to invest in more training or education in order to raise their productivity. The resulting increase in human capital has a positive impact on growth and, consequently, employment. Cahuc and Michel (1996) show that a decrease in the minimum wage may even reduce growth. Cubitt and Hargreaves-Heap (1996) argue that the net employment loss of minimum wages may be zero for a given range of values of the minimum wage since they will increase investment by firms in physical capital and by individuals in human capital. Acemoglou and Pischke (1998) also show that minimum wages may increase firm-provided training to low-skilled employees.

Minimum wages have also been analysed using a *job-search framework*. Within this framework, the sign of the employment effects depends on the level of minimum wage and its impact on the intensity of job search, the level of acceptance wages and the job offer probability. Swinnerton (1996) presents an equilibrium search model where firms have downward-sloping labour demand curves, labour productivity varies from firm to firm, and the unemployed have imperfect information and search randomly and sequentially for jobs. The author shows that, because of a rise in average labour productivity, positive welfare effects may still arise even in those cases where negative employment effects occur.

wage relative to workers' productivity, the more elastic the demand for labour, the less elastic the supply of labour, and the smaller the investment responses of firms and individuals. The larger the elasticity of substitution between skilled and unskilled labour, the larger the negative employment effects for the less skilled are likely to be. Consequently, the size and the sign of any employment effects may differ across firms, individuals (by age and skill levels) and geographical areas, and according to the level of the minimum wage.

One final issue concerns the short-run and long-run impacts of changes in the minimum wage. Many of the theoretical models compare the new equilibrium level of employment with the old. However, given adjustment costs, the short-run effects may be much more muted than predicted by theory. Moreover, as some of the human capital models suggest, dynamic responses, such as increased investment in education and training, may alter the simple predictions of long-run responses based on more static models.

These theoretical considerations have several implications for the empirical study of the employment effects of minimum wages. First, it is important to allow for the possibility of both positive and negative employment responses. Second, there may be a certain degree of non-linearity in employment responses, with positive effects occurring for minimum wages below a certain level, but job losses occurring thereafter. Third, disemployment effects may vary according to a worker's age, skills, industry and region of employment. In particular, the possibilities of substitution between workers of different skill levels imply that aggregate job losses may be more muted than for specific groups of workers. Finally, it is important to distinguish between short-run and long-run employment effects.

2. Recent empirical studies on minimum wages and employment

An overview of recent empirical studies is provided in Annex 2.B (Table 2.B.1). Earlier studies, based predominantly on time-series data for the United States, were summarised by Brown et al. (1982). They concluded that a 10 per cent increase in the level of the minimum wage reduced teenage employment by a range of 1 to 3 per cent. These and other results have been challenged by the work of Card and Krueger (1995) on the basis of both methodological considerations and their own empirical findings of insignificant or small positive employment effects.

The work of Card and Krueger has, in turn, been subject to intensive scrutiny and launched a raft of further empirical work on the impact of minimum wages on employment. A range of new data sources has been tapped, and various methodological approaches have been adopted, each with its own strengths and weaknesses (see Box 3). While differences in methodology and data sources may account for some of the widely differing results which have emerged, it is more difficult to reconcile the contradictory results which have arisen even when similar data and estimation techniques have been used.

Most empirical studies focus on the employment effects for youth. This is partly because youth generally have fewer skills and less labour market experience than other workers and, hence, their labour demand is likely to be more sensitive to hikes in the minimum wage. On the basis of the available evidence, however, it is not clear that a rise in minimum wages has unambiguously led to job losses for youth in all circumstances. The results of the time-series and pooled, cross-sectional studies are especially contradictory, with some authors finding negative, but generally small, employment effects and others finding either statistically insignificant or small positive effects. Apart from the econometric issues of differences in specification and estimation techniques, it may be the case that in all of these studies the net, aggregate, employment response for youth masks more substantial job losses for the least skilled among them as a result of substitution of more skilled for less-skilled youth.

These substitution effects can be potentially identified or controlled for in the studies based on longitudinal data. In these studies, there appears to be greater agreement that individuals affected by a minimum-wage rise are less likely to be subsequently employed than other workers who are not affected by the rise.

For other groups of workers, there is much less empirical evidence. The scant evidence available indicates that employment of part-time workers has risen in the United States following increases in minimum wages [Ressler et al. (1996)]. Manning (1996) suggests that monopsony is likely to occur with respect to the employment of women. However, the evidence available to date on the employment effects of minimum wages for women does not permit one to draw clear conclusions [Nakosteen and Zimmer (1989); Myatt and Murrel (1990); Williams and Mills (1998)].

3. International evidence on employment effects

One of the main difficulties facing national studies based on aggregate time-series data is the lack of variation in minimum wages relative to other factors affecting employment outcomes. This makes it difficult to identify the employment effects with any precision using standard econometric techniques. A potential source of much greater variation is provided by the large differences *across* OECD countries in minimum relative to average wages.

Therefore, a number of pooled, cross-country, time-series regressions were carried out using annual data in which employment-population ratios for different demographic groups were regressed against the ratio of minimum to average wages and other explanatory variables to control for various cyclical and institutional factors believed to influence employment outcomes (see Annex 2.C for details of the specification used and estimation procedures).[7] The corresponding estimates of the elasticity of employment with respect to minimum wages are presented in Table 2.5. The analysis covers the period 1975 to 1996 for nine countries: Belgium, Canada, France, Greece, Japan, the Netherlands, Portugal, Spain and the United States. Separate regressions were carried out by gender (except for Portugal and Spain) for teenagers, young adults and prime-age adults. The minimum-wage ratio was calculated separately for men, women and all persons using the corresponding average wage for each group. For Portugal and Spain, however, long time series of average wages by gender were not readily available and so two sets of regressions were carried out according to whether these two countries were included or excluded.

The specifications follow the approach adopted in much of the time-series literature, but adapted to a cross-country context. While the methodology underlying this approach has been subject to criticism (see Box 3), its use permits greater comparability of the results with those of earlier studies. However, even within the standard approach, there has been considerable debate about the most appropriate specification and the estimated elasticities are very sensitive to differences in these specifications.

Box 3. **Estimating employment effects of minimum wages**

Much empirical work has adopted a *time-series* approach in which a measure of employment for a demographic group thought most likely to be affected by the minimum (*e.g.*, the employment/population ratio for youth) is regressed against the ratio of minimum to average wages and a set of other control variables. One advantage of the time-series approach is that, in theory, both short-run and long-run responses can be distinguished. However, the empirical findings from time-series models tend to be sensitive to the exact estimation methodology used and to the inclusion/exclusion of different explanatory variables, *e.g.* time trends and controls for the business cycle. An additional drawback is the possible endogeneity of the minimum/average wage ratio. In particular, this ratio may capture, not only variation in the level of the minimum wage, but also the impact of labour demand or supply shocks on the level of the average wage. More generally, the model specified does not normally bear a direct relation to the theory. Some studies have tried to avoid these latter problems by adopting a more structural approach that relies on estimating both wage and labour demand equations, and then extrapolating the employment effects of minimum wages [for example, Bazen and Martin (1991)].

Studies based on *pooled cross-section* or *longitudinal data* would appear to provide generally more reliable estimates in that they can allow for greater variation in relative minimum wages across individuals, industries, firms or regions. However, in many cases the endogeneity problem also applies because the estimating model involves regressing employment-population ratios on the minimum-wage ratio. Moreover, these studies often capture only short-term effects.

Some studies using pooled cross-section or longitudinal data adopt the so-called *natural-experiment* approach. This compares employment changes for specific regions, individuals or firms that experience a change in the minimum wage with that of similar regions, individuals or firms which are unaffected by the change, *i.e.* the control group. These studies have been carried out most often in the US, where changes in the level of the minimum wage in each State have frequently taken place at different times. In Europe, studies of this type have compared changes in employment for workers earning just below or just above the minimum, and across regions, industries or firms with a different incidence of low-paid workers. The main criticism of these studies is that it is difficult to control fully for factors other than the change in minimum wages which might explain different employment responses between the groups of workers affected and the "control" group. Furthermore, some of these studies have been criticised for covering too short a time span, which may not permit them to detect longer-run employment responses.

Finally, a few studies have used the so-called *Meyer-Wise* approach. Meyer and Wise (1983) estimated what the earnings distribution would look like in the absence of the minimum wage based on the actual distribution of earnings above the legal minimum. The employment effects of the minimum can then be inferred by taking the difference between the estimated number of workers with below minimum-wage earnings according to this counterfactual distribution and the actual number at or below the minimum. However, this method has been shown to be very sensitive to the functional form of the counterfactual distribution and the extent to which the minimum wage has spillover effects on wages higher up in the distribution [Dickens *et al.* (1994b)].

Therefore, no attempt was made to obtain a single "best estimate". Instead, the results in Table 2.5 are reported according to a range of specifications. For each specification, elasticities are reported with either the prime-age male unemployment rate (Columns 1 and 3) or the output gap (Columns 2 and 4) as controls for cyclical factors. For several countries, the prime-age male unemployment rate has also trended upwards over time and so may capture factors other that just cyclical ones. In addition, some of the results are adjusted for autocorrelation and heteroscedasticity (Columns 3 and 4). In all cases, the specifications include country-specific time trends and a range of variables to control for institutional factors. Country dummy terms have also been included in each regression to control for all other factors which vary across countries but are constant over time.

The results suggest that minimum-wage rises have a negative impact on teenage employment, although the magnitude of the reported elasticities varies significantly, from –0.3 to –0.6 when Spain and Portugal are excluded, and from 0 to –0.2 when they are included in the regression. In some of the specifications, negative employment effects are also found for groups of workers other than teenagers.

Tests on the equations for individual countries (not reported) point to serially correlated error terms. Correcting for autocorrelation and heteroscedasticity results in elasticities for prime-age adults that are close to zero (Columns 3 and 4 in

Table 2.5. **Estimated employment elasticities with respect to the minimum wage, based on cross-country regressions**[a]

	Linear specification				Log specification			
	(1)	(2)	(3)	(4)	(1)	(2)	(3)	(4)
Elasticities								
Excluding Spain and Portugal								
Teenagers, aged 15-19[b]	−0.58**	−0.37**	−0.41**	−0.27*	−0.42**	−0.32*	−0.40**	−0.31*'
Men	−0.43**	−0.22	−0.31**	−0.19	−0.38**	−0.26*	−0.38**	−0.28*'
Women	−0.70**	−0.49**	−0.48**	−0.30*	−0.40**	−0.33*	−0.40**	−0.33*'
Youth, aged 20-24	−0.14**	−0.04	−0.10*	−0.05	−0.12	−0.03	−0.07	−0.05
Men	−0.10	0.01	−0.10*	−0.06	−0.12	−0.02	−0.11	−0.05
Women	−0.20**	−0.11	−0.08	−0.04	−0.11	−0.05	−0.03	−0.04
Adults, aged 25-54	−0.09**	−0.04	0.00	0.01	−0.09**	−0.05*	0.00	0.00
Men	−0.01	0.05**	−0.01	0.05**	−0.02	0.03	0.00	0.04*
Women	−0.22**	−0.19**	−0.03	0.00	−0.18**	−0.17**	0.02	0.02
Including Spain and Portugal								
Teenagers, aged 15-19[b]	−0.11	0.10	−0.20*	−0.07	−0.01	0.01	−0.19**	−0.15*
Youth, aged 20-24	−0.08	0.06	−0.06	−0.03	−0.04	0.07	−0.03	−0.04
Adults, aged 25-54	−0.07**	−0.01	0.01	0.02	−0.06*	−0.01	0.01	0.01
Controls for								
Prime-age male unemployment rate	Yes	No	Yes	No	Yes	No	Yes	No
Output gap[c]	No	Yes	No	Yes	No	Yes	No	Yes
Institutional factors	Yes	Yes	Yes	Yes	Yes	Yes	Yes	Yes
Fixed country effects and country-specific time trends	Yes	Yes	Yes	Yes	Yes	Yes	Yes	Yes
Autocorrelation and heteroscedasticity	No	No	Yes	Yes	No	No	Yes	Yes
Number of observations								
Excluding Spain and Portugal	154	154	154	154	154	154	154	154
Including Spain and Portugal	198	198	198	198	198	198	198	198

** and * indicate significance at the 1 per cent and 5 per cent levels, respectively.

a) The regressions were carried out using data for 1975 to 1996 pooled across nine countries: Belgium, Canada, France, Greece, Japan, the Netherlands, Portugal, Spain and the United States. Portugal and Spain could not be included in the separate regressions for men and women as sufficiently long time series of average earnings by sex were not available for constructing the relevant minimum-wage ratios. In the case of the linear specification, the elasticities have been calculated with reference to the means of the minimum-wage and employment/population ratios. A value for teenagers of −0.58 in Column 1 (excluding Portugal and Spain) of the linear specification, for example, indicates that a 10 per cent rise in the minimum wage will, all else equal, result in a 5.8 per cent fall in their employment. See Annex 2.C for further details on specification and estimation.

b) 16-19 in Spain and the United States.

c) Ratio of actual to smoothed real GDP, using the Hoderick-Prescott filter with a smoothing factor of 1 000.

Sources: Secretariat estimates. See Annex 2.C for further details and for the sources of the data used in the regressions.

both the log and linear specifications). In the case of young adults, the elasticities are also lower and for men and women separately are either close to or not statistically different from zero. However, making these adjustments does not change the conclusion that negative and significant employment elasticities are estimated for teenagers for both sexes. The results in Columns 3 and 4 of the linear and log specifications suggest that a 10 per cent rise in the minimum wage, all else equal, is associated with a fall in employment for teenagers of between 2 and 4 per cent.

The results are generally quite robust to a number of changes in the basic specification (see the discussion in Annex 2.C). For instance, the estimated elasticities are little changed if the minimum

and average wage are entered as separate variables rather than as a ratio. There is also little evidence that negative employment effects are larger in relatively high minimum-wage countries as compared with relatively low minimum-wage countries. The results are more sensitive to whether the time trends are omitted or not and so in future work it would be of some interest to explicitly include other variables such as enrolment rates which may also be closely related to employment rates for teenagers and youth.

Bearing in mind the possible "fragility" of the results in Table 2.5, a number of tentative conclusions can be drawn. Firstly, the results suggest that a rise in the minimum wage has a negative effect on teenage employment. Secondly, negative employment effects for young adults are generally close to or insignificantly different from zero. Thirdly, for prime-age adults, the most plausible specifications suggest that minimum wages have no impact on their employment outcomes. Overall, these findings, especially for younger workers, are very similar to the results found by Brown *et al.* (1982).

At the same time, it is important to note that these estimated effects are relatively insignificant in terms of explaining the large decline that has occurred in the teenage employment-population ratio in some countries. In Table 2.6, the estimated contribution of minimum wages has been calculated on the basis of the regression results underlying the elasticities reported in Column 3 of the linear specification. In France, for example, the teenage employment-population ratio declined by over 18 percentage points between 1975 and 1996, but the rise in the minimum wage relative to average wages accounts for less than half a percentage point of this decline. An even more dramatic decline in teenage employment occurred in Spain, despite a fall in the relative value of minimum wages. Thus, the substantial difference across countries in teenage employment trends can only be marginally attributed to differences in the evolution of minimum wages and must be explained by other factors.

D. IMPACT OF MINIMUM WAGES ON EARNINGS AND INCOME DISTRIBUTION

1. Introduction

While considerable research has been devoted to the employment effects of statutory minimum wages, there are fewer studies of their impact on the distribution of earnings and income. Yet, historically, two important – though certainly not exclusive – goals of minimum-wage legislation have been to pay workers a "fair" compensation for their work effort and to raise the standard of living of low-paid workers and their families. Therefore, this Section examines the distributional impacts of minimum wages, first on individual earnings and then on household incomes.

2. Impact on the earnings distribution

How does the minimum wage affect the earnings distribution? Simple neo-classical models predict that if a statutory minimum wage is binding, the imposition of a minimum will lead to those workers whose productivity levels are below the minimum wage being laid off [Stigler (1946)]. This truncation of the earnings distribution leads directly to a measured reduction of the dispersion of the earnings of those in jobs.[8]

There are many nuances to this prediction. One example is the model of Teulings (1996), which takes into account workers of different skill types. An increase in the minimum wage leads to layoffs for workers at or near the old minimum wage. The increase, however, lowers the relative price of more skilled labour. Shifting demand toward more skilled labour implies that some workers with wages originally between the two minima will be able to find employment at or above the new minimum. Some workers initially earning above the new minimum wage will also be affected. Their wages increase as well, with such spillover effects weakening the further up the distribution one goes. The net effect is also a truncation of the earnings distribution below the minimum wage, but with some increase in the portion of the workforce earning above the new minimum wage.

Empirical work has, however, pointed to an impact of minimum wages on the earnings distribution that is not explained by either the simple or complex versions of the neo-classical model: the

Table 2.6. **Estimated impact of the minimum wage on teenage employment**[a]

Percentage point changes in teenage employment/population ratios

	Belgium	Canada	France	Greece	Japan	Netherlands	Portugal	Spain	United States
Actual change, 1975-1996	−14.5	−5.6	−18.5	−15.2	−4.7	0.5	−40.4	−34.5	0.3
Change explained by									
Minimum wage	1.1	1.1	−0.3	2.9	−0.5	2.1	−1.4	1.6	1.2
Other factors	−16.9	−4.7	−17.7	−17.4	−3.3	2.1	−34.3	−35.7	−1.7
Residual	1.2	−2.1	−0.5	−0.7	−0.9	−3.7	−4.6	−0.4	0.7

a) The estimated contribution of changes in the minimum-wage ratio to changes in the teenage employment/population ratio is based on the regression results reported for the linear specification in Column 3 of Table 2.5. Teenagers refer to persons aged 16 to 19 in Spain and the United States, and 15 to 19 in the other countries.

Sources: Secretariat estimates. See Table 2.5 and Annex 2.C for further details on estimation methodology and data sources.

presence of a spike at the minimum wage, indicating a high proportion of workers earning exactly that wage [Card and Krueger (1995); DiNardo et al. (1996)]. As the minimum wage increases, the spike moves to the new minimum, indicating that many of those previously earning a wage below the new minimum wage are now earning exactly the minimum wage. Though the theories explaining this shift are not easily summarised, the existence of a spike is a well established empirical regularity [Card and Krueger (1995)].[9]

Minimum wages can also affect earnings differentials among demographic groups. Groups with higher proportions of low-wage workers are likely to see their earnings increase relative to those of other groups when minimum wages are increased. They will receive a disproportionate share of the "pay increase" as well as a disproportionate loss of low-paying jobs if there are disemployment effects.

In sum, a minimum wage affects the earnings distribution in at least three ways: i) by reducing the proportion of the workforce earning below the minimum; ii) by increasing the proportion of workers earning exactly the minimum; and iii) through spillover effects that affect workers initially earning above the new minimum. The magnitude of these impacts is an empirical question.

The recent empirical literature on these issues is summarised in Annex 2.D (Table 2.D.1). Several approaches have been adopted. Meyer and Wise (1983) sought to measure the impact of minimum wages by examining the difference between the actual earnings distribution and that which would have existed in its absence. This method is very sensitive to the assumed functional form of the counterfactual distribution and other parametric assumptions and recent work has sought to minimise the use of such assumptions [Green and Paarsch (1996)]. Another approach is to simulate the effect of increases in minimum wages on the earnings distribution (sometimes including disemployment effects, sometimes not), and then to use this simulated distribution to calculate measures of dispersion and of differentials across different demographic groups. A third method relies on multivariate analysis to uncover correlations between the levels of, or changes in, the minimum wage and measures of earnings dispersion.

Taken as a whole, several key findings emerge from this literature. First, almost all studies find that minimum wages do lead to a compression of the earnings distribution. Second, how much earnings dispersion is reduced depends on how high the minimum wage is set relative to the rest of the distribution. One indication of this is shown in Chart 2.3. Countries with higher minima relative to median earnings have both a lower dispersion of

earnings and incidence of low pay. Third, minimum wages have tended to narrow the earnings differentials across demographic groups. These effects have been strongest in the cases of gender and age differentials, because the incidence of employment at low wages is greater for women than for men and for younger workers relative to older ones.

3.   Impact on poverty and income distribution

The links between minimum wages and income at the family or household level are more complex than the relationship between wage minima and the earnings distribution. As Neumark and Wascher (1997) discuss, a prerequisite for an increase in the minimum wage to raise the incomes of poor families and to reduce family income inequality is that minimum wages redistribute earnings toward low-wage workers. This will be the case if the increase in earnings accruing to those at a rate of pay between the old and new minima exceeds the loss in earnings among any low-wage workers who lose jobs or find their hours reduced as the result of the minimum-wage hike.

The absolute size of the elasticity of employment with respect to wages provides an indication as to whether this prerequisite is usually met.[10] But many other factors must also be considered. First, a minimum wage increase could affect the labour supply of other family members and, as a result, the family's total income, although in what direction and to what extent is not clear. Second, these economic changes may induce changes in family living arrangements, with resulting impacts on measured poverty. Third, changes in labour income may affect government transfers received by the family. In general, those families experiencing job loss as a result of a minimum wage hike may receive an increase in government assistance, though they may also lose in-work benefits.

Perhaps more importantly, how much of the minimum wage increase will flow to those in poverty and whether or not it reduces family income inequality depends on two additional factors. First, the higher concentration of low-wage workers in the bottom of the family income distribution the more likely that low-income families will benefit disproportionately from minimum-wage increases. Second, the proportion of low-income families that have low-wage workers is also of considerable importance, as families without labour income do not benefit directly from increases in the return to labour.

Recent studies focusing on one or more of these issues are summarised in Annex 2.D (second part of Table 2.D.1). As with the earnings distribution literature, a range of methods and data have

Chart 2.3.

Minimum wages, low pay and earnings dispersion, mid-1990s

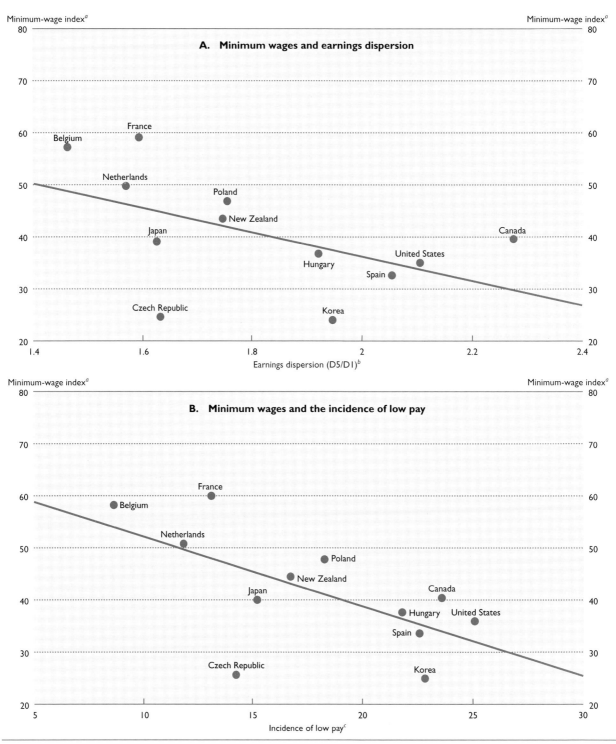

a)   Minimum wages as a percentage of median full-time earnings.
b)   Ratio of median earnings to the upper limit of earnings received by the bottom 10 per cent of full-time workers.
c)   Percentage of full-time workers receiving less than two-thirds of median earnings.
Sources: OECD Minimum Wage and Earnings Databases.

been used to attempt to answer different questions. Some view the minimum wage as one, among many, potential tools for improving the standard of living of those families where at least one individual is working. Thus, the focus is restricted to working families. For this group, minimum wages can have a visible impact on reducing poverty among families with low earnings, as well as on reducing the dispersion of family earnings. Others consider the impact of a minimum wage on poverty and income inequality among *all* families. Here, the impact will be smaller, as many families in the lower tail of the distribution have no earners present and, hence, cannot by definition benefit from a hike in the minimum wage.

Tables 2.7 and 2.8 show data on the overlap between those who are low paid and those who are in low-income households and, thus, provide an indication of where minimum wage hikes may have their greatest impact on poverty and the household income distribution when all households, not just working ones, are included. Because legal minimum wages do not exist across all the countries shown in the tables and to enhance comparability, the tables rely on a definition of low pay that is set equal to two-thirds of the median earnings of full-time, year-round workers. Poverty is also defined in a way that is consistent across countries, as those individuals with household incomes below one-half the median household income, adjusted for family size. Further

details on these calculations are contained in Annex 2.E.

The first four columns of Table 2.7 show the proportion of all individuals aged 16 or older in each part of the household income distribution who are low paid. For instance, the first row shows that in Belgium 1.9 per cent of adults that are members of poor households are low paid, with 2.7 per cent of

Table 2.8. **Distribution of low-paid workers**[a] **by household income, 1993**

| | Level of adjusted household income[b] | | |
	Below poverty	Low	Moderate to high
Belgium	7.3	9.9	82.8
Denmark	3.1	15.0	81.9
Germany	9.7	10.9	79.4
Greece	11.5	9.7	78.8
Spain	10.6	11.2	78.2
France	7.7	14.9	77.4
Ireland	3.3	3.8	92.9
Italy	18.4	10.4	71.2
Luxembourg	9.2	23.5	67.3
Netherlands	11.2	9.8	79.0
Portugal	13.7	9.5	76.8
United Kingdom	9.1	10.8	80.0
United States[c]	22.1	16.3	61.7

Notes and source: See Table 2.7.

Table 2.7. **Incidence of low-paid employment**[a] **by household income, 1993**

Percentages

| | A. Among all persons aged 16 and over | | | | B. Among all full-time, year-round employees | | | |
| | Level of adjusted household income[b] | | | | Level of adjusted household income[b] | | | |
	Below poverty	Low	Moderate to high	Total	Below poverty	Low	Moderate to high	Total
Belgium	1.9	2.1	2.9	2.7	64.9	30.8	7.8	9.1
Denmark	2.0	4.8	4.0	3.9	54.3	53.1	8.1	9.6
Germany	7.6	8.5	6.9	7.1	85.0	47.1	15.5	18.3
Greece	1.6	2.1	2.5	2.3	86.7	33.2	9.9	11.9
Spain	3.3	3.5	3.9	3.8	88.0	39.7	14.1	16.8
France	3.2	6.0	4.2	4.3	65.5	42.3	11.6	14.0
Ireland	1.7	1.3	5.8	4.8	89.9	30.9	18.1	18.9
Italy	3.8	2.8	2.7	2.9	73.4	20.3	9.2	11.7
Luxembourg	9.5	14.9	6.1	7.3	68.9	46.5	14.7	19.2
Netherlands	6.3	4.9	5.0	5.1	90.3	30.7	12.1	14.3
Portugal	4.0	4.9	5.7	5.3	61.6	28.7	13.0	15.4
United Kingdom	5.2	6.4	7.8	7.3	92.5	58.0	17.9	21.0
United States[c]	13.3	19.2	9.8	11.3	87.2	63.1	18.8	26.3

a) Low-paid employment refers to all employees working full-time, year-round and earning less than two-thirds of median earnings for this group.
b) Adjusted household income is calculated over all individuals. "Below poverty" refers to income of less than one-half the median adjusted household income; "Low" refers to income between one-half and two-thirds of the median; "Moderate to high" refers to income above two-thirds of the median.
c) 1995.
Source: See Annex 2.E.

all adults being low paid. Higher numbers imply a greater overlap between the working poor and the poverty population as a whole, suggesting a greater potential for minimum wages to improve the well-being of poor families. The incidence rate for adults in poverty ranges from under 2 per cent in Belgium, Greece and Ireland to over 13 per cent in the United States. Only Germany and Luxembourg have proportions exceeding one-half of that for the United States.

These numbers are low in part because low pay has only been measured for full-time, year-round workers and thus excludes those who work on a part-time or part-year basis or who are self-employed. The biggest reason, however, is the large number of individuals who do not work at all. The low incidence rates make it apparent why minimum wages cannot be considered – and are not designed to be – a tool to reduce poverty across all families: unless workers are present in a household, higher wages cannot affect that household's income.

The picture changes dramatically, however, when incidence rates of low pay are calculated among a group of workers, those employed full-time, year-round. The incidence of low pay among full-time, year-round workers in poverty – ranging from 54.3 per cent in Denmark to 92.5 per cent in the United Kingdom – indicates that the majority of low-income households with a worker present could potentially receive additional income from measures that boost the pay of low-wage workers.

Another interesting aspect of Table 2.7 is how the incidence rates of low-paid employment vary across the household income distribution. When the denominator is all adults, the incidence rate is usually higher for low-income individuals than for individuals in poverty. When the denominator is individuals working full-time, year-round, the incidence of low-paid employment falls with income, in some countries sharply so. The difference in the way the two incidence rates change with household income suggests that those without full-time, year-round work are a greater share of those individuals in poverty than of those with low incomes (also see Chapter 1).

The distribution of low-paid workers according to their household income is shown in Table 2.8 and provides an indication of the extent to which wage increases to the low paid will be concentrated among low-income households. Ireland stands out as having a particularly weak connection between low pay and low household income, with more than 90 per cent of low-wage workers living in households with moderate-to-high incomes. This result stems in large part from the fact that the incidence rate for low-paid employment for all individuals in moderate-to-high income families is more than four times

the comparable rate for low-income families. The data suggest that the labour force participation rate in Ireland's moderate-to-high income families relative to that in other families must be high in comparison to other countries. At the other end of the spectrum is the United States, which has more than one-fifth of its low-paid workers in poverty. Even here, the majority of any increases in wages paid to low-paid workers will accrue to individuals not living in poverty, as confirmed by many of the studies summarised in Table 2.D.1. The overlap between the low-paid and the poor increases, however, when attention is restricted to households with at least one worker.

In sum, in countries where there are large numbers of full-time/full-year "working poor," there is a greater potential for increases in the minimum wage to alleviate poverty and reduce the inequality of household income. A related question is the extent to which the level of the minimum wage contributes to cross-country differences in the overlap between those who are low-paid and those with low household incomes. As shown in Chart 2.3, those countries with higher minimum wages have narrower earnings distributions, which reduces the incidence of low pay. Similarly, countries with relatively high minimum wages have a lower incidence of low pay. Other factors – such as collective bargaining arrangements and differences in industrial structure – also affect the degree of earnings dispersion. Moreover, countries with similar levels of earnings inequality can be very dissimilar in terms of how the low paid are distributed across the household income spectrum, particularly if the rates of employment among individuals in low-income households are disparate. Though minimum wages undoubtedly influence cross-country differences in the extent to which those in poverty are working, other factors are clearly more important, including macroeconomic conditions, cultural norms and the generosity of public assistance.

4. The overlap of low pay and low incomes over the longer term

Tables 2.7 and 2.8 show the extent to which low-paid individuals reside in low-income households in a given year. This snapshot is incomplete. Over time, some workers will exit the ranks of the low paid, as either their pay increases or they lose jobs, while other workers will join these ranks. In addition, the composition of households changes frequently as well, as a result of children leaving the home, marriage, divorce and other such events. Therefore, to more fully assess the overlap between low pay and low household income, it is informative to follow individuals over longer periods of time. To do this, longitudinal data are required.[11]

Table 2.9 shows how the incidence of low-paid employment in different parts of the household income distribution (family income distribution in the case of the United States) varies as the time period expands. Because the composition of households often changes, it is necessary to follow the individual rather than the household. For each individual, an inflation-adjusted equivalent household income is calculated for each year and these incomes are summed over the period to form the household income distribution.

For each year, it is also determined whether an individual was among the low paid, defined as earnings below the low-pay threshold in any of the years under consideration. As the rates of low-pay inci-

dence are calculated over all adults rather than just adults in working families, they understate the extent to which working families are affected by low pay. For all countries, results are shown where the incidence of low pay was calculated using full-time, year-round workers. In addition, for the Netherlands, United Kingdom and the United States, calculations have also been made using all employees (see Annex 2.E for more details).

The first number in Table 2.9 indicates that for (west) Germany in 1993, low-paid (full-time, year-round) workers accounted for 3.6 per cent of all adults in poverty. The first number in the second row shows what happens to this incidence rate when the calculations are made over a two-year period. Thus, in Germany in 1992-1993, 5.5 per cent of those in poverty (measured by aggregate income over two

Table 2.9. **Incidence of low-paid employment by household income over one, two and five years**[a], **for all individuals aged 16 and over**

Percentages

	Period	Level of adjusted household income			
		Below poverty	Low	Moderate to high	Total
Low pay defined over full-time, year-round workers only					
Germany[b]	1993	3.6	3.8	2.8	3.0
	1992-1993	5.5	4.9	5.1	5.1
	1989-1993	11.6	10.3	9.3	9.5
Netherlands	1994	4.1	3.7	4.0	4.0
	1993-1994	5.0	5.0	6.2	6.0
	1990-1994	8.0	9.3	9.9	9.7
United Kingdom[c]	1995	1.7	7.0	9.2	8.4
	1994-1995	3.4	9.4	13.4	11.2
	1991-1995	6.0	12.1	20.3	17.1
United States[d]	1991	14.2	23.0	9.3	11.5
	1990-1991	20.5	34.0	13.0	16.4
	1987-1991	31.7	43.4	20.4	24.5
Low pay defined over all workers					
Netherlands	1994	12.5	6.6	7.7	8.0
	1993-1994	15.9	12.1	8.5	11.9
	1991-1994	20.5	17.8	17.7	17.9
United Kingdom[c]	1995	5.4	12.8	10.8	10.0
	1994-1995	8.4	17.4	15.4	14.4
	1991-1995	12.7	22.0	23.4	21.4
United States[d]	1991	33.3	32.6	13.4	18.9
	1990-1991	42.0	45.0	18.5	25.3
	1987-1991	52.9	56.3	28.1	35.0

a) Adjusted household income is summed over the relevant period and calculated over all individuals. The level of adjusted household income is classified as follows: "Below poverty" refers to income of less than one-half the median adjusted household income; "Low" refers to income between one-half and two-thirds of the median; and "Moderate to high" refers to income above two-thirds of the median. Low-paid employment is defined either among all employees or all employees working full-time, year-round (as indicated) and refers to all those earning less than two-thirds of the median earnings for the corresponding group. Low-paid employment can have occured in any year of the period. The results in this table are not directly comparable with those in Table 2.7 because of differences in data sources, definitions and reference years.
b) Western Germany only.
c) Low pay and full-time status are defined over the month rather than the year.
d) Adjusted family income is used instead of adjusted household income.
Source: See Annex 2.E.

years) were low paid in at least one of the two years. Given mobility into and out of low-paid employment, these incidence rates increase as the time period expands, for some countries dramatically so. This finding suggests that incidence rates for a single cross-section understate the portion of the population that is affected by policies designed to boost the earnings of low-paid workers.

The results in Table 2.8 suggested that for all countries the majority of low paid workers resided in households with moderate-to-high incomes. The results in Table 2.10 suggest that this finding holds even when the time period expands. In fact, there is evidence that low-paid workers are less concentrated among low-income households when the time period is lengthened. This result is driven by the fact that some individuals who are low paid in one year will find higher-wage employment in a later year, moving them up the income spectrum.

The second set of results for the Netherlands, the United Kingdom and the United States in Tables 2.9 and 2.10 suggests how the results would change if the definition of low paid is expanded to include employees working either part-time or part-year. The incidence of low pay is, not surprisingly, much higher using the broader definition. For instance, 4.1 per cent of adults in poverty in the Netherlands in 1994 were low paid using the narrower definition, versus 12.5 per cent for the broader definition. Low-paid workers are also more concentrated in poverty with the broader definition, although a majority of such workers resides in families with moderate- to high-incomes.

E. INTERACTIONS OF MINIMUM WAGES WITH THE TAX/BENEFIT SYSTEM

The impact of statutory minimum wages on employment and the earnings and income distribution will also depend on their interactions with the tax/benefit system. Several countries have accompanied a minimum-wage policy with either in-work benefits (e.g. Canada, New Zealand and the United States) or with payroll-tax reductions on low wages (e.g. Belgium, France and the Netherlands) in the hope of increasing labour demand for the low skilled, raising work incentives and alleviating in-work poverty.

Table 2.10. **Distribution of low-paid employment by household income over one, two and five years**[a]

Percentages

| | Period | Level of adjusted household income | | |
		Below poverty	Low	Moderate to high
Low pay defined over full-time, year-round workers only				
Germany[b]	1993	13.4	13.4	73.1
	1992-1993	10.0	11.6	78.3
	1989-1993	7.7	11.9	80.4
Netherlands	1994	9.9	11.7	78.3
	1993-1994	6.7	10.6	82.8
	1990-1994	4.8	12.2	83.0
United Kingdom[c]	1995	3.9	10.0	86.1
	1994-1995	5.4	9.1	85.5
	1991-1995	5.8	8.2	86.1
United States[d]	1991	23.2	18.3	58.5
	1990-1991	22.5	19.8	57.7
	1987-1991	21.3	17.5	61.3
Low pay defined over all workers				
Netherlands	1994	15.0	10.4	74.6
	1993-1994	10.6	12.8	76.6
	1991-1994	6.7	12.6	80.3
United Kingdom[c]	1995	9.7	14.0	76.2
	1994-1995	10.5	13.3	76.2
	1991-1995	10.0	11.9	78.1
United States[d]	1991	33.0	15.8	51.2
	1990-1991	30.0	17.0	53.2
	1987-1991	24.9	15.9	59.2

Notes and source: See Table 2.9.

Which of the two, subsidies for the low paid as opposed to employer subsidies, is the more suitable policy instrument to complement minimum wages will depend on the level of the minimum wage and the degree of earnings inequality. Countries with relatively low minimum wages, such as the United States, complement them with subsidies for the low paid in the form of in-work benefits. On the other hand, countries with higher levels of minimum wages, such as the Netherlands, have opted to subsidise the hiring of low-paid workers by reducing employers' payroll taxes on the low paid.[12] Countries with very compressed earnings distribution have tended not to implement in-work benefits since this has been seen as too costly because of the relatively large number of workers that would be entitled to the subsidy.

Both minimum wages and in-work benefits aim to ease the unemployment trap, *i.e.* the disincentives to work that arise from high, out-of-work, welfare payments relative to income from work.[13] Statutory minimum wages achieve this directly by raising gross earnings from low-paid jobs, whereas in-work benefits aim to " top up" net incomes from low-paid work either in the form of benefits or as a tax credit. At the same time, the two schemes have rather different implications in terms of financial costs for the public purse and the economic incentives they create for workers and firms. This has led some to argue that the two schemes may complement each other.

As discussed in the previous Section, minimum wages or in-work benefits cannot be expected to greatly reduce household poverty as many poorer households have nobody in work. However, their effectiveness in reducing income inequality among households with at least one person in work is greater. Even here, a rise in minimum wages may lead to substantial spillover to the non-poor, given the spread of minimum-wage workers throughout the income distribution. On the other hand, by raising incentives to work, minimum wages and in-work benefits could, in principle, shift some poorer, formerly, "workless" households out of poverty.

An advantage of in-work benefits is that they can be more closely targeted at the working poor [OECD (1997); Whitehouse (1996); Scholz (1996); Burkhauser *et al.* (1997)]. Nevertheless, they too face a number of drawbacks. High marginal effective tax rates associated with the phase-out range of the benefit give rise to disincentives to increase earned income beyond a certain limit. Moreover, since the benefits are usually means-tested on total family income, the spouses of the (potential) recipients may have an incentive to work a smaller number of hours or to drop out of the labour market in order for the family not to lose entitlement to the benefits. An

extensive system of in-work benefits might also provide an incentive for employers to lower wages for low-paid workers (sometimes termed "moral hazard"). This may occur directly or indirectly as a result of any increase in the labour supply stimulated by in-work benefits. An enforceable legal minimum wage could shift the benefits to workers, though possible disemployment effects would have to be considered. Take-up of in-work benefits may also be low because of stigma effects or lack of knowledge of the programme.[14]

Depending on the way they are implemented and the overall earnings distribution, in-work benefits can be very costly for the public purse and can involve administrative costs to avoid error and fraud. Minimum wages are instead paid by employers. It has been argued that the fiscal revenue from (higher) minimum wages could be used to cover part of the costs of in-work benefits schemes. However, if minimum wages also result in job losses, some of these gains may be offset by higher welfare expenditures. Moreover, the redistributive effects of relative price changes as a result of minimum wages would also need to be considered [Freeman (1996)].

It should also be remarked that minimum wages are paid to individuals, independently of the total family or household income, while in-work benefits are means-tested on total household income. In this respect, given the notable increase in household dissolution rates in all OECD countries in the past decades, means tests may be costly in the long-run because of larger scope for fraud and error and also because they may reinforce (married) women's dependency patterns with large costs for society in terms of lower participation rates, loss of human capital, lower earnings capacity and consequent dependency on social welfare benefits.

The advantages and disadvantages of each are summarised in Table 2.11. At first sight, it would appear that they may complement each other. In order to accurately assess the scope for complementarities, it is also important to take account of the "potential" beneficiaries of the two schemes. The incidence of minimum-wage work is greatest among teenagers, young adults, (married) women, and part-time workers though prime-age adults also account for a considerable proportion. Recipients of in-work benefits tend to be lone parents (60 per cent of recipients in the United States and 44 per cent in the United Kingdom) and one-earner couples with children (39 per cent in the United Kingdom). Although this distribution will tend to vary with different levels of minimum wages and different entitlement rules to in-work benefits, there seems to be a degree of complementarity in coverage between the two schemes. However, the two may be substitutes if, for example, the spouses (and the

Table 2.11. **Advantages and disadvantages of a statutory minimum wage and in-work benefits**

Positive effects and drawbacks	Minimum wage	In-work benefits
Positive effects		
Reduce in-work poverty	Limited	Yes
Ease the unemployment trap	Yes	Yes
Potential drawbacks		
Spillover to richer families	Yes	Limited
Reduce labour demand/employment	Yes (if set at a high rate)	No
Disincentives to increase earned income	No	Yes
Disincentives for spouses to work	No	Yes
May lower wages of low paid	No	Yes
Public budget/fiscal costs	No (if job losses small)	Yes
Scope for abuse and error	Limited	Yes
Stigma effects, low-take up	No	Yes (if implemented as a benefit rather than as a tax credit)

children) of low-wage workers have a disincentive to take-up or remain in work at the minimum wage, in order to allow their husbands to claim means-tested, in-work benefits.

The extent to which minimum wages and in-work benefits may complement each other will depend ultimately on the level at which they are set. The higher the level of the minimum wage and the lower the earnings thresholds that regulate entitlement to in-work benefits, the more likely they are to be substitutes rather than complements. However, it is extremely difficult to evaluate the overall net effects of such a policy mix given the complex interactions with other parts of the tax/benefit system and the resulting labour demand and supply responses. Microsimulations may provide some information on first-run effects of implementing various combinations of minimum wages and in-work benefits. However, they usually ignore longer-term behavioural responses.

In the United States, minimum wages and in-work benefits have co-existed for quite sometime, but little work on their possible interactions has been done. Burkhauser et al. (1997) simulate, separately, the effect of different levels of minimum wages and in-work benefits on the income distribution of households in the United States, using CPS data. They conclude that for the United States the Earned Income Tax Credit (EITC) is more effective than minimum wages in reducing household poverty. Bluestone and Ghilarducci (1996) simulate the impact of different levels of minimum wages and in-work benefits, implemented simultaneously, on the level of household income and hours of work for different household types. Negative employment effects are allowed for. The authors conclude that when considered in conjunction there are strong complementary effects between the minimum wage and the EITC.

In the United Kingdom, Family Credit has been in force since 1971 (originally under the name of Family Income Supplement). In the recent debate over the introduction of a national minimum wage, possible interactions between the two schemes have attracted considerable attention. Sutherland (1997) simulates changes in household incomes and hours of work for different levels of the minimum wage, and given the existing in-work and housing benefits schemes. She concludes that, unless minimum wages are set at a very high level, the benefit system must continue to subsidise low-income households to bring them out of poverty. Therefore, there is scope for complementarities. However, the author points out that means-tested benefits may create poverty traps and are very expensive to administer. Therefore, she argues, other policy tools, such as a higher non-means-tested child benefit or increased progressivity in the tax and national insurance systems, may be more effective in alleviating poverty, especially in the long-run.

The effectiveness of a combined policy of in-work benefits and minimum wages will depend on a number of other factors. The wider the earnings distribution, the greater the likelihood that in-work benefits will increase aggregate labour supply and at a lower cost [OECD (1997)]. Good access to child-care facilities and the provision of universal child allowances may cancel out or reduce the disincentives to work or to work longer hours for lone parents and for women married to low-paid men who are entitled to means-tested, in-work benefits. Finally, training courses may need to be made available to low-productivity workers to improve their skills and, thus, their chances of obtaining a job at the minimum wage and climbing the earnings ladder.

F. CONCLUSIONS

As with most policy measures, statutory minimum wages imply both benefits and costs. They can play a role in preventing wages from falling below socially unacceptable levels. They can also serve to improve incentives to take up work. However, if they give rise to large disemployment effects, their costs may outweigh the benefits. Their effectiveness in bolstering incomes of low-paid workers will also depend on their interactions with other policies designed to support low-income households.

Both theory and empirical evidence are inconclusive about the precise employment effects of minimum wages over some range relative to average wages. However, at high levels, there is general agreement that a statutory minimum wage will reduce employment. While sometimes conflicting, there is evidence that young workers may be most vulnerable to job losses.

The considerable diversity in the way in which minimum wages are set and operated in OECD countries suggests that there is some scope to limit the detrimental effect of minimum wages on employment. For example, reduced minimum rates exist for youths and apprentices in many countries, and special employment programmes may also allow employers to pay younger workers less than the statutory minimum.

There is also flexibility in the overall setting of minimum wages. While it may be politically difficult to cut minimum wages in nominal terms – if seen as too high – this has often occurred in real terms over time as a result of price inflation. In most countries, minimum wages have also fallen relative to average wages. Thus, it may be prudent for governments not to be locked into a rigid formula for regular adjustments of the minimum wage either in terms of price or wage inflation. This would need to be balanced against the possibility of a greater level of social conflict in the absence of a concrete commitment to adjust the minimum for changes in the cost of living or in line with productivity growth. In the Netherlands, for instance, this balance is struck by linking minimum wages to average wage increases, but subject to the inactivity rate remaining below a specified level. Some countries have also used reductions in employers' social security contributions to lower the cost of hiring low-paid workers while maintaining the real take-home value of the minimum wage.

Even if detrimental effects of minimum wages on employment can be mitigated, how effective are minimum wages as a policy instrument for raising the living standards of poorer workers? Countries with relatively high minimum wages have less earnings inequality and a lower incidence of low pay. In addition, minimum wages have been shown to narrow earnings differentials across demographic groups, particularly between young and older workers and male and female workers. There is also some evidence that minimum wages can help in reducing poverty among working families, as well as reduce income inequality for this group. Their impact on the income distribution for all families are less substantial, however, owing to the fact that many poor families do not have any workers present. The impact of minimum wages on the family income distribution depends importantly on whether those who are low paid also tend to be in families with low overall incomes. There is substantial variation across the OECD countries in this overlap.

The effectiveness of a statutory minimum wage in tackling low pay and poverty will also depend on its interactions with the tax/benefit system and should be assessed in the context of a policy package for tackling social inequities. In-work benefits, in particular, have received considerable attention as an alternative tool for alleviating working poverty. Both minimum wages and in-work benefits aim to increase work incentives by raising the rewards from work relative to unemployment income. At the same time, the two schemes have rather different implications in terms of financial costs for the public purse and the economic incentives they create for workers and firms, and they do not necessarily affect the same groups of people. This has led some to argue that the two schemes may possibly complement each other and, thus, achieve greater benefits than for any one measure in isolation. However, the interactions between minimum wages and tax/benefit systems are complex and designing the appropriate policy mix will depend on individual country circumstances.

In sum, there is considerably more flexibility across OECD countries than is often recognised in the setting of minimum wages and, hence, they can be tailored to limit some of their negative features. There is also scope to judiciously combine them with other policies to more effectively tackle growing social inequities.

Notes

1. It is not always easy to make a clear cut distinction between those countries with a statutory or national minimum wage and those without. For example, the Australian Industrial Relations Commission introduced a new Federal Minimum Wage in its April 1997 Safety Net Review Wages decision which applies to employees who work under Federal awards (around 40 per cent of all employees). Moreover, subsequent wage case decisions in all States except for Tasmania have applied the Federal Minimum Wage to workers under State awards. Nevertheless, there is no automatic link between the Federal Minimum Wage and wages set under State awards and so it was decided not to include Australia in this study as having a national minimum wage.

2. To a more limited extent than in Canada, Japan, Mexico and the United States, regional minima exist or existed in a few other countries. In Portugal, a separate rate was set for the Azores and continues to be set for Madeira. Separate minimum wage rates were also set for the French overseas departments and territories prior to 1996. Finally, for Turkey, regional minima were discontinued after 1973.

3. Japan is somewhat exceptional in that legal minimum wages are also set for certain industries in each prefecture in addition to the overall rate set for the prefecture. For 1997, the average of these industrial rates was almost 14 per cent higher than the average prefectural rate.

4. To a much more limited degree, separate occupational rates are also set in some Canadian provinces.

5. Indexation of the minimum wage in the Netherlands based on average wage growth was suspended from 1984 until 1990. The minimum wage was cut by 3 per cent at the beginning of 1984 and then frozen in nominal terms until 1990.

6. For example, the plausibility of monopsony has been questioned. Recent studies suggest that a certain degree of monopsony may exist in any case where individual firms face an upward-sloping labour supply curve [Boal and Ransom (1997)]. This may occur, for example, if information about job vacancies is imperfect and/or if job search and labour mobility are costly. Within the framework of imperfect information, some studies [e.g. Burdett and Mortensen (1989)] have put forward the idea of a dynamic monopsony, where employers who offer higher wages face lower quit rates and lower hiring costs. These elements lead to an elastic supply curve faced by these employers. Dolado *et al.* (1996) point out that "the important features of monopsony will be reproduced in any situation where firms have some discretion over the wages they pay". Dickens *et al.* (1994) develop a theoretical model where it is "labour market frictions" – meaning that labour supply to an individual firm will not be

perfectly elastic – that give firms some monopsony power. The authors conclude that the "optimal" minimum wage that maximises employment should vary from firm to firm and, in particular, it should differ for different types of workers. However, low-pay sectors are often characterised by high degrees of competition or high geographical density (*i.e.* retail trade outlets), offering highly substitutable products and employing similar workers. On the other hand, at the aggregate level, the empirical evidence suggests a steeply sloped or simply vertical (*i.e.* perfectly inelastic) labour supply curve and, thus, increases in the minimum wage may show up in higher wages with either little or negative effects on overall employment.

7. The institutional variables are: trade union density, *i.e.* the proportion of employees that belong to a trade union; the unemployment benefit replacement rate, *i.e.* the level of unemployment benefit entitlements relative to gross earnings, averaged across different family situations, durations of unemployment and earnings levels [for more details, see OECD (1994), Chapter 8, and OECD (1996), Chapter 2]; and the payroll tax rate, *i.e.* employer social security contributions as a proportion of total labour costs.

8. In the presence of disemployment effects, the two distributions will have different numbers of earners. It is, however, extremely difficult to calculate measures of earnings dispersion that include jobless individuals, as this would involve imputing wages to those without a job.

9. Card and Krueger (1995) discuss theories that are consistent with this feature of the wage distribution. Of course, if the minimum wage is so low as to be irrelevant, this spike is not likely to occur.

10. Neumark and Wascher (1997) point out that knowing whether an aggregate elasticity of employment with respect to wages is above −1 is not sufficient to determine whether labour earnings will be redistributed toward low-wage workers when the minimum wage is increased. That is because employment losses are likely to be concentrated among the low-wage group and because those workers earning between the old and new minimum wages may experience an increase in wages that is less than the rise in minimum wages.

11. Owing to differences in the underlying data sources, the estimates in Table 2.9 and 2.10 should not be regarded as directly comparable to those in Tables 2.7 and 2.8. Similarly, cross-country comparisons of incidence rates within Tables 2.9 and 2.10 should not be attempted, given important differences across surveys. Calculations using the British Household Panel Survey (BHPS) are particularly at variance with those from the other surveys, as the use of monthly data rather than annual data can lead to a very

different sample of workers being studied, with unpredictable effects on measures of low pay. See Annex 2.E for a description of the data sources and methods underlying the analysis in this sub-section. The Secretariat is particularly grateful to Richard Dickens (Centre for Economic Performance, London School of Economics and Political Science) for providing the estimates based on the BHPS.

12. Interestingly, in the Netherlands, there is currently a debate on introducing tax credits to the low-paid in order to create more incentives to work for the long-term unemployed [see the debate in *Economisch-Statistische Berichten*, 1998, 3-4].

13. In the Netherlands, however, the level of social benefits is linked to the statutory minimum wage and so increases in the minimum wage will be automatically reflected in increases in benefits. Thus, in proportionate terms, incentives to take up a minimum-wage job will not be increased.

14. A distinction should be made between benefits administered through the social security system or tax credits operated by the tax office. The latter seem to be associated with less stigma, have higher take-up rates and leave less scope for fraud or error [Scholz, (1996)].

ANNEX 2.A

Sources and definitions for minimum and average wage series in Charts 2.1-2.3

Table 2.A.1 gives the sources and definitions for the minimum and average wage series in Charts 2.1-2.3. Details are provided on adjustments to the average wage series in order to convert them to the same basis as the minimum wage in terms of a rate per hour, week, month, etc. The table also provides details on any splicing or interpolation that has been carried out in order to obtain a longer time series for the median or average wage.

Table 2.A.1. **Definitions and sources for minimum and median wage series**

	Minimum wage	Median wage	Adjustments to median wage	Supplementary wage series (W1 and W2)
Belgium	Minimum monthly wage – *Revenu minimum mensuel moyen garantie* (RMMMG) – for workers aged 21 and over. *Source*: Data provided by national authorities.	Median monthly earnings of full-time workers. *Source*: Institut National de Statistique, *Enquête sur la structure des salaires*, 1995.	Spliced with W1 prior to 1994 and with W2 for 1994 and for 1996 onwards.	W1: mean hourly wages of manual workers in industry. W2: hourly wage rate index for adult male manual workers in industry. *Sources*: ministère de l'Emploi et du Travail, "Le marché du travail en Belgique : salaires et durée du travail"; Institut national de statistique, *Bulletin de Statistique*.
Canada	Weighted average of provincial hourly minimum wages (weighted by labour force). *Source*: Data provided by national authorities.	Median annual earnings of full-year, full-time workers. *Source*: Data provided by Statistics Canada based on their *Survey of Consumer Finances*.	Divided by 2 184 potential hours of paid work per year (*i.e.* 52 weeks of 42 hours). Spliced with W1 prior to 1980 and for 1996.	W1: mean hourly earnings in manufacturing. *Source*: OECD, *Main Economic Indicators*.
Czech Republic	Minimum gross monthly wage. *Source*: Provided by national authorities.	Median monthly earnings of employees who worked at least 1 700 hours during the year. *Source*: Secretariat calculations based on Czech Statistical Office, *Earnings Survey, 1996*.	Spliced with W1 prior to 1996.	W1: mean gross monthly wage of all employees. *Source*: Provided by national authorities.
France	Net annual equivalent of the hourly minimum wage – *Salaire minimum interprofessionnel de croissance* (SMIC). *Source*: Provided by national authorities.	Median net annual earnings of full-time workers in the private and semi-private sector. *Source*: INSEE, *Séries longues sur les salaires*, 1996, as revised by INSEE.	No adjustment.	Not required.
Greece	Minimum daily wage for an unqualified, single, worker with no work experience. *Source*: Provided by national authorities.	Mean hourly wages in manufacturing. *Source*: Bank of Greece, *Bulletin of Conjunctural Indicators*.	Daily equivalent, assuming 8-hour work day.	Not required.
Hungary	Minimum gross monthly wage. *Source*: Provided by national authorities.	Median monthly earnings of full-time employees in May of each year. *Source*: Data provided by Ministry of Labour and National Labour Centre.	Interpolated using W1 as a guide for years where data not available.	W1: mean monthly earnings of full-time employees. *Source*: KSH, *Statistical Yearbook of Hungary*.
Japan	Weighted average of prefectural hourly minimum wages (weighted by employment). *Source*: Data provided by national authorities.	Median scheduled wage for June of each year (according to *Basic Survey on Wage Structure*). *Source*: Ministry of Labour, *Yearbook of Labour Statistics*.	Hourly equivalent, obtained by dividing by scheduled hours worked (taken from same source as for W1). Spliced with W1 prior to 1976.	W1: mean scheduled wage for June of each year (according to *Basic Survey on Wage Structure*). *Source*: Ministry of Labour, *Yearbook of Labour Statistics*.

Table 2.A.1. **Definitions and sources for minimum and median wage series** *(cont.)*

	Minimum wage	Median wage	Adjustments to median wage	Supplementary wage series (W1 and W2)
Korea	Minimum hourly wage. *Source:* Data provided by national authorities.	Median gross monthly wage, including overtime and all special payments (as reported in the *Wage Structure Survey*). *Source:* Ministry of Labour, *Yearbook of Labour Statistics.*	Hourly equivalent, obtained by dividing by hours worked (taken from same source as for W1). Spliced with W1 for 1996.	W1: mean monthly wage, including overtime payment but excluding special payments (according to *Monthly Labour Survey*). *Source:* Ministry of Labour, *Yearbook of Labour Statistics.*
Luxembourg	Minimum monthly wage – *Salaire social minimum* (SSM) – for single workers aged 18 and over. *Source:* Statec, *Annuaire Statistique.*	Mean hourly wages of manual workers in manufacturing. *Source:* Statec, *Annuaire statistique.*	No adjustment.	Not required.
Mexico	Weighted average of regional daily minimum wages (weighted by employment). *Source:* Data provided by national authorities.	Mean hourly wages of manual workers in manufacturing *Source:* INEGI, *Encuesta Industrial Mensual.*	Daily equivalent assuming 8-hour work day. Spliced with W1 prior to 1994 and with W2 prior to 1985.	W1: mean hourly wages of manual workers in manufacturing. W2: mean hourly earnings in industry. *Sources:* INEGI, *Encuesta Industrial Mensual;* INEGI, *Estadísticas Históricas de México.*
Netherlands	Minimum weekly earnings – *Minimumloon* – for persons aged 23 to 64. *Source:* CBS, *Sociaal-Economische Maand statistiek.*	Median gross annual earnings of full-time employees (including overtime payments). *Source:* CBS, *Sociaal-Economische Maand statistiek.*	Weekly equivalent (*i.e.* dividing annual wage by 52). Spliced with W1 prior to 1984 and with W2 prior to 1972.	W1: mean gross monthly earnings of full-time workers in industry and services. W2: mean gross weekly earnings of adult male workers in industry. *Sources:* CBS, *Vijfennegentig Jaren Statistiek in Tijdreeksen, 1899-1994;* CBS, *Negentig Jaren Statistiek in Tijdreeksen, 1899-1989.*
New Zealand	Minimum weekly wage for workers aged 20 and over. *Source:* Data provided by national authorities.	Median usual weekly earnings of full-time employees. *Source:* Data provided by the Department of Labour based on Statistics New Zealand, *Household Economic Survey.*	Spliced with W1 prior to 1984 and interpolated, also using W1, for missing observations for the odd years in the period 1984 to 1994.	W1: mean weekly earnings of employees excluding overtime payments. *Source:* Statistics New Zealand, *Monthly Statistics.*
Poland	Minimum monthly wage. *Source:* Data provided by national authorities.	Median gross monthly earnings of full-time workers. *Source:* Polish Central Statistical Office, *Statistical Yearbook.*	No adjustment.	Not required.
Portugal	Minimum monthly wage – *Salário Mínimo Nacional* (SMN) – for non-agricultural workers aged 20 and over. *Source:* Data provided by national authorities.	Mean monthly earnings in the business sector. *Source:* Ministério para a Qualificação e o Emprego.	Spliced with W2 prior to 1981 and with W1 after 1995.	W1: mean gross monthly earnings of full-time workers. W2: mean hourly earnings in manufacturing. *Sources:* Ministério para a Qualificação e o Emprego, *Inquérito aos Ganhos;* ILO, *Year Book of Labour Statistics.*

Table 2.A.1. **Definitions and sources for minimum and median wage series** *(cont.)*

	Minimum wage	Median wage	Adjustments to median wage	Supplementary wage series (W1 and W2)
Spain	Minimum monthly wage – *Salario Mínimo Interprofesional* (SMI) – for workers aged 18 and over. *Source:* Ministerio de Trabajo y Asuntos Sociales, *Boletín de Estadísticas Laborales.*	Median gross hourly earnings of full-time workers. *Source:* INE, *Encuesta Estructura Salarial, 1995.*	Monthly equivalent (*i.e.* dividing by 147.2 hours per month). Spliced with W1 both before and after 1995.	W1: mean gross monthly earnings. *Source:* Ministerio de Trabajo y Asuntos Sociales, *Boletín de Estadísticas Laborales.*
Turkey	Minimum daily wage for workers aged 16 and over. *Source:* Data provided by national authorities.	Mean daily earnings of manufacturing workers. *Source:* State Planning Organisation.	Spliced with W1 prior to 1988.	W1: mean monthly earnings of private sector manufacturing workers. *Source:* Bulutay (1995).
United States	Federal minimum hourly wage. *Source:* Data provided by national authorities.	Median usual weekly earnings of full-time employees. *Source:* US Bureau of Labor Statistics, *Employment and Earnings.*	Hourly equivalent assuming a 40-hour work week.	Not required.

ANNEX 2.B

Recent empirical studies of the impact of minimum wages on employment

An overview of recent empirical studies of the impact of minimum wages on employment is provided in Table 2.B.1.

Table 2.B.1. **Recent empirical studies of the impact of minimum wages on employment**

Time-series studies

	Country/Data sources	Outcome measures/Method	Main results	Comments
Bazen and Martin (1991)	France: Annual time series data, 1963/68-1986.	Structural time-series model with labour demand and wage equations and derived employment elasticities.	Employment elasticities are negative, but not robust for youths and zero for adults.	Assumption of a competitive labour market is imposed on the data.
Benhayoun (1994)	France: Time-series data, 1975-1991.	Time-series regressions.	No significant evidence of negative youth employment effects.	The minimum wage may be endogenous to the model. Results are sensitive to the specification adopted.
Koutsogeorgopoulou (1994)	Greece: Labour Force Survey, 1962-1987.	Applied the Bazen-Martin specification.	Employment elasticities of the minimum wage are negative for men and positive for women.	Assumption of a competitive labour market is imposed on the data.
Maloney (1995)	New Zealand: Labour Force Survey, 1985-1994. Minimum wages did not apply to youth (15-19) before 1994.	Regression of employment/population ratio for youth and young adults (20-24) on Kaitz index. School enrolment rate included among the regressors.	An increase in (adult) minimum wages raises youth employment rates and reduces young adult employment.	Possible endogeneity of the Kaitz index. School enrolment rates may be endogenous.
Mare (1995)	New Zealand: Labour Force Survey, 1985-1994.	Same regressions as Maloney.	Youth employment rates kept growing after youth minimum wage was introduced in 1993-1994. Maloney's results were explained by the cycle not by minimum wages.	Same critique that applied to Maloney's results.
Bell (1995)	Mexico and Columbia: monthly wages from Annual Industrial Survey of manufacturing firms, 1984-1990. Mexican Household Survey 1988.	Time series regression of employment/population ratio on Kaitz index. Panel data estimation of factor demand equations for unskilled and skilled labour. Fixed effects are assumed.	Significant negative employment elasticity for Columbia but insignificant for Mexico. Negative employment effects for the low skilled.	Robustness of the results not tested.
Card and Krueger (1995)	US: Time series data 1954-1993.	Time-series regressions.	No statistically significant teenage employment effects.	The minimum-wage ratio may be endogenous to the model. Results are sensitive to the specification adopted.
Deere et al. (1995)	US: Current Population Survey, 1985-93.	Regression of employment-population ratios on minimum wages.	Teenage employment falls as minimum wage rises.	The minimum wage may be endogenous to the model. Results are sensitive to the specification adopted.
Bazen and Marimoutou (1997)	US: Time-series data, 1954-1993.	Time-series regression. Re-estimated the Card-Krueger (1995) equations using several controls for seasonality and the cycle.	Significant negative employment elasticities for teenagers.	The estimates are sensitive to the method adopted.

Table 2.B.1. **Recent empirical studies of the impact of minimum wages on employment** (cont.)

	Country/Data sources	Outcome measures/Method	Main results	Comments
Pooled, cross-sectional studies				
Card (1992); Card and Krueger (1995)	US: Current Population Survey, 1987-1989. State data on employment and wages.	Employment of teenagers, low-paid workers and retail employees is compared across States with higher and lower fractions of workers earning between the old and new Federal minimum wage. Regressions of changes in employment.	In all cases, there is no significant reduction of employment in response to the rise in the Federal minimum.	Only short-term employment changes are captured.
Neumark and Wascher (1992)	US: 50 States and District of Columbia, 1973/77-1989. Information on State minimum-wage legislation; subminimum provisions.	Regressions of employment/population ratios on coverage-adjusted minimum wage. Year and state fixed effects.	Significant negative employment effects for teenagers and young adults employment – larger for teenagers. Subminimum wages imply more moderate effects.	School enrolment rate, included among the regressors, may be endogenous. If dropped, employment effects are positive (but insignificant) for teenagers and negative (significant) for young adults.
Machin and Manning (1994)	UK: New Earnings Survey, minimum wages levels in Wages Councils, 1979-1990.	Regressions of employment changes on Kaitz index. First differences and instrumental variables.	Positive relationship between minimum wages and employment.	There may be other (uncontrolled) factors explaining these results. Wage Councils were modified substantially before their abolition.
Bazen and Skourias (1997)	France: Cross-section time series data from Labour Force Survey, 38 industrial sectors, 1980-1984.	Investigate changes in proportions employed at minimum and subminimum wages.	Significant negative youth employment effects.	Other factors explaining youth employment levels are not taken into account such as, for example, sectoral labour demand, output growth, prices.
Dolado et al. (1996)	France: Labour Force Survey data grouped by education, age and gender. 1981-1985 minimum wage increase compared with 1985-1989. Regional data also used.	Regressions of employment/ unemployment rate on proportion paid at or below the minimum wage for each cell. Regression of employment growth on initial wages, regional data.	The increase in minimum wages in the 1980s has no substantial effects on employment.	The authors find some econometric evidence that youth unemployment increased in the eighties, but attribute this mainly to the recession rather than to higher minimum wages.
	Netherlands: Labour Force Survey, 1981 and 1983, when youth minimum wages were reduced.	Descriptive analysis of youth employment changes in low-wage sectors.	Youth employment rose in low-wage sectors, which are assumed to be more affected by the fall in youth minimum wages.	No attempt is made to control for other factors that may explain employment changes.
	Spain: Panel of industrial sectors. Data on employment and wages, 1967-1994.	Regression of change in employment on Kaitz index with sector fixed effects. Estimated by Instrumental Variables.	The Kaitz index has a significantly negative impact on youth employment but a positive impact on adult employment. Total employment rises with higher minimum wages.	Year fixed effects are not controlled for.

Table 2.B.1. **Recent empirical studies of the impact of minimum wages on employment** (cont.)

	Country/Data sources	Outcome measures/Method	Main results	Comments
Burkhauser et al. (1997)	US: Current Population Survey and Survey of Income and Program Participation, 1990-1992. Monthly data, pooled cross-sections.	Regressions of employment/population ratios on minimum wage.	Significant negative effects on employment of teenagers, young high-school dropouts and young blacks, but insignificant effects for prime-age workers.	Short period of time covered. Possible endogeneity of the minimum wage.
Baker et al. (1997)	Canada: Data from Labor Canada and Statistics Canada, 1975-1993.	Regression of teenagers employment/population ratio on Kaitz index. Fixed effects assumed for provinces and years.	Significant negative employment elasticities for teenagers.	The estimated effect varies in sign and significance depending on which specification is used.
Longitudinal studies				
Card and Krueger (1995, 1997)	US: Authors' own ad hoc survey and BLS ES-02 datafile for data on wages and employment in fast food restaurants in New Jersey and Pennsylvania, before and after minimum-wage increases in New Jersey in 1992; before and after minimum wage increase in Pennsylvania in 1996.	Regressions of changes in employment on New Jersey dummy and/or wage gap (from initial wages to new minimum wage level).	Employment increased (insignificantly) in New Jersey, relative to Pennsylvania in 1992. No evidence of employment losses in Pennsylvania in 1996.	Timing of surveys too close to legislated changes to observe possible long-run adjustments in labour demand.
Neumark and Wascher (1995)	US: Current Population Survey data 1979-1992. Matched surveys to construct longitudinal data for individuals.	Estimate effect of minimum wages on transitions of teenagers in and out of education and work. Multinomial logit models.	Employers substitute less-skilled teenagers with more skilled teenagers. Employment of the low-skilled is reduced and enrolment rates fall.	Unobserved individual characteristics may be difficult to control for.
Currie and Fallick (1996)	US: National Longitudinal Survey of Youth, 1979-1987. Pooled cross-sections.	Panel data model of the impact of minimum wages on the transitions between employment and unemployment.	Individuals affected by the minimum wage in 1979-80 were less likely to be employed a year later.	Missing employment data may affect estimation results (wage data are valid for only 30% of the sample in 1979 and 46% in 1980).
Abowd et al. (1997)	US: Current Population Survey, 1981-1987. France: Labour Force Survey, 1981-1989. Longitudinal, individual data.	Multinomial logits of transitions into and out of employment for workers paid below and above the minimum wage.	Youth paid at minimum wages have significantly lower employment probabilities then those paid marginally above in both countries.	Unobserved individual characteristics may be difficult to control for.
Chapple (1997)	New Zealand: Quarterly time series data 1985-1997; panel of industries 1980-1997.	Time-series model. Panel data model.	Negative employment effects for 20-24 years-old, but results are not robust.	There might have been a structural break in the nineties; time series data cover a relatively short period.

Table 2.B.1.   **Recent empirical studies of the impact of minimum wages on employment** *(cont.)*

	Country/Data sources	Outcome measures/Method	Main results	Comments
Other studies				
Van Soest (1994)	Netherlands: Macro time series and Dutch Socio-Economic Panel, 1984 and 1987.	Multinomial choice model: employment, unemployment, education. Potential wages are also estimated and wages allowed to be endogenous.	There is a significantly negative impact of minimum wages on youth employment.	The negative outcome is built into the structural model.
Dickens *et al.* (1994)	UK: Cross-sectional data on the distribution of wages.	Estimate employment losses by comparing the actual wage distribution with the hypothetical wage distribution in the absence of the minimum wage.	Negative employment effects of minimum wages, but not robust.	Estimates are sensitive to the functional form of the distribution of wages. The method relies on the assumption that workers earnings above the minimum are not affected by the minimum wage.

ANNEX 2.C

Cross-country regressions: specification and sensitivity of the results

1. Specification and data sources

In Table 2.5, employment-population rates for different groups were regressed against the ratio of minimum to median wages, with controls for the business cycle (prime-age male unemployment rate and/or output gap), different institutional features (trade union density, the gross unemployment benefit replacement rate and payroll taxes), trend effects (time and time interacted with country dummies), and fixed country effects. The minimum-wage ratio was calculated separately for men, women and all persons using the corresponding average wage for each group. Minimum wages were also calculated separately for each age-group taking into account reduced rates for youth rates in some countries. The regressions were carried out using data for 1975 to 1996 pooled across nine countries: Belgium, Canada, France, Greece, Japan, the Netherlands, Portugal, Spain and the United States. Portugal and Spain could not be included in the separate regressions for men and women as sufficiently long time series of average earnings by sex were not available for constructing the relevant minimum-wage ratio. In the linear specifications, the regressions have been run with respect to the levels of each variable. In the log specifications, the log of each variable has been used, except for time trends and country dummies. In the case of the linear specification, the elasticities have been calculated with reference to the means of the minimum-wage and employment-population ratios. The corrections for autocorrelation and heteroscedasticity were carried out using Generalised Least Squares (GLS) estimates and assuming country-specific, first-order, autocorrelation for the error terms and heteroscedasticity across countries, but not over time. Otherwise, Ordinary Least Squares (OLS) estimation was used.

The general specification underlying the cross-country regressions results reported in Table 2.5 is:

$$EP_{it} = \alpha + \beta\, MIN_{it} + \delta\, CY_{it} + \phi\, BEN_{it} +$$
$$\lambda\, UNION_{it} + \gamma TAX_{it} + \sum_i \tau_i DUM_i TIME +$$
$$\nu\, TIME + \sum_i \omega_i DUM_i + \varepsilon_{it}$$

where:

EP_{it} = employment-population ratio for country i at time t;

MIN_{it} = ratio of minimum to average wages for country i at time t;

CY_{it} = business-cycle indicator for country i at time t (either the prime-age male unemployment rate or the output gap);

BEN_{it} = gross unemployment benefit replacement ratio for country i at time t;

$UNION_{it}$ = trade union density for country i at time t;

TAX_{it} = non-wage labour costs as a proportion of total labour costs for country i at time t;

DUM_i = dummy for country i (except for Belgium which was chosen as the reference country);

$TIME$ = time trend; and

ε_{it} = error term.

The data sources are as follows:

EP: OECD, *Labour Force Statistics*, Part III; EUROSTAT, *Labour Force Survey Results*. Data for Greece was provided by the Greek national authorities. Some adjustments were made by the Secretariat to the data for Belgium, Greece, the Netherlands and Spain to take account of various breaks in the series;

MIN: OECD Minimum Wage Database;

CY: The prime-age male unemployment rate is taken from the same sources as for EP. The output gap refers to the ratio of actual to smoothed real GDP, using the Hoderick-Prescott filter with a smoothing factor of 1000. Real GDP is taken from the OECD Economic Outlook Database;

BEN: OECD database on tax and benefit entitlements;

UNION: Visser (1996) with revisions and updates by the Secretariat; and

TAX: OECD, *The Tax/Benefit Position of Production Workers*, various editions.

2. Sensitivity of the results

A number of supplementary regressions were carried out in order to check the sensitivity of the results presented in Table 2.5 to alternative specifications.

Card and Krueger (1995) have suggested that, if minimum wages and average wages are not entered as separate variables, equations of the type presented above may be misspecified. Therefore, the regressions were re-run with the denominator and numerator of the ratio of minimum to average wages entered separately. This resulted in very little difference in any of the estimated elasticities in Table 2.5.

A second concern is the possibility that there may be some non-linearity in the relationship between minimum wages and employment. As discussed in Section C, a relatively low minimum wage may have little effect on employment, but the effect could be greater if it is set at a relatively high level. This possibility was investigated by dividing the countries included in the regression results reported in Table 2.5 into two groups: a "high" minimum-wage group comprising Belgium, France and Greece; and a "low" minimum-wage group comprising the remaining six countries. An additional variable was then added to the basic specification as presented above in the regressions for teenagers and youth, consisting of the minimum-wage ratio interacted with a dummy variable for whether each country was in the "high" or "low" group. The coefficient on this variable was not statistically significant indicating that employment effects do not appear to be significantly greater in the "high" minimum-wage group of countries than in the "low" minimum-wage group.

The regressions were also re-run without the institutional variables with very little change with respect to the reported elasticities in Table 2.5. The results were also little changed when the total tax wedge was substituted for the payroll tax rate in the regressions. The results were more sensitive, however, to whether time trends are included or not. The elasticities are much higher without time trends for adult women and, in the log specification, for youth. The fact that the elasticities decline substantially when time trends are added suggests there may be omitted variables which are required to explain overall country trends in employment-population ratios. In many countries, the employment-population ratio for teenagers and youth has declined substantially while their participation in education has been rising and so an obvious "missing" variable to add to the regressions would be the school enrolment rate. However, these data are not readily available and problems of possible endogeneity between enrolment rates and employment prospects would have to be dealt with. It would also be useful to control for youth participation in active labour market programmes which, in countries such as France, have increased significantly over time, but unfortunately long time-series on a consistent international basis are not available. In the case of women, factors such as the timing and average number of births, availability of child-care facilities and educational levels may all be important factors which, ideally, should be included.

ANNEX 2.D

Recent empirical studies of the impact of minimum wages on the distribution of earnings and income

An overview of recent empirical studies of the impact of minimum wages on the distribution of earnings and income is provided in Table 2.D.1.

Table 2.D.1. **Recent empirical studies of the impact of minimum wages on the distribution of earnings and income**

	Country/Data sources	Outcome measures/Method	Main results	Comments
Earnings Distribution				
Green and Paarsch (1996)	Canada: Survey of Work History 1981; Survey of Union Membership, 1984; Labour Market Activity Survey, 1986-1987, 1988-1990.	Effect of the minimum wage on the distribution of teenage wages.	For male teenagers, it is estimated that the probability of observing wages between the minimum and one dollar above the minimum is decreased and the probability of observing wages higher than that level is increased. They find no such effects for female teenagers.	Econometric method used seeks to minimise functional form restrictions imposed by Meyer and Wise (1983).
Shannon (1996)	Canada: Labour Market Activity Survey, 1986.	Changes in the gender gap in hourly wages resulting from the existence of a minimum wage are estimated using Meyer and Wise (1983) method.	For 16-24 year-olds, the log wage gap would be nearly double, while for adults the wage gap would be about 10% higher in the absence of a minimum wage.	The method, which estimates what the wage distribution would have looked like in the absence of a minimum wage, has been criticised because of its sensitivity to functional form assumptions.
Dickens, Machin and Manning (1994)	UK: New Earnings Survey, 1975-1990, focusing on a panel of industries covered by Wages Councils.	Changes in the wage distribution resulting from the existence of a minimum wage using the method of Meyer and Wise (1983).	Find some compression of the wage distribution.	The authors argue that estimates of the impact of minimum wages are very sensitive to parametric assumptions about the form of the wage distribution.
Machin and Manning (1994)	UK: New Earnings Survey used to create a panel of industries covered by Wages Councils between 1979 and 1990.	Partial correlation between wage dispersion and "toughness" of minimum wage is estimated using regression analysis.	Decline in the "toughness" of minimum wages has contributed to an increase in wage dispersion.	
Card and Krueger (1995)	US: Current Population Survey, annual demographic and outgoing rotation group files, various years.	Partial correlation between the proportion affected by 1990-1991 minimum wage increase, on the one hand, and the inequality of the wage and family earnings distributions, on the other.	Greatest compression of wage and family earnings inequality tended to occur in states with higher proportions of workers affected by minimum wage.	Difficult to control for all factors leading to changes in wage distribution across states.
DiNardo, Fortin and Lemieux (1996)	US: Current Population Survey, hourly wage data from May and outgoing rotation group files, various years.	Semi-parametric methods used to assess what wage distribution would have looked like in the absence of a decline in the value of the minimum wage.	The authors estimate that between 1979 and 1988, the decline in the real value of the minimum wage accounts for up 25% of the change in the standard deviation of men's log wages and up to 30% for women's wages.	Assume no spillover effects, nor any disemployment effects.

Table 2.D.1. **Recent empirical studies of the impact of minimum wages on the distribution of earnings and income** *(cont.)*

	Country/Data sources	Outcome measures/Method	Main results	Comments
Horrigan and Mincy (1993)	US: Current Population Survey, March 1981 and 1988.	Comparison of actual change in the share of earnings held by each quintile between 1987 and 1980 and that which would have occurred if minimum wage had been indexed by inflation is made via simulation. The analysis is done separately for men and women.	Small impact on both the male and female earnings distribution. Small reduction in age- and occupation-differentials, and almost no impact on education differentials.	Labour demand elasticities are used to estimate disemployment effects of minimum wage increases. Spillover effects are not incorporated.
Mishel, Bernstein, and Rassell (1995)	US: Current Population Survey, outgoing rotation group file, 1993.	Changes in indicators of hourly-wage inequality, such as quantile ratios and education-earnings differentials are simulated.	Boosts in the minimum wage would narrow the gap between those in the 10th percentile and those higher paid, for both men and women. Minimum wages have very little impact on the college-high school wage differential, but have a greater impact on the college-high school dropout differential, particularly for women.	Spillover effects are incorporated, to reflect the impact of minimum wage boosts on portions of the distribution above the minimum wage. Employment effects are ignored.
Income Distribution				
Gosling (1996)	UK: Family Expenditure Survey, 1994-95.	Impact of various minimum wages on the distribution of net disposable equivalent income for all "benefit units" and for "benefit units" with at least one worker are simulated using Institute for Fiscal Studies (IFS) tax and benefit model.	A minimum wage that would affect 30 per cent of the workforce would only reduce the proportion of benefit units with less than two-thirds of mean income by 1.4 percentage points. Much of the gains accrue to the middle of the income distribution.	Possible employment effects and spillover effects are ignored.
Sutherland (1995)	UK: Family Expenditure Survey, 1991.	Percentage of gains from national minimum wage that would accrue to each decile of the distribution of equivalent disposable household income are simulated using the tax-benefit model POLIMOD.	The higher the level of minimum wage simulated, the more the gains are spread across household income levels, with the bulk going to middle-income households.	No behavioural changes taken into account.
Addison and Blackburn (1996)	US: Current Population Survey, annual demographic files, 1984-1992.	Calculated (partial) correlations between measured poverty rates and minimum wages, making use of variation in such wages over time and across states.	Do not find evidence that minimum wages have significant impacts on poverty rates, even amongst those groups most likely to be affected by minimum wage changes.	Use a reduced-form approach, which while avoiding some of the assumptions used in simulation exercises, does not allow an examination of individual channels by which minimum wages may affect poverty.

Table 2.D.1. **Recent empirical studies of the impact of minimum wages on the distribution of earnings and income** *(cont.)*

	Country/Data sources	Outcome measures/Method	Main results	Comments
Burkhauser, Couch and Wittenburg (1996)	US: Current Population Survey, outgoing rotation group file for March 1990.	Effect of increase in minimum wage on individuals classified on the basis of equivalent family income.	Workers who live in poor families are 3.6 times more likely to be helped by the minimum wage hike than is the average worker, but the majority of the working poor not helped by the increase. Roughly two-fifths of the benefits of a minimum-wage hike accrue to workers in poor families.	Employment and spillover effects not incorporated.
Card and Krueger (1995)	US: Current Population Survey, annual demographic and outgoing rotation group files, various years.	Partial correlations between the proportion affected the 1990-1991 minimum wage increases and changes in poverty, by state.	Find that reductions in poverty were faster in states where more workers affected by minimum wage increase, but estimates are imprecise.	
Horrigan and Mincy (1993)	US: Current Population Survey, March 1981 and 1988.	Comparison of actual change in percentage of family income held by each quintile between 1987 and 1980 and that which would have occurred if minimum wage had been indexed by inflation is made via simulation.	Higher minimum wage would have had almost no impact on family income inequality.	Labour demand elasticities are used to estimate disemployment effects of minimum wage increases. Spillover effects are not incorporated.
Mishel, Bernstein, and Rassell (1995)	US: Current Population Survey, outgoing rotation group file for March 1994.	Share of wage gains from proposed minimum wages increases accruing to each quintile of the income distribution of those families with at least one earner is simulated.	Some 60% of the gains would accrue to the bottom 40% of families with at least one worker, with the remaining gains persisting across the entire distribution of families with at least one worker.	Employment effects not incorporated, though spillover effects are. No account taken of families with no earner present.
Neumark and Wascher (1997)	US: Matched March Current Population Survey annual demographic files, 1986-1995.	The authors use logit analysis to see if, *ceteris paribus*, the level of the minimum wage (both current and lagged) affect the probabilities of transitions into and out of poverty.	Over a one-to-two year period, higher minimum wages increase both the probability that poor families escape poverty and the probability that previously non-poor families become poor. On net, no significant effects on the proportion of families that are poor.	The authors make use of variation in the minimum wages across states and over time. Some have argued that this variation is insufficient to estimate impacts with confidence.

ANNEX 2.E

Sources, definitions and methods for Tables 2.7-2.10

1. Data sources, definitions and methods for Tables 2.7 and 2.8

European Union: European Community Household Panel (ECHP), 1994 wave.

The ECHP is an annual survey of a representative panel of households and individuals in each country. The survey is based on a harmonised questionnaire, the Community version of which was drawn up by EUROSTAT, and subsequently adapted by "national data collection units" depending on the institutional peculiarities of each country. For the purposes of the ECHP, a *household* is defined in terms of two criteria: sharing the same dwelling; and common living arrangements. These can include meals taken together or a shared room, and/or a joint budget, and/or the use of common equipment.

Calculations involving household income make use of *total net monetary income.* This concept covers all market incomes plus social transfers received, including all types of pensions plus private transfers received, minus social insurance contributions and income taxes deducted at source. For France, all income taxes, including those remitted by households and individuals, are taken out.

Since income data refer to receipts during the year preceding the interview (1993) the labour force characteristics of households also refer to that year, except for the Netherlands. In this country, information on the labour force situation of households during the year preceding the interview was not asked and the employment profile characteristics of persons and households refer to a reference week in the year of the survey (1994).

Earnings refer to annual net earnings (net of social security contributions and income taxes deducted at source) including all overtime payments, paid leave, monthly and annual bonuses, etc. For France, annual earnings are net of social security contributions deducted at source, but not of income taxes.

United States: Current Population Survey (CPS), March 1996.

The CPS is a monthly survey of about 50 000 households conducted by the US Bureau of the Census for the Bureau of Labor Statistics. The sample is representative of the civilian non-institutional population. For the purposes of the CPS, a *household* consists of all the persons who occupy a house, an apartment, or other group of rooms, or a room which constitutes a housing unit. The measure of *household income* used in the CPS includes all forms of money income and government transfers, but does not exclude taxes that are paid.

Earnings refer to money received for work performed as an employee during the previous year. This includes wages, salary, Armed Forces pay, commissions, tips, piece-rate payments, and cash bonuses earned, before deductions are made for taxes, bonds, pensions, union dues, etc.

For all individuals in each survey (including children), adjusted household income (W_j), is calculated, using total income (TI_j), size of the household (S_j), and the following formula:

$$W_j = TI_j / S_j^{0.5} \qquad [1]$$

The exponent for S_j, 0.5, is the equivalence elasticity, which adjusts for the presence of economies of scale at the household level.

All adults are classified in terms of their employment status, with those individuals working as a full-time wage and salary employee for at least 10 months in the year (40 weeks in the case of the United States) counted as full-time, year-round workers. For this group, the average gross monthly salary income (including overtime, paid leave, bonuses, etc.) is calculated.

In Tables 2.7 and 2.8, all individuals aged 16 and over with incomes that are one-half or less than the median are classified as below poverty. "Low income" encompasses individuals with incomes above one-half, but below two-thirds of the median, with the remaining individuals put in the group for "moderate to high income". Full-time, year-round workers whose earnings are no more than two-thirds of the median earnings for this group are classified as low paid.

2. Data sources, definitions and methods for Tables 2.9 and 2.10

Germany: German Socio-Economic Panel (GSOEP).

The GSOEP is a representative longitudinal study of private households in Germany. The income variable used is total household income after taxes and transfers. This variable has been computed by researchers at Syracuse University and is the sum of labour earnings, asset flows, private transfers, public transfers, imputed rental value of owner-occupied housing and other income of all individuals within a given household minus federal income and payroll taxes [see Burkhauser, Butrica and Daly (1995)]. Low pay is defined over all employees working full-time for 10 or more months during the year.

Netherlands: *Socio-Economic Panel* (SEP).

The SEP is a representative random sample of Dutch households. Household disposable income is constructed on the basis of detailed questions on incomes. The household disposable income information used here was constructed by the SZW group at Tilburg University. Ruud Muffels, Rob Alessie and B. Mikulic provided valuable information on these calculations. Each wave of the SEP asks for information on gross annual earnings and months of work in the previous year. Data on hours worked, however, relate to contractual weekly hours in the job held at the time of the survey. As a result, when computing hourly earnings, it is necessary to combine data from successive waves of the SEP. Low pay is defined over two universes: all employees usually working 30 hours or more for 10 or more months during the year; and all employees.

United Kingdom: *British Household Panel Survey* (BHPS).

The BHPS is an annual survey of a nationally representative sample of households. The BHPS provides earnings data from the month preceding the survey. Household income, which is measured on a gross basis, is income for the month. Low pay, measured on the basis of monthly earnings, is defined over two groups: all employees who are working full-time during the month; and all employees. Richard Dickens of the Centre for Economic Performance, London School of Economics and Political Science, provided the results of calculations using the BHPS.

United States: *Panel Survey of Income Dynamics* (PSID).

The PSID is a longitudinal survey of a representative sample of individuals and the families in which they reside. Because most of the questions are based on a family concept, the income for a family is used instead of that for a household. The PSID defines a family as a group of individuals living together who are related by blood, marriage or adoption. In addition, cohabitors are considered to be part of the family if the couple is living together for more than one interview. Income refers to total money income, including government transfers, but not taking account of taxes. The survey asks about income and labour force information for the year preceding the time of the survey. Low pay is defined over two universes: all who worked 40 or more weeks and who usually worked 35 or more hours; and all employees.

To as great extent as possible, the same methodology for these tables was followed as for Tables 2.7 and 2.8, but extended to apply to periods longer than one year. In each case, adjusted household income for each individual was summed over the relevant period. Cut-offs for inclusion in various income categories were then made using this aggregate income. Aggregate adjusted household incomes that are one-half or less than the median are classified as below poverty. "Low income" encompasses individuals with incomes above one-half, but below two-thirds of the median, with the remaining individuals put in the group for "moderate to high income". Individuals had to be over 16 years of age for each year of the period and also have valid data for all years.

Bibliography

ABOWD, J.M., KRAMARZ, F., LEMIEUX, T. and MARGOLIS, D.N. (1997), "Minimum Wages and Youth Employment in France and the United States", National Bureau of Economic Research, Working Paper No. 6111.

ACEMOGLU, D. and PISCHKE, J.S. (1998), "The Structure of Wages and Investment in General Training", National Bureau of Economic Research, Working Paper No. 6357.

ADDISON, J. T. and BLACKBURN, M. L. (1996), "Minimum Wages and Poverty", mimeo, September.

BAILY, M.C., HULTEN, C. and CAMPBELL, D. (1992), "Productivity Dynamics in Manufacturing Plants", Brookings Papers on Economic Activity: Microeconomics, No. 1, pp. 187-267.

BAKER, M., DWAYNE, B. and STANGER, S. (1997), "The Highs and Lows of the Minimum Wage Effect: A Time Series-Cross Section Study of the Canadian Law", mimeo, Toronto University.

BALDWIN, J.R. (1995), The Dynamics of Industrial Competition: A North American Perspective, Cambridge University Press, New York.

BAZEN, S. and MARTIN, J.P. (1991), "The Impact of the Minimum Wage on Earnings and Employment in France", OECD Economic Studies, No. 16, pp. 199-221.

BAZEN, S. and BENHAYOUN, G. (1994), "Low Pay and Minimum Wages", International Journal of Manpower, No. 2/3, pp. 62-73.

BAZEN, S. and MARIMOTOU, V. (1997), "Looking for a Needle in a Haystack? A Re-examination of the Time Series Relationship Between Teenage Employment and Minimum Wages in the United States", mimeo, Université Montesquieu Bordeaux IV, France.

BAZEN, S. and SKOURIAS, N. (1997), "Is There a Negative Effect of Minimum Wages in France?", European Economic Review, No. 41, pp. 723-732.

BELL, L. A. (1995), "The Impact of Minimum Wages in Mexico and Columbia", The World Bank Policy Research Working Paper, No. 1514, Washington D.C.

BENHAYOUN, G. (1994), "The Impact of Minimum Wages on Youth Employment in France Revisited: A Note on the Robustness of the Relationship", International Journal of Manpower, No. 15, pp. 82-85.

BERNSTEIN, J. and SCHMITT, J. (1997), "The Sky Hasn't Fallen: An Evaluation of the Minimum Wage Increase", Economic Policy Institute Briefing Paper, Washington, D.C., July.

BINGLEY, P. and WALKER, I. (1997a), "Labour Supply with In-Work and In-Kind Transfers", Centre for Labour Market and Social Research, Working Paper No. 97-02, Äarhus, Denmark.

BINGLEY, P. and WALKER, I. (1997b), "The Labour Supply, Unemployment and Participation of Lone Mothers in In-Work Transfers Programmes", The Economic Journal, No. 107, pp. 1375-1390.

BLUESTONE, B. and GHILARDUCCI, T. (1996), "Making Work Pay: Wage Insurance for the Working Poor", Public Policy Brief, The Jerome Levy Economics Institute of Bard College, No. 28.

BOAL, W.M. and RANSOM, M.R. (1997), "Monopsony in the Labor Market", Journal of Economic Literature, March, pp. 86-112.

BROWN, C. (1988), "Minimum Wage Laws: Are They Overrated?", Journal of Economic Perspectives, No. 3, Summer, pp. 133-47.

BROWN, C., GILROY, C. and COHEN, A. (1982), "The Effect of the Minimum Wage on Employment and Unemployment", Journal of Economic Literature, June, pp. 487-528.

BURDETT, K. and MORTENSEN, D. (1989), "Equilibrium Wage Differentials and Employer Size", mimeo, University of Sussex.

BURKHAUSER, R. V., BUTRICA, B. A. and DALY, M. C. (1995), "The Syracuse University PSID-GSOEP Equivalent Data File: A Product of Cross-National Research", All-University Gerontology Center, Syracuse University, Cross-National Studies in Aging Program Project Paper No. 25, New York, July.

BURKHAUSER, R. V., COUCH, K. A. and GLENN, J. A. (1996), "Public Policies for the Working Poor: The Earned Income Tax Credit versus Minimum Wage Legislation", Research in Labour Economics, Vol. 15, pp. 65-109.

BURKHAUSER, R. V., COUCH, K. A. and WITTENBURG, D. C. (1996), "Who Gets What" from Minimum Wage Hikes: A Re-Estimation of Card and Krueger's Distributional Analysis in Myth and Measurement: The New Economics of the Minimum Wage", Industrial and Labor Relations Review, April, pp. 547-553.

BURKHAUSER, R. V., COUCH, K. A. and WITTENBURG, D. C. (1997), "Who Minimum Wage Increases Bite: An Analysis Using Monthly Data from the SIPP and the CPS", mimeo, Center for Policy Research, Syracuse University, New York.

CAHUC, P. and MICHEL, P. (1996), "Minimum Wage Unemployment and Growth", European Economic Review, August, pp. 1463-1482.

CALLENDER, C., COURT, G., THOMPSON, M. and PATCH, A. (1994), "Employees and Family Credit", Research Report No. 32, Department of Social Security, HMSO, London.

CARD, D. (1992), "Using Regional Variation in Wages to Measure the Effects of the Federal Minimum Wage", *Industrial and Labor Relations Review*, October, pp. 38-54.

CARD, D. and KRUEGER, A. (1994), "Minimum Wages and Employment: A Case Study of the Fast Food Industry in New Jersey and Pennsylvania", *American Economic Review*, September, pp. 772-793.

CARD, D. and KRUEGER, A.B. (1995), *Myth and Measurement: The New Economics of the Minimum Wage*, Princeton University Press, Princeton, N.J.

CARD, D. and KRUEGER, A.B. (1998), "A Reanalysis of the Effect of the New Jersey Minimum Wage Increase on the Fast-Food Industry with *Representative* Payroll Data", Industrial Relations Section, Princeton University, Working Paper No. 293.

CARD, D., KATZ, L.F. and KRUEGER, A. (1994), "Comment on David Neumark and William Wascher – Employment Effects of Minimum and Subminimum Wages: Panel Data on State Minimum Wage Laws", *Industrial and Labour Relations Review*, April, pp. 487-497.

CHAPPLE, S. (1997), "Do Minimum Wages Have an Adverse Impact on Employment? Evidence from New Zealand", *Labour Market Bulletin*, No. 2, pp. 25-50.

COHEN, D., LEFRANC, A. and SAINT-PAUL, G. (1997), "French Unemployment: A Transatlantic Perspective", *Economic Policy*, No. 25, pp. 265-293.

CUBITT, R. P. and HARGREAVES-HEAP, S. P. (1996), "Minimum Wage Legislation, Investment and Human Capital", mimeo, Economics Research Centre, University of East Anglia, Norwich, UK.

CURRIE, J. and FALLICK, B. C. (1996), "The Minimum Wage and the Employment of Youth: Evidence from the NLSY", *Journal of Human Resources*, Spring, pp. 404-428.

DEERE, D., MURPHY, K. M. and WELCH, F. (1995), "Reexamining Methods of Estimating Minimum Wage Effects: Employment and the 1990-91 Minimum Wage Hike", *American Economic Review Papers and Proceedings*, May, pp. 232-237.

DICKENS, R., MACHIN, S. and MANNING, A. (1994a), "The Effect of Minimum Wages on Employment: Theory and Evidence from Britain", Centre for Economic Performance, Discussion Paper No. 183.

DICKENS, R., MACHIN, S. and MANNING, A. (1994b), "Estimating the Effect of Minimum Wages on Employment from the Distribution of Wages: A Critical Review", Centre for Economic Performance, Discussion Paper No. 203.

DICKERT, S., HOUSER, S. and SCHOLZ, J.K. (1995), "The Earned Income Tax Credit Transfer Programs: A Study of Labor Market and Program Participation", in Poterba, J.M. (ed.) *Tax Policy and the Economy*, MIT Press, Cambridge, Mass.

DINARDO, J., FORTIN, N. and LEMIEUX, T. (1996), "Labor Market Institutions and the Distribution of Wages, 1973-1992: A Semi-parametric Approach", *Econometrica*, September, pp. 1001-1044.

DOLADO J., KRAMARZ, F., MACHIN, S., MANNING, A., MARGOLIS, D. and TEULINGS, C. (1996), "The Economic Impact of Minimum Wages in Europe", *Economic Policy*, October, pp. 319-370.

FREEMAN, R.B. (1995), "Comment: What will a 10% ... 50% ... 100% Increase in the Minimum Wage DO?", *Industrial and Labor Relations Review*, July, pp. 842-849.

FREEMAN, R.B. (1996), "The Minimum Wage as a Redistributive Tool", *The Economic Journal*, May, pp. 639-649.

FRY, V. and STARK, G. (1993), "The Take-Up of Means-Tested Benefits 1984-90", mimeo, Institute for Fiscal Studies, London.

GOSLING, A. (1996), "Minimum Wages: Possible Effects on the Distribution of Income", *Fiscal Studies*, November, pp. 31-48.

GREEN, D. A. and PAARSCH, H .J. (1996), "The Effect of the Minimum Wage on the Distribution of Teenage Wages", University of British Columbia, Department of Economics, Discussion Paper No. 97-02.

GRILICHES, Z. and REGEV, H. (1995), "Firm Productivity in Israeli Industry, 1979-1988", *Journal of Econometrics*, January, pp. 175-203.

HORRIGAN, M. W. and MINCY, R. B. (1993), "The Minimum Wage and Earnings and Income Inequality", in Danziger, S. and Gottschalk, P. (eds.) *Uneven Tides: Rising Inequality in America*, Russell Sage Foundation, New York, pp. 251-75.

ILO (1992), *General Survey of the Reports on the Minimum Wage-Fixing Machinery Convention (No. 26) and Recommendation (No. 30), 1928; the Minimum Wage Fixing Machinery (Agriculture) Convention (No. 99) and Recommendation (No. 89), 1951; and the Minimum Wage Fixing Machinery Convention (No. 131) and Recommendation (No. 135), 1970, Report III (Part 4 B)*, International Labour Conference 79th Session, Geneva.

JACKMAN, R. and LEROY, C. (1996), "Estimating the NAIRU: The Case of France", mimeo.

THE JOSEPH ROWNTREE FOUNDATION (1997), "Evidence to the Low Pay Commission", mimeo, London.

KENNAN, J. (1995), "The Elusive Effects of Minimum Wages", *Journal of Economic Literature*, December, pp. 1949-1965.

KOUTSOGEORGOPOULOU, V. (1994), "The Impact of Minimum Wages on Industrial Wages and Employment in Greece", *International Journal of Manpower*, No. 2/3, pp. 86-99.

MACHIN, S. and MANNING, A. (1994), "The Effects of Minimum Wages on Wage Dispersion and Employment: Evidence from the U.K. Wage Councils", *Industrial and Labor Relations Review*, January, pp. 319-329.

MACHIN, S. and MANNING, A. (1996), "Employment and the Introduction of a Minimum Wage in Britain", *The Economic Journal*, May, pp. 667-676.

MALONEY, T. (1995), "Does the Adult Minimum Wage Affect Employment and Unemployment in New Zealand?", *New Zealand Economic Papers*, No. 1, pp. 1-19.

MANNING, A. (1996), "The Equal Pay Act as an Experiment to Test Theories of the Labour Market", *Economica*, No. 63, pp. 191-212.

MARCEAU, N. and BOADWAY, R. (1994), "Minimum Wage Legislation and Unemployment Insurance as Instruments for Redistribution", *Scandinavian Journal of Economics*, No. 1, pp. 67-81.

MARE, D. (1995), Comments on Maloney, T., 'Does the Adult Minimum Wage Affect Employment and Unemployment in New Zealand', New Zealand Department of Labour, mimeo.

MEYER, R.H. and WISE, D.A. (1983), "Discontinuous Distributions and Missing Persons: The Minimum Wage and Unemployed Youth", Econometrica, November, pp. 1677-1698.

MISHEL, L., BERNSTEIN, J. and RASSELL, E. (1995), "Who Wins with a Higher Minimum Wage", Economic Policy Institute Briefing Paper, Washington D.C., February.

MYATT, A. and MURREL, D. (1990), "The Female/Male Unemployment Rate Differential", Canadian Journal of Economics, XXIII (2), pp. 312-322.

NAKOSTEEN, R.A. and ZIMMER, M. A. (1989), "Minimum Wages and Labour Market Prospects of Women", Southern Economic Journal, 56 (2), pp. 302-314.

NEUMARK, D. and WASCHER, W. (1992), "Employment Effects of Minimum and Sub-minimum Wages: Panel Data in State Minimum Wage Laws", Industrial and Labor Relations Review, October, pp. 55-81.

NEUMARK, D. and WASCHER, W. (1995), "Minimum Wage Effects on Employment and Enrolment: Evidence from Matched CPS Surveys", National Bureau of Economic Research, Working Paper No. 5092.

NEUMARK, D. and WASCHER, W. (1997), "Do Minimum Wages Fight Poverty?", National Bureau of Economic Research, Working Paper No. 6127.

OECD (1994), The OECD Jobs Study: Facts, Analysis, Strategies, Paris.

OECD (1996), Employment Outlook, Paris, July.

OECD (1997), The OECD Jobs Strategy. Making Work Pay: Taxation, Benefits, Employment and Unemployment, Paris.

O'RAVN, M. and SORENSEN, J. R. (1995), "Minimum Wages: Curse or Blessing", Center for Economic Policy Research, Discussion Paper No. 1212.

PALLEY, I. T. (1997), "The Positive Employment and Distributional Effects of the Minimum Wage", mimeo, Public Policy Department, AFL-CIO, Washington D.C.

RESSLER, R. W., WATSON, J. K. and MIXON, F. G. Jr. (1996), "Full Wages, Part-Time Employment and the Minimum Wage", Applied Economics, November, pp. 1415-1419.

REBITZER, J. and TAYLOR, L. (1995), "The Consequences of Minimum Wage Laws: Some New Theoretical Ideas", Journal of Public Economics, February, pp. 245-255.

ROORDA, W.B. and VOGELS, E. (1998),"Werknemerstoeslagen versus loonkostensubsidies", ESB, 13 February 1998.

SCHOLZ, J. K. (1996), "In-Work Benefits in the United States: The Earned Income Tax Credit", The Economic Journal, January, pp. 130-141.

SHANNON, M. (1996), "Minimum Wages and the Gender Wage Gap", Applied Economics, December, pp. 1567-76.

SKOURIAS, N. (1992), "Un réexamen des incidences du SMIC sur l'emploi, la participation et le chômage des jeunes", Centre d'Economie Régionale, Groupe de Recherches sur l'Internationalisation, la Formation et l'Emploi, No. 7, September.

SKOURIAS, N. (1993), "Salaire minimum et emploi des jeunes : l'expérience française", Centre d'Economie Régionale.

SLOANE, P. J. and THEODOSSIOU, I. (1996), "Earnings Mobility, Family Income and Low Pay", The Economic Journal, May, pp. 657-666.

SMITH, R. E. and VAVRICHEK, B. (1992), "The Wage Mobility of Minimum Wage Workers", Industrial and Labor Relations Review, October, pp. 82-88.

SORENSEN, P. B. (1997), "Public Finance Solutions to the European Unemployment Problem?", Economic Policy, No 25, pp. 223-264.

STEWART, M. B. and SWAFFIELD, J. K. (1997), "Low Pay Dynamics and Transition Probabilities", mimeo, Warwick University, UK.

STIGLER, G. (1946), "The Economics of Minimum Wage Legislation", American Economic Review, Vol. 36, pp. 358-365.

SUTHERLAND, H. (1995), "Minimum Wage Benefits", New Economy, Winter, pp. 214-219.

SUTHERLAND, H. (1997), "A National Minimum Wage and In-Work Benefits", Employment Policy Institute, Economic Report, April.

SWINNERTON, K. A. (1996), "Minimum Wages in an Equilibrium Search Model with Diminishing Returns to Labor in Production", Journal of Labor Economics, No. 2, pp. 340-355.

TEULINGS, C.N. (1996), "A Generalized Assignment Model of Workers to Jobs for the US Economy", Department of Microeconomics, University of Amsterdam, mimeo, January.

VAN SOEST, A. (1994), "Youth Minimum Wage Rates: the Dutch Experience", International Journal of Manpower, No. 2/3, pp. 100-117.

VISSER, J. (1996), "Unionisation Trends Revisited", University of Amsterdam, mimeo.

WILLIAMS, N. and MILLS, J. A. (1998), "Minimum Wages Effects by Gender", Journal of Labor Research, XIX, pp. 397-412.

WHITEHOUSE, E. (1996), "Designing and Implementing In-Work Benefits", The Economic Journal, January, pp. 130-141.

CHAPTER 3

Getting started, settling in: the transition from education to the labour market

A. INTRODUCTION AND MAIN FINDINGS

1. Introduction

Improving the transition from initial education to the labour market has long been a policy priority of OECD countries and many reforms have been enacted to facilitate this transition. At the same time, social and economic changes appear to have led to the transition becoming more difficult and prolonged. The 1996 *Employment Outlook* chapter on youth showed that participation and employment rates had declined over the past two decades, most particularly among men, while unemployment rates had also showed little improvement. The theme of a longer and more varied transition was developed further in the 1996 *Education at a Glance – Analysis*. Indeed, a wide-ranging thematic review of the transition, involving in-depth country-specific studies, is currently being undertaken at the OECD.

The aim of this chapter is to extend previous OECD analyses, by focusing specifically on the transition from school to work. Most importantly, it considers the integration of young people only *after* they have left the educational system. This is different from the large bulk of comparative analysis which tends to focus on all young people, whether or not they are in school. Such a focus does, however, preclude analysis of what youth bring with them to the labour market from the initial education system as well as the decision to leave school, even though both are important [Caspi *et al.* (forthcoming); Shavit and Müller (1998)]. The chapter analyses labour market outcomes of new school leavers with respect to jobs and unemployment, both in the very short-term or roughly one year after exiting the school system and, using longitudinal data, over the longer-term of three to six years after permanently leaving school.

Section B first sets the stage for the empirical analysis by describing some of the central attributes of education/training systems and labour market policies aimed at youth. Section C provides a detailed analysis of the initial transition to the labour market for 16 countries. It explores whether school leavers in the 1990s have faced greater difficulty in finding jobs compared with the 1980s, and considers some of the factors underlying success or failure. Finally, Section D uses longitudinal data for seven countries to enhance our knowledge of the longer-term process of settling into the labour market, and how and whether that varies across countries and groups of young people.

2. Main findings

One year after leaving education, youth in Finland, Greece, Italy, Portugal and Spain face a very high risk of unemployment, while in Austria, Germany, Luxembourg, Norway and the United States the risk is considerably lower. But, new school leavers are far from a homogeneous group and there is a very wide dispersion of outcomes according to age, gender and educational attainment.

Higher levels of initial education generally not only reduce the risk of unemployment, they also increase the chance of obtaining a full-time job with a permanent contract. That said, in many countries temporary and part-time jobs are on the rise across the board. Currently, about one-half of jobs found by new school leavers are temporary while one-third are part-time. Over the period covered in this chapter, there were moves in several countries to liberalise the possibility of using temporary contracts. Spain is the best example: currently, over 80 per cent of new school leavers in jobs are on temporary contracts. Many temporary contracts, especially in those countries where apprenticeships are important, are often combined with training.

The job prospects of new school leavers are also highly sensitive to the overall state of the labour market. The damaging effects of high and persistent unemployment are particularly evident for those with fewer educational qualifications and women. Institutional factors matter as well. The analysis suggests that co-ordinated/centralised collective bargaining structures are better contexts for new school leavers to get into employment compared with decentralised structures, as are well-developed apprenticeship systems. Similarly, employment protection legislation that is too strict can hinder youth employment.

Viewed over the larger haul, the longitudinal data reinforce many of these findings. In all countries, less educated youth start off with poorer job prospects, although differences tend to diminish over time, especially among young men. However, cross-country differences are also evident, especially at lower levels of education where young Germans have higher, often considerably so, employment rates compared with their counterparts in Australia, Ireland, France or the United States. There is also evidence of persistent cross-country differences which show up as quite large differences in the cumulative time spent in work or unemployed. Finally, while causality is difficult to establish, starting off in the labour market as unemployed, regardless of ones' level of education, almost "guarantees" employment problems in the future. In this context, the role of temporary jobs in easing the initial transition is of some interest. While data are limited, for some youth such jobs do ultimately lead to more permanent jobs and better prospects compared to being unemployed. But there is also a downside to temporary jobs: some never make the transition to permanent jobs and some bounce back and forth between temporary contracts and unemployment. In short, for a significant minority of youth, settling into the labour market, let alone good careers, proves quite difficult.

Some interesting policy orientations and questions emerge from the analysis. One clear result is that apprenticeship/dual-type systems work best in giving non-university-bound young people a good start in the labour market. In spite of the challenges they currently face, dual systems provide an attractive model. However, establishing large-scale apprenticeship systems in countries lacking any such tradition of strong government/employer/union linkages is very difficult. Although the creation of training opportunities comparable to apprenticeship will be of importance, especially for at-risk youth, countries need to consider possibilities for developing solid programmes within their existing institutions and with the co-operation of all the main actors.

There is an important question mark concerning the use of fixed-term/temporary contracts as a route for getting youth settled into the labour market. They appear to be a useful route for some, but not for others. An urgent task for research is to investigate the reasons for this mixed record of fixed-term/temporary contracts and suggest ways of making them a better route. The challenge is to improve the chances that an initial foothold into the world of

work, even for a short period, raises long-term employment and career prospects. The analysis in this chapter has not been able to probe very deeply into these issues so any conclusion must be seen as tentative. However, trying to ensure that temporary jobs involve a training dimension may be worthwhile pursuing.

B. THE LAUNCHING PAD: EDUCATION AND TRAINING SYSTEMS AND YOUTH LABOUR MARKET POLICIES

1. Schooling, youth policies and the transition from education to the labour market

Policies aimed at youth are related to the institutional links between school and the labour market and the common thread in initiatives to improve the transition has been attempts to develop more flexible paths between education/learning and employment [OECD (1996b)]. These paths can include reducing barriers between general and vocational tracks and improving opportunities to return to education after spending time in the labour market.

Educational systems, thus, play a crucial role in the transition [Shavit and Müller (1998)]. For the purposes of this chapter, they are divided into two groups with the emphasis on non-university-bound youth. One is the well-known dual system, which exists in Austria, Denmark, Germany, Luxembourg and Switzerland, where students have the choice between an academic or vocational pathway at an early stage. The latter is designed to give young people a combination of training at the workplace and school-based education.

The other group includes systems characterised by a range of relations between school and work experience. Countries such as France, Italy and Spain have systems that offer training in school, but often lack solid institutional bridges from school to work. Some other countries, e.g. the United States and Japan, have little in the way of vocational training at the level of initial education and only a small minority of a given youth cohort follow a vocational path. The assumption is that additional training or skills will be readily acquired upon entering the labour market. Despite the distinction presented here, it should be noted that, in almost all countries, general education is the track followed by the large majority of young people.

In the initial transition, sometimes beyond, labour market policies have come to play an important role in helping youth who exit school (government spending on youth labour market measures and the number of participants on such schemes can be found in Table J of the Statistical Annex). Measures include: training/apprenticeship programmes; active labour market programmes; policies on temporary or fixed-term contracts; and measures to lower labour costs (see Chapter 2).[1] The remainder of this section gives an overview of these policies.

Training and apprenticeship schemes

There are four possible sources of training: the educational system; the firm; specific government-financed labour market programmes; and individually financed training. Countries differ greatly in the elements emphasized [Blossfeld (1992); Lynch (1994a, b)]. Some initial training systems are school-based and youth obtain qualifications largely on the basis of theoretical instruction. Other systems integrate the various sources of training (e.g. the dual system). Specialised schools and government-led labour market programmes are often implemented when the sources of training are considered insufficient and produce unsatisfactory outcomes.

Examples of mainly school-based systems to aid the transition are found in Denmark, Norway and Sweden (Table 3.1). They are normally organised around a package of activities, school training and workshops. Sometimes they are tailored individually, giving orientation on skills acquisition and job-search assistance. Over time, these countries have tended to combine school-based training with on-the-job training.

There are several mainly workplace-based systems. The dual system of vocational training, typically associated with Germany, but also with Austria, Denmark, Luxembourg and Switzerland, is best known and many young people in these countries go through the system. It integrates a variety of elements at an early stage of initial education: workplace training is combined with vocational schooling and, often, there are public subsidies for firms who hire apprentices. There is also a well-defined use of low training wages for youth. A crucial feature is that all the key actors – employers, unions and the government – are involved and supportive of the principles of the system. Concerning the school-based component, the government, at various levels, often provides financial support.

The dual system is often touted as key to the successful integration of non-university-bound youth. However, some critics have argued that those who do not get the diploma can face difficulties in the labour market, although this is surely also true of other systems [Blossfeld (1992); Lynch (1994b)]. It has also been argued that the youth unemployment problem in countries with a dual system is simply displaced from teenagers to young adults, though the empirical evidence in support of this assertion is not clear-cut [Franz et al. (1997); Blau and Kahn

(1997)]. The relative lack of second-chance opportunities for drop-outs from the system and youth who have failed is also a perennial issue, though this problem confronts all OECD countries. Finally, Blossfeld (1992) argues that the German dual system is not flexible enough to adapt quickly to current changes in the occupational structure.

Where the dual system has a long tradition, policy makers and the social partners are well aware that reforms are necessary in order to preserve and reinforce it. Some potentially adverse developments include the fact that the dual system attracts relatively declining numbers of young people, that high-quality training is sometimes perceived as too expensive by many employers under changing conditions of international competition, and that apprenticeship places tend to be offered in declining and low-skilled sectors [Bundesministerium für Bildung, Wissenschaft, Forschung und Technologie (1997); OECD (1998a)].

Denmark has a tradition of combining a system of apprenticeship and vocational education, with government-led programmes [Hummeluhr (1997); Westergård-Nielsen and Rasmussen (1997)]. The apprenticeship system is based on a three- to four-year contract with an employer and youths spend ten weeks per year in vocational school. The employer pays the apprentice a wage whose level is negotiated between national labour unions and employer federations. At the same time, subsidies are used to compensate employers who hire apprentices. In 1996, a school-based practical training programme was started for those not qualifying for an ordinary training place. More recently, a major reform has been implemented, with a package of "activation measures" aimed at unemployed youth (see below).

Despite being mainly workplace-based, the Japanese system does not have much in common with the dual system. The most distinctive feature of the Japanese model is the almost exclusive reliance on firm-based skill formation and strong school-firm links for the recruitment of those leaving education [Hashimoto (1994)].

The American training system is highly decentralised and has little formal structure [Carnevale et al. (1990); Ryan and Büchtemann (1996); Lynch (1994a, b); Bailey (1995)]. Post-school training decisions are taken by workers or firms and training can be formal or informal, on-the-job or off-the-job, government programmes (e.g. the Job Training Partnership Act) and private institutions. More recently, links between learning and training at school and at work have been attempted via the 1994 School-to-Work Opportunities Act. One premise underlying this legislation is the belief that excessive labour market "churning" is costly for both youth trying to

Table 3.1. **Youth training systems after leaving initial education, selected countries**

System	Countries	Basic characteristics	Comments
Mainly school-based			
Government funded training run by local government institutions, combined with "activation measures"	Denmark Norway Sweden	Public centres of remedial education, vocational and general training. Reallocation grants, assistance and supervision, to promote mobility into growing sectors.	• Denmark: Special school-based training for those who cannot find a place in the ordinary dual system. Remedial education, training and activation measures. Public labour market programmes work only if they are implemented in tandem with workplace training [Hummeluhr (1997)]. • Norway: Since 1994, more workplace training has been introduced in the programmes. Two years of education in school are followed by one or two years of training as apprentices in a company [Hummeluhr (1997)]. • Sweden: Municipal programmes (youth < 20), since 1995.
Proprietary institutions	United States	Individual autonomy on training investments (Job Training Partnership Act). No general certification of skills.	• 60% of youth receive no additional formal school training. 30% of youth receive off-the-job training [Lynch (1993, 1994b)].
Government funded training combined with apprenticeship contracts	Belgium France Greece Italy Portugal Spain	Public institutes of training are government-funded and provide theoretical school-based training, combined with practical training in private and public enterprises. This programme comes in tandem with packages of regulated apprenticeship contracts specific for youth, with very low (or nil) labour costs to the employer.	• Greece: The vocational training organisation (OAED) runs a 6 semester programme for youth aged 15-18. Under supervision of OAED, trainees sign contracts with enterprises. • Italy: Programmes are planned by universities, district and public schools, training centres, local offices of the Ministry of Labour, etc. Low participation in the South. • Spain: Training programme run by the public employment office (FIP). In 1996, 23% of unemployed youth aged < 25 participated in the FIP. 62% of them found a job at the completion of the programme.
Mainly workplace-based			
Dual system of apprenticeship	Denmark Germany Austria Luxembourg Switzerland	It is part of the initial educational system. Employers, unions and government play key roles in the training decisions and programming. Both firms and workers invest in training (the system gives incentives to both). Certification of skills. Low training wages paid. Employers' subsidy for hiring apprentices. Youth have to find apprentice slots.	• Denmark: In 1997, 40% of youth got apprenticeship training. Wages and unemployment rates of this group differ significantly from workers who did not. After introducing a subsidy to employers, the demand for apprentices increased by 7% [Westergård-Nielsen and Rasmussen (1997)]. • Germany: about 75% of youth enter formal apprenticeship or governmental training after leaving school. • In general: Firms invest in marketable skills because there is low labour mobility, low variance of wages, high firing costs and less poaching [Harhoff and Kane (1994); Soskice (1994); Franz and Soskice (1995); OECD (1996e)].
Hybrid system, with firm-specific training	Japan	Close co-ordination between schools and employers. Firms recruit youth directly from school and give them specific training. Firms are willing to give training because of the absence of poaching behaviour (low turnover). Thus, training is embedded in the production process.	• Using survey (retrospective) data from 1989. 75% of the workforce had received training; and within one year of employment 61% of workers received training [Hashimoto (1994)]. The Japanese system gives strong incentives to workers to be co-operative and productive [Hashimoto (1994)].
Learning by doing	United States	Firm training is led by the firm's own initiative. Alternatively, individuals may finance their own training. High turnover and the risk of poaching can lead to low incentives for firms to invest in training.	• 14% of men and 8% of women had received formal company training in 1988 by the age of 25 [Lynch (1993)]. Education is positively correlated with training [Lynch (1993, 1994a, b)]. Training increases job mobility, especially if it is not financed by employers [Lynch (1993); Veum (1997)].

Sources: European Commission (1997b); Lynch (1993, 1994a, b); Ryan and Büchtemann (1996); Fay (1996); and OECD Active Labour Market Policy database.

establish careers and society at large, and that facilitating better schooling-workplace links will ultimately lead to better job matching. The most ambitious work-based training programme is youth apprenticeship, where participants spend part of the time in paid work, with the guidance of supervisors who advise them on employment issues. However, participation in this programme is low [see Bailey (1995) for a good overview].

Some European countries, especially those with mainly school-based systems, rely on employers' subsidies or tax relief conditional on work-place training, combined with special school-based training programmes. A commonly-used practice is specific training/apprenticeship contracts aimed at youth. This practice has been used to varying degrees in Belgium, France, Greece, Italy, Portugal and Spain.

Temporary apprenticeship/training contracts aimed at youth

Specific temporary or fixed-term contracts aimed at youth, with apprenticeship and training components (called "youth contracts" hereafter), are central to the debate about non-university-bound young people getting a foothold in the world of work in some OECD countries. In Scandinavian countries and those with a dual system of vocational training, however, these contracts are just a small part of the broader institutional context defining general school-to-work and training strategies. There is another group of countries, including France, Italy and Spain, that see fixed-term contracts in general, and apprenticeship and training contracts in particular, as a central policy tool to combat youth unemployment and ease the insertion of youth into the labour market. Youth contracts in these countries attempt to meet three goals: augment youth entry-level employment and experience (through hiring incentives via lower labour costs); give opportunities for solid insertion into the labour market (through incentives for transformation of the fixed-term into permanent contracts); and give training opportunities (through an obligation on the employers to train).

Table 3.2 considers only countries where these contracts seem to be a key policy tool and focuses on the most important programmes. It shows that they are designed for young job seekers, especially early school leavers. Most have a duration ranging from six months to four years. If training occurs, it is normally given in a school setting. Evaluation of the training content of these contracts is, unfortunately, very limited.

Financial incentives to hire young workers under such contracts vary across countries and are based on the assumption that lower labour costs (via lower payroll taxes, sub-minimum wages and/or subsidies) will have a significant impact on the hiring of youth and reduce the economic burden of training on firms. In France, Italy, Portugal and Spain, firms' social security contributions are often considerably reduced. In addition, low firing costs have been introduced in Italy and Spain. This does not imply de-regulation of such contracts in terms of wage setting: wages of apprentices/trainees are set as a proportion of minimum wage in France and Spain or a proportion of the normal full wage in Italy. Moreover, subsidies to employers who hire youth with specific contracts are common in France, Greece and Portugal.

Despite these apparent incentives, the importance of these contracts varies significantly across countries. As shown in Table 3.2, in the mid-1990s youth contracts accounted for almost 25 per cent of youth employment in Italy. They accounted for only 20 per cent in Greece, 12 per cent in France and in Spain, 7 per cent in Portugal and 3 per cent in Belgium. One explanation for the low take-up of apprenticeship and training contracts in Spain (despite the large incentives attached to them) is that alternative fixed-term contracts targeted at the whole population are even more attractive to firms because they do not involve an explicit training obligation [Adam and Canziani (1998)].

Another cross-country difference with such contracts concerns the presence or absence of incentives to transform them into permanent contracts. This is of some importance for the debate on whether temporary jobs can become traps for some people who move from one such job to another interspersed by periods of unemployment [OECD (1996a)]. There are no explicit incentives in France and Greece. On the other hand, Belgium, Italy, Portugal and Spain have built-in some incentives to employers to retain workers and give them permanent contracts. Fiscal benefits, subsidies and reductions in (or exemptions from) social security contributions are offered in all four countries. In Italy and Spain, there is an explicit mandate for converting temporary into permanent contracts such that an insufficient number of conversions reduces the possibility of further hirings with youth contracts. Despite similar incentives, the proportion of conversions differs dramatically. In Italy, 56 per cent of trainee contracts and 25 per cent of apprenticeship contracts were transformed into permanent ones in 1993. In Spain, only 12 per cent of training contracts and 28 per cent of learning contracts were so converted in 1997. Considering the low proportion of employed Spanish youth on these contracts, they do not actually affect the vast majority of young

Table 3.2. **Main temporary apprenticeship/training contracts aimed at youth, selected countries**

	Description	Incentives to hire on these contracts	Importance of the contract	Incentives for renewal into ordinary contracts	Renewals into ordinary contracts
Belgium					
Youth Training Scheme (*Stages des jeunes*)	Employers in the private (public) sector, in a medium/large firm must hire first-time job seekers (aged <30) and give them training, up to a target of 3% of the total number of employees. Duration: 6 months (renewable once) in the private sector; 12 months in the public sector.	The cost of training was gradually reduced for employers who pay the trainee 90% of the wage of an equivalent worker. The employers' social security contributions are also reduced.	3% of young workers aged 15-29 in 1990 and 2% in 1997 [Source: MET (1997)].	Some reduction of social security contributions.	Not known.
France					
Apprenticeship Contracts (*Contrats d'apprentissage*)	Training is undertaken in specialised centres. All employers can use these contracts. There is an apprenticeship tax. Targeted on those aged 16-25 with secondary school. Duration: 1 to 3 years.	The employer does not have to take care of training. Employment subsidies. Low labour costs: i) wages set at 25 to 78% of legal minimum wage (SMIC); ii) lower or nil social security contributions (depending on the firms' size).	9% of young workers aged 16-25 in 1996 (Source: INSEE, DARES).	None.	In 1993, 10% of apprentices were renewed into ordinary contracts [Vialla (1997)].
Skill Training Contracts (*Contrats de qualification*)	Contracts aimed at acquiring recognised skills. The employer cannot be the State. Training undertaken in specialised centres. Targeted on those aged 16-26. Duration: 6 to 24 months.	Employment subsidies. Training is partially paid by the state. Low labour costs: i) wages set at 30 to 75% of legal minimum wage (SMIC); ii) lower or nil social security contributions.	3% of young workers aged 16-26 in 1996 (Source: INSEE, DARES).	None.	Not known.
Greece					
Apprenticeship Contracts	Training in specialised centres and working activities are combined. Targeted on those aged 15-18.	Wages set at 20 to 50% of normal full wages. 15 days of holidays. 9-months' subsidies are paid to employers.	20% of young workers aged 15-19 in 1995.	None.	Not known.

Table 3.2. **Main temporary apprenticeship/training contracts aimed at youth, selected countries** *(cont.)*

	Description	Incentives to hire on these contracts	Importance of the contract	Incentives for renewal into ordinary contracts	Renewals into ordinary contracts
Italy					
Trainee Contracts (*Contratti di Formazione e Lavoro, CFL*)	Goals are to hire first-time job seekers and train young workers. Combination of work and training. The ultimate goal is that workers are hired on a regular basis by the firm. Targeted on the unemployed aged 15-29 with at least upper secondary education. Duration: 1 year.	Lower social security contributions, which vary from 25 to 50% reduction of the contributions paid by employers for regular employees.	5% of young workers aged 15-29 in 1995.	Fiscal benefits proportional to wages. Since 1997, reductions of social security contributions are extended for further 12 months if CFL transformed. Hirings with CFL are conditional upon renewal of at least 50% of previous CFL in the last 2 years. Automatic renewal if the activity lasts longer than the duration of the CFL. Renewal by court when employer does not comply with training requirements.	In 1993, 56% of CFL were renewed into ordinary contracts in the same firm (67% in 1992). Among those not renewed in the same firm, 13% found an ordinary contract with another firm in less than 3 months (19% in 1992).
Apprenticeship Contracts (*Contratti d'Apprendistato*)	Targeted on the unemployed aged 16-24. Duration: 18 months to 4 years.	Reduction of social security charges (greater than those if hiring with CFL), conditional on training. Low firing costs. Wages set at 80 to 92% of normal full wage.	20% of young workers aged 15-24 in 1996.	None.	In 1993, 25% of apprenticeship contracts were renewed into ordinary ones in the same firm (35% in 1992). Among those not renewed in the same firm, 18% found an ordinary contract with another firm in less than 3 months (27% in 1992) [Source: ISFOL, using the Social Security records (INPS)].
Portugal					
Skill Training Contracts (STC) and Apprenticeship Contracts (AC)	STC: 16-18 year-olds, inexperienced. 19-25 year-olds unemployed and experienced or trained. AC: Administrative authorisation is required in order to use these contracts. Limited number of contracts allowed. Wages fixed by public administration. Targeted on 14-24 year-olds with completed primary studies. Duration: 4 years.	Employer subsidies, conditional on giving training. Exemptions of 50% of social security contributions.	10% of young workers aged 15-24 in 1990, and 7% in 1995.	Subsidies of 12 times the minimum wage for every young unemployed who is hired with a permanent contract. Exemption from social security contributions (during 36 months) if the employer hires youth aged 16-30 with a permanent contract.	Not known.

Table 3.2. **Main temporary apprenticeship/training contracts aimed at youth, selected countries** *(cont.)*

	Description	Incentives to hire on these contracts	Importance of the contract	Incentives for renewal into ordinary contracts	Renewals into ordinary contracts
Spain					
Training Contracts (*Contratos de Formación*) (Apprenticeship contracts before 1997)	Goal: Give training to school drop-outs and unskilled. Combination of working and training activities (15% of the time), and workers are not eligible for unemployment and other benefits. Targeted on those aged 16-21. Duration: 2 years.	Substantially reduced social security contributions. No severance payments. Firings cannot be referred to labour courts. Wages above statutory minimum wage except for < 18 year olds, who get a salary of 85% of the minimum wage.	10% of young workers aged < 25 in 1997 (Source: INEM).	Employer gets a 50% reduction in social security contributions for 2 years if worker is given a permanent status upon expiry of the maximum period of the contract. If no renewal, for one year the employer cannot fill the position using a fixed-term contract.	12% of apprenticeship contracts transformed into permanent ones in 1997 (Source: INEM).
Learning Contracts (*Contratos de Practicas*)	Designed for workers who recently graduated from educational and training programmes. Targeted on those aged < 30. Duration: 2 years.	No severance payments. Firings cannot be referred to labour courts. Wages are set at 60% and 70% in the first and second year, respectively, of the wage agreed in collective bargaining. Wages cannot be lower than the minimum.	2% of young workers aged < 30 in 1997 (Source: INEM).	*Idem* (see training contracts).	28% of the contracts transformed into permanent ones in 1997 (Source: INEM).

Sources: MISEP (1996, 1997); OECD (1996d, 1997b); European Commission (1997b).

people (most young employed Spaniards are on general, non-targeted, temporary contracts).

Thus, in Italy, France and Spain youth contracts, as defined here, may serve to give entry-level employment to some fraction of the population, although many fewer Spanish youth acquire a training-based contract. However, in Italy, probably because they are aimed at skilled youth, these contracts may serve as real bridges for solid insertion into the labour market (Section D presents longitudinal evidence on these issues).

Direct job creation measures

Some OECD countries also use (public sector) direct job creation schemes as a complementary policy tool in hopes of giving youth experience and contact with the labour market. Examples include France, with specific subsidised contracts, Scandinavian countries, via some labour market programmes, and programmes of subsidised jobs in the Netherlands. The French employment-solidarity contracts (CES), although not targeted only on youth, are aimed at inserting disadvantaged youth into the labour market through employing them in socially useful activities. Youth are hired on fixed-term half-time contracts for a period of 3 to 12 months. The government is the formal employer and also takes responsibility for any training costs. The wage paid on such contracts is set equal to 50 per cent of the minimum wage of a full-time worker. Other examples are "city jobs" (*Emplois ville*) and consolidated employment contracts (CEC). The former were established in 1996 and are targeted exclusively at unskilled youth aged 18-26 years living in disadvantaged areas. They provide subsidised non-market jobs for periods of up to five years. The CEC are aimed at the more disadvantaged among youth who have also participated in a CES.

A Scandinavian example of direct job creation is the 1992 Swedish *Youth Practice* programme. It provides work in the private and public sectors for youth aged 18-25 years for a maximum period of six months [Hummeluhr (1997)]. Employers are heavily subsidised to hire youth, but there are no particular incentives to retain the young worker after the six months are up. Workers are paid an allowance well below the level of prevailing wages, unless they are also entitled to unemployment benefits. The young worker has to be searching actively for a job to be eligible for the programme, and has to participate in guidance and counselling activities. A similar measure, the *Workplace Introduction Programme*, was implemented in 1995. This consists of four months of work experience followed by a job, subsidised by the state if necessary, for youth aged 20-24 years. Access

to the programme is guaranteed if the person has been unemployed for more than 100 days.

Since 1991, the Netherlands has had a programme of direct job creation, the *Youth Employment Guarantee Act*, which is implemented by municipalities and offers combined training and work experience to young unemployed aged 16-21 years and school leavers aged 21-23 years who have been unemployed for six months. The programme offers places in the public sector, non-profit sector and, in some cases, in the private sector. More recently, the Netherlands introduced the 1998 *Jobseekers Employment Act*; it too operates at the municipal level with the co-operation of the public employment service. The instruments are many, including social activation and training-to-work experience positions in private enterprises.

As with many youth programmes, the effectiveness of many direct job creation programmes as a tool to improve the transition is in doubt. In practice, they are not only costly, but they also rarely lead to integration into the regular labour market and sometimes serve to simply re-establish eligibility for unemployment benefits. However, for some disadvantaged groups, they may be the only route into a job when all other possibilities have failed.

2. Recent youth-specific policy developments

In recent years, many countries have begun implementing new policies and programmes. The rationales and aims of the policies range from the simple desire to reduce youth unemployment to improving the transition from school to stable work.

Denmark introduced wide-ranging changes in its active labour market policies in 1994 and 1996, which, among other population groups, target unemployed youth [Björklund (1998); OECD (1996d, 1997c)]. The 1994 reform provided that, after six months of unemployment, an individual action plan is formulated for persons under the age of 25. Youths are offered either 18 months of education, 18 months of on-the-job training or a two-year grant to start their own enterprise. In 1996, unemployment insurance (UI) eligibility was changed for youth aged 24 years or less. A young person under the age of 25 can now receive benefits for only six months, and at only one-half of the normal compensation level. Moreover, low-skilled young workers "must" take training immediately following their first six months of unemployment.

During the 1990s, Sweden introduced a number of measures with some workplace training content. This year, a package of decentralised "activation measures" was implemented, very much in the same vein as the Danish reform. Activation plans on a full-time basis are offered to unemployed youth aged 20-24 years. Municipalities, local employment services and these youths take the responsibility to set up the plan within 90 days. The plan can last for a maximum of one year and, when completed, active job search or full-time regular education must follow. During the "activation plan", income support is given to youth who are not eligible for unemployment benefits or social assistance.

France launched a new package of measures in 1997, the Plan Emplois-jeunes, both for youth aged 18-26 years and for 26-30-year-olds, provided the latter have not worked long enough to qualify for UI benefits. The plan provides for five-year non-renewable contracts in the public, para-public and non-profit sectors. The government pays 80 per cent of the minimum wage and the remainder is paid by the employer.

In 1997, Italy launched the Treu Package of employment promotion measures. Apart from modifications in the areas of training and apprenticeships, it includes a set of measures for unemployed youth living in disadvantaged areas (Mezzogiorno). They consist of direct job creation involving socially useful tasks. The programme is aimed at first-time job seekers aged 21-32 years who have been unemployed for more than 30 months and live in areas where the unemployment rate is above the national average.

New policy measures have also been started in the United Kingdom. One of the four target groups of the New Deal is the young unemployed aged 18-24 years. The aim is to achieve a reduction in their level of long-term unemployment and to improve their employability. For this target group, there are four options: a subsidised job with an employer (the employer gets £60/week), with at least one day per week spent in education and training; a job for six months on the Environment Taskforce, with day-release education/training; a job for six months with a voluntary sector employer, with day-release education/training; or full-time education or training on an approved course for 12 months.

The European Council agreed at the 1997 Luxembourg Jobs Summit to adopt a set of employment guidelines for Member states. One such guideline states that they must make efforts "to improve employability" of youths. The most important implication is that governments "must offer every young unemployed person either training, retraining, work experience or another employability measure within the six months of becoming unemployed". The guidelines also include "orientations", e.g. member governments "must reduce the number of young people who leave the education system early", and

they "must make sure that young people are able to adapt to technological and economic changes".

Outside of Europe, there have also been many recent policy initiatives. In 1998, Australia introduced a number of initiatives. They include the implementation of income support arrangements for youth, the Youth Allowance, which covers unemployed youth aged less than 21 years and full-time students under the age of 25 years. In addition, youth aged 18 or over might be assisted in undertaking full-time education, training, job search or an approved combination of the three. New so-called "mutual obligation" arrangements also are being launched. After six months of unemployment, youth aged 18-24 years will be required to combine their job-search activity with a "mutual obligation" activity, such as part-time work, voluntary work, education or training etc. Youth can make their own arrangements, with the advice of a council. Third, the 1996 training reform is attempting to develop a new apprenticeship system, involving training and paid employment while in school. Finally, the Jobs Pathway Programme is designed to assist the transition from school to work.

Canada has also introduced new programmes since 1997. For example, the Youth Internship and the Student Summer Job Action provide wage subsidies to employers who give work experience to unemployed and underemployed youth. The latter programme also provides loans to start summer businesses. The Youth Service programme provides funding to organisations who create community service projects for groups of youth at risk. Finally, the Opportunity Strategy is a programme that aims to give equal opportunities to participate in a changing labour market. This is to be accomplished mainly through the following measures: providing financial assistance to students; and providing help to manage student debt via interest relief or extensions of repayment periods.

C. GETTING STARTED: LABOUR MARKET OUTCOMES ONE YEAR AFTER LEAVING EDUCATION

1. Introduction

A decisive event in the life of most young people is when they leave school and enter the labour market. Accordingly, this section concentrates on labour market outcomes of young people soon after leaving initial education, hereafter called new school leavers (see the Box and Annex 3.A for details on the definitions and limitations of the data). The focus is on quantity outcomes – how many among them are

---

**New school leavers and the school-to-work transition as captured
in labour force surveys**

New school leavers are defined as those individuals who were in initial education about one year before the survey, but who are not at the time of the survey. More precisely, the time since leaving school is close to nine to ten months in European Union countries, and about six months for Norway and the United States. Labour force surveys in about one-half of OECD countries contain questions which allow one to estimate this over-the-period flow. These data are not perfect, but they do permit analysis based on common concepts and definitions [Join-Lambert (1995)].

The most important drawback of the approach adopted here is that the transition process is captured in a snapshot survey and it does not follow that the individuals in question have permanently left initial education. Young adults, more so in some countries than others, and more so for some levels of education than others, can and do return to the educational system. This seems to occur frequently in the Scandinavian countries [OECD (1996c)]. Consequently, some "new school leavers", as defined here, are not first-time entrants in the labour market, but re-entrants with some work experience. There are two separate issues here. Quite apart from apprenticeships, there are large cross-country differences in the numbers of youth combining schooling and paid employment. Combining the two is much more frequent in Anglo-Saxon countries, Denmark and the Netherlands compared with most of Continental Europe. In addition, these data can classify as new school leavers young people who had "left" education one or more times in the past, tested the job market for awhile, returned to education and are now leaving again. Finally, information at the *time* of the survey is based on the usual ILO conventions and definitions, but that for one year earlier is based on respondents' recall and self-assessment. It is, however, unlikely that being in school or not one year before is that difficult to remember. Perhaps more problematic is the delimitation of youths' situation into either employed, unemployed or inactive. This is particularly the case for youth participation in labour market programmes. Very few labour force surveys directly collect information on programme participation. Hence, whether programme participants are counted as employed, unemployed or inactive is not generally known.

Importantly, in these data, apprentices are never counted as being in education, but are counted as employed. Countries such as Austria, Denmark, Germany and Luxembourg where the apprenticeship system is well-established, therefore, tend to have higher employment probabilities for new school leavers, as defined here.[3] In these countries, the majority of youth leave the general education system and continue to improve their education in the dual system.

---

employed, unemployed or inactive – and not on wage/earnings outcomes (see Chapter 2).[2]

The questions reviewed are: How well have new school leavers fared? Do their employment and unemployment probabilities differ much across country, gender, level of educational attainment and the overall state of the labour market? Have "entry conditions" changed over time? What is the mix of part-time or full-time jobs, and permanent or temporary jobs? Do new school leavers choose to work part-time and on temporary contracts or are they accepted *"faute de mieux"*?

2. Profiles of new school leavers

Data on new school leavers by gender, age and level of educational attainment have been gathered for 16 OECD countries. The age group considered refers to persons aged 16-29 years. This broad age span is used because the school-to-work transition has been progressively delayed in many countries

and now starts in the late teens and often ends after the mid-twenties.

Table 3.3 shows new school leavers as a proportion of all persons aged 16-29 years.[4] On average in 1995, this proportion was 10 per cent for men and 9 per cent for women. The figures for Denmark and Finland are more than twice this average, probably reflecting the fact that individuals seem to move more in and out of the initial education system in these two countries. Conversely, in Austria, Belgium, Greece (women) and Luxembourg, new school leavers represent a relatively smaller proportion of the 16-29 age group.

The proportion of less-qualified new school leavers varies a lot across countries [Barreiros and Ramprakash (1995); Freysson (1997)]. In 1996, it ranged from just over one-half in Denmark and the United Kingdom to around 15 per cent in Belgium and Greece. Apprenticeship countries appear to have more new school leavers leaving the general education system without qualifications than the

Table 3.3.   **Characteristics of new school leavers among the population aged 16-29 years**

Percentages

	Proportion of the age group, 1995			Educational attainment,[a] 1996								
				Total			Men			Women		
	Total	Men	Women	A	B	C	A	B	C	A	B	C
Austria	5.6	6.3	4.9	31.4	56.2	12.4	35.0	54.0	11.0	28.2	58.1	13.7
Belgium	5.5	6.2	4.7	15.7	41.6	42.7	17.4	45.5	37.1	13.7	36.9	49.4
Denmark	22.2	21.0	23.5	51.8	36.4	11.8	54.3	34.7	11.0	49.4	38.2	12.4
Finland	23.7	23.5	23.9	41.3	51.4	7.3	40.7	53.3	6.0	41.9	49.4	8.7
France	8.5	9.3	7.7	25.3	43.0	31.7	30.1	43.6	26.3	19.9	42.4	37.7
Germany[b]	7.1	8.0	6.2	42.4	40.3	17.3	42.2	40.6	17.2	42.7	39.9	17.4
Greece	6.6	8.7	4.8	15.2	64.1	20.7	19.3	60.5	20.2	8.7	69.9	21.4
Ireland	9.7	9.5	9.8	26.5	40.9	32.6	27.9	41.3	30.8	25.0	40.5	34.5
Italy	7.5	8.3	6.7	27.6	61.5	10.9	33.5	56.7	9.8	21.2	66.8	12.0
Luxembourg	4.7	4.0	5.4	30.2	37.7	32.1	21.1	46.8	32.1	40.3	27.7	32.0
Netherlands[c]	9.4	10.4	8.5	37.1	48.5	14.4	32.4	51.5	16.1	43.6	44.3	12.1
Portugal	6.2	6.5	5.9	42.4	37.0	20.6	51.0	33.7	15.3	32.9	40.7	26.4
Spain	8.1	8.8	7.4	34.8	33.9	31.3	44.3	30.5	25.2	23.3	37.8	38.9
United Kingdom	10.6	10.6	10.7	52.7	26.8	20.5	55.1	25.1	19.8	50.3	28.5	21.2
United States[b]	8.6	8.4	8.8	27.9	27.8	44.4	29.6	29.1	41.3	26.2	26.4	47.4
Unweighted average	**9.6**	**10.0**	**9.3**	**33.5**	**43.1**	**23.4**	**35.6**	**43.1**	**21.3**	**31.2**	**43.2**	**25.7**

a)   The level of educational attainment is not necessarily the final level achieved because individuals may return to the educational system. **A:** Less than upper secondary; **B:** Upper secondary; and **C:** University/tertiary.
b)   Data refer to 1995.
c)   Refers to 1994 for educational attainment.
Source: See Annex 3.A.

average, but, as emphasized in the Box, this is a quirk in the data and, in fact, many will actually get their qualifications on-the-job in the dual system. About one-third of new school leavers in France, Ireland, Luxembourg and Spain, and over 40 per cent in Belgium and the United States are classified as university/tertiary. It does not, however, follow that they have or will get degrees. For instance, in the United States in 1995, nearly 30 per cent of the population entering college after high school had never obtained any degree.

3.   Labour force status of new school leavers

Today's transition from school to work is often described as a turbulent and uncertain period for young people [OECD (1996b); EUROSTAT (1997); Galland (1997); Urquiola et al. (1997)]. The state of the labour market when they leave school and seek their "first job" is often a crucial factor in determining the ease in finding a job, although there is a good deal of debate as to whether some cohorts are permanently at a disadvantage compared with others because of different conditions at the time of entry [OECD (1986); Korenman and Neumark (1997); Gautié (1997); Poulet (1997); INSEE (1997)]. However, as will be shown later, there is little doubt that

aggregate economic conditions at the time of entry affect significantly the likelihoods of employment and unemployment for new school leavers [Benoît-Guilbot et al. (1994); Gitter and Scheuer (1997); Williams and Collins (1997)].

Chart 3.1 shows the unemployment probability of new school leavers. This probability exhibits a "cyclical" pattern in Belgium, France, Portugal and Spain. In the majority of countries, the late 1980s was a period of declining unemployment probabilities, while the early 1990s witnessed increases. The mid-1990s can be qualified as a period of stable unemployment probabilities, with Ireland and Luxembourg the only two countries showing a strong decrease.

Probability levels differ greatly across countries. In Finland, Greece, Italy, Portugal and Spain, between one-third and one-half of new school leavers are unemployed shortly after leaving education. Austria, Germany, Luxembourg, Norway and the United States are at the opposite end with only around 10 per cent of new school leavers unemployed.

The risk of unemployment is only one indicator of adverse labour market outcomes. Another is the probability of being out of the labour force alto-

Chart 3.1.

Unemployment probabilities[a] for new school leavers one year after leaving education, 1983-1996

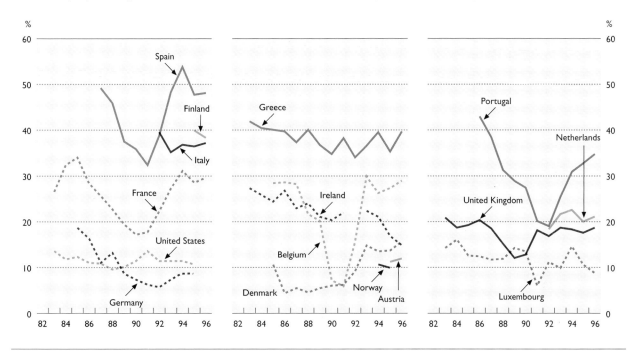

a)   Unemployed new school leavers as a proportion of all new school leavers.
Source: See Annex 3.A.

gether. In some countries, this likelihood is considerably higher than the risk of being unemployed, especially among young women. This is true in Germany, Ireland, Luxembourg and the United States. Inactivity is usually considerably higher among less qualified young women. The United States provides a striking example: in 1995, 9 per cent of all women counted as new school leavers were unemployed, while 19 per cent were inactive. Among young women who had not completed upper secondary education, the percentages were 17 and 41, respectively. These patterns could reflect discouragement over labour market prospects, though there is little direct evidence either for or against this proposition. Inactivity among less educated compared with more educated women could also reflect the fact that the former are more likely to acquire family responsibilities sooner, coupled with lack of access to good child care [Joshi and Paci (1997)]. Problems of accurate measurement of the different labour force states may also be important. There can be a thin borderline between inactivity and unemployment, making the two difficult to distinguish in labour force surveys.

Many analysts believe that employment probabilities are a better indicator of the true situation of youth on the labour market. There are, of course, borderline classification cases, such as apprenticeships and participation in some active labour market measures, which make cross-country comparisons less than perfect. Indeed, in this section, employment includes apprenticeship and labour market measures which offer a labour contract. Nevertheless, Table 3.4 and Chart 3.2, taken together, do provide a good basis to assess whether a country is performing well or poorly in integrating its new school leavers into a job. Starting with the Chart, Germany performs the best concerning the proportion of youth employed soon after having left school while Italy is at the bottom. Table 3.4 shows that four other countries do nearly as well as Germany. Three are also apprenticeship countries (Austria, Denmark and Luxembourg) and the other is the United States: between 70 and 80 per cent had a job soon after leaving school, although this level is reached in the United States only by higher educated youth. Closer to Italy, lie Finland, which went through a particularly deep recession in the early

Table 3.4. **Employment probabilities of new school leavers aged 16-29 years one year after leaving education**

Percentages

	1989			1996		
	Total	Men	Women	Total	Men	Women
Belgium	68.8	68.9	68.7	57.9	62.6	52.3
Denmark	86.6	90.7	82.8	71.2	72.5	70.0
France	70.0	73.3	65.8	58.3	61.8	54.3
Germany[a]	78.5	81.8	73.3	81.7	82.5	80.7
Greece	46.0	53.2	33.9	38.7	44.3	29.9
Ireland	52.3	53.2	51.4	66.0	67.9	64.0
Luxembourg	78.1	78.8	77.4	78.2	84.5	71.2
Portugal	59.1	67.0	49.1	50.3	53.7	46.5
Spain	44.3	51.3	33.5	37.2	42.2	31.1
United Kingdom	75.4	74.3	76.6	67.6	65.3	70.1
United States[b]	77.2	80.8	73.5	74.6	77.1	72.7
Unweighted average of the above 11 countries	**66.9**	**70.3**	**62.4**	**62.0**	**64.9**	**58.4**
Austria	..	..	..	78.6	76.2	80.7
Finland	..	..	..	37.6	39.4	35.7
Italy	..	..	..	30.0	38.5	20.6
Netherlands	..	..	..	52.5	54.0	50.9
Norway[c]	..	..	..	57.8	55.8	60.0
Unweighted average of the above 5 countries	**..**	**..**	**..**	**51.3**	**52.8**	**49.6**
Unweighted average of all the above countries	**..**	**..**	**..**	**58.6**	**61.1**	**55.7**

.. Data not available.
a) Data refer to 1990 and 1995. The data for 1990 refer to western Germany, while the data for 1995 refer to the whole of Germany.
b) Data refer to 1989 and 1995.
c) Data refer to 1994.
Source: See Annex 3.A.

1990s, Greece and Spain: only around one-third of new school leavers were in work in these countries.

The employment prospects of new school leavers have changed considerably (Table 3.4). Between the cyclical peak year 1989 and the mid-1990s, the probability of being employed decreased, on average, from 67 to 62 per cent.[5] The drop was greatest in Denmark[6] – although starting from a very high level – followed by Belgium and France. In these three countries, the probability fell by more than 10 percentage points, while in Greece, Portugal, Spain and the United Kingdom, the drop was between 7 and 9 percentage points. Only Germany and Ireland show rising employment probabilities.

Employment prospects also differ by gender. On average in 1996, employment prospects for women one year after leaving school were lower than for men. Only Austria, Norway and the United Kingdom show higher figures for women. The countries with very poor labour market prospects for women *relative* to men are Belgium, Greece, Italy, Portugal and Spain. However, between 1989 and 1996 the situation tended to deteriorate more for men than for women, with the male-female differential narrowing in the majority of countries. Particularly large declines in male employment

probabilities compared with women were recorded in Denmark, Greece, Portugal, Spain and the United Kingdom.

Low educational attainment is especially associated with poor prospects of quickly finding a job, though there are differences across countries. Chart 3.2 shows several patterns. First, the higher the level of initial education, the higher the employment probability, especially in Belgium, Finland, Ireland, the Netherlands and the United States. Although the "employment gap" is far from the same everywhere, this pattern suggests a "queuing for jobs", with the more educated first in line. The gap is most pronounced in Belgium and Finland and, particularly among women, in Ireland and the United States. Other countries show a much more disparate pattern, very often with a gender differentiation. In France, Greece, Italy, Spain and the United Kingdom, there is very little difference for men, but a more pronounced difference for women. Apprenticeship countries (Austria, Denmark, Germany and Luxembourg) not only have some of the highest overall probabilities rates, but also show little dispersion by gender or by educational attainment.

Chart 3.2.

Employment probabilities[a] of new school leavers one year after leaving education by educational attainment and gender, 1996

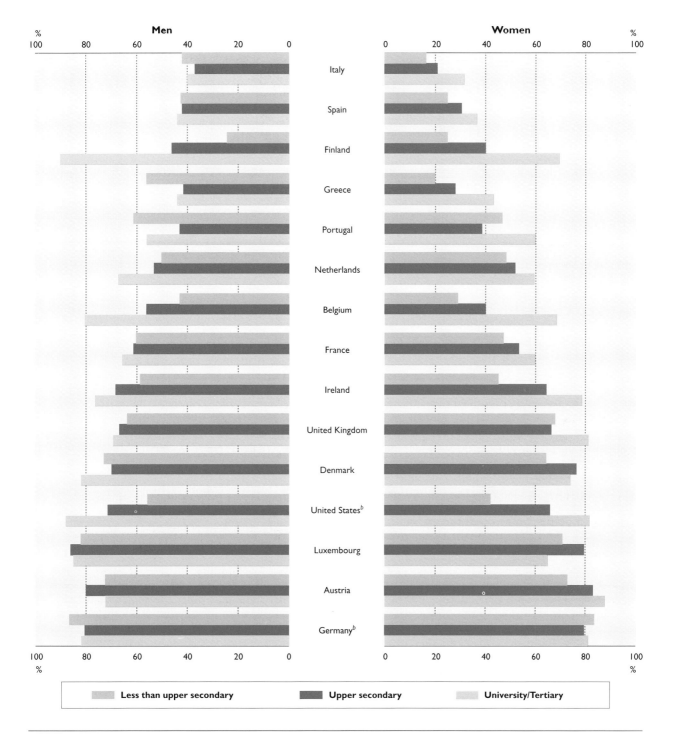

Countries are ranked in ascending order of the overall probability of being employed.
a)   Employed new school leavers as a proportion of all new school leavers.
b)   Data refer to 1995.
Source: See Annex 3.A.

4. Entry-level jobs held by new school leavers

Getting a job is a first foothold in the transition, but the kind of job can also be important for the medium- and longer-term integration into the labour market. This subsection, therefore, considers the kinds of jobs new school leavers hold and how they have changed over the past decades. It is well known that young people in some countries are used to getting into the labour market via a succession of temporary contracts, very often on a part-time basis. Labour market programmes, including training with some remuneration, aimed at youth are also often designed to offer them what is hoped to be a stepping-stone into the labour market (see Section B for a discussion of some of these programmes). While they can also be used simply as a temporary respite from unemployment, some programmes can speed up integration into secure jobs for some young people, though others seem to go from one temporary job to another interspersed by periods of unemployment [DARES (1997); Magnac (1997); OECD (1996a)].

Table 3.5 shows that, in 1996, one-half the jobs held by new school leavers were on temporary contracts, while some 30 per cent were part-time (the two categories are not mutually exclusive). Not surprisingly, young women work part-time more frequently than do young men.

It is instructive to consider the reasons young people give for taking temporary and part-time work. A little more than one-third of temporary contracts cover a period of training. Almost the same proportion of them are involuntary, in the sense that these youth could not find permanent jobs. Involuntary temporary contracts are slightly more frequent for women compared with men. Part-time work is due more to the person undergoing school-based education or training: on average, training reasons are cited by 56 per cent of part-timers, while 20 per cent could not find a full-time job. Again, involuntary part-time work is, on average, more frequent for women than for men.

These averages conceal substantial cross-country differences. In Chart 3.3, countries are ranked in ascending order according to the proportion of temporary contracts in all jobs held by new school leavers (also see Table 3.5). In 1996, this proportion ranged from around 26 per cent in the United Kingdom to around 86 per cent in Spain. The countries where temporary contracts are largely associated with training include, not surprisingly, the "apprenticeship countries" (Austria, Denmark, Germany and Luxembourg), but also Belgium and Italy, mainly for young men.

Conditional upon being in work, the type of job varies by educational attainment, but differences

are not very pronounced. The overall average for the incidence of temporary work is 54 per cent for those who had not attained upper secondary, 51 per cent for those with upper secondary education and 46 per cent for those with some higher education. Differences by level of educational attainment are often less within, than between, countries with the exceptions of Austria, Belgium and Germany. Moreover, new school leavers with an educational level below upper secondary are more frequently on a temporary contract compared with more educated ones in only one-half of the countries.

Country differences in the incidence of part-time work are quite clear (see Chart 3.4 and Table 3.5). In 1996, the proportion of employed new school leavers working part-time ranged from 78 per cent in the Netherlands to 13 per cent in Portugal. Taking part-time work for education/training purposes is the predominate reason given by new school leavers in Denmark, Luxembourg, the Netherlands and the United Kingdom. By contrast, this reason is given by less than 35 per cent of employed new school leavers in Belgium, Greece, Spain and the United States.

Chart 3.4 also shows whether working part-time varies by level of educational attainment. Highly educated new school leavers in jobs work part-time much less frequently than lower educated ones. In 1996, the respective proportions were: 20 per cent for higher education; 33 per cent for upper secondary; and 37 per cent for less than upper secondary. Dispersion within countries is particularly pronounced in Belgium and in countries where the incidence of part-time work is high, such as Denmark, Finland, Ireland, the Netherlands and the United Kingdom.

5. Summary of factors underlying the employment and unemployment probabilities facing new school leavers

The chance of youths getting started in jobs after leaving school is on average three in five, but for one-half of them, it is a temporary job and for one-third it is part-time. New school leavers are, however, far from a homogeneous group. Low educational attainment is associated with relatively poor prospects of getting integrated quickly into the labour market.

While education is important in terms of an individual's labour market prospects, it is not the only factor. OECD (1996a) highlighted the disproportionately large response of youth employment and unemployment to changes in overall unemployment and other indicators of aggregate economic activity. The purpose of this subsection is to take that analysis a bit further using regression analysis to examine

Table 3.5. **Entry-level jobs held by new school leavers aged 16-29 years one year after leaving education, 1996**

Percentages

	Men						Women					
	Temporary jobs			Part-time			Temporary jobs			Part-time		
	Total[a]	of which: (per cent of total)		Total[a]	of which: (per cent of total)		Total[a]	of which: (per cent of total)		Total[a]	of which: (per cent of total)	
		for training[b]	involuntary[c]		for training[d]	involuntary[e]		for training[b]	involuntary[c]		for training[d]	involuntary[e]
Austria	45.1	80.3	1.2	13.1	75.9	18.2	35.2	59.6	9.1	24.1	33.9	8.3
Belgium	38.8	50.2	18.0	12.8	59.1	24.6	45.6	33.2	20.1	23.2	11.5	55.5
Denmark	44.2	52.1	17.2	45.6	82.3	4.7	31.3	31.4	39.2	55.8	80.0	7.5
Finland	67.4	24.4	49.6	33.5	69.0	25.5	65.9	11.4	56.3	52.7	68.7	26.6
France	68.3	33.5	..	21.8	..	40.6	66.3	28.9	..	40.3	..	48.5
Germany[f]	62.8	68.0	..	16.3	69.0	5.3	69.9	71.8	..	21.1	61.9	6.1
Greece	38.0	23.2	55.3	11.5	33.8	37.5	41.9	34.5	42.4	20.1	32.3	51.0
Ireland	39.4	36.6	19.2	32.1	63.7	13.6	42.1	33.1	24.3	40.2	65.8	17.7
Italy	32.8	53.5	17.7	15.7	42.2	29.7	51.9	41.4	25.2	25.6	36.8	37.8
Luxembourg	42.5	65.1	9.6	14.8	90.4	9.6	22.5	61.7	7.1	13.6	87.6	..
Netherlands	57.3	10.9	29.3	68.8	90.9	4.5	54.7	1.7	25.7	88.7	94.6	2.3
Portugal	54.5	10.8	62.2	9.2	48.7	24.5	62.1	28.2	53.0	17.6	43.5	45.3
Spain	85.8	15.5	69.4	19.4	36.5	18.9	87.4	14.6	71.0	33.2	27.1	19.4
United Kingdom	27.3	11.7	25.9	45.3	88.4	7.1	25.7	10.0	25.3	54.1	84.0	10.2
United States[f]	..	..	..	21.3	19.9	18.8	..	..	..	35.3	11.8	19.7
Unweighted average	**50.3**	**38.3**	**31.2**	**24.0**	**60.7**	**17.6**	**50.2**	**33.0**	**33.2**	**34.0**	**52.0**	**22.4**

.. Data not available.
a) As a percentage of all jobs held.
b) Refers to a contract covering a period of training (apprentices, trainees, research assistants, etc.).
c) The person could not find a permanent job.
d) Refers to persons working part-time and undergoing school-based education or training.
e) The person could not find a full-time job.
f) Data refer to 1995.
Source: See Annex 3.A.

Chart 3.3.

Proportion of employed persons one year after leaving education in temporary jobs by educational attainment, gender and reasons for taking a temporary job, 1996

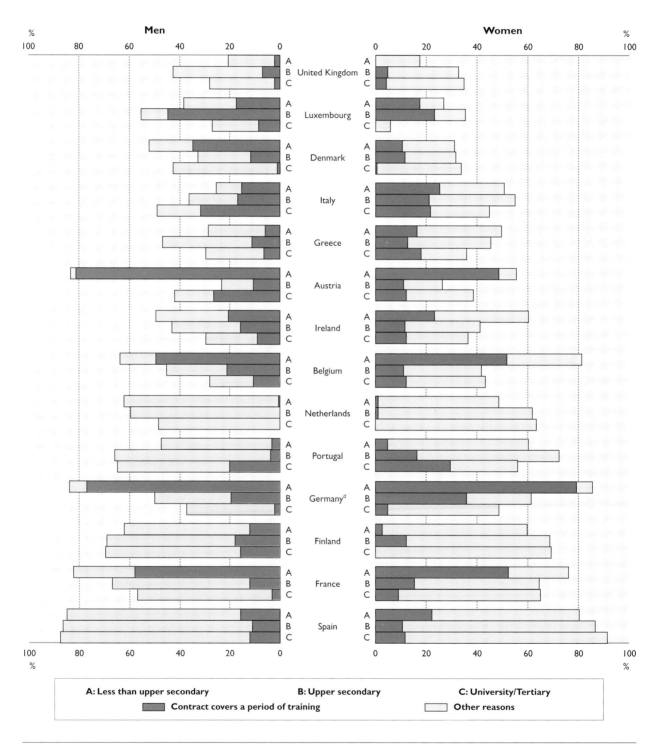

Countries are ranked in ascending order of the proportion of the employed with temporary contracts.
a)   Data refer to 1995.
Source: See Annex 3.A.

Chart 3.4.

Proportion of employed persons one year after leaving education in part-time jobs by educational attainment, gender and reasons for taking a part-time job, 1996

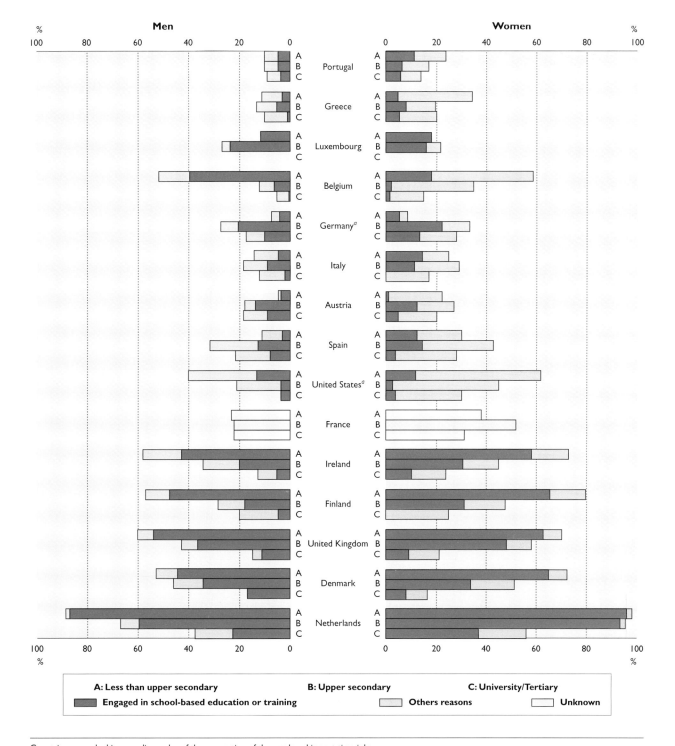

Countries are ranked in ascending order of the proportion of the employed in part-time jobs.
a)   Data refer to 1995.
Source: See Annex 3.A.

a range of potential factors affecting new school leavers employment and unemployment prospects (see Annex 3.A for the definitions of all variables).

Table 3.6 shows results on employment and unemployment probabilities from a pooled cross-section, time-series model for 14 countries. The table records OLS regression coefficients on the adult unemployment rate and the level of public expenditure on youth programmes (as a per cent of GDP), and dummy variables for gender, education, age, whether or not a country has a developed apprenticeship system, and a time-invariant measure of the overall strictness of employment protection legislation (EPL).

There is little ambiguity as to the effect of the adult unemployment rate on the probability of new school leavers to be employed or unemployed. The first decreases significantly with adult unemployment while the second is positively related to adult

unemployment. The coefficient of youth ALMPs suggests that more spending is associated with lower unemployment and lower employment, but these estimates are difficult to interpret. For one thing, they take no account of possible simultaneity problems since governments are likely to change spending on ALMPs when unemployment changes. In addition, most youth measures are highly targeted on particular groups of this population and this targeting cannot be captured by a measure of overall spending. Coefficients of the dummy variables make clear that men fare significantly better in a statistical sense than women, and that school leavers with the lowest educational level are at a disadvantage versus higher educated ones, particularly concerning the probability of getting a job. Both relatively low and medium levels of EPL are associated with higher levels of employment and lower levels of unemployment compared with very strict EPL, consistent with Scarpetta (1996). Finally, coun-

Table 3.6. **Some underlying factors influencing the employment and unemployment of new school leavers one year after leaving education**[a, b, c]

OLS estimates

	Employment		Unemployment	
Adult unemployment rate	−1.3**	(19.1)	1.2**	(24.4)
Youth measures (% of GDP)	−6.0**	(3.4)	−2.6*	(2.0)
Gender	6.7**	(13.3)	−2.8**	(7.6)
Level of educational attainment				
Less than upper secondary	−8.7**	(10.3)	3.7**	(5.8)
Upper secondary	−7.0**	(9.5)	2.7**	(4.9)
Age				
16	2.6	(1.5)	−4.3**	(3.4)
17	4.4*	(2.6)	−2.3	(1.9)
18	5.1**	(3.1)	−1.7	(1.4)
19	5.6**	(3.4)	−0.6	(0.5)
20	6.8**	(4.1)	−1.2	(1.0)
21	8.3**	(5.1)	−1.9	(1.5)
22	9.2**	(5.6)	−2.5*	(2.0)
23	9.5**	(5.7)	−2.7*	(2.2)
24	8.5**	(5.1)	−2.2	(1.8)
25	5.3**	(3.1)	0.0	(0.0)
26	7.1**	(4.0)	−3.0*	(2.3)
27	3.0	(1.7)	0.6	(0.5)
28	3.2	(1.7)	−2.8*	(2.0)
Employment protection legislation				
Low	12.6**	(18.8)	−13.3**	(27.1)
Medium	2.5**	(3.5)	−3.0**	(5.7)
Dual system	16.3**	(21.5)	−14.2**	(25.3)
Trend	0.4**	(4.1)	−0.2**	(2.9)

a) ** and * indicate significance at the 1 per cent and 5 per cent levels, respectively. T-statistics are in parentheses and in absolute values. The two dependent variables are the proportion of new school leavers employed and the proportion unemployed.
b) The reference groups for the dummy variables are women, university/tertiary education, aged 29 years, high level of strictness of employment protection legislation and not having an extensive apprenticeship system.
c) Fourteen countries are included: Austria, Belgium, Denmark, Finland, France, Germany, Greece, Ireland, Italy, the Netherlands, Portugal, Spain, the United Kingdom and the United States.
Source and definitions: See Annex 3.A.

Table 3.7. **Impact of institutions on the employment and unemployment of new school leavers one year after leaving education**[a, b, c]

OLS estimates

	Employment			Unemployment		
Adult unemployment rate (%)	-1.7** (10.0)	-1.6** (9.7)	-0.8** (8.0)	2.1** (18.6)	2.0** (18.3)	1.5** (21.0)
Youth measures (% of GDP)	-33.2** (7.6)	-25.6** (8.5)		19.6** (6.7)	12.4** (6.1)	
Net replacement rate for youth (%)	-0.1* (2.4)			0.1** (3.4)		
Collective bargaining structure						
Intermediate	-2.8 (1.5)	-3.4 (1.9)	2.9 (1.8)	-4.1** (3.3)	-3.4** (2.8)	-6.9** (6.3)
Centralised/co-ordinated	7.7** (2.6)	5.4 (1.9)	12.3** (5.5)	-11.1** (5.5)	-8.9** (4.7)	-13.7** (8.9)
Collective bargaining coverage (%)	0.4** (4.9)	0.2** (4.4)	0.0 (0.5)	-0.3** (6.0)	-0.2** (5.0)	-0.1** (3.0)
Trade union density (%)	-0.1* (2.0)	-0.2** (4.2)	-0.3** (9.4)	0.1* (2.6)	0.1** (5.4)	0.2** (10.3)
Employment protection						
Low	32.7** (12.1)	29.1** (12.9)	26.8** (13.7)	-23.0** (12.6)	-19.6** (12.9)	-20.6** (15.2)
Medium	13.4** (5.9)	14.8** (6.8)	18.7** (10.4)	-0.9 (0.6)	-2.3 (1.5)	-5.2** (4.2)
Dual system	7.5** (2.8)	10.5** (4.3)	15.2** (6.7)	-0.1 (0.1)	-3.0 (1.8)	-4.6** (2.9)
Trend	0.9** (6.1)	0.9** (5.9)	0.8** (7.0)	-0.3** (2.9)	-0.3* (2.6)	-0.4** (5.3)

a) ** and * indicate significance at the 1 per cent and 5 per cent levels, respectively. T-statistics are in parentheses and in absolute values. The dependent variables are as in Table 3.6. The equations also include dummy variables for age, gender and educational attainment.

b) The reference groups for the dummy variables shown are decentralised/un-coordinated collective bargaining structure, high level of strictness of employment protection legislation and not having an extensive apprenticeship system.

c) Because of data availability, the regressions include only Belgium, Denmark, France, Germany, Italy, the Netherlands, Spain, the United Kingdom and the United States.

Source and definitions: See Annex 3.A.

tries with strong apprenticeship systems show significantly higher employment and lower unemployment probabilities.

A wider range of institutional factors are considered in Table 3.7. The list includes measures of the
structure of collective bargaining, trade union density, collective bargaining coverage rates and a time-
invariant measure of net unemployment benefit
replacement rates for youth, in addition to the other
variables used in Table 3.6. This specification is
motivated by the debate on the causes of high and
persistent unemployment [see, for example, Alogoskoufis *et al.* (1995); Bertola and Rogerson (1995); Esping-Andersen (1998); Layard *et al.* (1991); Nickell
(1997); Scarpetta (1996)]. However, data limitations
restrict this analysis to just nine countries.

The results show that collective bargaining
structures matter, with more centralised/co-ordi-
nated countries "outperforming" more decentralised ones in terms of delivering better labour market outcomes for new school leavers in the short-
term. There is also little evidence, consistent with
OECD (1997d), that intermediate systems do worse
than decentralised ones; in fact, the results suggest
they do better with respect to unemployment. The
results for EPL and apprenticeship systems are similar to those shown in Table 3.6. Although the
coefficients are quite small, higher levels of collective bargaining coverage are associated with higher
employment and lower unemployment, while the
opposite pattern is estimated for trade union
density.

D. SETTLING IN: A LONGER-TERM VIEW
OF THE TRANSITION

1. Introduction

The previous section took a short-run perspective to youth insertion into the labour market. The
purpose of this section is to extend that analysis by
following youth over time using longitudinal data for
Australia, France, Germany, Ireland, Italy, Spain and
the United States (see Annex 3.B).

The main questions addressed are: What are
individuals' employment and unemployment experiences over a three to six-year period after "permanently" leaving initial education? How does that
experience vary across countries and levels of educational attainment? How much time do youths
spend employed and is there any evidence of "persistence" in labour force status?

Before taking up these questions, some background on the methods used in this section is necessary. For each country-specific data set, with the

exception of Italy, youths in education were followed over successive interviews to determine
when they were no longer in school, including
apprenticeship programmes. Once that point was
determined, those individuals were then followed
over successive interviews to ensure that they were
"permanently" out of school (the Irish data, however, are based largely on retrospective information). Thus, this analysis is based on dating
"entrance into the labour market" as the first interview in which individuals no longer report any additional education. All the data sets allow retrospective reconstruction of individuals' labour market
history month-by-month. However, unless otherwise
noted, all calculations here refer to labour force status at the *time* of each survey. It was also necessary
that individuals be in the sample continuously and
provide responses to all labour force and schooling
questions. This raises the problem of sample attrition and, on average, individuals with less educational qualifications are more likely to have been
non-respondents. It can probably be assumed that
they are also more likely to have greater difficulty in
the labour market.

The different data sets preclude any uniformity
in the timing of permanent entry. For example, the
Australian data refer to labour market entry between
1989-1990, while the timing for American youth
ranges between 1981-1988. No formal attempt has
been made to determine whether or not the year of
entering the labour market had any lasting impact
on these young people, although visual inspection
of the German and American data found little evidence for the proposition. Finally, this section measures the evolution of certain labour market outcomes from the date of permanent entry to the
labour market. This puts individuals in a similar time
frame with a similar exposure to the labour market.
Another possibility would consider people at a
given age and measure cumulative experience
obtained by each age [Pergamit (1995)].

2. Incidence of employment and
unemployment – the first three-five years
after permanently leaving education

Tables 3.8 and 3.9 record the evolution of
employment and unemployment rates for this select
group of permanent school leavers. Concerning
employment, three tendencies are apparent. First,
with the exception of Germany, there are large
differences in *first-year* employment rates by educational attainment, with rates going from low to high
as qualifications increase. American youth with less
than an upper secondary education (*i.e.* high school
dropouts) have quite low employment rates.[7] Blau
and Kahn (1997) find similar American-German

Table 3.8.   **Employment rates**[a] **over the first three to five years after leaving initial education by gender and educational attainment**

	Men			Women		
	First year	Third year	Fifth year	First year	Third year	Fifth year
Less than upper secondary						
Australia	65.1	65.9	75.9	55.4	45.5	39.2
France[b]	77.5	81.3	78.1	68.3	73.0	69.0
of which: in subsidised jobs	25.0	16.3	7.2	30.6	24.0	10.0
Germany	87.5	91.9	88.5	73.7	79.2	72.6
Ireland	75.9	81.0	78.4	62.7	64.9	61.2
United States	49.5	64.8	79.8	31.6	31.9	39.3
Upper secondary						
Australia	74.9	74.9	82.5	78.2	75.4	74.2
France	. .	. .	. .	. .	. .	. .
Germany	88.2	96.3	95.0	83.6	89.9	86.0
Ireland	68.1	90.3	87.1	62.0	87.6	88.5
United States	71.6	77.7	85.9	61.1	68.0	71.1
University/tertiary						
Australia	78.2	84.0	87.0	79.0	77.6	77.6
France[c]	80.4	94.4	95.5	77.6	91.2	91.2
Germany	85.9	87.7	99.7	75.4	82.7	86.9
Ireland	73.7	83.6	. .	78.6	94.0	. .
United States	87.1	94.7	95.4	81.0	86.9	81.8

.. Data not available.
a) Defined as the percentage of the sample with a job.
b) Subsidised jobs refers to *Travaux d'utilité collective, Contrats emploi solidarité, Contrats d'adaptation* and *Contrats de qualification.* Time spent in obligatory national service is excluded.
c) Data refer to the first, third and fourth year after leaving initial education at the university/tertiary level.
Source: See Annex 3.B.

Table 3.9.   **Unemployment rates**[a] **over the first three to five years after leaving initial education by gender and educational attainment**

	Men			Women		
	First year	Third year	Fifth year	First year	Third year	Fifth year
Less than upper secondary						
Australia	30.5	29.7	19.6	28.7	23.9	21.6
France	15.4	16.7	20.2	23.5	21.0	24.0
Germany	11.7	7.7	13.0	15.5	8.9	16.9
Ireland	22.4	18.7	21.4	30.9	25.6	25.7
United States	42.2	29.4	14.9	47.9	34.6	28.1
Upper secondary						
Australia	22.6	22.6	14.8	16.0	13.8	9.9
France	. .	. .	. .	. .	. .	. .
Germany	9.8	1.8	3.7	9.0	5.9	5.9
Ireland	17.4	6.8	11.3	19.7	6.7	5.4
United States	20.5	15.8	8.6	21.5	14.4	11.0
University/tertiary						
Australia	21.2	14.5	9.5	17.0	13.3	10.5
France	14.4	4.4	3.8	17.2	5.4	5.3
Germany	4.9	12.3	3.7	17.9	0.6	0.0
Ireland	9.2	7.5	. .	8.5	7.5	. .
United States	10.0	3.5	2.6	9.7	5.7	4.2

.. Data not available.
a) Defined as the percentage of the labour force who are unemployed.
Notes and source: See Table 3.8.

differences over the 1980s and 1990s using synthetic cohorts aged 18-29 and 25-36 years old. Second, there are gender differences. Women's employment rates are lower than men's, with the absolute differences generally greater at lower levels of educational attainment (the exception is Irish women with some university/tertiary education). This gap is particularly pronounced in Australia and the United States. Finally, though much more so among young men, the rates tend to rise over time and the absolute gap between those with less and more education does narrow. However, differences do persist: five years after entering the labour market, between 13 and 25 per cent of young men at the lower end of the education scale are not employed compared with only 1 to 13 per cent of those with some university/tertiary education.

France is an interesting case because it is the one country for which the data set contains information on participation in subsidised jobs and, as emphasized in Section B, such measures add an important dimension to understanding youth labour markets. The first year after leaving school one-third or more of young French persons without even the general *Baccalauréat* were employed in subsidised jobs. Other research shows that fully one-half of this cohort went through at least one programme [Werquin (1997)]. Although employment rates for this group of school leavers change little over time, recourse to programmes declines dramatically, while integration into jobs with a permanent contract tends to increase, though fully one-third never obtained such a contract. Not surprisingly, French research has shown that programmes close to regular employment, *e.g. contrats de qualification*, have a higher probability of leading to regular jobs [DARES (1997)].

Some of the tendencies observed with employment are mirrored in unemployment rates (Table 3.7). The latter, as in cross-section data, decline as educational qualifications increase. But, there are again large differences across countries, which are more pronounced at lower levels of education. Finally, unemployment rates tend to decline over time among less-educated youths, except in France, Ireland and Germany.

Thus far, only labour market experience after leaving school has been considered. In some countries where the apprenticeship system is of little importance, one topic for debate on improving the school-to-work transition has centred on the role of employment opportunities while in school [Ruhm (1997)]. Research has focused on both the direct effects of acquiring work experience while in school and the indirect effects of working on final educational attainment. Ruhm (1997), for example, argues that, in the United States, there is a positive and

long-term impact from such in-school work experience, though it varies a lot across different groups. For example, among those who work in the later stages of high school and do not go on to higher education, the impact is positive and considerably larger compared with persons moving on to university. He also finds that working while in school is more prevalent the more *advantaged* ones' family background, a finding not replicated in British research [Dustmann *et al.* (1996)].

There are numerous analytical complexities in considering the impact of school-work combinations on *long-term success rates* in integrating into employment and constructing good careers. A very simple illustrative approach is adopted here. Data are available on employment while in school in both the German and American longitudinal datasets. The text table below shows employment rates in both the first and fifth year after leaving school for individuals who did and did not work in paid employment during their last year in education (the proportion of the samples working their last year in school was almost 80 per cent in Germany and 53 per cent in the United States):

Employment rates

	First year	Fifth year
Worked last year in school		
Germany	87.3	87.9
United States	87.1	87.7
Did not work last year in school		
Germany	64.7	84.6
United States	67.3	75.0

There are quite large differences, of the order of 20 percentage points or more, in the first year after leaving education. However, they are much less pronounced, only 3 percentage points in Germany and almost 13 percentage points in the United States, after five years in the labour market. The interesting question is why German youths who were not working their last year in school caught up much faster with those who were working than was the case for young Americans. The difference may well point to a more structural set of institutions for integrating young people more quickly into the labour market in Germany via a range of well-known and accepted standards of certification and assessment of youths' abilities, whereas in the United States early "hands on" work experience of any kind is the main signal employers have in assessing young people's work habits or abilities. However, much more comparative work is necessary before reaching any firm conclusions.

3. Time spent in work

The evolution of employment and unemployment rates over time is only one part of the picture of how well or poorly youth become integrated into the labour market. The total amount of time spent in jobs or job-seeking, and whether or not there is persistence in status are also important elements in any judgement about getting a firm foothold in the world of work.

Table 3.10 shows the average time spent in employment. The figures are calculated conditional upon whether these youths were employed, unemployed or not in the labour force in their first year in the labour market. The closer the values are to one, the closer are these youths to having been continuously in work at the moment of each of the three to six annual interviews [the Irish data, however, refer to the total time spent employed over a 36- (university/tertiary) and a 60-month period].

The overall results are clear. Irrespective of education or gender, getting a job in the first year after school is associated with a greatly increased likelihood of being employed at the moment of each subsequent annual interview compared with youth starting off without a job. To some degree, this "persistence" is also higher among the more educated, though the difference is small. The table also shows calculations for full- and part-time employment. In general, though the differences are often small, part-time working tends to mean less stable employment histories compared with working in a full-time job.

In terms of these youth cohorts overall, the figures in columns one and six of Table 3.10 should be combined with the very large cross-country differences in employment rates in Table 3.8. Thus, while youth who do start the transition in a job spend a similar cumulated amount of time in employment in all countries, this covers a significantly larger proportion of youth, especially those

Table 3.10. **Average cumulative time employed over the first three to six years after leaving initial education by gender and educational attainment conditional upon labour force status in the first year**[a]

Proportion of time

| | Men | | | | | Women | | | | |
| | Employed the first year | | | Unemployed the first year | Not in labour force the first year | Employed the first year | | | Unemployed the first year | Not in labour force the first year |
	Total	Full-time	Part-time			Total	Full-time	Part-time		
Less than upper secondary										
Australia	0.78	0.78	0.63	0.40	0.36	0.79	0.85	0.54	0.20	0.08
France[b]	0.86	..	..	0.50	0.61	0.79	..	..	0.49	0.42
of which: in subsidised jobs	0.17	..	..	0.15	0.11	0.22	..	..	0.14	0.13
Germany	0.93	0.94	0.80	0.56	0.37	0.88	0.88	0.93	0.49	0.47
Ireland[c]	0.88	..	..	0.38	0.62	0.83	..	..	0.23	0.20
United States	0.86	0.87	0.81	0.50	0.37	0.64	0.75	0.51	0.23	0.19
Upper secondary										
Australia	0.83	0.85	0.76	0.51	0.56	0.84	0.87	0.76	0.42	0.40
France	..	..	..	..	..	..	..	..	..	..
Germany	0.98	0.98	0.99	0.58	0.37	0.88	0.92	0.81	0.67	0.66
Ireland[c]	0.90	..	..	0.60	0.64	0.89	..	..	0.59	0.65
United States	0.89	0.90	0.88	0.55	0.42	0.84	0.86	0.79	0.44	0.36
University/tertiary										
Australia	0.89	0.91	0.75	0.53	0.33	0.84	0.85	0.75	0.56	0.41
France	0.96	..	..	0.62	0.54	0.94	..	..	0.61	0.43
Germany	0.96	0.96	0.99	0.80	0.71	0.92	0.91	0.95	0.78	0.18
Ireland[c]	0.92	..	..	*d*	*d*	0.90	..	..	*d*	*d*
United States	0.97	0.97	0.93	0.69	0.65	0.92	0.93	0.85	0.56	0.45

..   Data not available.
a)   The figures refer to the per cent of time employed over a four-year interview period for Australia and France (university/tertiary), a five-year interview period for Germany and the United States, and a six-year interview period for France (less than upper secondary). Labour force status is determined at the time of each annual survey. The first year is included in the average cumulative time.
b)   Time spent in subsidised jobs is included, while time in obligatory national service is excluded.
c)   The figures refer to the per cent of months spent mainly in employment over a five-year period (less than upper secondary and upper secondary) and over a three-year period (university/tertiary). The data are based on retrospectively constructing annual work histories.
d)   The sample size is too small for reliable estimates.
Source: See Table 3.8.

with fewer educational qualifications, in Germany, France, and to some extent Ireland, compared with the other countries.

Starting off unemployed or not in the labour force leads in all five countries to significantly less cumulated time in employment. There are, however, some cross-country and cross-education differences. Whether the experience of unemployment itself causes further unemployment – the so-called "scarring" hypothesis – has been the subject of considerable debate and some empirical research. Although the evidence is not conclusive, the balance seems to lean towards some evidence of a scarring effect [Franz *et al.* (1997); Gardecki and Neumark (1997); Werquin *et al.* (1997)]. Though the data in Table 3.10 cannot be used to prove rigorously that early problems in finding a job *cause* later problems, they do point in this direction.

Another dimension of persistence is shown in Table 3.11. It records the *distribution* of employment and unemployment. Very few young men, regardless of educational background, were never employed. However, the distribution shows large cross-country differences. At the lower end of educational attainment, over 85 per cent of German men and over 75 per cent of German women were in work during at least four of the annual surveys (these figures are obtained by adding the proportion employed for four and five periods). This compares with 70 per cent for Irish men and 50 per cent for Irish women, and 69 per cent for French men and 63 per cent for French women. The equivalent proportions are much lower for young men and women in Australia and the United States with less than upper secondary education. As educational attainment increases, these cross-country differences diminish among both genders. Results are, not surprisingly, similar for time spent unemployed. Multiple "periods" of unemployment are far more prevalent among American, Australian and French youth. In all countries, the likelihood of being unemployed at any of the survey dates declines with educational attainment.

A useful summary measure which highlights these large differences is to compute how much of this five-year period is spent in employment on average. For men with less than upper secondary education in both Australia and the United States, only about two-thirds of the period was spent in work compared with almost 90 per cent in Germany. Moreover, in the first two countries the distribution is highly unequal, with roughly one-half of the total time spent in employment being accounted for by just one-third of these youths. In France, where a six-year period is considered, men with less than upper secondary education spent only half of the total period in employment. The distribution is also

highly unequal, with one-half of the total time in employment being accounted for by a little more than one-quarter of these French youth.

The experience of unemployment, although very different across countries, is rather concentrated. Taking the same group as above (men with less than upper secondary education), roughly one-third of the total time spent in unemployment is accounted for by 8 per cent of those with some unemployment in Australia and the United States; the equivalent fraction is 4 per cent in Germany and 5 per cent in France.

4. Transitions in and out of temporary jobs and the time spent in them

One of the debates on the integration of youth into jobs concentrates on the role of temporary contracts. The question is whether they provide youths with a stepping-stone to more stable employment. This subsection analyses this issue in two ways. First, it considers flows into and out of these jobs. Second, as is in the previous subsection, it examines the time spent in temporary jobs and compares this with youth starting off in permanent jobs or unemployed.

The longitudinal data used covers only France, Italy and Spain, and there are considerable problems of data comparability to keep in mind. For example, the Italian and Spanish data refer to all youths leaving education, while the French data refer to low-skilled youth with less than an upper secondary education. The time over which individuals are observed also differs. It is a six-year period for France and Italy, but just 15 months for Spain. Finally, the Italian data cover only wage and salary workers. Tables 3.12 and 3.13 show the information on the labour force status transition matrix and the average cumulative time spent in work or unemployment, respectively.

The most interesting results of this exercise are as follows. Taking Table 3.12 first shows that low-skilled French youth employed on a temporary contract during their first year out of school are both less likely to be in a job six years later and, if working, less likely to have a permanent contract compared with those who started in a permanent job. That said, over 60 per cent of these youths who found a temporary job after leaving school were in a permanent one six years later. Moreover, they tend to do better, defined as having a permanent job, than those who started on a labour market programme, and they do considerably better than the unemployed.

The results for Spain and Italy are somewhat different. In Spain, the likelihood of being employed

Table 3.11a. **Distribution of time spent employed over the first three to six years since leaving initial education by gender and educational attainment**

Percentages

| | Men | | | | | | | Women | | | | | | |
| | Total | Never employed | Employed | | | | | Total | Never employed | Employed | | | | |
			One period	Two periods	Three periods	Four periods	Five periods			One period	Two periods	Three periods	Four periods	Five periods
Less than upper secondary														
Australia[a]	100	8.3	7.4	14.8	16.7	15.7	37.1	100	37.3	12.7	6.9	4.9	7.8	30.4
France[b]	100	2.9	6.1	9.7	12.4	21.6	47.4	100	5.4	9.1	10.5	11.9	15.4	47.7
Germany[a]	100	1.5	2.5	1.7	7.2	20.8	66.3	100	7.9	2.4	6.3	4.7	33.4	45.3
Ireland[c]	100	6.5	3.8	5.9	13.2	15.2	55.4	100	16.9	7.8	9.6	14.2	8.4	43.1
United States[a]	100	7.8	8.8	12.1	18.6	21.9	30.9	100	29.1	25.3	12.8	15.9	10.6	6.4
Upper secondary														
Australia[a]	100	4.4	5.0	6.3	15.0	16.9	52.4	100	6.4	5.6	6.0	10.3	18.9	52.8
France	:	:	:	:	:	:	:	:	:	:	:	:	:	:
Germany[a]	100	0.0	2.0	2.2	2.7	12.1	81.1	100	0.7	1.9	7.7	5.8	20.8	63.1
Ireland[c]	100	2.1	2.3	4.4	9.4	28.4	53.4	100	2.4	2.5	4.6	9.4	30.2	50.9
United States[a]	100	2.9	5.4	8.3	12.9	22.1	48.4	100	8.4	9.4	13.3	13.4	19.9	35.5
University/tertiary														
Australia[a]	100	5.2	3.9	3.9	7.8	13.0	66.2	100	2.0	11.2	8.4	13.3	13.3	51.8
France[d]	100	6.7	4.9	18.7	38.1	31.6	:	100	3.6	3.7	7.4	21.6	63.7	:
Germany[a]	100	0.0	0.0	0.0	4.5	25.2	70.2	100	5.2	2.1	0.0	9.0	27.8	55.9
Ireland[e]	100	12.3	5.3	16.2	66.2	:	:	100	1.7	3.0	15.5	79.8	:	:
United States[a]	100	0.5	0.7	1.8	3.5	17.2	76.3	100	3.1	2.7	5.4	9.9	18.7	60.2

: Data not available.
a) Data refer to the first five-year interview period since leaving education.
b) Data refer to the first six-year interview period since leaving education. The column "five periods" reports values for five to six periods. Especially for men. these figures are underestimates of those with three or more periods employed because those going directly into obligatory national service are excluded.
c) Data refer to the first five years since leaving education.
d) Data refer to the first four-year interview period since leaving education. Especially for men, these figures are underestimates of those with three or more periods employed because those going directly into obligatory national service are excluded.
e) Data refer to the first three years since leaving education.
Source: See Table 3.8

Table 3.11b. Distribution of time spent unemployed over the first three to six years since leaving initial education by gender and educational attainment

Percentages

	Men							Women						
			Unemployed							Unemployed				
	Total	Never unemployed	One period	Two periods	Three periods	Four periods	Five periods	Total	Never unemployed	One period	Two periods	Three periods	Four periods	Five periods
Less than upper secondary														
Australia[a]	100	39.8	18.5	16.7	16.7	2.8	5.5	100	65.7	14.7	11.8	2.0	2.9	2.9
France[b]	100	52.3	23.1	12.4	7.7	2.7	1.8	100	37.2	23.5	15.8	13.3	6.4	3.9
Germany[a]	100	71.8	16.4	6.4	1.7	3.7	0.0	100	72.9	18.1	4.2	2.7	2.0	0.2
Ireland[c]	100	58.7	12.6	12.8	5.9	3.8	6.2	100	60.2	10.4	8.9	4.9	5.2	10.4
United States[a]	100	38.0	28.5	19.9	6.1	5.1	2.3	100	43.6	31.2	16.1	6.1	2.1	1.0
Upper secondary														
Australia[a]	100	58.1	15.0	13.8	4.4	5.0	3.7	100	68.2	14.2	6.4	3.0	2.6	5.6
France	..	..	..	..	..	..	..	..	..	..	..	..	..	..
Germany[a]	100	85.1	9.6	3.6	1.5	0.2	0.0	100	79.4	15.4	4.1	0.6	0.0	0.6
Ireland[c]	100	70.6	18.5	5.8	2.0	1.9	1.2	100	76.0	16.8	3.7	2.0	0.9	0.6
United States[a]	100	58.3	22.7	12.8	4.3	1.7	0.2	100	62.0	23.4	9.8	3.6	0.8	0.4
University/tertiary														
Australia[a]	100	68.8	13.0	7.8	5.2	3.9	1.3	100	62.9	21.7	7.7	5.6	2.1	0.0
France[d]	100	83.9	12.7	2.4	0.8	0.3	..	100	77.4	16.5	4.3	1.3	0.5	..
Germany[a]	100	79.5	20.5	0.0	0.0	0.0	0.0	100	81.6	17.9	0.5	0.0	0.0	0.0
Ireland[e]	100	82.2	13.1	0.0	4.7	..	..	100	89.5	7.8	1.8	0.9	..	..
United States[a]	100	82.2	14.6	2.0	0.6	0.4	0.2	100	80.3	14.8	3.3	1.4	0.1	0.0

.. Data not available.
a) Data refer to the first five-year interview period since leaving education.
b) Data refer to the first six-year interview period since leaving education. The column "five periods" reports values for five to six periods. Especially for men, these figures are underestimates of those with three or more periods unemployed because those going directly into obligatory national service are excluded.
c) Data refer to the first five years since leaving education.
d) Data refer to the first four-year interview period since leaving education. Especially for men, these figures are underestimates of those with three or more periods unemployed because those going directly into obligatory national service are excluded.
e) Data refer to the first three years since leaving education.
Source: See Table 3.8.

Table 3.12. **Labour force status of youth after leaving initial education distributed by their status _t_ years later, by type of contract and gender**[a]

Percentages

Status at first interview	Status _t_ years after leaving school											
	Men						Women					
	Total	Employed (all)	Permanent	Fixed-term	Unemployed	Not in the labour force	Total	Employed (all)	Permanent	Fixed-term	Unemployed	Not in the labour force
France, less than upper secondary education[b]												
Employed (all)	100	83.2	71.6	11.6	8.2	8.7	100	71.3	64.5	6.8	18.6	10.1
Permanent	100	89.6	81.9	7.7	5.6	4.9	100	88.2	78.9	9.3	9.1	2.7
Fixed-term	100	77.8	62.5	15.3	9.7	12.6	100	64.8	59.9	4.9	24.1	11.1
Subsidised jobs	100	69.4	55.7	13.7	21.4	9.3	100	57.4	48.9	8.5	24.6	17.9
Unemployed	100	52.8	42.3	10.5	30.8	16.4	100	51.5	44.5	7.0	21.1	27.4
Italy[c]												
Employed (all)	100	54.6	46.9	7.3	..	..	100	52.9	45.1	4.7	..	..
Permanent	100	48.7	45.1	3.2	..	..	100	47.7	42.7	2.8	..	..
Fixed-term	100	63.1	49.3	13.4	..	..	100	61.4	50.1	8.1	..	..
Spain[d]												
Employed (all)	100	52.5	21.7	24.0	21.7	25.8	100	54.0	14.7	28.8	28.2	17.8
Permanent	100	43.4	17.2	19.2	22.2	34.4	100	52.6	19.3	21.1	33.3	14.1
Fixed-term	100	43.1	15.6	21.1	23.9	33.0	100	51.4	8.1	33.8	39.7	8.9
Unemployed	100	50.0	21.8	17.3	33.6	16.4	100	47.7	20.2	19.3	34.9	17.4

.. Data not available.

a) The data for France and Italy refer to labour force status at the starting date and six years later. The data for Spain refer to the starting date and five quarters later.

b) All employed in France refers only to wage and salary workers with either a permanent or temporary contract. There may be a small number of persons counted as not in the labour force who are in subsidised jobs, in self-employment or are unpaid family workers.

c) Italian figures are taken from the social security records. Therefore, non-dependent employment, the unemployed and certain types of public employment are not included.

d) All employed in Spain includes the self-employed, unpaid family workers and employment where the contractual arrangement is not known.

Source: See Annex 3.B.

Table 3.13. **Average cumulative time spent in employment or unemployment over the first five quarters to six years after leaving initial education conditional on status the first year**[a]

Proportion of time

Status at first interview	Men					Women				
	Employment (all)	Permanent	Fixed-term	Other employment	Unemployment	Employment (all)	Permanent	Fixed-term	Other employment	Unemployment
France, less than upper secondary education[b]										
Employed (all)	0.75	..	..	..	0.09	0.78	..	..	..	0.13
Permanent	0.83	0.77	0.06	..	0.06	0.90	0.79	0.11	..	0.06
Fixed-term	0.70	0.36	0.34	..	0.12	0.72	0.39	0.33	..	0.17
Subsidised jobs	0.41	0.32	0.09	..	0.14	0.37	0.28	0.09	..	0.22
Unemployed	0.32	0.22	0.10	..	0.43	0.34	0.25	0.09	..	0.44
Italy[c]										
Employed (all)	..	0.38	0.11	..	..	..	0.43	0.08	..	..
Permanent	0.59	0.47	0.10	..	..	0.58	0.49	0.05	..	..
Fixed term	0.57	0.33	0.21	..	..	0.72	0.43	0.25	..	..
Spain[d]										
Employed (all)	0.55	0.25	0.28	0.12	0.17	0.68	0.24	0.30	0.14	0.20
Permanent	0.53	0.40	0.17	0.06	0.16	0.70	0.44	0.16	0.10	0.19
Fixed-term	0.56	0.17	0.42	0.07	0.18	0.64	0.13	0.44	0.07	0.22
Unemployed	0.41	0.14	0.19	0.08	0.41	0.45	0.17	0.19	0.09	0.42

.. Data not available.
Notes and source: See Table 3.12.

at both dates differs little by type of contract. However, unlike the case of France, the probability of moving from a temporary to a permanent contract is not particularly high, especially among women. Indeed, many youth, who started in permanent jobs, were 15 months later in temporary ones. Italy is altogether different: starting off with a fixed-term contract is actually associated with a higher probability of being employed six years later compared with those on a permanent contract. There are two likely reasons for this. First, these Italian fixed-term contracts are designed for a rather select group of skilled youth. Second, as shown in Section B, there is a legal requirement on firms that they must transform at least one-half of these contracts into permanent ones.

To a very great degree, these differences also show-up in differences in the amount of time spent in employment (Table 3.13). Thus, in France the low-skilled who start off with fixed-term contracts spend considerably less time in any job and more time unemployed compared with low-skilled youths who started off in permanent jobs. In Spain, there is little difference between the two groups, each spends about the same time in work and out of work. But, both fare much better than the unemployed.

5. Summary

The longitudinal data reveal important national differences in how well the transition "works". This is especially true among individuals who do not go to university. It is clear that German youth are more quickly integrated into work. They have higher rates of employment and are much more likely to have been in work "continuously" over the period. Young Australians and Americans are much more likely to experience more time out of work, particularly in their initial transition years. France and Ireland tend to lie in-between. These differences cannot be simply ascribed to attributes of the German apprenticeship system – the really large differences show-up among youth with low levels of qualifications. What may underlie these differences is an open question. In all countries, however, getting into a job quickly is important. While causality cannot be proven, the lack of success early on is quite clearly associated with continued problems of finding and holding down a job. In this context, the role of temporary contracts is complicated. Looked at solely from the standpoint of employment *per se*, starting off with a fixed-term contract seems, on average, clearly preferable to unemployment. From a comparative perspective, whether such jobs are stepping-stones to permanent employment is less clear. However, the results for less educated French youths is instructive. Quite a large proportion who left school to a

temporary job had, six years later, made the jump to a permanent one. They had, however, also spent considerably more time out of work during those six years compared with those who began with a permanent contract. Whether their longer term career trajectories have been scarred as a result, remains an open, but important, question.

E. CONCLUSIONS

The evidence presented in this chapter suggests that the transition from school to work is a turbulent and uncertain period for young people, even if many of them start on the right track. The latter are lucky enough to have a higher level of education or to enter the labour market in a good year. These conditions are necessary, but often not sufficient, for a successful transition as the longitudinal data analysis in Section D shows clearly.

"Starting off" in the labour market as unemployed is the case, on average, for one new school leaver in four in the 16 OECD countries for which data are available. Judging from the longitudinal analysis, such a start foreshadows reduced future employment prospects for men and women and for all educational groups. However, there is a wide variation across countries in the probability of starting off as unemployed and it is unlikely that the differences can be explained solely in terms of the educational attainment youths bring to the labour market.

The damaging effects of persistence in unemployment and inactivity in the first years of the transition process are particularly worrying. Nonetheless, the proportion of youth employed does rise over time, especially among men, in all educational groups. Unemployment is also rather concentrated among a relatively small group of young people, even though in some countries, like Australia and the United States, the experience of unemployment in the early years is more widespread than in other countries. Augmenting the quality of initial education and, especially, reducing early exits from education clearly must remain of prime importance in tackling such problems.

But greater success in these objectives, on their own, will not be sufficient. Tackling overall high and persistent unemployment is an essential part of any "youth-oriented" policy package, but will also not be sufficient. In addition, the large cross-country differences evident in the data point towards the important role of labour market institutions in aiding the integration process, including "systems" of apprenticeships, collective bargaining, the strictness of employment protection legislation and youth labour market policies. The debate on the appropriate policies to tackle the problems faced by youth in making the transition to the job market needs, in many countries, to be more focused as to objectives. Should they simply seek to "maximise" short-run employment opportunities? Should they rather be geared to promoting institutional arrangements to assist youth to get into stable employment more

quickly? Two key points need to be addressed. First, it is important to study further the roles of these institutions in some detail, especially in a cross-country perspective. Secondly, however, the aim is not to simply transfer "institutions", which, in any case, poses numerous problems, but to learn from different country experiences.

Notes

1. In reality, youth measures are often a combination of active and passive (*i.e.* income-support) policies. The policy mix varies across countries, but the general tendency has been to try to reduce the importance of passive measures in favour of active policies. Moreover, passive measures are becoming more integrated with active measures. For example, youth (unemployment) allowances in Scandinavian countries are often included in packages of "activation policies".

2. Wage/earnings outcomes of new school leavers are not available from most of the labour force survey data sources used in Section C. They are, however, available in some national labour force surveys. For example, a recent study using the French labour force survey has argued that young people starting work in 1995 faced more difficult conditions than those who entered the labour market at the beginning of the decade [Ponthieux (1997)]. The differences include not only rising unemployment, job insecurity and an increase in part-time work, but also lower average wages, even though those starting work in 1995 were generally more highly qualified than their predecessors.

3. In these countries, apprentices also have a high probability of ultimately being hired with a regular contract by the firm where they were apprentices. In most countries, an apprenticeship system, despite efforts, is hardly well established. Since 1987, apprenticeships have been extended to all diploma levels in France. These kinds of contracts have generated interest in new segments of services, such as financial institutions, consulting firms, hotel chains, and mass marketing firms [Simon-Zarca (1996)]. However, in 1993, 27 per cent of all apprenticeship contracts were terminated before completion. Among those who completed the apprenticeship, only 30 per cent were hired by the employer where they were apprentices, and only 10 per cent obtained a regular contract [Vialla (1997)].

4. Although not shown here, in most countries by far the highest incidence of school leaving occurs between the ages of 18-22 years. This has shifted towards the higher end of this age group as school staying-on rates have generally increased [OECD (1996a)].

5. Similar results, not presented here, are found if one considers employment probabilities by single year of age. For example, the employment probabilities for 19- and 23-year-old school leavers were 59 and 66 per cent, respectively, in 1989 compared with 54 and 61 per cent in 1996. Viewed over the entire 16-29 age group, the probability of being in a job tends to increase with age while unemployment probabilities by age are rather constant.

6. Since 1996, Denmark has developed a broad range of "activation policies" for unemployed youth, which are considered by the European Commission as best practices [see Section B and European Commission (1997a)]. Therefore, more up-to-date data might show a different picture.

7. American youth with less than upper secondary education comprise 9 per cent of the sample, whereas they account for 18 and 22 per cent of the samples in Germany and Australia, respectively. Calculating employment rates for the bottom quintile of educational qualifications would reduce those differences, but they would still remain substantial.

ANNEX 3.A

Definitions, data sources and regression specifications
for the analysis in Section C

1. Definitions

Data have been gathered by single year of age for young people aged 16-29 for 16 OECD countries. With the exception of Norway, the data are from labour force surveys. The flow measure, "new school leavers", refers to individuals classified as being in initial education or training at time T-1 who were classified as not being in initial education one year later, or at the time of the survey. More precisely, most labour force surveys are conducted in the Spring whereas students tend to leave school in June. Thus, the time since leaving school is close to nine to ten months. The exceptions are Norway and the United States, where the time period is about six months.

New school leavers comprise a subgroup of any particular age group. Hence, analysis of their insertion into the labour market within the first year after leaving the education system does not correspond to the more traditional analysis of young people's labour force status. One example makes the distinction clear. In Belgium for 1995, new school leavers aged 16-24, as defined here, made up 8 per cent of all persons aged 16-24. This is because many youth, particularly teenagers, remained in school at both points in time, and because others had left the education system a number of years prior to the survey or had moved into and out of the education system several times. The recorded labour force status of the two "groups" is not the same. The probability of these new school leavers having a job in 1995 was 58 per cent whereas, as shown in Table C of the Statistical Annex, the employment rate of all Belgian youth aged 15-24 was just 27 per cent.

There are clear benefits of focusing on the subgroup of new school leavers as opposed to the more traditional focus on all youth *per se*. This focus permits one to analyse more precisely the ease or difficulty faced by young people in making their initial transition from education to the labour market. The short-term or over-the-year definition applied here enables such an analysis to be undertaken, unencumbered by the mixing together of youth still in education and of youth who had "permanently" left education many years ago.

There are certain limits to the data and analysis to bear in mind. While the data are based on common concepts, definitions and methods, the information is still limited to labour market outcomes about one year after exiting the initial schooling system. It does not follow that the data capture only those who have "permanently" left the education system. Some of those counted as having left education may well return at a later date and, indeed, many OECD countries have systems in place designed to foster opportunities to return to full-time education as well as to undertake part-time continuing education and training. Aspects of the longer-term and more permanent process of insertion into the labour market are reviewed in Section D, which uses longitudinal data to trace out the first three to six years of labour market experience. In addition, it is important not to confuse the idea of new school leavers used here with that of new entrants to the labour market. As previous work has shown, some young people work or search for a job while also attending school, a combination that differs a lot across countries [OECD (1996a)]. Thus, being a new school leaver is not always the same as having no prior work experience.

2. Data sources

European Union countries

The data were provided by EUROSTAT on the basis of each country's regular labour force survey. Data are available for all the EU countries except Sweden. The periods covered vary by country. The information is based on persons who were students in initial education or training or were conscripts in compulsory military or community service in the previous year and were not in initial education or training at the time of the survey. Initial education and training refer to schooling which takes place during or immediately after compulsory schooling or which is interrupted only by compulsory military or community service. Importantly, apprenticeships are not considered as being in initial education or training in these data.

The usual information on labour force status at the time of the survey has been supplemented by more detailed data on those counted as employed. In particular, data are available on whether the job is a full-or part-time one and whether it is temporary or permanent. Information on the reasons for part-time work and temporary contracts is also available. However, it should be borne in mind that the definitions of part-time work and temporary contracts are not uniform across countries [OECD (1996a, 1997d)]. Data are also analysed on new school leavers by their recorded level of educational attainment at the time of leaving the education system, although such data are only available from 1992 forward. Educational attainment is defined as: less than upper secondary (ISCED 0-2); upper secondary (ISCED 3); and university/tertiary (ISCED 5-7) [see OECD (1997a) for the country-specific definitions of these ISCED levels].

Norway

Data for 1993 and 1994 were provided by Statistics Norway on the basis of registration information which shows detailed labour force and schooling status in November of persons who completed initial education in May or June. In order to arrive at a definition of new school leavers more or less comparable to that for other countries, adjustments were made to these data. Persons who had left education in May or June, but in November were counted as in ordinary education or as combining education and part-time employment were considered to be still in the educational system. Persons counted as combining education and full-time employment were considered to be part of the new school leaver group. Persons counted as being on government measures were treated as follows: 42 per cent were counted as still being in some form of education – this is the group in qualifications programmes who, in the Norwegian labour force survey, would be counted as inactive and in education. The remainder were considered as new school leavers. Finally, all registered unemployed were counted as new school leavers.

The labour force status of new school leavers was based on the following definitions: Employed refers to persons in regular employment, 36 per cent of those on government measures (an estimate of those in subsidised jobs), and all persons in education, but working full-time. Unemployed refers to persons registered as unemployed and 22 per cent of those on government measures (an estimate of how they would be classified in the labour force survey). Not in the labour force is a residual of "others" from the registration data, including persons in military service and unpaid household workers. Data on educational attainment were not considered sufficiently robust to be included in the analysis.

United States

Data have been calculated from the October supplement to the Current Population Survey on school enrolment and cover the period 1983-1995. In this supplement, respondents are asked if they are currently enrolled in school and if they were also enrolled one year ago. New school leavers are defined as persons enrolled one year ago who were not enrolled at the time of the survey. Besides the usual information on labour force status at the time of the survey, data have been assembled on part-time and full-time work. Part-time employment is defined in this chapter as persons who usually work less than 35 hours per week. In addition, information on the reasons for part-time work is available. Educational attainment is defined as follows: less than upper secondary (up to and including the 12th grade, but without having completed high school); upper secondary (high school graduate); and university/tertiary (some college, but no degree; Associate's degree in college; Bachelor's degree in college; Master's degree; Professional school degree; and Doctorate degree).

3. Estimating the employment and unemployment probabilities of school leavers by pooling cross-section and time-series data

As is clear from the preceding description, the data contain both a cross-section and a time-series component. This has been taken advantage of by, for each country and for all countries together, pooling the data to greatly expand the number of observations available (see Table 3.A.1). OECD (1996a) provides more information on this procedure. The econometric method employed throughout is that of pooling both dimensions. All equations were estimated by OLS (ordinary least squares) using SAS software.

The dependent variables of interest are the probability of being employed and the probability of being unemployed for new school leavers. Two specifications are tested, the first for the 16 countries included in the database, except Norway and Luxembourg, the second for 9 countries (Belgium, Denmark, France, Germany, Italy, the Netherlands, Spain, the United Kingdom and the United States), for which all of the institutional variables are available.

Specification for 14 countries

The independent variables are the adult unemployment rate as a proxy for the cycle, public spending on youth labour market measures as a per cent of GDP and a set of socio-demographic dummy variables – gender, educational attainment, and age – designed to "control" for omitted variables specific to each cross-section unit. The equation also includes two, time-invariant, variables designed to account for two features of the institutional environment: a measure of the strictness of employment

Table 3.A.1. **Details of data files used in regressions**

	Years	Number of years	Number of observations[a]
Austria	1995-1996	2	168
Belgium	1985-1996	12	616
Denmark	1985-1996	12	616
Finland	1995-1996	2	168
France	1983-1996	14	672
Germany[b]	1985-1995	11	532
Greece	1983-1996	14	672
Ireland	1983-1991 and 1993-1996	13	588
Italy	1992-1996	5	420
Netherlands	1992-1996	5	420
Portugal	1986-1996	11	588
Spain	1987-1996	10	560
United Kingdom	1983-1996	14	672
United States	1983-1995	13	1 092
All			**7 784**

a) In every country and year, data are available for 14 single years of age, gender and three levels of educational attainment (1992 forward only for EU countries).

b) Data refer to the whole of Germany from 1991 onward.

protection legislation; and a variable indicating the presence of a well-established apprenticeship system. The equation is:

$$Y_{it} = \alpha_i + \beta_1(Ua_{it}) + \beta_2(Ym_{it}) + \beta_3(Gender_{it}) + \beta_4(Educ_{it}) + \beta_5(Age_{it}) + \beta_6(EPL_i) + \beta_7(DUAL_i) + \beta_8T + \varepsilon_{it}$$

where:

Ua_{it} = adult unemployment rate of country i at time t;

Ym_{it} = youth measures as a per cent of GDP of country i at time t;

$Gender_{it}$ = (1,0) gender dummy;

$Educ_{it}$ = (1,0) level of educational attainment dummy;

Age_{it} = (1,0) age dummy;

EPL_i = time-invariant (1,0) employment protection dummy;

$DUAL_i$ = time-invariant (1,0) apprenticeship dummy;

T = time trend; and

ε_{it} = stochastic error term.

Employment protection legislation (EPL). Countries are grouped into three categories: low, medium and high strictness of EPL. The criterion used to define the groups is the following. Take the standard deviation of the OECD index presented in column two of Table 6.7 (Panel B) of OECD (1994), and calculate the confidence intervals around the mean (at a 95 per cent significance level). Then three EPL groups can be formed, according to whether countries fall within, above or below, the confidence interval. The groups are:

Low EPL: Denmark, Ireland, the United Kingdom and the United States

Medium EPL: Austria, Belgium, Finland, France, Greece and the Netherlands

High EPL (reference group):   Germany, Italy, Spain and Portugal

Dual apprenticeship countries (DUAL). Austria, Denmark and Germany are classified as DUAL countries.

Specification with a full range of institutional variables for nine countries

The specification of the second regression includes a larger set of institutional variables in addition to the adult unemployment rate, public spending on youth labour market measures and socio-demographic dummies. Since this information is not available for all the countries of the dataset, only nine countries are included.

Youth net replacement rate. This variable indicates, for 1995, the unemployment benefit entitlements of young unemployed single people, in their first month of unemployment, assuming that waiting periods are met. The rate

is estimated at two-thirds of the average production worker level, including social assistance and housing benefits, and is net of taxation [OECD (1998b), Table 3.7].

Collective bargaining structure. Three dummies are created to capture the level of co-ordination and centralisation of collective bargaining over three different time periods. The reference group is those countries with a decentralised and uncoordinated bargaining structure. The distribution of countries across the three levels changes over time [OECD (1997d), Chapter 3].

Until 1989:	Co-ordinated/centralised:	Denmark and Germany
	Intermediate:	Belgium and the Netherlands
	Uncoordinated/decentralised:	France, Italy, Spain, the United Kingdom and the United States
1990 to 1993:	Co-ordinated/centralised:	Germany
	Intermediate:	Belgium, Denmark, France and the Netherlands
	Uncoordinated/decentralised:	Italy, Spain, the United Kingdom and the United States
From 1994:	Co-ordinated/centralised:	Germany and Italy
	Intermediate:	Belgium, Denmark, France and the Netherlands
	Uncoordinated/decentralised:	Spain, the United Kingdom and the United States

Collective bargaining coverage: Proportion of workers who are covered by collective bargaining agreements in 1980, 1990 and 1994 [OECD (1997d), Table 3.3].

Trade union density: Proportion of workers belonging to trade unions in 1980, 1990 and 1994 [OECD (1997d), Table 3.3].

Employment protection legislation (EPL). Countries are grouped in three categories: low, medium and high EPL based on the same method as above. The groups are:

Low EPL: Denmark, the United Kingdom and the United States

Medium EPL: Belgium, France and the Netherlands

High EPL: Germany, Italy and Spain

Dual apprenticeship countries (DUAL). Defined as above.

$$Y_{it} = \alpha_i + \beta_1(Gender_{it}) + \beta_2(Educ_{it}) + \beta_3(Age_{it}) + \beta_4(Ua_{it}) + \beta_5(Ym_{it}) + \beta_6(\text{Youth net replacement rate}_i) + \beta_7(\text{Collective bargaining structure}_{it}) + \beta_8(\text{Collective bargaining coverage}_{it}) + \beta_9(\text{Trade union density}_{it}) + \beta_{10}(EPL_i) + \beta_{11}(DUAL_i) + \beta_{12}T + \varepsilon_{it}$$

ANNEX 3.B

Definitions and data sources for the longitudinal analysis in Section D

1. Overview of definitions

Section D analyses the longer term labour market integration of young people after having permanently left the initial education system and, therefore, requires longitudinal data. While an overview of the country-specific data is provided below, the use of longitudinal data raises several data quality concerns that deserve mention.

The first is analytical and concerns the dating of labour market entry. Such dating is inherently ambiguous because young people can garner work experience while in education and because some youth will return to education after a period in the labour market. A natural starting point is to regard entry into the labour market as the first year in which a young person is observed in panel data to have "permanently" left the education system, including apprenticeships. That is, "permanent exit" from the education is defined as when they are observed as being out of education for the duration of the panel observations. For purposes of the analysis in this chapter, that is generally taken as a three- to six-year period during which respondents report no additional education. Hence, the sample consists of youth in education at time T and who had left education at time T+1 or the next interview and were never recorded as having returned to education over the period.

For a variety of reasons, some individuals in a panel dataset will be lost from the sample over time. This can effect the representiveness of the remaining sample. The German data provide fairly sophisticated probability weights designed to correct for sample attrition bias and are used for all the calculations. For the United States, the weights for the end-point year have been used. In principle, one could attempt to recompute all individual weights based upon persons for whom complete information is available in order to deal with this problem. This was not feasible. The data for Australia, France, Ireland, Italy and Spain are unweighted. A check of several of the calculations used in this chapter suggested that this made no qualitative difference to the percentages shown.

A final form of general sample restriction must be noted. To be included in the analysis, valid information was required for all variables of interest – age, gender, educational attainment, schooling status and employment status – for all years. Individuals missing information on one or more of these variables for even one wave were dropped from the analysis. Detailed analysis of this form of attrition suggests that it is more important among persons with fewer initial educational qualifications, i.e. those most likely to have more difficulties in constructing suc-

cessful labour market careers. For example, in the data for the United States, 783 persons with less than an upper secondary education were identified as leavers from the education system, but about 40 per cent of them are excluded from the analysis because of missing data over the full five-year period. This compares with an exclusion rate of only about 20 per cent for persons with university/tertiary education.

Finally, the periods covered differ across the countries. The Australian data refer to 1989-1994, France to 1989-1994 for those with less than upper secondary education and 1988-1991 for those with university/tertiary education, Germany to 1984-1995, Ireland to the 1992 follow-up survey of 1985/1986 school leavers, and the United States to 1979-1993. This may be of some importance because the timing of permanently leaving education and entering the labour market will tend to be dissimilar across countries, as well as across groups of youth classified by their final educational attainment. Since business cycle and other economic conditions change over time and differ across countries, this could affect the comparability of the results.

2. Data sources

Australia

The data are based on the Australian Youth Survey, 1989-1994, and were calculated by Matthew Gray of the Australian National University. This panel is based on annual interviews with a cohort of youth aged 16-19 in 1989, with a new sample of 16-year-olds added each year from 1990-1994. Information for this survey – questionnaires, user's guides and data definitions – are available from the Social Science Data Archives, Research School of Social Sciences, The Australian National University, Canberra, ACT.

New leavers from the initial education system are defined as follows: First, it is determined if individuals in the sample are in education at the time of the survey. Being in education refers to persons saying they were still in secondary school or were engaged full-time in any post-secondary education, which can include apprenticeships or traineeships as well as tertiary and university-level education. This group is then followed until they have left the education system and remain so for the remaining years.

The definitions of the final level of initial educational attainment are as follows: Less than upper secondary refers to pre-primary, primary and lower secondary, with the latter referring to year ten or less. Upper secondary refers to having completed years 11 and 12. University/tertiary refers all other post-secondary education.

The definitions of labour force status are as follows: Employed persons are those working at the time of the survey or who had a job, but were not at work due to circumstances such as sickness or holidays. Unemployed persons are those not working, but who had searched for work at some point during the four weeks prior to the survey. Not in the labour force is the residual. Part-time employment refers to person who worked less than 30 hours during the reference week. Data on permanent and fixed-term contracts were not available for the analysis.

France

The data were provided by Patrick Werquin of the *Centre d'Études et de Recherches sur les Qualifications* (CEREQ). For those with less than upper secondary education, a representative sample of those who left school during the 1988-1989 school year is used. Less than upper secondary can include *bacheliers professionnels, bacheliers technologiques* and persons who went through an apprenticeship training centre (*Centre de formation d'apprentis*), but excludes the *baccalauréat général*. These persons, subject to the fact that there is attrition of the sample, were interviewed in each year from 1990, usually during the month of December. All data for 1989 were gathered retrospectively. For those counted in this chapter as university/tertiary education, the data are based on a survey carried out by a mail questionnaire in 1991 of a sample of persons who had left the French "Enseignement supérieur" in 1988. There are two other important points concerning this sample. First, it only includes those who obtained degrees and excludes some specific types of higher education. Second, during the period covered for this group, there was little in the way of labour market programmes for them to enter and no attempt is made to distinguish programmes from other forms of employment. In addition, France has a community or military service obligation for men in particular, though there are exemptions. Therefore, a considerable proportion of men spent some time in military service over the time periods covered. In this chapter, military service is excluded from all calculations, although labour market activity prior to and after leaving national service is included in all calculations except those shown in Tables 3.11-3.13.

Labour force classification is based on individuals responses to a question concerning their situation at the time of the interview. Employment refers to having a job irrespective of the type of contract, including certain remunerated labour market programmes listed in Table 3.8. Permanent contracts refer to those with an indefinite duration (CDI). Fixed-term contracts refer to those with a fixed duration (CDD), although there is scope for their renewal. Unemployment refers to the response *au chômage*, while not in the labour force is a residual.

Germany

Data are based on the German Socio-Economic Panel survey from 1984-1995 and refer only to western Germany. This panel covers the whole population aged 16 and over

with interviews conducted once a year. The sample is renewed each year with a new cohort and, thus, is representative of the population each year. For detailed information on this survey, see the *German Socio-Economic Panel User Handbook*, German Institute of Economic Research, Berlin.

New leavers from the initial education system are defined as follows: First, all persons aged 16-30 are selected and it is determined if they are in education. Being in education means that, at the time of the survey, respondents said they were in general education, college, vocational school, apprenticeship, trade school, receiving training in health care or in civil service training. Going to night school is excluded. This group is then followed until it is determined that they have left the education system and remain so for at least five consecutive years. Not being in education at the time of the survey means that they were not in education at all or that they were following a further education course, career training, going to a specialised school such as a master apprenticeship or were following other further career training. These latter categories are considered to be apart from the formal initial educational system and, rather, represent individuals labour market career trajectory.

The definitions of the final level of initial educational attainment are as follows: Less than upper secondary refers to a school-leaving degree corresponding to *hauptschulabschluss, realschulabschluss, anderer abschluss* or *kein abschluss*. Upper secondary refers to a school leaving degree corresponding to *fachhochschule* or *abitur*, or a vocational degree corresponding to *lehre, berufsfachschule* or *sonstige ausbildung*. University/tertiary education refers to a vocational degree corresponding to *schule gesuntheitswesen, fachschule* or *beamtenausbildung*, or a completed college education corresponding to *fachhochschule* or *universitat*.

The definitions of labour market status are as follows: Employed refers to persons who were in gainful employment at the time of the survey and were not registered as unemployed. Gainful employment refers to being in full-time employment, having a regular part-time job, currently following career training or retraining within a company, and occasionally/irregularly employed. Unemployed are those not in gainful employment as defined above and who are registered as unemployed at the time of the survey. Not in the labour force are those not in gainful employment and not registered as unemployed. Part-time employment refers to persons in wage or salary jobs who said they worked less than 30 hours a week. It was not possible to use the data available on temporary or permanent contracts.

Ireland

The data are based on the Irish 1992 follow-up survey of school leavers in 1985/1986 and were supplied by Damian Hannan of the Economic and Social Research Institute. The data presented in this chapter are based on respondents' recall of their labour market history between the time of leaving education and the 1992 survey.

In all instances, educational attainment refers to the level of education achieved at the end of the initial period of full-time education. Less than upper secondary refers to having received a junior certificate or less. Upper secondary refers to the senior cycle of secondary education which comprises two years of a Leaving Certificate programme preceded by an optional transition year. It can also encompass one to two years of post-leaving certificate education, apprenticeship training and private business schools. University/tertiary includes all primary and bachelor degree programmes and above.

For Tables 3.8, 3.9, 3.11a and 3.11b, labour force status refers to one month during each year since leaving full-time education. Employed refers to having any kind of paid job and unemployed includes participation on a small number of government schemes. For Table 3.10, the entire three to five year retrospective history has been used based on respondents filling out their activity over the 36-60 months since leaving full-time education. Information on the nature of the employment contract was not available for the analysis undertaken here.

Italy

The data in Tables 3.12 and 3.13 are drawn from the Italian social security records (INPS, Istituto Nazionale di Previdenza Sociale), and cover the period 1987 to 1992. Data were provided by Claudio Malpede of Ricerche e Progetti at Turin.

The data cover only dependent employees. Although the entire private sector is covered, public sector coverage is incomplete. The database consists of one record for each individual employment spell. Individuals enter the sample as soon as they enter their first job. Thus, unemployed first-job seekers are not observed. Note that the data does not contain information on education qualifications or age of entry in the labour market.

A random sub-sample has been used for the analysis. Sample selection was made using scale 1:90, based on the date of birth. The sample includes only youth aged less than 30, who entered the work force in 1987. The definition of permanent school leavers as defined for other countries has not been used for Italy because the characteristics of the data do not make it possible. However, the sub-sample includes only young people who were not in education during the period analysed.

Spain

Figures for Spain in Tables 3.12 and 3.13 are drawn from matched files of the labour force survey, EPA (Encuesta de la Población Activa). This is a quarterly survey with a rotating sample with one-sixth of the sample replaced every quarter. Thus, individuals are observed for no more than six quarters.

For the purposes of this chapter, the sample selection was the following: Individuals under the age of 30 who were interviewed for the first time in the first quarter of 1995 or later, who responded to six consecutive interviews, who where students in the first interview, and who were not students in the subsequent five interviews were selected. Individuals who joined the military service after leaving school are not included. This selection is as close as possible to the definition of "permanent school leavers" described earlier in this annex.

Labour force status is based on the time of each quarterly survey. Employed persons are those who worked for pay or profit during the reference week. The fixed-term or permanent nature of the contract is based on responses as to whether the person has a temporary contract or job. Unemployment refers to persons without a job who actively looked for work during the four weeks prior to the survey.

United States

The data come from the National Longitudinal Survey of Youth, an annual survey of a cohort of youth aged 14-21 in 1978. The data analysed refer to the period 1979-1993. For detailed information on this survey see NLS Users' Guide, 1995, Center for Human Resource Research, Ohio State University, Columbus, Ohio, June 1995.

New leavers from the initial education system are defined as follows: Being in education refers to enrolment status as of 1 May of the survey year (note that this does not necessarily correspond to the actual time of the interview). Enrolled in education refers to those who said they were enrolled in high school or enrolled in college (college encompassed university and community colleges). This group was then followed until it was determined that they were no longer enrolled in education and remained so for at least five consecutive years. Not enrolled in education refers to those who said they were not enrolled as of 1 May of the survey year. A second definition was also constructed. Final educational attainment in years of schooling given in the 1993 survey was first calculated. Then the year of "labour market entry" was defined as: (AGE1993–YEARS of EDUCATION1993–6)+1. The figure in brackets corresponds to a traditional human capital formulation. Calculations on labour market status were done for both definitions with very similar results. Results using the first definition are reported in the chapter as it is felt to give a more accurate rendition of the actual time of permanent entry into the labour market from the education system.

The definitions of final level of educational attainment are as follows: Less than upper secondary refers to the highest grade completed as of 1 May of the survey year as 1-11 and no grade completed (persons with 12 years education, but no high school diploma are classified as having less than an upper secondary education). Upper secondary refers to having completed 12 years of education and having received a high school diploma. University/tertiary refers to having completed some college or university.

The definitions of labour force status are as follows: The analysis uses the Current Population Survey-based employment status recode and refers to status during the week of the survey. Employed refers to persons working or with a job, but not at work during the reference week. Unemployed refers to persons without a job and looking for work. Not in the labour force refers to persons neither working or looking for work who said they were keeping house, going to school, unable to work or other. The armed forces are excluded from the analysis. Part-time employment is defined as usually working less than 30 hours per week. No information is available on the type of employment contract.

Bibliography

ADAM, P. and CANZIANI, P. (1998), "Partial De-regulation: Fixed-term Contracts in Italy and Spain", Centre for Economic Performance, Discussion Paper No. 386.

ALOGOSKOUFIS, G., BEAN, C., BERTOLA, G., COHEN, D., DOLADO, J. and SAINT-PAUL, G. (1995), *Unemployment: Choices for Europe*, Centre for Economic Performance, London.

BAILEY, T. (ed.) (1995), "Learning to Work: Employer Involvement in School-to-Work Transition Program", *Brookings Dialogues on Public Policy*, Washington DC.

BARREIROS, L. and RAMPRAKASH, D. (1995), "Poverty and Social Exclusion Amongst Youth: A Conceptual Framework", Contribution to the Siena Group Seminar in Oslo, June 8th-9th, mimeo.

BENOÎT-GUILBOT, O., RUDOLPH, H. and SCHEUER, M. (1994), "Le chômage des jeunes en France et en Allemagne", *Travail et Emploi*, No. 59, pp. 48-63.

BERTOLA, G. and ROGERSON, R. (1995), "Institutions and Labor Reallocation", mimeo.

BJÖRKLUND, A. (1998), "Denmark and Sweden", mimeo.

BLAU, F.D. and KAHN, L.M. (1997), "Gender and Youth Employment Outcomes: The US and West Germany, 1984-91", National Bureau of Economic Research, Working Paper No. 6078.

BLOSSFELD, P. (1992), "Is the German Dual-system a Model for a Modern Vocational Training System? A cross-national comparison of how different systems of vocational training deal with the changing occupational structure", *International Journal of Comparative Sociology*, No. 3-4, pp. 168-181.

BUNDESMINISTERIUM FÜR BILDUNG, WISSENSCHAFT, FORSCHUNG UND TECHNOLOGIE (1997), *Berufsbildungsbericht* 1997, Bonn, May.

CARNEVALE, A., GAINER, L. and VILLET, J. (1990), *Training in America*, Jossey-Bass, San Francisco.

CASPI, A., WRIGHT, B.R.E., MOFFITT, T.E. and SILVA, P.A. (forthcoming), "Early Failure in the Labor Market: Childhood and Adolescent Predictors of Unemployment in the Transition to Adulthood", *American Sociological Review*.

DARES (Direction de l'Animation de la Recherche, des Études et des Statistiques) (1997), *La politique de l'emploi*, La Découverte, Paris.

DUSTMANN, C., MICKLEWRIGHT, J., RAJAH, N. and SMITH, S. (1996), "Earning and Learning: Educational Policy and the Growth of Part-Time Work by Full-Time Pupils", *Fiscal Studies*, February, pp. 79-104.

ESPING-ANDERSEN, G. (1998), "Unemployment and Employment Regulation: A Review of the Evidence from Comparative Research", mimeo.

EUROPEAN COMMISSION (1997a), *Proposal for Guidelines for Member States Employment Policies* 1998, Background Key Paper for the Jobs Summit in Luxembourg, October.

EUROPEAN COMMISSION (1997b), "Employment and Labour Market", *Employment and Social Affairs*. Series No. 1.

EUROSTAT (1997), *Youth in the European Union. From Education to Working Life*, Luxembourg, March.

FAY, R. (1996), "Enhancing the Effectiveness of Active Labour Market Policies: Evidence From Programme Evaluations in OECD Countries", *Labour Market and Social Policy Occasional Papers*, No. 18, OECD, Paris.

FRANZ, W. and SOSKICE, D. (1995), "The German Apprenticeship System", in Buttler, F., Franz, W. and Schettkat, R. (eds.), *Institutional Frameworks and Labor Market Performance*, Routledge, London, pp. 208-234.

FRANZ, W., INKMANN, J., POHLMEIER, W. and ZIMMERMANN, V. (1997), "Young and Out in Germany: On the Youths' Chances of Labor Market Entrance in Germany", National Bureau of Economic Research, Working Paper No. 6212.

FREYSSON, L. (1997), "Labour Market Exclusion of the Young: Some Illustrations of the Situation in the European Union", Annual Workshop of the European Research Network on Transition in Youth, Dublin, mimeo.

GALLAND, O. (1997), "L'entrée des jeunes dans la vie adulte", *Problèmes Politiques et Sociaux*, La Documentation Française, December.

GARDECKI, R. and NEUMARK, D. (1997), "Order from Chaos? The Effects of Early Labor Market Experiences on Adult Labor Market Outcomes", National Bureau of Economic Research, Working Paper No. 5899.

GAUTIÉ, J. (1997), "Insertion professionnelle et chômage des jeunes en France", *Regards sur l'actualité*, La Documentation Française, July-August, pp. 12-25.

GITTER, R.J. and SCHEUER, M. (1997), "US and German Youths: Unemployment and the Transition from School to Work", *Monthly Labor Review*, March, pp. 16-20.

HARHOFF, D. and KANE, T.J. (1994), "Financing Apprenticeship Training: Evidence from Germany", National Bureau of Economic Research, Working Paper No. 4557.

HASHIMOTO, M. (1994), "Employment-based Training in Japanese Firms in Japan and in the United States: Experiences of Automobile Manufacturers", in Lynch, L. (ed.), *Training and the Private Sector*, University of Chicago Press, Chicago, pp. 109-148.

HUMMELUHR, N. (1997), "Youth Guarantee in the Nordic Countries", OECD, Paris, mimeo.

INSEE (1997), "Les trajectoires des jeunes: distances et dépendances entre générations", *Économie et Statistique*, No. 304-305.

JOIN-LAMBERT, E. (1995), "Les bilans formation-emploi depuis 1973", *Emploi-Revenus*, No. 79-80, INSEE Résultats, Paris, pp. 107-118.

JOSHI, H. and PACI, P. (1997), "Life in the Labour Market", in Bynner, J., Ferri, E. and Shepherd, P. (eds.), *Twenty-Something in the 1990's, Getting On, Getting By, Getting Nowhere*, Ashgate, Aldershot, UK, pp. 31-52.

KORENMAN, S. and NEUMARK, D. (1997), "Cohort Crowding and Youth Labor Markets: A Cross-National Analysis", National Bureau of Economic Research, Working Paper No. 6031.

LAYARD, R., NICKELL, S. and JACKMAN, R. (1991), *Unemployment: Macroeconomic Performance and the Labour Market*, Oxford University Press, Oxford.

LYNCH, L. (1993), "Entry-Level Jobs: First Rung on the Employment Ladder or Economic Dead End?", *Journal of Labour Research*, No. 3. pp. 249-263.

LYNCH, L. (ed.) (1994a), *Training and the Private Sector*, University of Chicago Press, Chicago.

LYNCH, L. (1994b), "Payoffs to Alternative Training Strategies at Work", in Freeman, R. (ed.), *Working under Different Rules*, Russell Sage Foundation, New York, pp. 63-96.

MAGNAC, T. (1997), "Les stages et l'insertion professionnelle des jeunes: une évaluation statistique", *Économie et Statistique*, No. 304-305, pp. 75-94.

MET (Ministère de l'Emploi et du Travail) (1997), "La politique fédérale de l'emploi. Rapport d'évaluation", Belgium.

MISEP (1996), *Tableau de Bord*, Employment Observatory, European Commission, Brussels.

MISEP (1997), *Tableau de Bord*, Employment Observatory, European Commission, Brussels.

NEUMARK, D. and WASCHER, W. (1995), "The Effects of Minimum Wages on Teenage Employment and Enrollment: Evidence from Matched CPS Surveys", National Bureau of Economic Research, Working Paper No. 5092.

NICKELL, S. (1997), "Unemployment and Labour Market Rigidities: Europe versus North America", *Journal of Economic Perspectives*, Summer, pp. 55-74.

OECD (1986), *Employment Outlook*, Paris, September.

OECD (1991), *Employment Outlook*, Paris, July.

OECD (1994), *The OECD Jobs Study: Evidence and Explanations*, Paris.

OECD (1996a), *Employment Outlook*, Paris, July.

OECD (1996b), *Education at a Glance – Analysis*, Paris.

OECD (1996c), *Lifelong Learning For All*, Paris.

OECD (1996d), *The Public Employment Service in Denmark, Finland and Italy*, Paris.

OECD (1996e), *The Public Employment Service in Austria, Germany and Sweden*, Paris.

OECD (1997a), *Education at a Glance – Indicators*, Paris.

OECD (1997b), *The Public Employment Service: Belgium*, Paris.

OECD (1997c) *Economic Survey: Denmark*, Paris.

OECD (1997d), *Employment Outlook*, Paris, July.

OECD (1998a), *Pathways and Participation in Vocational and Technical Education and Training*, Paris.

OECD (1998b), *Benefits and Incentives*, Paris.

PERGAMIT, M. R. (1995), "Assessing School to Work Transition in the United States", *Statistical Journal of the United Nations Economic Commission for Europe*, No. 3-4, pp. 272-287.

PONTHIEUX, S. (1997), "Débuter dans la vie active au milieu des années 90: des conditions qui se dégradent", *Économie et Statistique*, No. 304-305, pp. 37-51.

POULET, P. (1997), "Repères sur l'emploi des jeunes", *Note d'information*, No. 97.09, Direction de l'évaluation et de la prospective, Paris.

RUHM, C. (1997), "Is High School Employment Consumption or Investment", *Journal of Labor Economics*, October, pp. 735-776.

RYAN, P. and BÜCHTEMANN, C. (1996), "The School-to-Work Transition" in Schmid, G., O'Reilly, J. and Schömann, K. (eds.), *International Handbook of Labour Market Policy and Evaluation*, Edward Elgar, Cheltenham, UK, pp. 308-347.

SCARPETTA, S. (1996), "Assessing the Role of Labour Market Policies and Institutional Settings on Unemployment: A Cross-Country Study", OECD *Economic Studies*, No. 26, pp. 45-97.

SHAVIT, Y. and MÜLLER, W. (eds.) (1998), *From School to Work*, Clarendon Press, Oxford.

SIMON-ZARCA, G. (1996), "Apprenticeship in France: Between tradition and innovation", *Training & Employment*, Centre d'Études et de Recherches sur les Qualifications, No. 25, Autumn.

SOSKICE, D. (1994), "Reconciling Markets and Institutions: The German Apprenticeship System", in Lynch L. (ed.), *Training and the Private Sector*, University of Chicago Press, Chicago, pp. 25-60.

URQUIOLA, M., STERN, D., HORN, I., DORNSIFE, C., CHI, B., WILLIAMS, D., MERRITT, D., HUGHES, K. and BAILEY, T. (1997), *School to Work, College and Career: A Review of Policy, Practice and Results 1993-1997*, National Center for Research in Vocational Education, University of California, Berkeley, CA.

VEUM, J.R. (1997), "Training and Job Mobility among Young Workers in the United States", *Journal of Population Economics*, No. 10, pp. 219-233.

VIALLA, A. (1997), "Apprentissage: ruptures, enchaînements de contrats et accès à l'emploi", *Note d'information*, No. 97.22, Direction de l'évaluation et de la prospective, Paris.

WERQUIN, P. (1997), "1986-1996 : Dix ans d'intervention publique sur le marché du travail des jeunes", *Économie et Statistique*, No. 304-305, pp. 121-136.

WERQUIN, P., BREEN, R. and PLANAS, J. (eds.), (1997), *Youth Transitions in Europe: Theories and Evidence*, Centre d'Études et de Recherches sur les Qualifications, No. 120.

WESTERGÅRD-NIELSEN, N. and RASMUSSEN, A.R. (1997), "Apprenticeship Training in Denmark - the Impacts of Subsidies", Centre for Labour Market and Social Research, University of Aarhus and Aarhus School of Business, Working Paper 97-07.

WILLIAMS, J. and COLLINS, C. (1997), The Economic Status of School Leavers, 1994-1996, Results of the School Leavers' Survey, Department of Enterprise, Trade and Employment, the Economic and Social Research Institute, Dublin, December.

CHAPTER 4

Work-force ageing in OECD countries

A. INTRODUCTION AND MAIN FINDINGS

1. Introduction

Expanding the range and quality of employment opportunities available to older workers will become increasingly important as populations age in OECD countries. Accordingly, there is a need to understand better the capacity of labour markets to adapt to ageing work forces, including how it can be enhanced.

Both the supply and demand sides of the labour market will be important. It is likely that pension programmes and social security systems in many OECD countries will be reformed so that existing incentives for early retirement will be reduced or eliminated. Strengthening financial incentives to extend working life, together with a large increase in the older population and improvements in their health, means that the supply of older workers will increase sharply in the coming decades. The *demand* for older workers, along with the efficacy of labour markets in matching supply and demand, will determine their employment and earnings prospects, as well as the impact of work-force ageing on aggregate productivity and income.

Section B assesses how the supply of older workers is likely to change over the next several decades, confirming that significant labour-force ageing is in prospect. Section C presents a conceptual framework for analysing the implications of this for employment and earnings. The empirical relationships between compensation and age, and productivity and age are taken up in Sections D and E, respectively. Section F then analyses mobility patterns among older workers. The final section presents some concluding remarks.[1]

2. Main findings

Labour force ageing in OECD countries is likely to be substantial over the next several decades. In many countries, labour force growth will also slow and educational attainment among older workers will rise rapidly. Pension policy changes designed to raise the *effective* retirement age will magnify labour

force ageing, but offset part of the projected fall in labour force growth.

OECD labour markets have adapted to significant shifts in the age structure of the labour force in the past. However, the ageing projected over the next several decades is outside the range of recent historical experience. Hence, it is uncertain how easily such a large increase in the supply of older workers can be accommodated, including the implications for the earnings and employment of older workers.

There is only weak evidence that the earnings of older workers are lower relative to younger workers in countries where older workers represent a larger share of total employment. This may indicate that workers of different ages are close substitutes in production, so that an increased supply of older workers can be employed without a significant fall in their relative wages. However, a number of factors affect the demand for older workers at any given relative wage and greater relative wage flexibility may sometimes be an important component of an overall programme to adapt to work-force ageing.

Improved job skills and access to training could help reduce the risks of unemployment and low pay for older workers. Work-force ageing also means that OECD countries will have to rely increasingly on mid- and late-career workers to meet emerging skill demands. This heightens the importance of improving the opportunities of older workers to develop new skills and to renew and re-deploy old skills. The limited evidence currently available suggests that older workers with adequate educational attainment and a history of participation in on-the-job training appear to be good training prospects, and training rates do not fall off strongly until workers approach conventional retirement ages.

However, older workers do encounter significant difficulties if they lose their job, as reflected in a high incidence of long-term unemployment and the large earnings losses experienced by older displaced workers, when they do find a new job. If their labour market mobility remains limited, these problems could increase as the work-force ages, since it is likely that increasing numbers of older workers will experience lay-offs.

Firms' pay, training, recruiting and other personnel practices will be key factors in determining the employment and earnings opportunities of older workers. Furthermore, proactive strategies, emphasising the skill base with which workers enter the later stages of their careers, are likely to be more effective than remedial measures after older workers have encountered employment problems. Thus, the training and other personnel practices of employers, as well as the career planning of workers, need to begin now to adapt to the prospect of work-force ageing. Governments have an important educational and co-ordinating role to play in facilitating these adjustments.

B. WORK-FORCE AGEING OVER THE NEXT SEVERAL DECADES

1. Future scenarios of the size and age composition of the labour force

This section uses UN population projections to assess the likely impact of population ageing on labour supply in OECD countries. Simple projections through the year 2030 are considered that illustrate the implications of population ageing for the size and composition of the future labour force (see Annex 4.A). Population trends alone are insufficient, however, to determine labour force trends. If labour force participation rates continue to evolve differently at different ages, the labour force will not age in lock-step with the total population. In particular, the extent to which population ageing will result in older labour forces depends critically on the future evolution of the effective age of retirement, which is uncertain.[2] The plausible range of trends in retirement patterns can be assessed accurately enough, however, to construct illustrative scenarios.

In most OECD countries, it appears that pension and social security programmes will be adjusted so that possibilities for early retirement will be more limited or less attractive, and that workers will respond to these changes in incentives by seeking to delay retirement. Hence, the trend among men toward younger retirement ages could cease or reverse. The scenarios examined below are based on the assumption that this pattern becomes general and make no allowance for specific national factors that might suggest a different evolution.

The "baseline" scenario assumes that age-specific participation rates remain unchanged at their current levels. Under the "later-retirement" scenario, it is assumed that much of the recent trend among men toward retiring at younger ages is gradually reversed. It is assumed that the 1995 patterns of

labour force exit after age 45 – calculated separately for men and women – make a smooth transition to the 1970 pattern for men between 2000 and 2020.[3] These scenarios, in conjunction with population forecasts from the UN, are used to examine the future rate of growth of the labour force and its age composition.

This simple exercise suggests that the rate of growth of the labour force in the early 21st Century will be considerably lower than in the recent past in many Member countries (Chart 4.1). Under the baseline assumption, labour force growth decelerates in all countries except Hungary, often sharply. It could even become negative in a substantial number of European countries and Japan. In most countries, labour force growth is projected to be significantly stronger under the later-retirement scenario, since the combination of a rapid increase in the older population with an increase in retirement ages results in a large increase in the number of older workers. Only in Hungary and Poland is the projected labour force growth more rapid than recent historical experience. Thus, many OECD countries will experience a significant reduction in labour force growth over the next three decades.

Labour forces will also likely become significantly older in the next several decades, although the strength of this effect varies markedly across countries (Table 4.1). Even under the more conservative baseline scenario, the OECD average share of workers aged 45 to 59 years rises from 26 to 32 per cent between 1995 and 2030, while the share aged 60 years and older rises from 5 to almost 9 per cent. Thus, firms will need to employ both a greater share of workers aged 45 to 59 years and a greater share of retirement-age workers (*i.e.* aged 60 years and over). A key question is how successfully firms can adjust to such a major shift in the composition of their work forces.

Comparing the two scenarios confirms that the extent to which the labour force will age will be strongly influenced by trends in retirement patterns. The OECD average share of workers aged 60 years and older in 2030 is 9 per cent under the baseline assumption, but rises to 17 per cent if retirement patterns return to those of 1970. Policy measures to encourage delayed retirement imply substantial shifts in the age composition of the work force that lie considerably outside the range of recent historical experience. Conversely, a continued trend toward earlier retirement could off-set the direct effect of the changing age structure of the population on the age composition of the labour force. However, large reductions in participation rates generally would be required, implying undesirable and, possibly, unsustainable increases in retirement dependency ratios [OECD (1998*b*)].

Chart 4.1.

Labour force growth: recent experience and two future scenarios[a]
Average annual percentage change

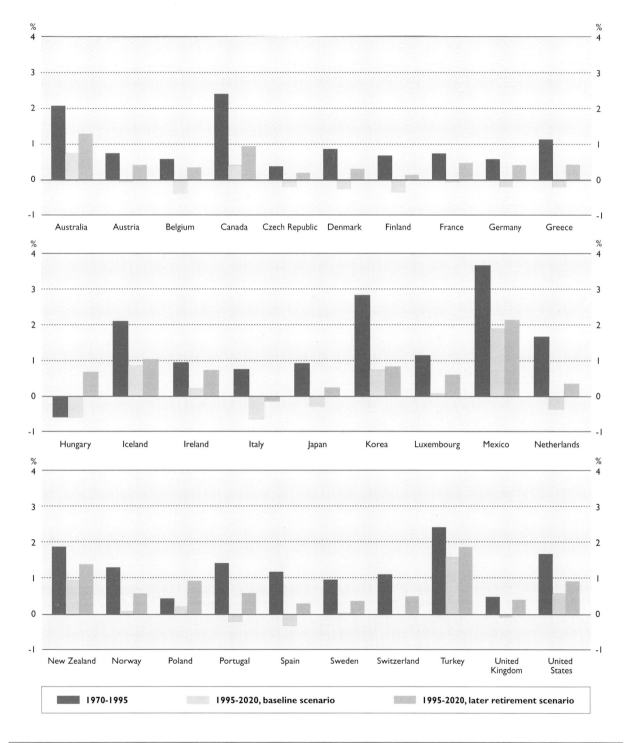

a) The labour force is based on persons aged 15 and over. The baseline scenario assumes that age-specific participation rates remain unchanged at their current levels, while the later retirement scenario assumes that much of the recent trend towards earlier retirement gradually reverses (details in the text).

Sources: Secretariat estimates based on the ILO Labour Force Database and the UN Population Database.

Table 4.1. **Labour force shares of older workers, 1970-2030**[a]

Percentage of total labour force

	Share of workers aged 45 to 59 years				Share of workers aged 60 years and older			
	1970	1995	2030 Baseline scenario	2030 Later retirement scenario	1970	1995	2030 Baseline scenario	2030 Later retirement scenario
Australia	24.2	23.9	28.6	29.4	6.4	3.6	6.3	14.5
Austria	25.9	25.4	34.2	34.9	5.6	1.2	2.7	10.4
Belgium	25.6	23.8	28.9	32.7	5.8	1.7	2.9	10.6
Canada	24.5	24.3	29.9	29.4	6.9	4.2	8.1	16.5
Czech Republic	26.2	28.9	37.1	37.3	7.5	3.8	5.8	11.8
Denmark	26.6	29.5	29.7	27.8	9.8	4.5	7.6	18.5
Finland	25.4	31.4	32.2	30.3	6.1	2.8	4.7	13.9
France	25.0	28.2	35.1	33.7	7.9	2.5	4.0	14.0
Germany	23.8	28.6	34.8	32.0	9.3	2.9	5.5	18.4
Greece	24.1	26.1	34.7	32.5	11.2	6.9	10.3	21.8
Hungary	23.0	26.4	34.5	32.1	12.2	0.4	0.6	22.2
Iceland	22.1	23.2	28.6	25.7	10.5	11.3	17.5	21.2
Ireland	24.9	22.7	32.9	31.5	14.1	5.7	9.3	18.4
Italy	24.6	25.2	34.3	36.0	5.9	4.3	8.7	14.6
Japan	21.9	33.1	34.5	31.1	9.3	12.5	20.7	30.1
Korea	19.7	22.3	33.6	32.4	4.9	6.2	16.2	19.0
Luxembourg	24.6	24.4	31.1	32.8	4.0	1.7	2.5	6.0
Mexico	16.0	15.6	25.8	26.1	9.4	6.2	12.6	16.9
Netherlands	23.3	24.9	29.5	30.2	6.4	1.7	4.0	14.9
New Zealand	25.0	25.3	30.1	29.9	6.5	3.3	5.3	12.7
Norway	29.9	27.9	30.0	28.2	12.5	6.9	11.5	20.2
Poland	22.7	24.1	32.9	31.9	12.1	8.1	11.0	21.7
Portugal	21.5	24.0	32.5	30.3	11.5	7.7	11.5	25.1
Spain	24.1	22.6	36.4	34.8	8.5	4.6	8.2	19.3
Sweden	29.8	32.3	31.1	29.2	9.5	6.3	9.6	16.5
Switzerland	23.7	28.3	32.1	28.6	10.4	6.0	12.3	24.1
Turkey	17.6	15.6	26.8	27.6	9.8	7.2	13.1	17.2
United Kingdom	28.9	28.2	30.6	29.7	9.0	5.3	8.1	16.4
United States	27.7	25.0	28.9	27.9	9.1	5.8	9.8	16.1
Unweighted average:								
North America[b]	22.8	21.6	28.2	27.8	8.4	5.4	10.2	16.5
European Union	25.2	26.5	32.5	31.9	8.3	4.0	6.6	15.9
OECD Europe	24.7	26.0	32.3	31.4	9.1	4.7	7.8	17.1
Total OECD	24.2	25.6	31.8	30.9	8.7	5.0	8.6	17.3

a) The total labour force is aged 15 years or more. See note to Chart 4.1. and text for an explanation of the two scenarios.
b) North America comprises Canada, Mexico and the United States.
Sources: Secretariat estimates based on the ILO Labour Force Database and the UN Population Database.

2. Scale of the required adjustments

This sub-section uses recent historical experience to provide a qualitative assessment of the scale of the adjustments required. Some indication of the capacity of OECD labour markets to adapt to these projected changes can be made by comparing the labour market performance of countries whose labour supply trends have differed in the past. This requires a summary index of the rate of change in the age structure. One such index is examined in Chart 4.2, which reports the ratio of the forecast rate of change in age composition to the actual change experienced in recent years.[4]

Several lessons emerge. First, OECD labour markets have faced considerable changes in the age structure in recent decades. It is possible that the rate of change will actually decelerate (yielding a ratio below 1.0) in many countries under the baseline scenario. Second, there are large cross-country differences. Italy, Mexico and Turkey stand out for the extent to which labour markets will likely need to accommodate a sharp acceleration in the rate of change. Third, the later-retirement scenario shows that reversing the trend toward earlier retirement will significantly increase the rate of change in age composition in all countries compared with the trend over the period 1970-1995. Finally, there are

Chart 4.2.

Change in the age structure of the labour force, 1995-2020 projections relative to 1970-1995

Ratio of 1995-2020 index to 1970-1995 index,[a] values above 1.0 indicate accelerating change

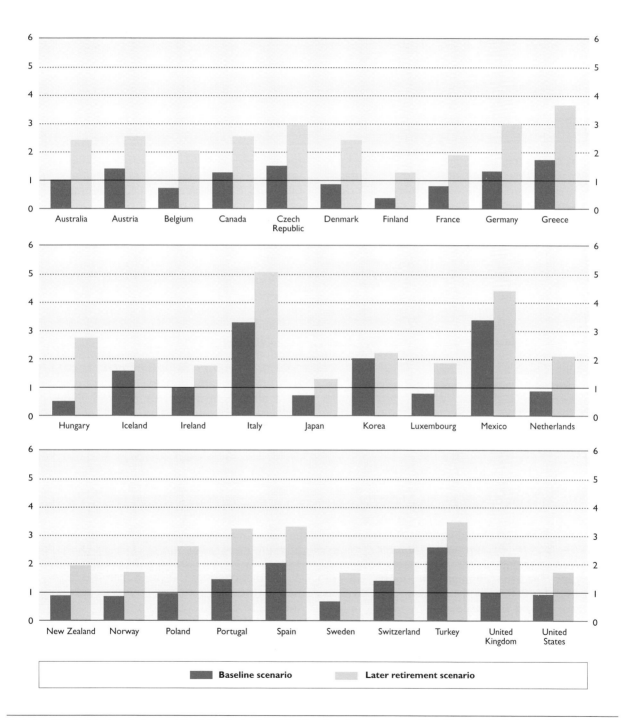

a) Index of the absolute change in the cumulative distribution function of the labour force by age (see note to Chart 4.1. and text for further details).
Sources: Secretariat estimates based on the ILO Labour Force Database and the UN Population Database.

Table 4.2. **Cross-country correlations between measures of demographic change and measures of labour market performance, 1970-1996[a]**

Labour market performance	Working-age population[b]	
	Average annual growth rate	Change in the age structure[c]
Average unemployment rate, 1970-1996	0.20	−0.29
Change in unemployment rate, 1970-1996	−0.38	−0.20
Average annual growth in employment, 1970-1996	0.75*	0.16
Average employment/population ratio, 1970-1996	−0.24	0.42*
Change in employment/population ratio, 1970-1996	−0.20	0.45*

* Significant at the 5% level.
a) Correlations are across all OECD Member countries except the Czech Republic, Hungary, Korea, Luxembourg, Mexico and Poland.
b) 15-64 years.
c) The index of age structure is based on the 1970-1996 changes in the distribution function of the population by the finest age-group disaggregation possible (see text).
Sources: Secretariat estimates based on the OECD Analytical Database and the UN Population Database.

important qualitative differences between the forecast changes in age composition and the changes already experienced, which the summary index does not capture. Between 1970 and 1995, most countries experienced the labour market entry and initial ageing of the baby-boom generation, and a strong trend toward earlier retirement. By contrast, 1995-2020 will be characterised by increases in the shares of older workers.

There has not been a strong association in the past between these two types of labour supply changes and unemployment (Table 4.2). Consistent with this finding, labour supply growth was positively correlated with employment growth.[5] Strong conclusions cannot be drawn from these simple correlations, since no attempt was made to control for other determinants of labour market performance. Nonetheless, they provide a useful reminder that modern economies appear to have considerable capacity to adapt to different demographic conditions.

Several caveats to this optimistic appraisal are required. The demographic changes that will characterise labour supply in the next several decades are qualitatively different from past changes. Also, the fact that different national economies have accommodated quite different demographic environments in the past need not imply that abrupt *changes* in demographic trends will not require a difficult transition period. Finally, even if the macro indices of employment and unemployment examined here should not be greatly affected by work-force ageing, older workers could encounter increased employment difficulties.

3. The changing educational profile of older workers

The cohort of workers aged 45-64 years in 2015 will be better educated than their counterparts today (Table 4.3).[6] The share not having completed upper secondary schooling is likely to fall by over one-third (the unweighted OECD average falls from about 44 to 27 per cent). This trend is likely for all OECD member countries, although large international differences in the distribution of education levels will persist.

Rising educational attainment should ease the absorption of larger groups of older workers. Recent decades have witnessed a strong increase in the demand for more educated workers and a concomitant deterioration in the opportunities for less-educated workers [OECD (1997a, Chapter 4)]. Poorly-educated youths, particularly men, appear to have been most disadvantaged. However, older workers have also been negatively affected. Older workers displaced from production jobs, a group with low educational attainment on average, are at a high risk of remaining jobless for an extended period of time and typically experience large earnings losses if they do become re-employed [Podgursky and Swaim (1987); Jacobson, LaLonde and Sullivan (1993); Carrington and Zaman (1994); Fallick (1996)].

The forecast improvement in educational attainment of older workers is good news, perhaps especially for men, but a word of caution is in order. A "prediction" that the rapid increase in the educational levels of older workers is likely to expand their employment opportunities is potentially subject to a fallacy of composition. For a given cohort, more educated workers fare better on average than less educated ones. If this is due to so-called "screening" by employers, then it need not follow that an upwards shift in the amount of schooling received by a cohort will result in improved employment prospects for the cohort as a whole.[7] Section E examines the implications of education and training for ageing in more detail.

Table 4.3. **Distribution of educational attainment of the labour force aged 45 to 64 years, 1995 and 2015**

Percentages

	1995				2015[a]			
	Less than upper secondary	Upper secondary	Non-university tertiary	University	Less than upper secondary	Upper secondary	Non-university tertiary	University
Australia	44.8	29.0	11.6	14.6	37.1	31.8	12.1	18.9
Austria	33.0	58.7	1.5	6.8	17.5	69.8	2.8	9.8
Belgium	46.2	27.0	13.3	13.5	25.7	35.6	19.1	19.6
Canada	27.7	24.8	29.3	18.2	14.1	30.1	33.8	21.9
Czech Republic[b]	15.2	72.4	..	12.4	7.1	78.3	..	14.6
Denmark	35.5	42.4	6.1	15.9	23.5	49.6	8.3	18.6
Finland	43.4	36.0	8.6	12.0	17.9	56.2	10.5	15.4
France	38.4	44.0	6.5	11.1	15.4	57.8	11.0	15.8
Germany	15.4	58.1	11.7	14.8	8.6	63.5	10.8	17.1
Greece	71.4	14.4	3.6	10.6	41.5	29.6	9.9	19.1
Ireland	61.3	18.9	8.5	11.3	36.4	31.4	15.1	17.1
Italy[b]	67.2	21.9	..	10.9	44.6	42.3	..	13.1
Korea[b]	65.0	24.8	..	10.2	22.6	51.7	..	25.6
Luxembourg[b]	62.0	20.1	..	17.9	53.2	25.8	..	20.9
Mexico	85.1	7.0	0.5	7.4	64.7	16.7	1.9	16.7
Netherlands[c]	36.9	38.1	..	25.0	23.5	46.1	..	30.4
New Zealand	41.6	31.1	17.3	9.9	31.1	41.1	14.2	13.6
Norway	20.6	51.2	11.2	16.9	9.4	53.2	13.1	24.2
Poland	34.5	49.6	2.4	13.5	12.7	69.9	4.8	12.6
Portugal	84.0	5.2	3.8	7.0	67.8	14.7	4.3	13.2
Spain	78.8	7.1	2.7	11.5	49.5	20.1	8.4	22.0
Sweden	35.8	37.4	11.5	15.3	14.7	54.3	16.4	14.6
Switzerland	19.4	57.9	14.2	8.5	10.8	63.5	14.0	11.7
United Kingdom	27.6	51.3	9.9	11.2	13.0	61.3	9.4	16.4
United States	12.4	51.0	7.6	29.0	9.2	51.7	9.5	29.6
Unweighted average	44.1	35.2	9.1	13.4	26.9	45.9	11.5	18.1

.. Data not available.
a) The distribution of the labour force in 2015 is based on applying education-specific participation rates for individuals aged 45-64 years in 1995 to the population aged 25-44 years in 1995.
b) Data for non-university tertiary education are included in university education.
c) Non-university tertiary education is not applicable.
Sources: OECD Education Database except for Mexico where data were provided by the national authority as part of the OECD project on ageing populations.

C. CONCEPTUAL FRAMEWORK FOR ASSESSING THE EFFECTS OF WORK-FORCE AGEING

Economic theory provides a useful framework for analysing the earnings and employment consequences of work-force ageing [also see Disney (1996)]. This section, therefore, reviews economic models relevant for analysing, in turn, the labour market effects of *individual* ageing (*i.e.* individual employment histories and how they would change if workers desired to delay retirement) and *group* ageing (*i.e.* a shift in the age distribution of the work force, whether due to population ageing or an rise in the effective age of retirement). Subsequently, the determinants of the age at which workers wish to retire are reviewed.

1. Individual ageing

The basic model of competitive labour markets implies that, at any point in time, workers' wages

reflect their productivity. Human capital theory reconciles this equilibrium condition with the empirical tendency for earnings to rise over a large portion of most careers by positing that workers and their employers invest in on-the-job training that enhances future productivity. When the model is extended to incorporate the depreciation of skills and/or an eventual decline in productivity associated with biological ageing, it can generate realistically shaped age-earnings profiles: initially rapid earnings growth gradually slows, potentially even turning negative beyond a certain age. When this is combined with a rising disutility of working beyond a certain age, it creates an incentive for workers eventually to retire. So long as wages adjust to equal productivity at all ages, employers will find it profitable to employ older workers.

Analysing training choices as an optimal investment problem reveals incentives to concentrate training investments early in a worker's career. Both the shorter time horizon remaining for an older worker to employ any newly acquired skills and any age-related diminution in the ability to learn new skills would reduce the economic returns to training. However, the returns to training older workers may be enhanced by other factors. If firms finance training or it imparts *specific* skills (*i.e.* skills that enhance productivity with the current firm, but would not do so in other firms), the time horizon over which the profitability of training is assessed is the worker's expected remaining tenure with that employer, which may be much shorter than their total expected remaining working life, especially for young workers. In these circumstances, the lower quit rate of older workers would raise the expected returns to training them, relative to that for younger workers. Similarly, rapidly changing skill requirements would reduce the importance of a long pay-back period to the selection of trainees, but magnify the importance of any age-related decline in the ability to learn new skills.

The distinction between general and specific skills has two additional implications for ageing. As workers age, skills learned on the job become more important relative to skills learned in school. On-the-job training tends to impart less general skills than formal education, however, implying that the human capital of older workers is less "portable" and they, therefore, risk large earnings losses if they change employers. Second, firms may under-invest in general skills because some of the returns accrue to other firms, who have an incentive to recruit workers after they have received general training from their current employers. This potential market failure has implications for workers of all ages, but could particularly disadvantage older workers by discouraging employers from investing to maintain the "trainability" of workers as they age, or providing them with skill credentials that are recognised in the external labour market.

Long-duration employment relations may facilitate investments in on-the-job training, but may also change how compensation varies with age. Many workers stay with the same employer for long periods and firms may prefer to pay these workers wages that do *not* correspond to their productive contributions at all points during their careers. A "back-loaded" compensation structure, in which pay is lower than productivity for junior workers, but rises more steeply and eventually surpasses productivity, potentially increases economic efficiency by strengthening incentives for workers to work more diligently, to remain with the same firm or to invest in firm-specific skills.[8] Clearly, older workers generally are not disadvantaged by implicit contracts of this type, since both life-time and current earnings are increased. However, difficulties could

arise for older workers attempting to delay retirement or to change jobs because:

- employers will only find it profitable to enter into back-loaded pay schemes if a predetermined maximum retirement age prevails, which limits the period of time during which compensation exceeds productivity.[9] Accordingly, the existence of such incentive schemes could create employment difficulties if future cohorts of older workers should desire to work beyond the retirement age targeted by employers. If pension reforms and related policies cause many mid- and late-career workers to revise upwards their desired age of retirement, it might prove difficult – at that late point – to modify the implicit contract with their employer. Reforms announced sufficiently in advance would be more easily accommodated, because wage profiles could be reconfigured to a later retirement age [Lazear (1984)][10]; and

- employers who use back-loaded compensation schemes may prefer not to hire older job seekers, either because it is infeasible to offer an array of seniority pay schedules that are tailored to workers entering the firm at different ages or because this type of implicit contract creates a fixed cost of hiring and, hence, an incentive to hire younger workers whose expected future tenure with the employer is greater [Hutchens (1986, 1988)].[11]

The argument that fixed hiring costs may disadvantage older job seekers is more general. The bias could also result from the costs of recruiting new employees or of providing initial job training [Oi (1962)]. Fixed hiring costs typically may increase the job security of older workers who are already employed, since the firm will want to amortize that investment over as many years as possible. However, firms may have a preference to shed their oldest workers when downsizing, because the "match capital" lost when a worker leaves the firm is larger the longer the worker would be expected to remain with the firm. This time horizon effect may be one reason that early retirement schemes are frequently used as a way to accommodate structural change [Handa (1994); OECD (1995a)].

Older workers may also face pay and employment disadvantages that result from *age discrimination*, defined as lesser opportunities of older workers that do not reflect lower productivity [Cain (1986)]. Negative age stereotypes might particularly disadvantage older job seekers, since prospective employers may have difficulty assessing their past job performance or other credentials. As with gender and ethnic discrimination, it has proven difficult to find direct measures of age discrimination and most empirical estimates are based upon residual intergroup differences in pay or employment, after taking account of other explanations. Such estimates are inherently fragile, however, because it is never certain that all other factors have been adequately accounted for. This difficulty is particularly severe in the case of age discrimination, because the relationships between age, productivity and earnings are so complex.

2. Group ageing

The theory of factor demand with heterogeneous labour has been used to assess the quantitative implications of changes in the age structure of the work force for the employment and earnings levels of workers of different ages [see Hamermesh (1993)]. The starting point for this analysis is a production function summarising how much output can be produced for different combinations of factor inputs, including workers of different ages. Intuitively, a high degree of substitutability between workers of different ages would imply that firms could accommodate large shifts in the age mix of their work force with little effect on overall productivity and, hence, that relatively small adjustments in relative wages would be sufficient to maintain labour market equilibrium. If substitutability is more limited, expansion of the relative number of older workers would significantly reduce their marginal product, implying that their relative wage would need to fall considerably if they are not to be at an increased risk of unemployment.

The econometric evidence on substitution patterns for workers of different ages is limited to a few countries and is neither entirely consistent nor easily extrapolated to the future. Overall, this evidence suggests that workers of different ages are quite good substitutes in production. To the extent this finding is reliable, it suggests that modest declines in the relative earnings of older workers would be sufficient to secure their employment in the future.[12] Any such changes in the wage structure would also provide an incentive for employers to adjust recruitment and training practices so as to take fuller advantage of the potential contribution of older workers. However, this research provides little guidance about how efficiently the human resource practices of firms will respond to the market signals created by work-force ageing, or whether public policies can facilitate those adjustments.

The production function approach adopts a static notion of skill requirements that side-steps the difficult issue of whether an older work force will be less adaptable. While future skill needs cannot be forecast with precision, it is virtually certain that the introduction of new technologies and the constant flux of product market competition will create an ongoing need for workers to learn new skills and to move from declining to growing firms. The models of human capital, implicit contracts and fixed hiring costs discussed above suggest that older workers, being more heavily invested in their current jobs and specific skills than younger workers, find it more costly to make these sorts of adjustments. Therefore, younger and low-tenure workers provide a disproportionate share of the work force's overall adaptability. As the share of younger workers falls, it is likely that older workers will have to provide more of these adjustments. If there are age-related disadvantages in adaptability, access to training or job search, they may have increasingly adverse consequences for the employment and earnings security of older workers, and for the overall adaptability of the economy.

3. Desired age of retirement

A large literature applying the theory of labour/leisure choices to retirement has clarified how economic incentives affect labour supply near the end of the working life. One of the key empirical findings is the importance of pensions for the timing of retirement [Gruber and Wise (1997); OECD (1998c)]. Public and private pensions often create strong incentives for workers to retire at the age of first benefit entitlement, because of high effective tax rates on earnings. In some OECD countries, unemployment and disability benefit systems, or special early retirement programmes, also create strong incentives for workers to withdraw from the labour force in advance of conventional retirement ages. Past increases in the generosity of these income transfers and, especially, the extension of eligibility to younger workers appear to explain an important share of the secular trend toward earlier retirement in most countries. Estimates of the effect of pension systems on the age at which workers retire vary considerably, however, and some studies conclude that other factors, such as the secular rise in wage levels, changes in preferences, or shifts in the job structure towards sectors where earlier retirement is typical, account for the majority of the reduction in effective age of retirement [Anderson et al. (1997)]. Another complicating factor in assessing the independent impact of expanded pension benefits on lowering the effective age of retirement is that the expansion of benefits has sometimes been a response to the employment difficulties of some groups of older workers (OECD, 1995b).[13]

The empirical research suggests that much of the recent trend toward earlier retirement is potentially reversible. Changes to public pensions or other social security programmes that either reduce the income support provided for early retirement or provide financial incentives for later retirement probably would cause many workers to prefer to retire somewhat later or more gradually. It is more difficult to assess how readily firms would accommodate such a reversal. It is clear, however, that changes would not occur overnight. The theories of on-the-job training and implicit contracts imply that the *anticipated* age of retirement affects recruitment, training and pay practices throughout a career. Mistaken expectations about the timing of retirement could be costly and governments may be able to facilitate the labour market adjustment to work-force ageing by providing timely information to workers and employers that help them anticipate the implications of demographic trends and policy changes for the timing of retirement.

D.   AGE, RELATIVE EARNINGS AND EMPLOYMENT

As noted in the previous section, compensation is a potentially key factor affecting the employability of older workers. This section examines how earnings vary by age. The risk of low-paid employment for older workers is also assessed.

1.   Relative earnings of older workers

Chart 4.3 shows age-earnings profiles in 1995 for 20 OECD countries. They tend to have an inverted U-shape, with lower earnings among younger workers, rising to a peak around age 50 and then declining. National differences are quite large, however, both in how steeply wages rise between labour market entry and prime-earning ages and in the extent to which wages subsequently fall.[14]

Table 4.4 reports ratios of average earnings for workers in three age groups. The ratio of earnings in what are often the peak-earnings years (aged 45 to 54 years) to the earnings of recent entrants into the labour force (aged 25 to 29 years) averages 1.4. The ratio of earnings of individuals aged 55 to 64 to those aged 45 to 54 indicates that earnings of older workers fall an average of 9 per cent. There is considerable variation in these ratios across countries, however.

Since educational attainment differs between cohorts, the overall relationship between age and average earnings confounds pure age effects with the returns to education. Chart 4.4 shows age-earnings profiles separately by level of education in 1995 for the G7 countries. They are flatter and lower for workers with lower education levels. When ratios of the average earnings of 45 to 54 year-olds ("peak

earners") and 25 to 29 year-olds ("recent entrants") are calculated by level of education, there is a strong tendency for this ratio to rise with the level of education (Table 4.4). Averaging over all countries, the earnings premium of peak-earnings workers relative to recent entrants rises from 23 per cent for workers with only a lower secondary education to 89 per cent for those with a university degree. The variability across countries also appears to be higher for higher educational levels.

Controlling for educational attainment weakens the tendency for age-earnings profiles to slope downward late in the working life. However, average earnings still tend to fall between ages 45 to 54 years and 55 to 64 years in five of the G7 countries, especially for the higher education groups. But this pattern is either absent or weak in Germany and Italy.

Table 4.5 shows that the earnings premium of peak-earnings workers relative to recent entrants has tended to rise recently in the three countries for which time-series data are available. Between 1980 and 1995, this premium rose 35 percentage points in France, 10 percentage points in Japan and 31 percentage points in the United States. In France and the United States, the change in the earnings ratio is in the same direction for workers at all levels of education. The pattern is more mixed in Japan, where the relative earnings ratio for peak-earnings workers with tertiary-level education declined. Across these three countries there does not appear to be any clear trend in the earnings of late-career workers (aged 55 to 64 years) relative to peak-earnings workers.

The recent tendency for the earnings premium received by peak-earnings workers to rise illustrates that these relativities do not adjust in lock-step to changes in the age mix of the work force. Indeed, a quite strong downward trend in the relative supply of younger workers over the past few decades generally has not led to an increase in their relative earnings [OECD (1996, Chapter 4)]. While recent trends in relative earnings by age do not confirm a tendency for relative wages to adjust quickly to changes in the age structure, market forces for such an adjustment may strengthen as ageing proceeds, particularly if there is a significant trend toward later retirement.

Whether higher earnings of older, relative to younger, workers reduces the employment opportunities of older workers is an important and complicated issue. There is no significant cross-country correlation between the earnings premium of older relative to younger workers, and the share of older workers in total employment (data not shown here). However, these correlations are always negative. There is also a positive correlation between the

Chart 4.3.

Age-relative earnings profiles, 1995[a]

Average gross annual earnings = 100

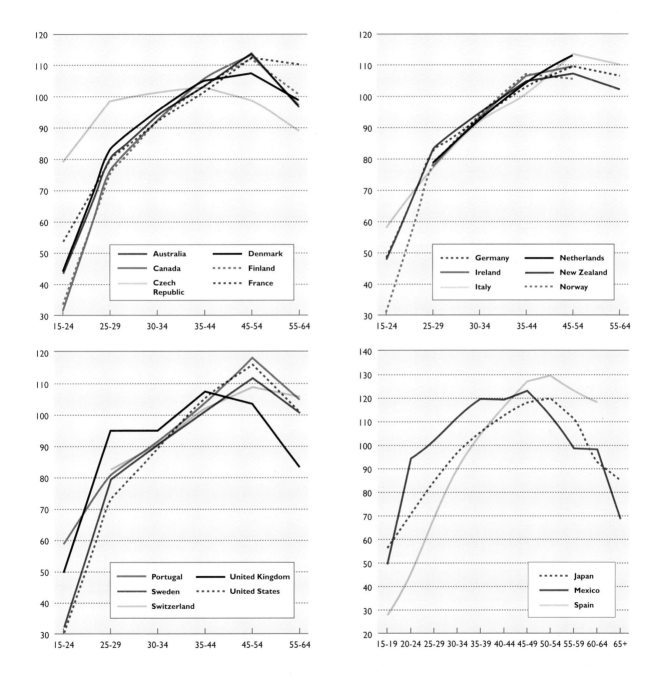

a) For Japan, Mexico and Spain, earnings for each age group are calculated relative to all workers aged 15 and over; for other countries they are calculated relative to workers aged 25-64. For Ireland and the Netherlands, data are for 1993. For Finland and Portugal, data are for 1994. Data are not available for the following groups: Ireland 15-24 and 55-64; the Netherlands, 15-24; Norway, 55-64; Switzerland, 15-24. For the Netherlands, the age group 45-54 refers to 45-64, while for Spain, the age group 60-64 refers to 60 and over.

Sources: Data for Australia, France, Japan and Mexico were provided by national authorities as part of the OECD project on population ageing. Data for Spain were supplied by the Instituto Nacional de Estadistica (INE) from the European Structure of Earnings Survey. Data for other countries are from the OECD Education Database.

Table 4.4. **Earnings ratios by age group and level of educational attainment, 1995**

Gross annual earnings before taxes

	45-54 years/25-29 years					55-64 years/45-54 years
	Less than upper secondary	Upper secondary	Non-university tertiary	University	Overall	Overall
Australia	1.30	1.26	1.35	2.06	1.42	0.85
Canada	1.05	1.46	1.37	1.96	1.48	0.86
Czech Republic[a]	0.99	0.99	..	1.42	1.00	0.90
Denmark	1.21	1.23	1.29	1.60	1.29	0.92
Finland[b]	1.43	1.36	1.69	2.11	1.49	0.90
France	1.18	1.47	1.45	1.95	1.38	1.07
Germany	0.97	1.28	1.10	1.76	1.33	0.97
Ireland[c]	1.24	1.59	1.59	2.25	1.41	..
Italy[a]	1.27	1.64	..	2.60	1.46	0.97
Japan	1.23	1.44	1.64	1.99	1.42	0.86
Mexico	1.13	1.61	1.33	1.65	1.16	0.84
Netherlands[c, d]	1.19	1.41	..	1.73	1.43	..
New Zealand	1.25	1.39	1.16	1.93	1.29	0.95
Norway	1.10	1.26	1.88	1.67	1.35	..
Portugal[a, b]	1.56	1.89	..	1.80	1.46	0.89
Spain[a]	1.75	2.09	..	2.61	1.86	0.94
Sweden	1.38	1.26	1.67	1.70	1.40	0.90
Switzerland	1.06	1.25	1.52	1.80	1.32	0.97
United Kingdom	0.93	1.09	1.41	1.50	1.09	0.81
United States	1.29	1.28	1.39	1.67	1.48	0.89
Unweighted average	1.23	1.41	1.46	1.89	1.38	0.91

.. Data not available.
a) Data for non-university tertiary education are included in university education.
b) Data refer to 1994.
c) Data refer to 1993.
d) Non-university tertiary education is not applicable.
Sources: France, Japan and Mexico: national authorities, as part of the OECD project on ageing populations.
 Spain: Instituto Nacional de Estadistica (INE), European Structure of Earnings Survey.
 United States: Bureau of Labour Statistics, Current Population Survey, unpublished data.
 Other countries: OECD Education Database.

earnings of workers aged 45 to 54 years relative to those aged 25 to 29 and the risk of a layoff leading to joblessness for the older group. Consistent with earlier research on substitutability in production (see Section C), these simple correlations provide, at best, weak evidence that cross-country differences in the relative earnings of older workers have been associated with greater employment difficulties, despite quite large cross-country differences in the relative earnings of older workers.

2. Low-paid employment

Like unemployment or involuntary retirement, low earnings when employed is also a potential threat to the living standards of older workers and their families. Flexibility in the level and composition of the compensation received by older workers – including possible reductions in earnings towards the end of the working life – might help labour markets to employ an ageing labour force, but could also increase the risk of earnings levels too low to

meet family income needs. Low pay and earnings mobility were extensively analysed in both the 1996 and 1997 Employment Outlook. The implications of that analysis for ageing are:

– in all countries, younger, female and low-skilled workers are more likely to be employed in low-paid jobs than older, male and high-skilled workers. However, in some countries the risk of being low paid does rise near the end of a career. In Japan, 20 per cent of full-time workers aged 55 and older were low paid, double the incidence among workers aged 25 to 54. Low-pay incidence also rises between prime and older ages in Australia, New Zealand, the United Kingdom and the United States, but falls in Austria, Hungary and Sweden;

– older, low-paid workers have substantially worse prospects of moving up the earnings distribution than younger workers. Comparing estimates of average cumulated time in low pay over the period 1986-1991 shows that

Chart 4.4.

Average earnings by level of educational attainment and age, G7 countries, 1995[a]
Earnings of 30 to 34 year olds in ISCED 3 = 100

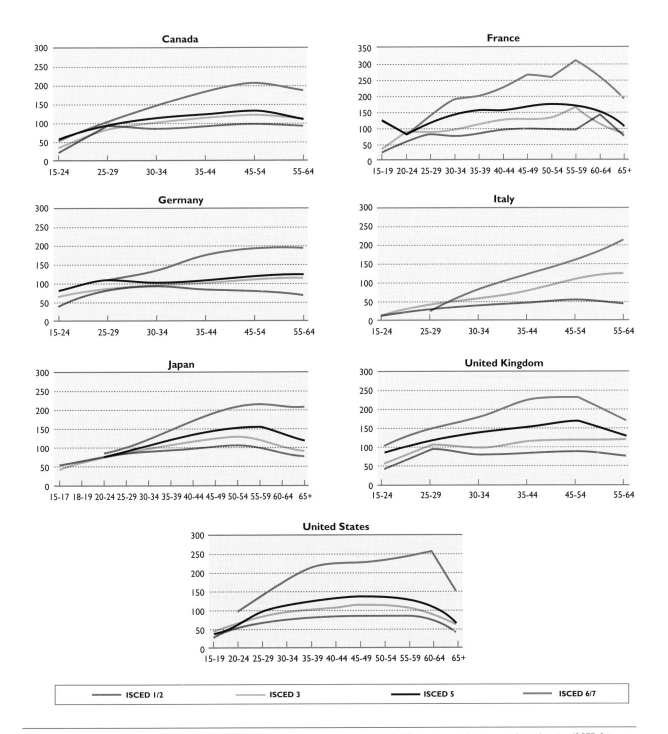

a)   Earnings are average annual gross earnings. Educational attainment is defined as follows: ISCED 1/2 is primary or lower secondary education; ISCED 3 is upper
    secondary education; ISCED 5 is non-university tertiary education; ISCED 6/7 is university education.

Sources: Data for France, Japan and the United States were provided by national authorities as part of the OECD project on population ageing. Data for other countries
    are from the OECD Education Database.

Table 4.5. **Farnings ratios by age group, level of educational attainment and year in three countries**

	45-54 years/25-29 years					55-64 years/45-54 years
	Less than upper secondary	Upper secondary	Non-university tertiary	University	Overall	Overall
France						
1982	1.03	1.17	1.19	1.49	1.03	0.97
1985	1.15	1.43	1.51	1.74	1.26	0.97
1990	1.27	1.47	1.43	1.81	1.35	0.96
1995	1.18	1.47	1.45	1.95	1.38	1.07
Change 1982-1995	**0.15**	**0.30**	**0.25**	**0.45**	**0.35**	**0.10**
Japan						
1976	1.14	1.41	1.87	2.10	1.26	0.82
1980	1.18	1.44	1.81	2.15	1.31	0.85
1985	1.25	1.49	1.79	2.19	1.38	0.86
1990	1.27	1.49	1.69	2.10	1.42	0.85
1995	1.23	1.44	1.64	1.99	1.42	0.86
Change 1980-1995	**0.05**	**0.00**	**−0.17**	**−0.16**	**0.10**	**0.01**
United States						
1975	1.04	1.04	1.07	1.23	1.00	0.87
1980	1.14	1.11	1.24	1.48	1.17	0.94
1985	1.24	1.19	1.25	1.38	1.21	0.91
1990	1.27	1.26	1.37	1.47	1.32	0.90
1995	1.29	1.28	1.39	1.67	1.48	0.89
Change 1980-1995	**0.15**	**0.17**	**0.15**	**0.20**	**0.31**	**−0.05**

Sources: *France and Japan:* national authorities, as part of the OECD project on ageing populations.
    United States: Bureau of Labor Statistics, Current Population Survey, unpublished data.

older workers experienced more time in low-paid employment than other workers, especially in Germany and the United Kingdom (Chart 4.5); and

– labour force ageing will probably tend to increase the risk of low-paid employment among older worker unless off-set by other factors. The increased supply of older workers may generate market pressures for their relative earnings to fall. If older workers also change jobs more frequently (see Section F), the risk of downwards earnings mobility may also increase. Thus, the incidence of low-paid employment among older workers may well rise and it is probable that older workers, once low paid, would continue to have relatively poor upward mobility prospects.

E.   AGE, TRAINING AND PRODUCTIVITY

The productivity of older workers, including their ability to learn new skills, will be an important determinant of their employability and earnings. It will also affect how well OECD economies will be able to meet evolving skill needs. In this section, evidence about how productivity changes with age is first considered. Training patterns by age are then analysed.

1.   Individual ageing and productivity

It is difficult to generalise about how productivity changes as individuals age, since job-skill requirements and individual capacities are so diverse. A large number of gerontological/psychological studies present direct measures of job performance and analyse their relationship to age. A recent survey of this literature concludes that there is no significant overall difference between the job performance of older and younger workers [Warr (1994)]. In almost every case, variations within an age group far exceed the average difference between age groups.

One of the causes of large productivity differences within age groups, namely, poor health, is significantly related to age. The risk of poor health and disability rises with age, and the onset of health problems affects the timing of retirement for a significant number of older workers [Bound *et al.* (1997); Burkhauser *et al.* (1997)]. However, recent increases in longevity appear to have been accompanied by a significant reduction in the incidence of disability at older ages [Manton *et al.* (1997)], suggesting that the extent to which poor health reduces the productivity of workers at any given age is trending downward. The shift of employment away from manual occupations may also diminish the significance of age-related health problems for job performance.

Chart 4.5.

Average cumulative years in low-paid employment during 1986-1991, by age[a]

Continuously employed full-time workers who were low-paid in 1986

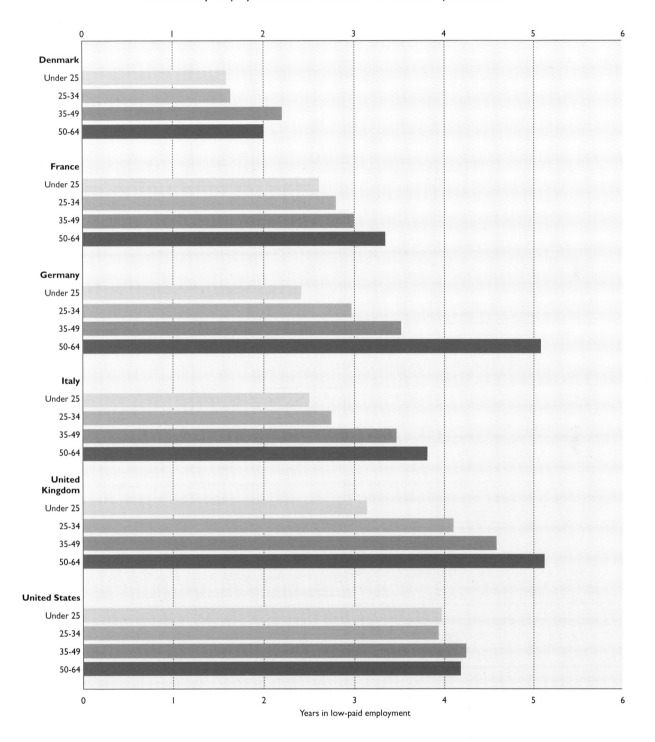

Years in low-paid employment

a)   Low pay is defined as below 0.65 median earnings.
Source: OECD (1997a), Chapter 2.

Economists have criticised the gerontological/psychological literature on age and productivity for paying insufficient attention to the economic significance of the performance measures that are analysed. An alternative research strategy is to infer how productivity varies with age from age-earnings profiles [Kotlikoff and Gokhale (1992)]. This approach may also be misleading, however, since earnings and productivity can follow rather different paths. A study that juxtaposes data on earnings with a direct measure of productivity found that earnings grew more steeply with seniority than did productivity [Medoff and Abraham (1981)], as is predicted by Lazear's theory of back-loaded compensation (see Section C).

An important aspect of how ageing affects productivity, especially in the context of policies designed to raise the effective age of retirement, is whether older workers have greater difficulty learning new skills. Even if ageing typically does not reduce a worker's ability to perform familiar job tasks, a declining ability to adapt to changing skill requirements would tend to lower their productive contribution over time. "Trainability", like productivity generally, defies easy measurement. Nonetheless, some indirect evidence is available.

The International Adult Literacy Survey (IALS) is an important source of evidence about the relationship between age, productivity and trainability [see OECD and Statistics Canada (1995c) for more information about the IALS]. The IALS provides continuous scores of several different dimensions of literacy (i.e. competencies using written and quantitative information) in realistic situations, such as are encountered on the job. A large body of research concludes that recent trends in work organisation and technology are increasing the importance for job performance of cognitive skills, such as the ability to comprehend, manipulate and communicate symbolic information. This inference suggests that the literacy skills measured by the IALS are an important determinant of worker productivity. Good literacy skills should also greatly enhance a worker's trainability, a key aspect of which is the ability to take in and process new information.

IALS literacy scores are substantially lower for older individuals, but these cross-sectional comparisons confound true ageing effects with other determinants of literacy, notably, the lower educational attainment of older cohorts.[15] Accordingly, a multivariate analysis was conducted using IALS data for ten countries, which attempts to isolate the causal effect of ageing on literacy by including a rich set of demographic and economic control variables – including educational attainment – in the equation.[16] The regression coefficients suggest that literacy skills generally decline only modestly

between ages 40 and 65 years, but more research is clearly needed on this important question.

Evidence from the IALS also indicates that literacy skills improve with practice and deteriorate if not used [OECD and Statistics Canada (1995c)]. This suggests a "use it or lose it" dynamic, with the ability to acquire new skills progressively deteriorating for workers in jobs where these skills are not well exercised. Workers employed in a "learning environment" appear much less susceptible to a decline in trainability. However, some gerontological research suggests that the ability to learn quickly is impaired with age, especially when the new material is qualitatively different from that previously mastered [Warr (1994)].

This review of how ageing affects individual productivity and trainability indicates that this critical relationship is not well understood. However, the evidence to date is largely reassuring. The productive potential of the older age groups does not appear to be substantially impaired by ageing per se. The most important concern related to the effect of ageing on work-force skills appears to be whether training practices will realise the productivity potential of older workers.

2. Training over the life-cycle

Incentives to train

Human capital theory indicates that older workers could receive little training either because it is efficient to concentrate training on younger workers, for whom the economic returns are greater, or because market failure leads to under-investment in training for workers of all ages. In both cases, low training could lead to low earnings or employability problems among older workers and, hence, raise equity concerns. In the case of market failure, policies providing older workers with increased access to training also have the potential to raise efficiency.

Two factors that could lower the returns to training older workers are a decline in trainability with age or a shorter pay-back period due to the imminence of retirement.[17] The previous subsection presented evidence suggesting that a substantial decline in trainability is unlikely to occur for most workers who have continued to acquire new job skills through the course of their careers. In order to assess the effect of age on the effective pay-back period, Table 4.6 presents evidence about how expected future tenure with the firm varies with age, which is the time horizon of greatest relevance for employers considering a training investment. These five-year retention rates measure the percentage of workers of different ages who were still with their current employer five years later [see OECD

Table 4.6. **Five-year retention rates by age and tenure, 1990-1995**

Percentages

	Australia[a]	Canada	Finland	France	Germany[b]	Japan	Spain	Switzerland[a]	United States[a]
All ages	41.3	47.9	42.8	49.9	60.7	64.2	42.8	55.2	48.6
45+ years	48.1	51.9	40.6	47.6	65.4	62.8	45.7	69.8	56.2
Length of tenure (years)									
All ages									
|5-10|/|0-5|	33.1	36.4	35.5	28.1	49.9	58.2	28.6	46.5	39.7
|10-15|/|5-10|	63.0	71.3	55.9	90.2	73.9	68.3	73.7	72.1	64.6
|15-20|/|10-15|	61.8	76.0	62.9	77.6	74.2	75.6	73.0	72.8	68.3
45+ years									
|5-10|/|0-5|	40.2	39.6	34.8	29.6	63.9	60.5	26.5	63.3	47.3
|10-15|/|5-10|	59.2	65.2	45.6	68.8	65.4	63.6	65.6	83.9	63.2
|15-20|/|10-15|	56.2	65.7	48.2	57.7	66.8	65.3	69.4	67.0	67.8

a) 1991-1996.
b) 1989-1994.
Sources: See OECD (1997a).

(1997a)]. The retention rate for workers aged 45 years and older is higher than that for younger workers in six of the nine countries for which data are available. Data not shown here indicate that retention rates remain relatively high and comparable with those of prime-age workers through approximately age 50-54 years. Beyond the age of 55, the probability of an older worker remaining a further five years with the same employer declines substantially. Apparently, the pending retirement of these workers significantly shortens the amortisation period and may discourage further skill training. However, late-career trainees (aged 45 to 54 years) may be preferable to younger trainees, at least when an important share of the potential returns are expected to accrue over the first five years.

The high overall retention rate for older workers compared with younger workers reflects, in part, the greater stability of older recent hires relative to younger recent hires, as measured by the retention rate between 0-5 and 5-10 years of job tenure (Table 4.6). Thus, the need to provide significant initial training to new recruits may not be a general barrier to hiring older workers. However, the bottom line is that little is known about how firms assess the potential life of skill investments.

Incidence of training

Table 4.7 presents several measures of participation in job-related continuing education and training from the IALS. The share of workers receiving professional and career upgrading training in the previous year is about as high for those aged 45 to 54 years as for those aged 25 to 44 (21 versus 23 per cent in the unweighted averages). The rate falls to 15 per cent for the oldest group

(aged 55-64 years), which is close to the rate for the youngest workers (aged 15 to 24 years). Thus, these data suggest that firms – who finance nearly three-fourths of this training – generally do not view older workers as unsuited for training.[18] Though causality is not implied, the training rate does decline beyond approximately age 54, the age at which impending retirements cause the 5-year retention rates to begin falling.[19]

The age profile of training varies substantially between countries. The Netherlands stands out as having a very sharp reduction in training rates with age: whereas 15 per cent of workers aged 25 to 44 years participated in professional and career upgrading training, the corresponding rates were 12 per cent for those aged 45-54 years and just 2 per cent for those aged 55-64 years. The United States is at the opposite extreme, with training rates peaking for workers aged 45 to 54 years and only declining a little for those aged 55-64, but with only a third as many of the youngest workers receiving training. The reasons for these differences, as well as their implications for work-force productivity, are important topics for future research.

Workers with lower educational attainment are substantially less likely to receive training than more educated workers [OECD (1995c)]. While the poor training access of low-skilled older workers reflects general training patterns, the "use it or lose it" aspect of trainability may mean that this pattern is most detrimental to employment and earnings prospects near the end of the working life. At some point, many low-education workers whose previous work history includes little skill training may have to adapt to changed job requirements or search for new jobs, and they may be ill-prepared to do so. This source of the employment and earnings

Table 4.7. **Participation in job-related continuing education and training by age, 1994-1995**

Percentage of the labour force taking a course in the previous year (standard error in parentheses)

	Participation in job-related continuing education and training		Participation in professional and career-upgrading training	
	Total	Paid for by the employer	Total	Paid for by the employer
Australia	39.6 (0.5)	22.6 (0.5)	24.4 (0.5)	17.3 (0.4)
15-24 years	48.6 (1.4)	15.2 (1.1)	14.9 (1.1)	8.1 (0.9)
25-44 years	41.0 (0.8)	26.6 (0.7)	28.1 (0.8)	20.8 (0.7)
45-54 years	32.5 (1.4)	22.6 (1.3)	26.2 (1.3)	19.1 (1.2)
55-64 years	25.0 (2.2)	16.8 (2.0)	21.7 (2.1)	15.5 (1.9)
Belgium (Flanders)	18.2 (1.3)	12.4 (1.2)	10.5 (0.9)	7.4 (0.9)
15-24 years	11.4^a (4.1)	6.2^a (3.1)	7.2^a (3.5)	4.2^a (2.8)
25-44 years	18.5 (1.4)	12.0 (1.4)	11.6 (1.1)	7.9 (1.1)
45-54 years	19.8 (2.5)	14.9 (2.5)	9.5 (1.9)	7.6^a (1.7)
55-64 years	19.6^a (5.1)	17.6^a (4.8)	6.6^a (3.1)	6.4^a (3.1)
Canada	38.0 (1.7)	23.1 (2.1)	26.6 (1.8)	18.8 (1.6)
15-24 years	52.3 (3.6)	11.2 (3.2)	18.5 (3.3)	10.1 (3.1)
25-44 years	38.6 (2.2)	27.7 (3.8)	28.8 (2.6)	21.9 (3.6)
45-54 years	30.3 (4.3)	18.8 (1.9)	25.5 (4.6)	15.5 (1.5)
55-64 years	30.2 (9.4)	23.7^a (15.4)	28.4 (9.5)	21.7^a (15.9)
Ireland	23.9 (1.8)	13.2 (1.4)	11.9 (1.1)	7.6 (0.9)
15-24 years	33.4 (2.5)	12.7 (2.0)	10.9 (2.0)	5.8^a (1.0)
25-44 years	23.3 (2.2)	15.2 (1.8)	13.1 (1.0)	9.1 (1.0)
45-54 years	19.3 (3.4)	11.2^a (2.2)	11.8^a (2.8)	7.0^a (2.2)
55-64 years	11.0^a (3.4)	6.2^a (3.2)	6.7^a (2.7)	4.1^a (1.9)
Netherlands	33.3 (1.4)	22.9 (1.0)	13.9 (0.7)	9.5 (0.6)
15-24 years	38.5 (3.8)	15.6 (2.7)	18.4 (3.1)	9.7^a (2.5)
25-44 years	36.2 (1.5)	26.5 (1.5)	14.8 (1.0)	10.2 (0.9)
45-54 years	27.2 (2.8)	21.8 (2.6)	11.6 (1.9)	10.1 (1.9)
55-64 years	15.2^a (3.7)	12.7^a (3.5)	2.3^a (1.4)	1.7^a (1.3)
New Zealand	47.9 (1.5)	31.4 (1.3)	34.4 (1.4)	26.2 (1.3)
15-24 years	60.8 (4.2)	26.1 (2.7)	27.3 (3.6)	18.8 (2.5)
25-44 years	47.9 (1.5)	34.0 (1.6)	37.6 (1.5)	28.9 (1.6)
45-54 years	45.2 (3.2)	33.6 (3.4)	38.3 (3.1)	29.7 (3.2)
55-64 years	30.0 (4.8)	21.9 (3.4)	22.4 (3.1)	17.6 (2.7)
Poland	14.3 (1.0)	10.6 (0.6)	13.1 (1.0)	8.6 (0.5)
15-24 years	10.9^a (1.9)	7.2^a (1.3)	9.5^a (1.8)	3.7^a (1.3)
25-44 years	15.3 (1.5)	11.3 (1.1)	14.2 (1.4)	9.5 (0.9)
45-54 years	15.0 (1.7)	12.2 (1.8)	13.3 (1.7)	9.7 (1.9)
55-64 years	7.5^a (3.3)	5.7^a (3.0)	8.3^a (3.8)	6.5^a (3.3)
Switzerland	31.9 (1.0)	20.1 (1.0)	26.0 (1.2)	16.8 (1.0)
15-24 years	34.5 (5.2)	23.5 (3.1)	21.0 (3.9)	12.6^a (4.5)
25-44 years	33.9 (1.8)	20.9 (1.5)	28.7 (1.7)	17.8 (1.4)
45-54 years	29.7 (2.2)	18.9 (2.3)	25.6 (2.3)	18.8 (2.0)
55-64 years	25.2 (2.7)	15.9 (2.6)	20.7 (2.8)	12.9 (2.8)
United Kingdom	50.2 (1.4)	39.2 (1.3)	15.4 (1.0)	12.9 (0.9)
15-24 years	55.6 (3.5)	30.3 (3.0)	14.4 (2.0)	12.1 (1.7)
25-44 years	55.2 (1.7)	46.3 (1.8)	18.1 (1.4)	15.0 (1.4)
45-54 years	42.8 (2.3)	35.3 (2.4)	13.1 (1.4)	11.1 (1.3)
55-64 years	32.1 (2.4)	27.2 (2.5)	8.6 (2.1)	7.4 (1.9)
United States	44.5 (1.7)	31.7 (1.6)	29.7 (1.3)	24.1 (1.2)
15-24 years	42.4 (7.0)	11.7 (2.8)	9.4 (2.2)	6.2^a (2.0)
25-44 years	46.4 (1.9)	36.2 (1.9)	32.5 (1.8)	26.9 (1.7)
45-54 years	45.7 (2.6)	36.2 (2.3)	35.8 (2.5)	29.4 (2.0)
55-64 years	36.8 (4.0)	25.8 (4.5)	28.4 (3.9)	21.4 (4.2)
Unweighted average	34.2	22.7	20.6	14.9
15-24 years	38.8	16.0	15.2	9.1
25-44 years	35.6	25.7	22.8	16.8
45-54 years	30.8	22.6	21.1	15.8
55-64 years	23.3	17.4	15.4	11.5

a)   Estimate based on a maximum sample size of 30 observations.
Source: International Adult Literacy Survey, 1994-1995, unpublished estimates.

instability is likely to become increasingly important if pension reforms increase the desired age of retirement.

While it is clear that less-educated workers have less favourable employment and earnings prospects at all ages, the extent to which training magnifies this disadvantage among older workers is not known. Labour force participation rates are lower for less educated males at all ages, but the participation gap increases between prime working ages and the ages associated with early retirement (*e.g.* between ages 35-44 and 55-64) in most countries (Table 4.8). This pattern is consistent with the employability problems associated with low education becoming more severe with age. Similarly, earnings differences by educational level tend to rise with age (Section D). However, the greater propensity of lower education workers to retire early might reflect the structure of pension benefits, rather than increased difficulty in remaining employed [OECD (1998c)]. Differences in the timing of retirement may also distort pay comparisons among older workers.

The adaptation of training practices to work-force ageing

Training practices will have to adapt in order to minimise any adverse effects of ageing on overall productivity, while also accommodating any preference of older workers to delay retirement. The analysis of training rates by age suggests that firms' training investments reflect their predictions about the time of retirement. As an important complement of pension reforms designed to encourage later retirement, governments may have an important role to play in informing both firms and workers to anticipate such a shift and to begin as soon as possible to adapt training practices. By increasing the perceived pay-back period for investments in older workers, this information – if credible – could raise the age threshold beyond which training rates start to fall in anticipation of retirement.

Even if firms look more favourably on investing in training older workers, they may still be unwilling to invest much in those with low educational attain-

Table 4.8. **Labour force participation rates by educational attainment and age, 1995**

| | Men aged 35 to 44 years | | | | Men aged 55 to 64 years | | | |
| | Participation rate for educational attainment less than upper secondary (Percentage) | Increase in participation rate relative to educational attainment less than upper secondary (Percentage point difference) | | | Participation rate for educational attainment less than upper secondary (Percentage) | Increase in participation rate relative to educational attainment less than upper secondary (Percentage point difference) | | |
		Upper secondary	Non-university tertiary	University		Upper secondary	Non-university tertiary	University
Australia	88.5	5.9	8.0	9.0	57.9	5.0	12.3	19.3
Austria	92.1	5.3	5.2	6.2	40.0	4.5	19.6	43.9
Belgium	91.0	5.9	8.3	7.5	25.8	17.2	17.5	39.4
Canada	83.6	9.4	11.1	12.9	51.2	9.7	12.9	20.6
Czech Republic	88.0	9.0	..	10.8	39.6	13.5	..	32.4
Denmark	85.4	9.5	11.6	12.3	59.9	8.3	16.2	24.6
Finland	88.9	4.7	8.4	9.0	40.3	10.6	14.0	28.8
France	92.6	4.8	5.7	5.0	34.5	10.5	18.7	34.6
Germany	95.4	2.1	3.5	3.3	47.9	6.7	17.1	27.6
Greece	96.0	2.2	1.8	2.8	64.0	−15.6	−18.4	−1.1
Ireland	87.8	8.1	10.0	8.8	61.4	7.5	10.9	21.5
Italy	94.2	3.5	..	4.7	41.7	15.5	..	36.4
Korea	94.5	3.0	..	3.9	79.4	−0.5	..	2.9
Mexico	96.5	1.9	2.8	2.2	80.7	−7.3	16.9	2.0
Netherlands	90.2	6.4	..	7.1	35.5	7.8	..	19.0
New Zealand	87.2	8.0	7.8	8.1	61.3	8.8	11.7	21.1
Norway	83.3	10.5	12.9	14.5	59.4	14.3	21.9	32.6
Poland	85.5	6.7	12.4	12.8	42.6	−3.3	1.9	21.5
Portugal	95.1	2.3	4.2	4.1	60.6	−6.5	7.5	13.4
Spain	93.5	3.8	4.4	5.3	53.0	8.7	10.2	21.6
Sweden	93.7	2.3	2.8	3.4	83.7	0.0	−1.0	5.1
Switzerland	93.1	5.2	6.5	4.6	76.9	5.5	6.5	11.4
United Kingdom	83.4	11.2	12.6	15.2	53.9	11.5	14.0	14.6
United States	75.7	16.2	18.4	21.4	50.9	15.7	21.7	26.9
Unweighted average	89.8	6.2	7.9	8.1	54.3	6.2	11.6	21.7

.. Data not available.
Sources: OECD Education Database except for Mexico where unpublished data were supplied by STPS-INEGI, *Encuesta Nacional de Empleo.*

ment These individuals may become increasingly vulnerable to skill obsolescence, especially if they attempt to delay retirement, and the market incentives for firms to address this risk may be quite weak. Rising educational attainment among future cohorts of older workers should be a positive factor mitigating this risk, but it seems probable that low-skilled older workers will represent a major challenge for labour market programmes.[20]

F. MOBILITY OF OLDER WORKERS

This section considers whether the mobility of older workers is a problem in the context of work-force ageing. The extent to which limited mobility currently is a cause of long-duration joblessness is first examined. Empirical evidence on hiring patterns are then examined in order to assess whether older job seekers are disadvantaged in competing for jobs. Finally, attention turns to whether older workers may have to change employers more frequently in the future.

1. Long-term unemployment

Table 4.9 presents data on the unemployment rate and the incidence of long-term unemployment. The unemployment rate for older workers is lower

Table 4.9. **Unemployment rates and the incidence of long-term unemployment, 1996**

	Unemployment rate (Percentage of labour force)		Unemployed for 12 months or more (Percentage of unemployed)	
	15 to 64 years[a]	45 to 64 years[b]	15 to 64 years[c]	45 to 64 years[b]
Australia	8.5	6.4	28.4	44.8
Austria	5.3	5.4	25.6	37.0
Belgium	9.5	5.9	61.3	76.6
Canada	9.7	7.3	13.9	21.6
Czech Republic	3.8	2.6	31.6	37.6
Denmark	6.9	5.6	26.5	43.6
Finland	16.2	16.4	39.3	61.8
France	12.1	8.0	39.5	62.0
Germany	8.9	10.0	47.8	57.8
Greece	9.9	3.9	56.7	54.6
Hungary	9.8	6.5	54.4	58.8
Iceland	3.7	2.6	18.4	40.0
Ireland	11.9	9.5	59.4	72.4
Italy	12.3	4.5	65.6	61.2
Japan	3.5	2.8	19.5	27.4
Korea	2.0	0.8	3.6	5.7
Luxembourg[d]	3.5	1.8	26.8	33.3
Mexico	4.5	2.4	2.2	5.1
Netherlands	6.5	5.1	50.0	60.5
New Zealand	6.2	3.9	20.8	34.6
Norway	4.9	2.3	15.4	35.7
Poland	12.7	7.6	39.0	47.4
Portugal	7.7	5.1	53.1	64.8
Spain	22.4	12.8	55.7	62.9
Sweden	8.1	5.9	17.1	27.0
Switzerland	3.9	3.5	25.0	..
Turkey	6.3	2.6	43.6	45.1
United Kingdom	8.3	5.9	39.8	52.2
United States	5.5	3.3	9.3	14.6
Unweighted average:				
North America[e]	6.6	4.3	8.5	13.8
European Union	10.0	7.1	44.3	55.2
OECD Europe	8.8	6.1	40.5	52.0
Total OECD	8.1	5.5	34.1	44.5

.. Data not available.
a) Unemployment rates for Australia, Canada, France, Germany, Ireland, Korea, Luxembourg and the United Kingdom differ from those in Table B of the Statistical Annex since they are estimated from different data sources or have a different upper age limit.
b) Australia, Canada and Korea, 45 years or more; France, 50 years or more; Luxembourg 45 to 54 years; Switzerland 55 to 64 years.
c) Estimates differ from those in Table G of the Statistical Annex for a number of countries due to differences in the upper age limit.
d) Data for duration of unemployment are based on small sample sizes.
e) North America comprises Canada, Mexico and the United States.
Sources: OECD Unemployment Duration and Labour Force Databases (see notes to Table G of the Statistical Annex).

than the overall rate in most countries. However, they are significantly more at risk of entering the ranks of long-term unemployment.

Unemployment rates for older workers may either over- or understate the difficulties they have in changing jobs. The measured incidence of long-term unemployment will overstate the difficulties to the extent that it reflects supply-side incentives to remain jobless. For example, the special unemployment benefits sometimes available to older workers may function as a form of pension for workers who are effectively retired. Conversely, measured unemployment will understate the extent of involuntary joblessness, if significant numbers of older workers withdraw from the labour force following redundancies, because their job-search prospects are poor.

Though difficult to distinguish, both involuntary job loss and voluntary labour force withdrawal appear to be important routes to joblessness for older workers. Among older workers who left a job in the previous 6 months and were not yet re-employed, the reason reported for separating from the previous job gives an indication of the relative frequencies of involuntary job loss and voluntary departures as causes of joblessness (Chart 4.6). In 1995, the risk of joblessness stemming from layoff (2.1 per cent) was higher than the risk of retirement (1.2 per cent), early retirement for economic reasons (0.8 per cent), quits (0.7 per cent) or illness (0.7 per cent). Beginning in 1991, there was a significant increase in the percentage of older workers laid-off and jobless, which probably reflects the recession of the early 1990s, but may also reflect a

Chart 4.6.

**Persons aged 45-64, currently without a job,
by reason for leaving their last job, selected European countries**[a]

Percentage of employment

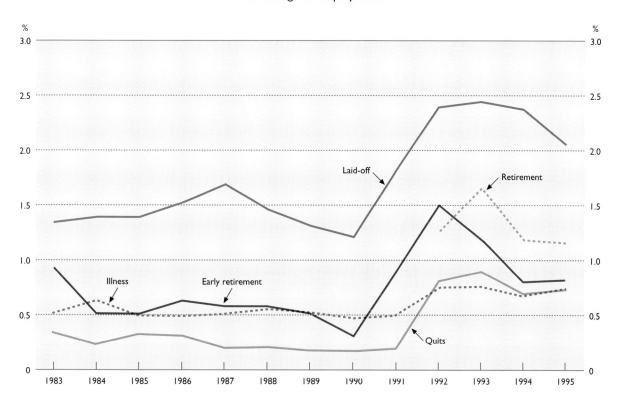

a) Persons currently without a job refers to those currently unemployed or not in the labour force who left their job during the previous six months. Data are a weighted average for Belgium, Denmark, France, Germany, Greece, Ireland, Italy, Luxembourg, the Netherlands and the United Kingdom. Data for retirement are unavailable prior to 1992.
Source: Unpublished data provided by EUROSTAT on the basis of the European Union Labour Force Survey.

secular increase in job displacement for older workers [Farber (1996)].

2. Hiring of older workers

To what extent does the high incidence of long-term unemployment among older job seekers reflect disadvantages they face in finding new jobs? Data on employers' recruitment choices among job applicants of different ages generally are not available, so this subsection considers broader comparisons of hiring patterns by age.

Older workers account for a smaller share of new hires than of total employment (Table 4.10). Among workers aged 45 to 64 years, their hiring share ranges from a low of 28 per cent of their employment share in Belgium to a high of 56 per cent in Australia. By comparison, the share of young workers (aged 15 to 24 years) in recent hires is more than twice their share of employment, while they are almost equal for prime-age workers. The disproportionately low share of older workers among recent hires illustrates that many firms who employ a significant number of older workers, nevertheless, tend not to hire them [Hutchens (1986)]. This pattern need not result from a preference among employers to recruit younger workers. If older workers are less likely to leave one job and search for another, that too would cause under representation in hiring, even if recruiting practices were age-neutral.

Multivariate analysis can provide a better indication of whether employers are less likely to hire older workers from among other candidates. A regression equation predicting hiring shares by age was estimated that also contained controls for a host of other factors believed to influence hiring, including differences by age in the share of workers who actively search for a new job. The econometric results imply that, on average across nine EU countries, the share of older workers in recent hires is almost 13 percentage points lower than that of prime-age workers.[21] This analysis suggest that employer preferences for younger job candidates is one of the reasons why older job losers experience long jobless spells and larger earnings losses once re-employed.

The apparent tendency for some employers to prefer younger job applicants, controlling for observable characteristics, suggest that older job seekers may be disadvantaged in hiring. There are many potential reasons for this finding – declining skills or productivity with age, higher costs associated with hiring older workers, such as fixed hiring costs or a higher cost of providing non-wage benefits, or age discrimination – but research to

Table 4.10. **Relative hiring intensities by age group, 1995**

Ratio of share of new hires to share of total wage and salary employment[a]

	15-24 years	25-44 years	45-64 years
Australia[b]	1.7	1.0	0.6
Austria	2.3	0.9	0.4
Belgium	3.7	0.9	0.3
Canada	2.5	0.9	0.4
Denmark	2.1	1.0	0.4
Finland	3.3	1.0	0.4
France	3.4	0.9	0.4
Germany	2.2	1.0	0.4
Greece	2.9	0.9	0.5
Ireland	2.3	0.7	0.4
Italy	3.3	0.9	0.3
Japan	3.0	0.7	0.5
Luxembourg	2.9	0.9	0.3
Netherlands	2.5	0.8	0.3
Portugal	2.6	0.9	0.4
Spain	2.2	1.0	0.5
Sweden	3.1	1.0	0.4
Switzerland	2.8	1.0	0.3
United Kingdom	2.3	0.9	0.5
United States[b]	2.3	0.9	0.5
Unweighted average	2.6	0.9	0.4

a)   Workers with tenure less than one year are defined as new hires.
b)   Data refer to 1996.
Sources: Data from the European Union Labour Force Survey were supplied by EUROSTAT. For Australia, Canada, Japan, Switzerland and the United States, see OECD (1997a).

date provides little help in assessing their importance.

3. Future trends

It appears likely that work-force ageing will create an increased need for older workers to change jobs because more will be laid-off. Layoffs occur when firms' downsizing needs cannot be met by voluntary attrition. Job losses due to downsizing and firm closure are relatively high in most OECD countries, in the range of 10 per cent of total employment annually, and show no downward or upward trend [OECD (1996)]. By contrast, work-force ageing may cause voluntary attrition to fall, since voluntary quits are relatively infrequent among older workers [Devine and Kiefer (1991, Chapter 8); OECD (1997a, Chapter 5)]. The combination of stable job loss rates and falling attrition implies a tendency for layoffs to rise, and the falling share of younger workers over the next few decades suggests that it will become more difficult for employers to protect older workers from these layoffs.

If more older workers do experience job loss, the economic costs resulting from their limited mobility would tend to increase. Greater proactive training investments to maintain trainability and acquire general skills probably could improve the mobility of older job changers. However, little is known about what sort of training would generate the highest returns and market incentives may be inadequate to induce the desired response.

G. CONCLUSIONS

OECD labour forces will become significantly older over the next several decades. The work-force ageing due to population ageing will be strongly amplified to the extent that the trend toward earlier retirement reverses. Such a reversal would limit the growth in the number of retirees relative to the number of active workers, which is one of the keys to avoiding the potentially negative impact of population ageing on living standards [OECD (1998a)]. Reforms to pension and other social security programmes that reduce significantly or eliminate existing incentives for early retirement probably would generate a significant increase in labour supply at older ages. However, the full potential benefits of such policies will only be realised if labour markets are able to generate enough good jobs for an unprecedentedly large number of older workers.

Proactive measures by workers, employers and governments to enhance the employability of older workers will be an essential complement to pension reform.

There is a striking disproportion between the importance of the challenge to expand the employment opportunities of older workers and the limited success of economic research at providing guidance for policy making. A number of important relationships between ageing and recruitment, training and pay have been identified, including potentially important equity and efficiency concerns. However, relatively little is known about the actual magnitudes of these potential problems nor about the best policies to redress them. The relationship between age and job performance, including how it is shaped by training practices, appears to be critical, but is not well understood. Limited mobility also appears to be an important concern, but the extent and causes of the apparent disadvantage of older job seekers are not well understand either. Further research on these and related topics deserves high priority.

Even with the present limited state of knowledge, several preliminary judgements appear justified. First, the preponderance of the evidence on ageing and productivity suggests that most workers have the potential to remain productive up to and beyond currently standard retirement ages, provided they receive adequate training. Second, although the market signals created by work-force ageing will tend to cause recruitment, training and pay practices to adapt in desirable ways, these adjustments may well not go as far, or proceed as rapidly, as desirable. In particular, there is a danger that insufficient investments will be made in maintaining the trainability and mobility of workers as they age. Finally, even if firms and workers make all desirable provisions for ageing, it will remain true that older workers face elevated risks of skill obsolescence and poor health. Advocates of reforming pensions so as to encourage later retirement have rightly emphasised that unemployment and disability benefit programs need to be tightly regulated, to ensure that they do not become substitute sources of *de facto* early retirement benefits. It should be understood, however, that raising the age of pension eligibility will expand the legitimate demand for these benefits.

Notes

1. The analysis in this chapter was conducted under the aegis of a comprehensive OECD study of the policy implications of population ageing [OECD (1998a, b)]. That study concludes that the implications of ageing are deep and pervasive, and recommends that governments take actions across a broad range of economic, financial and social policies. One of the guideposts offered for these reforms is that "active ageing" should be promoted by increasing the opportunities of older individuals to contribute to society and the economy. The labour market issues examined here are part of that broader agenda. The chapter's coverage of issues is partial, however, even within the subtopic of work-force ageing. Important issues, such as the labour supply effects of pensions, disability and "flexible retirement" receive only cursory attention; they are, however, covered in OECD (1998c).

2. The trend toward earlier retirement among men in recent decades, along with increasing employment of younger women, has meant that the initial stage of population ageing generally has not been associated with an increase in the share of the labour force at or above historical retirement ages. It seems unlikely, however, that future changes in labour force participation patterns will continue to decouple the age composition of the labour force from that of the underlying population in most OECD countries. A continuation of simultaneous trends toward greater longevity and retirement at progressively earlier ages is likely unsustainable in the long run, because it would imply that the "dependency" ratio of retirees to active workers rises without limit. Such a continuation would make it very difficult to address the pension "affordability problem" and could lower living standards generally.

3. The later-retirement scenario is potentially unrealistic, in the sense that it assumes a sharp reversal of recent trends. However, if no such reversal occurs, it will be very difficult to maintain the solvency of many national pension systems or overall fiscal balance [OECD (1998b)].

4. The index of the change in the age composition is based on the absolute change in the cumulative distribution function of the labour force by age and is calculated as:

$$I = \Sigma_{i = 1 \text{ to } N} \, |f_{i, t1} - f_{i, t2}|$$

where i denotes age group, $t1$ and $t2$ denote the beginning and ending years of the period and $f_{i, t}$ denotes the share of the labour force in age groups 1 to i in year t. This index provides a measure of the overall extent to which the age mix of the population has changed, but no information about which age groups expanded or contracted.

5. The significant positive correlation between changes in the age structure and the employment to population ratio are an example of this relationship: labour force participation rates increased most rapidly in countries where the age structure changed most, because there was a larger shift from the youngest age groups, for whom school enrolment is important, to prime working-age groups.

6. Educational attainment is not projected to 2030, since the cohorts who will constitute the older work force then have not yet completed their initial education. Further increases in educational attainment are likely between 2015 and 2030.

7. In a pure signalling model, educational attainment is used by firms as a criteria for recruiting, but has no intrinsic effect on productivity. Accordingly, an increase in the educational level of the labour force has no effect on the availability of employment or the level of wages.

8. These are sometimes referred to as "Lazear contracts" although the balancing of productivity and pay over a career is rarely, if ever, written explicitly into employment contracts. Lazear (1979) emphasised the desire of employers to reduce shirking and monitoring costs through increasing the cost to workers of dismissal, but efficiency gains resulting from reduced quit rates and the increased appropriability of the returns to training investments could also motivate implicit contracts of this type. Equity concerns of trade unions or informal work-place culture can also create a tendency for compensation to rise more rapidly with age than does productivity. The theory of specific human capital also provides a rationale for employers to redistribute the compensation paid to a worker over the life of the contract [Becker (1993)]. However, compensation rises less rapidly than productivity in these models, implying that employers find it profitable to continue employing older workers.

9. Lazear (1979) originally argued that employers needed an explicit policy of *mandatory* retirement and, hence, that age discrimination legislation outlawing such policies would be inefficient. More recent research suggests that employers can structure occupational pensions to induce retirement at the appropriate age, even in the absence of mandatory retirement [Neumark and Stock (1997)].

10. Human capital theory identifies an additional advantage of announcing reforms to encourage later retirement as far in advance as possible, since the returns to skill investments depend on the anticipated age of retirement.

11. Employer-sponsored, defined-benefit pension plans, which are an important form of deferred compensation in some countries, provide an example. The

annual contribution costs for enrolling a newly hired worker typically rise with age [Casey (1997)].

12. There is also some evidence that substitution between workers of different ages is more limited for workers with a university education than for less educated workers. This suggests that work-force ageing will have the greatest impact on the employment and earnings prospects of highly educated workers. However, most of the research about how educational attainment affects substitution patterns among workers of different ages has focused on the labour market difficulties encountered by "baby-boom" cohorts as they entered the American labour market in earlier decades [Freeman (1979); Welch (1979); Berger (1983, 1985); Connelly (1986)]. It is possible that an expansion in the supply of older, highly educated workers would be easier for labour markets to absorb, since there is more time for training, promotion and other personnel practices to anticipate it.

13. Conversely, pensions and retirement complicate the empirical analysis of the labour market difficulties encountered by older workers, because it is difficult to differentiate between supply and demand-side influences. Some older workers classified as unemployed in labour force surveys may have voluntarily retired, while some identifying themselves as "retired" may have left the labour force in response to poor employment prospects. Retirement behaviour also makes cross-age comparisons of earnings or training more difficult to interpret. If workers retiring at younger ages differ from those retiring later, cross-sectional comparisons between older and younger workers may not provide a reliable picture of how earnings or training vary over the course of a career. Similarly, the earnings of older workers may provide a poor estimate of the potential earnings available to early retirees, if they were to seek work.

14. The lower annual earnings of the oldest workers could reflect lower annual hours worked or a tendency for the best-paid workers to retire younger, as well as a decline in wage rates.

15. The lower literacy scores of the current cohort of older workers probably reflect significant employment difficulties, but likely overstate the extent to which future cohorts will be so affected.

16. This regression analysis is based on a replication of the multivariate analyses presented in Willms (1997) and OECD, Human Resources Development Canada and Statistics Canada (1997b) for ten countries: Belgium (Flanders), Canada, Germany, Ireland, the Netherlands, New Zealand, Poland, Sweden, the United Kingdom and the United States.

17. The typically higher wages received by late-career and older workers might indicate a third reason why the returns to training fall with age. One of the costs of training is foregone production. If the higher wages of older workers reflect higher productivity, the hourly opportunity cost of training is also correspondingly higher. If the age/earnings premium exceeds productivity differences, however, relative wages overstate the true difference in the opportunity cost of training.

18. Lower training among the current cohort of older workers could be due to a number of factors, such as lower levels of education, in addition to age *per se*. A multivariate analysis (not shown here) of the probability of enrolling in a training course reveals that, when these are taken into account, the decline in the incidence of training between ages 45-54 years and 55-64 years is cut approximately in half.

19. The low training rate of the youngest workers is also associated with low retention rates. Data from business enterprises in the United States show a similar age profile for participation in training and suggest that annual hours devoted to training actually peak around age 50 [Lynch (1997)].

20. Another issue, about which little is known, is how effectively training practices will adjust so as to maintain the work force's adaptability in meeting shifts in job skill requirements or reallocations of employment across firms.

21. The estimated equation for the share in hiring of workers in age group j in country i at time t is:

Employment < 1 year$_{ijt}$ / Employment < 1 year$_{it}$) $= \alpha_i + \beta_1$Age$_{it} + \beta_2$(Employment$_{ijt}$ / Employment$_{it}$) $+ \beta_3$(Jobless < 6 months$_{ijt}$ /Jobless < 6 months$_{it}$) $+ \beta_4$(Early retirees$_{ijt}$ / Employment$_{ijt}$) $+ \beta_5$Country$_i + \beta_6$Year$_t + \beta_7$Gender$_{it} + \beta_8$Occupation$_{it} + \varepsilon_{it}$

where:

Age$_{it}$ = a vector of 2 dummy variables covering ages 15 to 24 and 45 to 64 years, with age 25-44 years being the omitted category;

(Employment < 1 year$_{ijt}$ / Employment < 1 year$_{it}$) = Employment of age group j with tenure less than one year as a percentage of employment of all ages with tenure less than one year, where j is age 15-24 years, 25 to 44 years and 45 to 64 years;

(Employment$_{ijt}$ / Employment$_{it}$) = Employment in age group j as a percentage of total employment;

(Jobless < 6 months$_{ijt}$ /Jobless < 6 months$_{it}$) = individuals in age group j jobless less than 6 months who were laid off or quit (excluding retirement and illness as a reason for leaving) as a percentage all those jobless less than 6 months for similar reasons;

(Early retirees$_{ijt}$ / Employment$_{ijt}$) = persons who have retired as a percentage of employment;

Country$_i$ = a vector of 8 country dummy variables, with Germany being the omitted category;

Year$_t$ = a vector of 3 dummy variables covering 1993 to 1995, with 1992 being the omitted category;

Gender$_{it}$ = a gender dummy variable;

Occupation$_{it}$ = a vector of 8 dummy variables covering the International Standard Classification of Occupations (ISCO), with managerial, administrative and legislative occupations being the excluded category;

ε_{it} = a stochastic error term.

The second, third and fourth independent variables control for differences by age in the share of workers who actively search for a new job. They measure, respectively, the employment share of age group j, their share of job separations and the extent to which older job leavers are more likely to leave the labour force rather than search for a new job. The results, using weighted least squares with employment as the weight, are as follows:

(Employment <1 year$_{ijt}$ / Employment < 1 year$_{it}$) = 16.05**+18.46** (15-24 years) −12.60 ** (45-64 years) + 0.70** (Employment$_{ijt}$ / Employment$_{it}$) + 0.32** (Jobless < 6 months$_{ijt}$ /Jobless < 6 months$_{it}$) − 0.01 (Early retirees$_{ijt}$ / Employment$_{ijt}$) − 0.065 (Belgium) + 0.063 (Denmark) − 0.031 (Spain) − 0.073 (Greece) − 0.043 (Ireland) − 0.081 (Italy) − 0.483 (Portugal) − 0.020 (United Kingdom) + 0.009 (1993) − 0.16 (1994) + 0.10 (1995) − 0.013 (women)   0.218 (professionals) − 0.262 (technicians and associate professionals) − 0.197 (clerks) − 0.195 (service and sales workers) − 0.327 (skilled agricultural workers) − 0.195 (craft and related trades) − 0.220 (plant and machine operators) − 0.208 (elementary occupations).

Adjusted R^2 = 0.89, No. of observations = 1 746

where ** and * indicate significance at the 1 and 5 per cent levels respectively using a two-tailed T test.

ANNEX 4.A

Data sources and methods used to project labour supply

The labour supply projections analysed in Section B are based on the medium-fertility population projections reported in *World Population Prospects* 1950-2050, United Nations, New York (the 1996 revision), in combination with two scenarios for the future evolution of labour force participation rates. These participation-rate scenarios are based on historical estimates of labour force participation rates by 5-year age groups and gender reported in *Economically Active Population* 1950-2010, Fourth Edition, Bureau of Statistics, International Labour Office, Geneva, December 1996 (computer file distributed on diskettes).

Under the baseline scenario, it is assumed that future participation rates are the same as those in 1995, the most recent year for which the historical estimates are available. The later-retirement scenario assumes a gradual return, during the period 2000 to 2020, to the retirement pattern among men in 1970. It is implemented as follows:

- For all years, the projected participation rates for ages 44 and younger are set at their 1995 values (as in the baseline scenario);

- For years 1996 to 1999, projected participation rates for ages 45 and older are set at their 1995 values (as in the baseline scenario);

- For years 2020 and later, projected participation rates for ages 45 years and older are calculated to yield the same proportionate rate of labour force withdrawal, relative to the participation rate for ages 40 to 44 years, as was observed for men in 1970. For example, if the participation rate for men aged 60 to 64 years in 1970 was 63 per cent, compared with 92 per cent for men aged 40 to 44 years, the participation rate for men aged 60 to 65 years was 68 per cent [*i.e.* (63/92)*100] that of men aged 40 to 44 years. Thus, if the 1995 participation rate for women aged 40 to 44 years was 57 per cent, the projected participation rate for women aged 60 to 64 years in 2020 would be 39 per cent (*i.e.* 68 per cent of 57 per cent); and

- For years 2000 to 2019, the projected participation rates for ages 45 years and older make a smooth transition (*i.e.* linear interpolation) between the rates projected for 1999 and 2020.

Bibliography

ANDERSON, P., GUSTMAN, A. and STEINMEIER, T. (1997), "Trends in Male Labor Force Participation and Retirement: Some Evidence on the Role of Pensions and Social Security in the 1970s and 1980s", National Bureau of Economic Research, Working Paper No. 6208.

BECKER, G. (1993), Human Capital: A Theoretical and Empirical Analysis, with Special Reference to Education (third edition), University of Chicago Press, Chicago and London.

BERGER, M. (1983), "Changes in Labour Force Composition and Male Earnings: A Production Approach", Journal of Human Resources, Spring, pp. 177-196.

BERGER, M. (1985), "The Effect of Cohort Size on Earnings: A Re-Examination of the Evidence", Journal of Political Economy, June, pp. 561-573.

BOUND, J., SCHENBAUM, M.T., STINEBRICKNER, T. and WAIDMANN, T. (1997), "Measuring the Effects of Health on Retirement Behaviour", paper presented at International Health and Retirement Surveys Conference, Amsterdam, August.

BURKHAUSER, R.V., DWYER, D., LINDEBOOM, M., THEEUWES, J. and WOITTIEZ, I. (1997), "Health, Work, and Economic Well-being of Older Workers", paper presented at International Health and Retirement Surveys Conference, Amsterdam, August.

CAIN, G. (1986), "The Economic Analysis of Labor Market Discrimination: A Survey", in Ashenfelter, O. and Layard, R. (eds.), Handbook of Labor Economics, Vol. 1, North Holland, Amsterdam, pp. 693-785.

CARRINGTON, W. and ZAMAN, A. (1994), "Interindustry Variation in the Costs of Job Displacement", Journal of Labor Economics, April, pp. 243-275.

CASEY, B. (1997), "Incentives and Disincentives to Early and Late Retirement", paper prepared for the Joint ILO-OECD Workshop: Development and Reform of Pensions Schemes, 15-17 December, Paris.

CONNELLY, R. (1986), "A Framework for Analyzing the Impact of Cohort Size on Education and Labor Earnings", Journal of Human Resources, Fall, pp. 543-562.

DEVINE, T. and KIEFER, N. (1991), Empirical Labour Economics: The Search Approach, Oxford University Press, Oxford.

DISNEY, R. (1996), Can We Afford to Grow Older? A Perspective on the Economics of Ageing, MIT Press, Cambridge MA.

FALLICK, B.C. (1996), "A Review of Recent Empirical Literature on Displaced Workers", Industrial and Labor Relations Review, March, pp. 5-16.

FARBER, H.S. (1996), "The Changing Face of Job Loss in the United States", National Bureau of Economic Research, Working Paper No. 5596.

FREEMAN, R. (1979), "The Effect of Demographic Factors on Age-Earnings Profiles", Journal of Human Resources, Summer, pp. 289-318.

GRUBER, J. and WISE, D. (1997), "Social Security Programs and Retirement around the World", National Bureau of Economic Research, Working Paper No. 6134.

HAMERMESH, D. (1993), Labor Demand, Princeton University Press, Princeton.

HANDA, J. (1994), Discrimination, Retirement and Pensions, Avebury, Aldershot.

HUTCHENS, R. (1986), "Delayed Payment Contracts and a Firm's Propensity to Hire Older Workers", Journal of Labor Economics, October, pp. 439-457.

HUTCHENS, R. (1988), "Do Job Opportunities Decline with Age?", Industrial and Labor Relations Review, October, pp. 89-99.

JACOBSON, L., LALONDE, R. and SULLIVAN, D. (1993), "Earnings Losses of Displaced Workers", American Economic Review, September, pp. 685-709.

KOTLIKOFF, L.J. and GOKHALE, J. (1992), "Estimating a Firm's Age-Productivity Profile using the Present Value of Workers' Earnings", Quarterly Journal of Economics, November, pp. 1215-1242.

LAZEAR, E.P. (1979), "Why is there Mandatory Retirement?", Journal of Political Economy, December, pp. 1261-1284.

LAZEAR, E.P. (1984), "Social Security and Pensions", National Bureau of Economic Research, Working Paper No. 1322.

LYNCH, L. (1997), "Too Old to Learn?", Tufts University, Boston, December.

MANTON, K.G., CORDER, L. and STALLARD, E. (1997), "Chronic Disability Trends in Elderly United States Populations: 1982-1994", Proceedings of the National Academy of Sciences USA, March, pp. 2593-2598.

MEDOFF, J.L. and ABRAHAM, K.G. (1981), "Are Those Paid More Really More Productive?", Journal of Human Resources, Spring, pp. 186-216.

NEUMARK, D. and STOCK, W. (1997), "Age Discrimination Laws and Labor Market Efficiency", National Bureau of Economic Research, Working Paper No. 6088.

OECD (1995a), The Transition from Work to Retirement, Social Policy Studies No. 16, Paris.

OECD (1995b), The Labour Market and Older Workers, Social Policy Studies No. 17, Paris.

OECD and STATISTICS CANADA (1995c), Literacy, Economy and Society – Results of the First International Adult Literacy Survey, Paris and Ottawa.

OECD (1995d), Employment Outlook, Paris, July.

OECD (1996), Employment Outlook, Paris, July.

OECD (1997a), *Employment Outlook*, Paris, July.

OECD, HUMAN RESOURCES DEVELOPMENT CANADA and STATISTICS CANADA (1997b), *Literacy Skills for the Knowledge Economy: Further Results from the International Adult Literacy Survey*, Paris.

OECD (1998a), *Maintaining Prosperity in an Ageing Society*, Paris.

OECD (1998b), *Maintaining Prosperity in an Ageing Society: Background Report*, Paris.

OECD (1998c), *The Retirement Decisions in OECD Countries*, ECO/CPE/WP1 (98)2, February, Paris.

OI, W. (1962), "Labor as a Quasi-fixed Factor", *Journal of Political Economy*, June, pp. 538-555.

PODGURSKY, M. and SWAIM, P. (1987), "Job Displacement Earnings Loss: Evidence from the Displaced Worker Survey", *Industrial and Labor Relations Review*, October, pp. 17-29.

WARR, P. (1994), "Age and Job Performance", in Snel, J. and Cremer, R. (eds.), *Work and Ageing: A European Perspective*, Taylor and Francis, London.

WELCH, F. (1979), "Effects of Cohort Size on Earnings: The Baby Boom Babies' Financial Bust", *Journal of Political Economy*, October, pp. S65-S97.

WILLMS, J.D. (1997), "Literacy Skills of Canadian Youth", Statistics Canada, Ottawa, May.

CHAPTER 5

Working hours: latest trends and policy initiatives

A. INTRODUCTION AND MAIN FINDINGS

1. Introduction

In recent years the debate over working hours has intensified in many OECD countries. Full-time employees in Anglo-Saxon countries, particularly those in the more skilled occupations, have been concerned about long working hours and their effects on family and community life. In some European countries where unemployment has been stubbornly high, interest has re-emerged in the potential of so-called "work-sharing" policies – reducing the average hours of work per person employed in order to increase the numbers of people in employment. Almost all countries have seen some increase in employee demand for non-standard working arrangements, notably part-time working, though concerns have been expressed about the quality of such jobs and the career prospects they offer.

Employers have shown sustained interest in enhancing the flexibility of working-time arrangements. This has almost always been a feature of such negotiated reductions in hours of work that have occurred. Increased flexibility has been seen not only as a means of reducing costs, for example by matching labour input more closely with that needed for production and avoiding overtime payments, but also as part of more wide-reaching changes in working arrangements, designed to increase the capacity of firms to innovate and to adapt to rapid changes in product markets.

Government policy has been focused, in general, on accommodating increases in the flexibility of working time. The aims have been both to promote the competitiveness of firms, and thereby employment, and also to accommodate individual aspirations for more diverse working arrangements. In addition, Japan has carried out a series of measures designed to achieve a substantial reduction in working hours. Recently, France began to introduce measures designed to reduce normal working hours with a view to raising employment levels, and similar policies are under active consideration in Italy.

This chapter documents changes in the duration and flexibility of working time, explores some of the causes for the changes, and discusses the scope for achieving increases in employment through decreases in normal working hours. "Normal hours" are taken to mean the level of hours beyond which overtime premia become payable. "Flexibility" is understood from the point of view of the firm, in the sense of working arrangements designed to meet the needs of the business, which allow hours to vary in ways which are not possible through the use of fixed-hours working by full-time workers alone. It encompasses overtime working, some part-time working, shift-working, and other forms of "unsocial hours" working, such as weekend, evening and night working.

Sections B and C document longer-term trends in the duration of working hours and in key forms of "flexibility". They are followed by three sections concerning the roles played by hourly productivity, employee preferences and government policies in determining working-time arrangements. Section G discusses the circumstances in which a reduction in normal hours might lead to an increase in employment.

2. Main findings

An examination of the trends in working hours over the past two to three decades suggests that:
– the long-term trend decline in average annual hours worked per person in employment has slowed significantly in recent decades in almost all OECD countries (Germany, Japan and the Netherlands are the main exceptions). In some countries, the decline appears to have stopped, in some others it continues mainly because of an expansion of part-time working, and in a few there has recently been an increase in hours;
– there has been a growing diversity in hours worked by employees. While the most commonly-reported workweek in OECD countries is still 40 hours, the proportion of employees working 40 hours has fallen. Many countries have seen increases in the proportion of men working very long and/or very short hours;

– part-time working has increased strongly in the large majority of countries. While a substantial proportion of part-time working can be considered to represent a form of flexible working, evidence is lacking of substantial, long-term increases in the other main forms of working practices providing flexibility to employers, such as shift-working and overtime working. However, in some countries, since the beginning of the current recovery, there may be indications of greater use of some forms of flexible working, including the annualisation of working hours;

– over the past three decades, the average rate of increase of hourly labour productivity has slowed in almost all OECD countries, restricting the scope for reductions in average hours without reductions in average earnings;

– the proportion of employees favouring reductions in hours of work has risen in most European Union countries, while there has been a long-term decline in the United States. However, in all countries, the preferences of most employees are still in favour of increased earnings, rather than reductions in hours;

– government policies in recent years have primarily been concerned to increase the flexibility of working hours. In particular, they have sought to widen the possibilities for the "annualisation" of working hours;

– some European countries, including Belgium and France, have introduced incentives for firms to reduce working hours while simultaneously increasing the size of their workforces. The take-up of most programmes of this type has been low, although schemes to encourage the hiring of part-time workers have achieved higher take-up rates. A few countries, including Belgium, Denmark and Finland, have seen substantial employee interest in innovative programmes using career breaks to provide temporary employment for unemployed people. However, few evaluations of any of these measures are available as yet; and

– there is little empirical evidence for the proposition that across-the-board reductions in normal hours of work imposed on firms will lead to the creation of large numbers of jobs.

B. TRENDS IN THE DURATION OF WORKING HOURS

1. The flattening trend in average working hours

Over the last three decades, the steady, long-term decline in average hours of work per person

employed, which Maddison (1995) has traced back over more than a century, slowed its pace in virtually all OECD countries, sometimes to the point of reversal (Chart 5.1). The chart illustrates the wide cross-country differences in both trends and levels. (Owing partly to differences in the type of source, the data are suitable for only the roughest comparisons of levels, as explained in Annex 5.A.)

Table 5.1 shows the degree to which the long-term decline in average annual hours of work per employed person has slowed down over the last three complete economic cycles.[1] The exceptions to this overall pattern are Japan, where the acceleration in the rate of decline can be attributed to recent government measures designed to reduce working hours, and Germany and the Netherlands, where the trend continued largely unchanged over the last two cycles, though at a lower rate of decline than that observed in the early 1970s. In the United States, the trend appears to have reversed, with the current level of annual hours close to that of the early 1970s. The increase in Sweden over the last cycle is due partly to the rising proportion of women part-timers working relatively long hours [Anxo (1995)] and partly to the sharp decrease in absences from work since the beginning of the last recession. The figures for the United Kingdom are influenced by the strong increase over the 1980s in the proportion of total employment represented by the self-employed, whose average hours are longer than those of employees.

These data reflect not only average weekly hours actually worked by full-time employees and by the self-employed, but also trends in paid vacations and in part-time working. In most European countries, the average number of days of paid vacation increased strongly from around 2 to 3 weeks in the mid-1950s to 4 to 6 weeks in the early 1980s. In the United States, the corresponding change was from around $1\frac{1}{2}$ weeks to $2\frac{1}{2}$ weeks [Green and Potepan (1988)]. However, from 1983 onwards, there have been few changes. According to EUROSTAT (1995a), the only change of any magnitude in EU Member States since 1983 has been an increase of just over one day of paid vacation in Germany (equivalent to a decrease of under 0.5 per cent in annual hours of work). In Japan, the average number of days of paid vacation actually taken has remained virtually constant, changing from 8.8 days in 1983 to 9.1 in 1994. For the United States, average paid holidays for full-time workers with five years tenure rose by just over one day between 1982 and 1993.

Part-time working, on the other hand, has made a significant contribution to recent trends in average annual hours. Table 5.2 presents the results of a shift-share calculation to determine what part of the

Chart 5.1.

Average annual hours actually worked per person in employment[a]

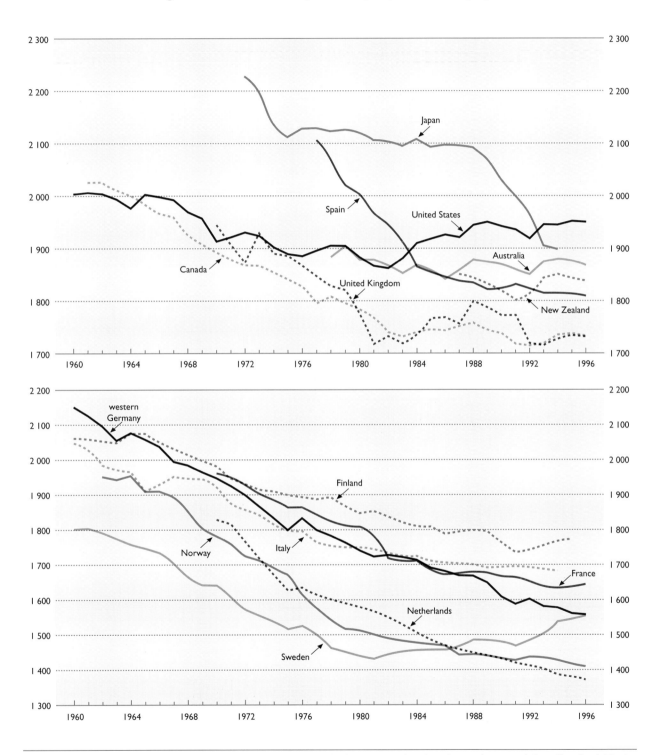

a) The concept used is the total number of hours worked over the year divided by the average number of people in employment, including self-employed. The data
   are intended for comparisons of trends over time. They are unsuitable for comparisons of the level of average annual hours of work for a given year, because of
   differences in their sources. Part-time workers are covered as well as full-time. Data for Italy and the Netherlands refer to dependent employment.
Source: OECD Annual Hours Database (see Table F of the Statistical Annex).

Table 5.1. **Trends in average annual hours worked per person in employment**

Average change from year to year

	Cycle[a]	Average change per year	Cycle[a]	Average change per year	Cycle[a]	Average change per year
Canada	1970-75	−9.6	1975-82	−12.5	1982-92	−1.3
Finland	1971-78	−8.0	1978-83	−12.6	1983-93	−8.5
France	1971-75	−21.7	1975-85	−19.6	1985-93	−4.7
Germany[b]	1971-75	−31.8	1975-82	−13.4	1982-94	−14.0
Japan[c]	1972-75	−41.2	1975-83	−3.1	1983-94	−19.7
Netherlands[d]	1972-75	−47.5	1975-83	−12.6	1983-93	−11.8
Norway	1970-75	−22.3	1975-82	−23.8	1982-90	−8.4
Spain	1971-75	..	1975-84	..	1984-93	−7.9
Sweden	1972-78	−16.4	1978-83	−2.1	1983-93	4.3
United Kingdom	1971-75	−2.6	1975-82	−24.1	1982-93	5.3
United States	1970-75	−5.3	1975-82	−3.9	1982-91	8.3

..   Data not available.
a)   The cyclical periods shown are taken from trough-to-trough. Years identified as troughs are those in which the Secretariat has identified a quarter corresponding to a trough in the growth rate of GDP. The growth rates during the trough-to-trough periods are estimated by a regression over time. The most recent trough years are provisional.
b)   Data refer to western Germany.
c)   Data for 1972 are used since data for the 1971 trough are not available.
d)   Employees only.
Sources: OECD Annual Hours Database (see Table F of the Statistical Annex) and OECD Statistics Directorate estimates of turning points (unpublished).

Table 5.2. **Contribution of part-time employment to recent changes in average annual hours of employees**[a]

Average change in hours from year to year

		Overall change in hours	Change attributable to:		
			Change in hours of full-timers	Change in hours of part-timers	Change in share of part-timers
Belgium	1983-1993	−7.5	−2.5	0.2	−4.9
Canada[b]	1983-1993	−1.1	0.7	0.5	−2.3
Denmark	1985-1993	−6.6	−7.1	−0.9	1.4
France	1983-1993	−4.1	0.4	0.7	−4.4
Germany	1983-1993	−10.9	−6.1	−0.9	−3.9
Greece	1983-1993	−1.0	−1.6	−0.4	1.3
Ireland	1983-1993	−7.4	−1.0	−0.4	−6.0
Italy	1983-1993	−3.7	−3.0	0.4	−0.9
Luxembourg	1983-1993	−2.1	−0.9	−0.1	−1.1
Netherlands	1987-1993	−6.6	0.0	3.2	−11.3
Portugal	1986-1993	−6.9	−6.5	0.6	−0.3
Spain	1987-1993	−6.0	−3.8	−0.4	−1.8
Sweden[b]	1987-1994	7.7	1.8	3.6	2.3
United Kingdom	1983-1993	−1.5	3.8	−0.5	−5.0
United States[b]	1983-1993	7.3	4.7	1.3	1.2
Unweighted average of above countries	1983-1993	−3.1	−1.4	0.5	−1.7

a)   The following formula is used to decompose the total change in hours:
H − h = (pr)(HP − hp) + (1 − pr)(HF − hf) − (PR − pr)(hf − hp) + (PR − pr)[(HP − hp) − (HF − hf)]
where H = (1 − PR)(HF) + (PR)(HP) and h = (1 − pr)(hf) + (pr)(hp)
h and H are the overall average hours of work in the first and second years, respectively, hp and hf are the average hours of part-time and full-time workers, in the first year, and pr is the proportion of part-time workers, in the first year, etc. The last term, not shown in the table, is the interaction term, which is generally small. It explains the difference between the first column and the sum of the other three. The figures shown are the sum of year-on-year changes, except where indicated.
b)   The results for Canada, Sweden and the United States are based solely on the two years shown and on the assumption that the ratio of annual hours of part-time workers to those of full-time workers is equal to the corresponding ratio for usual weekly hours (actual hours in the case of the United States). For Canada and Sweden, the results refer to all persons in employment.
Sources: EUROSTAT (1995a) for the European Union countries. For the other countries, the annual hours data are from the OECD Annual Hours Database. Supplementary data for Canada were taken from The Labour Force, various issues. For Sweden, data were supplied by Statistics Sweden. For the United States, data were taken from Employment and Earnings, various issues.

change in average annual hours of work can be ascribed to changes in the proportion of part-time working, and what part to changes in the average hours worked by full-time and part-time employees.[2] On the unweighted average for the fifteen countries shown, the average year-on-year decline of around three hours may be ascribed roughly equally to a decline in the working hours of full-time workers and to an increase in the proportion of part-time workers. However, the average conceals widespread variation between countries. All of the decline in France can be ascribed to increases in the proportion of part-time working. In Denmark, Italy and Portugal, virtually all the decline is attributable to falls in the hours of full-timers. The United Kingdom and United States are distinguished by sizeable increases in the hours worked by full-time employees.

2. Growing diversity of individual hours of work

Within the overall averages, there have been complex changes in the distribution of hours worked between individuals, reflecting an increased diversity of working schedules. Table 5.3 and Chart 5.2 show different facets of the changes in the distribution of "usual" weekly hours reported in labour force surveys. "Usual" hours refer to the hours usually worked in paid employment, including any overtime or extra hours that are usually worked. The concept is thus different from "normal" or "contractual" hours, which are specified in contracts of employment, and "actual" hours, which refer to hours actually worked. For international comparisons, usual hours have the advantage over actual weekly hours that they are not affected by special features of the survey week, such as public holidays.[3]

Table 5.3. **Usual weekly hours of work most frequently reported:[a] male employees in industry and services in their main job**

Hours and percentage working those hours

		1975		1980		1985		1990		1994	
		Peak	%	Peak	%	Peak	%	Peak	%	Peak	%
Australia[b]	major peak	40	42	40	32	40	22	40	20	40	18
Austria[c]	major peak	40	76	40	80	40	82	40	56	40	55
	minor peak	..	..	..	..	..	..	38	26	38	26
Belgium	major peak	..	..	..	..	38	46	38	55	38	53
	minor peak	..	..	..	..	40	27	40	21	40	23
Canada[d]	major peak	40	50	40	49	40	46	40	45	40	42
Denmark	major peak	..	..	..	..	40	77	38	56	37	60
Finland	major peak	..	..	..	..	35-40	77	35-40	76	35-40	71
France	major peak	..	..	40	..	39	50	39	53	39	55
Germany[d]	major peak	40	71	40	76	40	72	38	34	38	32
	minor peak	..	..	..	..	..	..	40	26	40	31
Greece	major peak	..	..	..	..	40	49	40	51	40	53
Ireland	major peak	..	..	..	..	40	64	40	53	40	32
	minor peak	..	..	..	..	35	25	..	..	39	22
Italy	major peak	..	..	36-40	54	40	60	40	57	40	51
Japan	major peak	43-48	32	43-48	30	43-48	28	49-59	25	35-42	26
Luxembourg	major peak	..	..	..	..	40	93	40	91	40	87
Netherlands	major peak	..	..	..	..	40	59	38	39	..	..
	minor peak	..	..	..	..	..	..	40	32	..	..
Norway	major peak	40-44	54	40-44	53	40-44	48	37-39	36	37-39	38
	minor peak	45+	28	45+	21	45+	24	45+	28	45+	26
Portugal[c]	major peak	..	..	..	..	45-49	54	45-49	47	40-44	27
	minor peak	..	..	..	..	40	21	40	25	..	..
Spain	major peak	..	..	41-44	33	40	45	40	76	40	71
Sweden[c]	major peak	..	..	..	..	40	63	40	61	40	58
United Kingdom	major peak	..	..	..	..	no peak	..	no peak	..	no peak	..
United States[e]	major peak	40	47	40	44	40	42	40	41	40	35

.. Data not available.
a) For example, for Australia in 1975, the data show that the most commonly reported level of hours was 40 and that 42 per cent of male employees reported working that number of hours.
b) Data refer to actual hours for all jobs, for all employed persons, in all industries, and are annual averages. 1976 instead of 1975.
c) 1976 instead of 1975.
d) 1987 instead of 1985.
e) 1993 instead of 1994.
Sources: Data for the EU-12 were supplied by EUROSTAT. All other data were supplied by national authorities.

Chart 5.2.

Proportion of workers working short and long usual hours, 1994 and 1985

Men

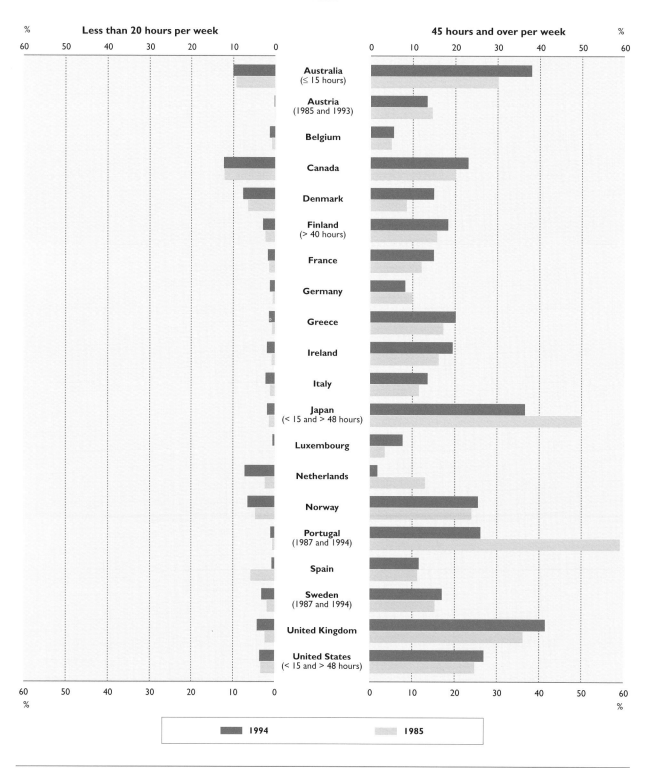

Chart 5.2. *(cont.)*

Proportion of workers working short and long usual hours, 1994 and 1985

Women

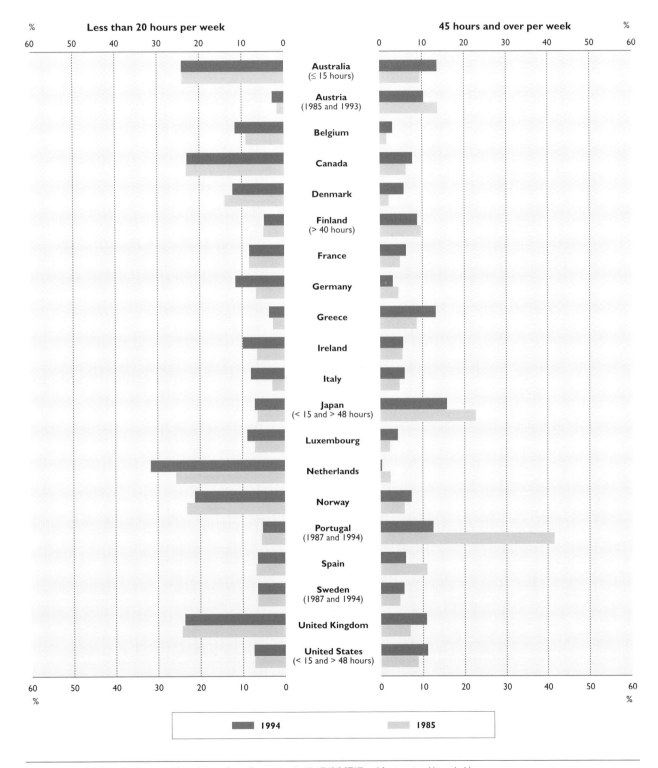

Sources: Data taken from the European Union Labour Force Survey supplied by EUROSTAT, and from national household surveys.

For men, the most frequently reported figure for usual hours in the main job is still 40 hours a week, in the majority of OECD countries (Table 5.3). However, since the beginning of the 1980s, there has been some decline in this peak value of usual hours for men in several countries including Denmark, Germany, Norway and Portugal. The largest falls are three hours for Denmark, to 37 hours, and two for Germany, to 38 hours (the figures for Norway are banded, so that the change cannot be assessed).

In many countries, the data suggest a widening in the distribution of usual hours, in the sense of a reduction in the proportion of men working the peak hours. For example, while "40 hours a week" was still the most frequent response in Australia in 1994, only 18 per cent cited it, as opposed to 42 per cent in 1975. An examination of the full distribution of hours indicates that, in almost all cases, this has been due to a tendency for slippage away from peak hours towards a lower figure. Canada, the United Kingdom and the United States are exceptions – the slippage from the peak figure of 40 hours has been upwards as well as downwards. For the United Kingdom, from 1985 onwards, it is no longer possible to identify a clear peak in the distribution of usual hours of work. Data for women also display a widening of the distribution, though the patterns are different because of the greater proportion of part-time working [Rubery *et al.* (1995)].

Another aspect of the diversification of working hours is that, in many countries, the proportion of men usually working long hours (defined as 45 hours and over) increased between 1985 and 1994 (Chart 5.2). The main exceptions were Japan (where there was legislation in favour of a general reduction in working hours), Portugal (where there were moves to five-day working), Austria, Germany and the Netherlands. There was also a widespread increase in the proportion of men reporting that they usually work short hours. For women, the picture is more mixed, with increases in the proportion of employees working long hours in just over half of the countries.

C. CHANGES IN "FLEXIBLE" WORKING ARRANGEMENTS

This section provides information on structural changes over the medium term in key forms of "flexible" working arrangements: part-time working, overtime working and shift-working, as well as indications of the direction of change in some of the other forms of flexible working mentioned above.

1. Part-time working

Many, but not all, forms of part-time working are likely to represent increases in flexibility, in the sense in which it is used in this chapter. Even when its schedules are fixed within the working day, part-time employment may add to flexibility if it can be arranged to coincide with peaks in labour requirements. This will not always be possible, *e.g.*, when part-time working is scheduled to allow mothers to work when their children are in school, as is common in Germany [Bosch (1996)]. Part-time working is also used to extend working hours into evenings, nights and weekends. For the European Union, calculations from the European Union Labour Force Survey (not reported here) show that, on average, one-third of all part-time workers work evenings, nights, weekends or shifts on a regular basis. This overall figure is slightly higher than for full-time workers. Compared with full-time workers, part-timers are particularly likely to work evenings, though less likely to work nights or shifts. They may also provide some forms of working hours flexibility at relatively low cost. In particular, extra hours worked by part-timers are very unlikely to attract overtime premia and may well be cheaper than the same hours worked by full-time workers. For most European countries, the proportion of part-time workers reporting having worked extra hours in any given week is roughly similar to that for full-timers [EUROSTAT (1997)].

Bielenski (1994) notes differences between types of part-time working which correspond to employers' perceived needs and those which respond to employees' wishes. In establishment surveys in a number of European countries, the majority of managers said that the primary reason for the introduction of part-time working was to meet the needs of the firm. In such circumstances, managers tended to favour shorter hours (under 20 a week), schedules which could be varied at short notice, and mainly saw a need for manual and low-skilled part-time workers. In the minority of cases where part-time working had been introduced in response to the wishes of employees, it was more likely to be characterised by longer hours and fixed schedules.

Since the beginning of the 1970s, most OECD countries have seen a growth in the proportion of the employed counted as working part-time (Table 5.4). In the Southern European countries, however, the figure has remained roughly constant at relatively low levels. In the Scandinavian countries, it may have reached a peak at the high level of around 25 per cent or more. In particular, for Sweden, there are signs of a fall in the incidence of part-time employment among women.[4]

While part-time working is associated particularly with service employment, in countries where there has been a rise in the proportion of part-time working it has occurred in all sectors [DARES (1997); OECD (1995); Walwei (1995)]. It has also increased

Table 5.4. **Part-time employment as a percentage of total employment, national and European Union definitions**[a]

	1973	1979	1983	1990	1993	1996
Australia	11.9	15.9	17.5 |	21.3	23.9	25.0
Austria	6.4	7.6	8.4	8.9	10.1	12.6
Belgium	3.8	6.0	8.1	10.9 |	12.8	14.0
Canada	9.7	13.8	16.8	17.0	19.1	18.9
Czech Republic	..	..	..	..	6.4	6.1
Denmark	..	22.7	23.8	23.3 |	23.3	21.5
Finland	..	6.6	7.7	7.2	8.6	7.9
France	5.9	8.1 |	9.6	11.9	13.7	16.0
Germany	10.1	11.4	12.6 |	15.2 |	15.1	..
Greece	..	..	6.5	4.1 |	4.3	..
Hungary	..	..	..	..	..	5.5
Iceland	..	..	..	..	27.3	27.9
Ireland	..	5.1	6.7	8.1 |	10.8	11.6
Italy	6.4	5.3	4.6	4.9 |	5.4	6.6
Japan	13.9	15.4	16.2	19.2	21.1	21.8
Luxembourg	5.8	5.8	6.8	7.0 |	7.3	7.6
Mexico	..	..	..	..	27.0	23.8
Netherlands	..	16.6 |	21.2 |	31.7 |	35.0	36.5
New Zealand	11.2	13.9	15.3	20.0	21.2	22.4
Norway	22.9	27.3	29.6 |	26.5	27.1	26.6
Poland	..	..	..	..	10.7	10.6
Portugal	..	7.8	..	5.9 |	7.4	8.7
Spain	..	..	..	4.9	6.6	7.7
Sweden	..	23.6	24.8 |	23.3 |	24.9	23.6
Switzerland	..	..	..	..	27.0	27.4
Turkey	..	..	..	20.6	27.7	23.9
United Kingdom	16.0	16.4	19.0	21.7 |	23.4	22.2
United States	15.6	16.4	18.4 |	16.9 |	17.6 |	18.3

.. Data not available.
\| Break in series.
a) These data should not be used for comparisons of levels because of differences in definitions. See Van Bastelaer, Lemaître and Marianna (1997).
Sources: OECD Full-time/Part-time Employment Database.

among both women and men. For men, the unweighted average for OECD countries has risen from under 5 per cent of total employment in the early 1970s to a current figure of 8 per cent, most of the increases occurring during recessions [OECD (1996a)]. For both sexes taken together, the proportion of part-timers in total employment has risen more strongly for the younger (under 25) and older (55 and over) age groups. One consequence of this interaction between age and the propensity to work part-time is that full-time workers in the 25-54 age bracket have become a larger proportion of total employment in virtually all OECD countries.

2. Paid and unpaid overtime working

Table 5.5 presents a number of indicators of trends in paid overtime, including the proportion of employees working overtime, weekly overtime hours per civilian employee and over-

time hours as a proportion of total hours. Despite the differences between the concepts, it is apparent that, where two indicators are available for the same country, their medium-term changes are similar.

There has been no uniform trend in paid overtime working. Italy and the United States are the only countries to show clear upward trends (in both cases the data apply only to manual workers). In Canada and the United Kingdom, movements appear to be largely cyclical. In Japan, the trend has fluctuated in direction: recent figures are close to those seen in 1975. For Australia, Finland, Germany and Japan, there are signs of a fall in overtime working over the recent cycle. In Germany, this is part of a long-term decline extending back to at least the 1960s. In some countries, annualisation may have tended to depress paid overtime working slightly over the recent period.[5]

Trends in paid overtime are not capable of explaining the widespread increases in the proportion of men reporting long hours in their main job (Chart 5.2). Hence, increases in unpaid overtime are clearly an important factor. For example, the proportion of professional and managerial workers in total employment is growing, and they are both likely to work long hours and to lack entitlement to overtime payments. Gregg (1994) shows that this is an important reason for the increase in hours of work since 1982 in the United Kingdom. Rubery et al. (1994) find that professional workers accounted for 18 per cent of men reporting usual weekly hours of 45 or more in the European Community in 1991. According to Duchesne (1997), Canadian teachers, managers, administrators and professionals in natural sciences, engineering and mathematics are the most likely to report extra hours, which are generally unpaid.

3. Shift-working

Shift-working may be defined as a situation where one wage earner replaces another at the same task within a 24-hour period. There are many different types of shift-working, and its incidence varies by sector, size and type of production process. It tends to be more common in larger firms and in those with a higher degree of capital intensity [Anxo et al. (1995)]. Its characteristics tend to change over time. Anxo and Taddéi (1995) conclude that where shift-work has grown, the increase is generally due to the growth of discontinuous, two-shift work patterns (two shifts per 24 hours), as opposed to more traditional, continuous and semi-continuous work patterns. International comparisons must be made with great caution, especially as the data sources vary considerably and have different types of bias.[6]

Table 5.5. **Trends in paid overtime**

Percentages

	1970	1973	1975	1979	1980	1981	1982	1983	1984	1985	1986	1987	1988	1989	1990	1991	1992	1993	1994	1995	1996	1997
A. All industries																						
Australia																						
Percentage of employees in survey working overtime	..	..	..	..	19.7	21.1	20.4	17.4	16.7	19.9	19.4	19.4	20.2	21.1	20.3	17.7	16.9	17.9	18.4	17.5	16.7	..
Weekly overtime hours per employee in survey					1.4	1.5	1.5	1.2	1.1	1.3	1.3	1.3	1.4	1.6	1.5	1.2	1.2	1.2	1.3	1.3	1.2	..
Canada																						
Weekly overtime hours per employee								0.36	0.37	0.39	0.39	0.46	0.51	0.51	0.47	0.39	0.37	0.40	0.44	0.46	0.51	0.59
Finland																						
Percentage of employees working overtime									9.6	10.2	9.8	9.9	9.9	10.3	9.6	8.7	7.9	7.4	7.7	8.8	8.0	8.2
Weekly overtime hours per employee									0.68	0.80	0.77	0.79	0.79	0.81	0.78	0.66	0.61	0.60	0.62	0.71	0.62	0.67
Germany																						
Weekly overtime hours per employee	3.0	2.4	1.9	1.8	1.5	1.4	1.3	1.2	1.3	1.3	1.3	1.2	1.2	1.3	1.3	1.3	1.2	1.1	1.3	1.3	1.2	1.2p
Overtime hours as proportion of total annual hours	8.3	7.0	5.7	5.4	4.7	4.5	3.8	3.8	4.0	4.1	4.1	3.8	4.0	4.3	4.4	4.2	4.0	3.8	4.4	4.6	4.2	4.3p
Japan																						
Weekly overtime hours per employee	3.9	3.6	2.4	3.0	3.1	3.1	3.0	3.1	3.3	3.4	3.3	3.4	3.6	3.6	3.6	3.4	2.9	2.6	2.5	2.6	2.8	..
United Kingdom																						
Percentage of male employees working overtime		45.3	41.5	42.6	39.3	33.5	35.0	35.5	37.6	39.1	39.1	38.6	39.6	40.4	38.9	35.4	35.0	34.0	35.1	35.2	34.8	35.4
Weekly overtime hours per male employee		4.5	3.8	4.3	3.8	2.9	3.1	3.0	3.3	3.5	3.4	3.4	3.6	3.8	3.6	3.0	3.1	2.9	3.1	3.2	3.1	3.2
B. Manufacturing																						
Australia																						
Percentage of employees in survey working overtime					29.2	29.7	28.9	23.7	28.0	33.2	33.5	34.4	37.2	39.1	36.5	30.3	32.3	33.8	37.9	33.9	32.1	..
Weekly overtime hours per employee in survey					2.2	2.3	2.2	1.8	2.2	2.7	2.5	2.6	2.9	3.3	3.0	2.3	2.5	2.7	3.2	2.9	2.7	..
Canada																						
Weekly overtime hours per employee								0.91	0.94	0.97	0.99	1.25	1.35	1.30	1.17	1.02	1.09	1.26	1.39	1.33	1.35	1.70p
Finland																						
Percentage of employees working overtime									10.5	11.8	11.3	11.7	11.4	12.5	11.1	9.1	9.6	9.8	10.0	11.3	10.6	11.5
Weekly overtime hours per employee									0.82	0.96	0.95	0.99	0.97	1.07	0.94	0.72	0.78	0.86	0.88	1.01	0.90	1.04
Italy																						
Overtime hours as proportion of total hours worked (manual workers in large industrial firms only)		4.6	2.8	2.9	3.2	3.0	2.8	3.0	3.4	3.7	4.3	4.4	..	5.6	5.1	5.1	4.6	4.4	4.6	5.5	5.0	5.4p
Japan																						
Weekly overtime hours per employee	4.4	3.9	2.1	3.6	3.8	3.7	3.6	3.7	4.2	4.2	3.9	4.0	4.5	4.6	4.5	4.2	3.3	2.8	2.8	3.1	3.4	..
United Kingdom																						
Percentage of male employees working overtime	63.6	61.2	56.5	58.5	54.3	46.8	49.3	49.8	52.5	54.4	54.4	54.8	56.8	58.0	56.9	52.1	52.4	51.9	53.6	54.8	53.3	54.5
Weekly overtime hours per male employee	6.4	6.4	5.5	6.2	5.6	4.4	4.8	4.6	5.0	5.3	5.2	5.4	5.7	6.0	5.9	5.1	5.3	5.1	5.4	5.6	5.3	5.5
United States																						
Weekly overtime hours per employee (production or non-supervisory worker)			2.6	3.3	2.8	2.8	2.3	3.0	3.4	3.3	3.4	3.7	3.9	3.8	3.6	3.6	3.8	4.1	4.7	4.4	4.5	4.8

.. Data not available.   p = provisional data.

Sources: *Australia:* Data for 1985 to 1996 were supplied by the Australian Bureau of Statistics from the Survey of Employee Earnings and Hours. Data for 1980 to 1984 are from the Australian Bureau of Statistics, *Job Vacancies and Overtime, Catalogue No. 6354.0.* All data refer to May. All industries excludes the group agriculture, forestry, fishing and hunting. There is a series break from 1983 to 1984.
Canada: Overtime hours were supplied by Statistics Canada, from the Survey of Employment, Pay and Hours. Data on wage and salary earners are from the OECD Labour Force Statistics Database.
Finland: Overtime data were supplied by Statistics Finland from the Monthly Labour Force Survey, annual averages. The classification of industries changed in 1989 and 1995. Weekly overtime hours were calculated using 52 weeks.
Germany: Data were supplied by the Statistisches Bundesamt, as calculated by the Institut für Arbeitsmarkt- und Berufsforschung der Bundesanstalt für Arbeit (IAB). Data refer to western Germany. Weekly overtime hours were calculated using 52 weeks.
Italy: Data up to 1987 were taken from the *Bollettino Mensile di Statistica* and *Statistiche del Lavoro,* various issues. Data for 1991 to 1996 were provided by the Instituto Centrale di Statistica.
Japan: Policy Planning and Research Department, Minister's Secretariat, Ministry of Labour, *Yearbook of Labour Statistics.* All data refer to establishments of 30 or more employees.
United Kingdom: *New Earnings Survey, Part A,* Table 1. Up to 1983, data refer to male full-timers aged 21 years and over and afterwards to those on adult rates of pay. For manufacturing, data refer to manual workers.
United States: Data were supplied by the Bureau of Labor Statistics and taken from the January issue of *Employment and Earnings.*

The incidence of shift-working in the economy as a whole seems to be little different from what it was twenty years ago, at least for the countries for which data are available. In addition to the data shown in Table 5.6, which indicate some long-term decline for Germany and Japan, changes over time can be estimated from comparisons of data from the 1993 European Union Labour Force Survey with those from a supplement on Working Conditions to the corresponding survey for 1975. These results (not presented here) suggest a slight decline in the overall proportion of people saying they engaged in shift-working on a "usual" basis for Belgium, Italy and Luxembourg, and stability for Denmark, Ireland and the United Kingdom. The data in Table 5.6 for longer term trends in the manufacturing sector show a different pattern, with upward trends in France

(data for manual workers only), Norway, Sweden, and the United Kingdom. For Germany, the data indicate stability, and for Japan, a slight decline.

Since the end of the 1980s, there have been some indications of an increase in shift-working for several countries, particularly in manufacturing industries (Table 5.6).[7] This is corroborated by the results of two employer-based surveys for Europe. Data from the European Union *ad hoc Labour Market Survey*, reported in OECD (1997a), show a slight increase in shift-working over the period 1989-1994 in the majority of countries. Responses to the Cranet-E surveys [Cranfield School of Management (1996) and further data supplied by Cranfield School of Management] indicate that, on average, around 20 per cent of firms increased their use of shift-working in the three years up to 1995, as against only 6 per cent reporting a decrease.[8]

4. Patterns of flexible working time across industries

Industries show different patterns of flexible working. Table 5.7 shows the incidence of part-time working, shift-working, Saturday and evening working by 2-digit industry groups ordered according to their contribution to total employment growth in 11 countries of the European Union over the period 1984-1994. Shift-working is more common in primary industries and in transport and communications, with a smaller, but still substantial, figure in manufacturing. Among service industries, it is widespread only in "health, sanitation and other services". Part-time and Saturday working, by contrast, are concentrated in many of the services industries. Evening working is more evenly spread.

The varying concentration of the different forms of working time in the faster- and slower-growing industries gives some indication as to their future development. If the patterns of employment growth and decline seen over the period 1984-1994 in Europe continued, they would favour the growth of part-time and Saturday working. This is in line with the results of the European Union *ad hoc Labour Market Surveys* of 1989 and 1994, and the recent Cranet-E survey [OECD (1997a); Cranfield School of Management (1996)].

Table 5.6. **Employees engaged in shift work**[a]

Percentage of employees

	1975	1980	1985	1990	1993
All industries					
Australia	..	..	12.1[b]	..	13.9
Finland	..	..	15.1[c]	..	17.9
France[i]	..	11.0	11.6	12.5	11.6
Germany[d]	15.3	..	..	12.0[e]	..
Japan	..	12.8[f]	..	8.5[g]	8.4[h]
United States[i]	..	..	15.9	17.8[e]	..
Manufacturing					
Australia	..	..	13.8[b]	..	17.1
Finland	..	..	19.9[c]	..	24.9
France[i]	31.3[k]	27.5[l]	30.4[b]	34.1	..
Germany[d]	18.6	..	..	18.2[e]	..
Japan	..	15.5[f]	..	12.3[g]	12.3[h]
Norway	14.4	..	21.8	24.4	25.0[h]
Sweden	22.4	22.4	23.6	25.3	..
United Kingdom	14.9	15.4	15.5	16.4	16.6
United States[i]	..	..	17.9	19.4[e]	..

.. Data not available.
a) This table, designed to indicate changes over time, should not be used for comparisons of the level of shift-working.
b) 1986.
c) 1984.
d) Data cover western Germany and regular shift-workers only.
e) 1991.
f) 1979.
g) 1989.
h) 1992.
i) Data for full-time workers only.
j) Data for manual workers only.
k) 1974.
l) 1981.
Sources: *Australia*: ABS (1988 and 1994).
  France: Cette (1995).
  Finland: Statistics Finland, *Annual Labour Force Survey*, Autumn 1984 and 1993.
  Germany: Bosch and Stille (1995).
  Japan: Policy Planning and Research Department, Minister's Secretariat, Ministry of Labour, *Yearbook of Labour Statistics*. Data refer to enterprises of 30 or more employees.
  Norway: Golombek and Nymoen (1995).
  Sweden: Anxo and Sterner (1995).
  United Kingdom: Bosworth (1995) and *New Earnings Survey*.
  United States: Mellor (1986) and BLS (1991).

D. LONG-TERM TRENDS IN PRODUCTIVITY GROWTH AND HOURS

Trends in hourly productivity growth have an important bearing on the length of the work week. Assuming that the share of real national income represented by real compensation of employees remains constant, an increase in hourly productivity

Table 5.7. **Incidence of shift, evening, Saturday and part-time work for 2-digit industries, European Union, 1994**[a]

Percentages

	Proportion of employees engaged in:				Industry employment as proportion of total	Average annual employment growth rate 1984-1994
	Shift work	Evening work	Saturday work	Part-time work		
Business, computer, research	2.7	8.9	8.9	18.7	7.4	7.4
Health, sanitation, other services	13.8	16.7	23.2	29.9	12.1	1.3
Wholesale, retailing	3.0	8.0	29.4	23.2	13.2	1.0
Education	3.0	8.8	20.4	20.7	8.7	1.5
Public admin., extra-territ. orgs.	9.3	7.7	18.2	10.9	9.6	1.3
Recreational activities	4.3	19.9	22.3	29.0	1.6	3.1
Hotels, restaurants	9.0	33.2	43.2	32.3	3.5	1.3
Financial intermediation	1.3	3.3	10.3	9.4	2.7	1.3
Wood, furniture	4.3	4.6	7.7	6.4	1.8	1.9
Land and water transport	15.9	18.2	22.3	6.6	4.2	0.6
Instrument engineering	4.5	5.4	2.7	7.1	0.5	4.1
Paper, printing	12.6	14.0	9.1	11.8	1.9	0.9
Post and telecommunications	8.9	8.1	22.9	11.2	2.2	0.6
Rubber and plastic products	22.9	15.5	7.1	5.2	1.0	1.0
Water	6.4	6.4	10.3	4.8	0.2	0.1
Metal ores	5.2	2.6	2.6	0.0	0.0	−8.6
Oil and natural gas	10.8	18.9	11.8	3.4	0.1	−3.2
Coke, oil products, nuclear fuel	16.1	10.6	8.9	5.2	0.2	−2.1
Air transport	29.4	23.9	30.1	7.2	0.3	−1.4
Office machinery	5.4	8.0	8.8	3.4	0.3	−1.4
Other mining	8.0	6.7	9.1	4.6	0.2	−3.4
Non-metallic mineral products	17.0	9.5	10.7	4.1	0.9	−1.5
Coal mining	12.8	12.8	5.5	1.1	0.1	−15.9
Electricity, gas, etc.	8.7	5.7	7.9	3.4	0.9	−1.9
Insurance	1.4	6.5	7.7	9.5	0.8	−2.4
Chemicals	14.9	11.7	7.8	4.5	1.5	−1.3
Other transport equipment	8.9	8.3	3.5	2.5	0.8	−3.6
Food, drink, tobacco	12.8	11.3	19.9	9.2	2.7	−1.4
Motor vehicles	27.8	16.3	3.9	2.0	1.2	−3.5
Metal products	15.2	9.6	7.7	3.8	2.9	−1.7
Construction	1.7	2.4	7.1	4.2	6.5	−0.9
Agriculture, fishing	3.7	5.7	36.3	17.8	1.8	−5.8
Engineering	9.0	7.4	3.5	4.0	3.5	−3.2
Textile, footwear and clothing	10.1	5.6	6.9	6.4	3.1	−3.7
Weighted average, all industries[b]	8.1	10.5	18.0	15.6	98.6	0.3

a) Figures refer to the 11 countries for which data were available. Austria, Finland, Germany and Sweden are excluded. The data refer to people who report that they regularly work shift, evenings or Saturdays. For details of the special industrial classification, based on Nace Revision 2, see European Commission (1995b). The industries are ordered according to their contribution to total employment between 1984 and 1994 (this is approximately equal to the product of the last two columns).
b) The proportions do not add to 100 per cent because not all industry employment could be assigned to the categories of the classification.
Source: Data from the European Union Labour Force Survey were supplied by EUROSTAT.

may be reflected in an increase in average real wages (or other forms of employee compensation), a decrease in average hours, or a combination of the two. However, over the short-run, it is not clear which way the direction of causality runs – from productivity gains to hours reductions, or the other way round. White (1987) presents evidence for a small number of countries showing that rapid productivity gains tend to occur after a reduction in hours rather than before. This does not imply that reductions in hours are the primary cause of increases in hourly

labour productivity over the long-term. A deceleration in hourly productivity over the past three decades is apparent in all countries, irrespective of the trends in working time (Table 5.8).[9] However, it is possible that, following a technological advance, a re-organisation of working arrangements may be helpful in realising the potential productivity gains [OECD (1996a); Betcherman (1997)]. It is frequently argued that such re-organisations can be facilitated by reductions in average working time [Cette and Taddéi (1997)].

Table 5.8.   **Growth in productivity, worker compensation and hours worked**[a]

Average annual percentage changes

	Productivity	Compensation per worker	Annual hours per worker	Compensation relative to GDP		Productivity	Compensation per worker	Annual hours per worker	Compensation relative to GDP
Canada					**Netherlands**				
1961-1969	2.6	2.4	−0.7	0.6	1960-1969	..	..	..	..
1970-1979	2.0	1.4	−0.6	0.0	1970-1979	4.4	3.6	−1.6	0.8
1980-1989	1.5	1.1	−0.3	−0.1	1980-1989	2.4	0.0	−1.0	−1.3
1990-1996	0.9	0.2	−0.1	−0.6	1990-1996	1.5	0.4	−0.7	−0.4
Finland					**Norway**				
1960-1969	4.8	5.3	−0.4	0.9	1962-1969	4.9	4.6	−1.1	0.9
1970-1979	3.3	3.6	−0.7	1.0	1970-1979	4.8	3.6	−1.8	0.6
1980-1989	3.1	2.7	−0.3	−0.1	1980-1989	2.2	2.0	−0.5	0.4
1990-1995	2.9	2.0	0.1	−1.0	1990-1996	3.2	1.9	−0.3	−1.0
France					**Sweden**				
1960-1969	..	..	..	..	1960-1969	4.9	5.1	−1.0	1.2
1970-1979	3.7	4.0	−0.9	1.2	1970-1979	2.4	2.0	−1.4	0.9
1980-1989	2.9	1.1	−0.8	−1.0	1980-1989	1.2	0.8	0.3	−0.7
1990-1996	1.5	1.4	−0.2	0.1	1990-1996	1.9	1.7	0.8	−1.0
Germany[b]					**United Kingdom**				
1960-1969	5.2	4.9	−1.0	0.7	1960-1969	..	..	..	..
1970-1979	4.0	3.6	−1.1	0.8	1970-1979	2.8	2.0	−0.7	−0.1
1980-1989	2.2	0.8	−0.6	−0.7	1980-1989	2.0	1.3	0.1	−0.8
1990-1994	2.0	0.7	−0.5	−0.8	1990-1996	2.2	0.9	−0.4	−1.0
Italy					**United States**				
1960-1969	6.8	7.3	−0.6	1.0	1960-1969	2.9	3.1	−0.3	0.5
1970-1979	4.0	3.6	−1.1	0.7	1970-1979	1.0	0.7	−0.1	−0.2
1980-1989	2.6	1.2	−0.4	−1.0	1980-1989	0.8	0.9	0.4	−0.3
1990-1994	1.9	0.4	−0.2	−1.4	1990-1996	0.9	0.8	0.1	−0.1
Japan					**All countries (unweighted average)**				
1960-1969	..	..	..	..	1960s	4.6	4.7	−0.7	0.8
1972-1979	3.8	4.9	−0.7	1.8	1970s	3.3	3.0	−1.0	0.7
1980-1989	3.0	2.4	−0.3	−0.2	1980s	2.2	1.3	−0.3	−0.5
1990-1994	2.3	1.8	−1.7	1.2	1990s	1.9	1.1	−0.3	−0.5

..   Data not available.

a)   Productivity = real gross domestic product (GDP)/total hours worked per year by all persons in employment. Compensation per worker = total compensation of employees/total persons in employment. Annual hours per worker = total hours actually worked per year per person in employment, except for Italy and the Netherlands where it is per dependent employee. Compensation relative to GDP = total compensation of employees/real GDP. The percentage changes in the table were calculated using logarithms so that the following identity holds: change in productivity = |change in compensation per worker| − |change in annual hours per worker| − |change in compensation relative to GDP|.

b)   Data refer to western Germany; comparable figures for the whole of Germany for 1991-96 are respectively 2.5, 1.5, 0.0 and −1.0.

Sources: OECD Annual Hours Database (see Table F of the Statistical Annex) and OECD Analytical Database.

In the 1960s and 1970s, hourly productivity grew relatively fast, at the same time as the share of employee compensation in total national income was rising. This was reflected in both substantial average real employee compensation gains and in a marked shortening of working hours. By contrast, over the past 15 years or so, the relatively modest productivity gains (which occurred during a time when the share of employee compensation in national income often fell) have appeared mainly as increases in real compensation. Within this general pattern, there are large cross-country differences. In Sweden and the United States, recent productivity gains have been reflected almost entirely by higher average real employee compensation. In Germany, the Netherlands and, more recently, Japan, the balance has been more towards lower hours.

In order to test whether, over the short-term, changes in hourly productivity precede changes in hours, or *vice versa*, a Granger causality test was applied to the two series for those countries for which relatively long runs of data were available. Only for Germany were the results consistent with the presence of causality running from short-term changes in productivity growth to changes in the level of hours. The results for France, Sweden and the United Kingdom were inconclusive. For France and Sweden, the hours and productivity series were found to be independent, while in the United Kingdom, there appeared to be evidence of causality operating in both directions. Finally, for Canada, the results were consistent with a direction of causality from changes in hours to changes in productivity.

In sum, these findings appear consistent with the view that, over the long-term, given continued growth in average real earnings, hours reductions are constrained by long-term trends in hourly productivity growth. However, over the short-term, the situation may be different. In some cases, industrial relations systems may allow a smooth allocation of emerging productivity gains into rises in real earnings and reductions in hours of work. However, in other cases, reductions in hours may trigger changes in work organisation which are necessary to allow technological advances to be translated into increased productivity growth.

E.   EMPLOYEE PREFERENCES, COLLECTIVE BARGAINING SYSTEMS AND WORKING TIME

Other factors which may be important for explaining the wide differences between trends and levels of hours of work across countries are employee preferences, union objectives and the state of collective bargaining arrangements. This subsection begins by considering the possible effects of employee preferences.

Data on employee preferences, which are obtained from attitude surveys, must be interpreted with particular care. They are very sensitive to the precise wording of the questions, to individual circumstances and to the economic climate [Nätti (1995)]. With these *caveats*, international comparisons of preferences are possible on the basis of sets of similar surveys commissioned by the European Commission (Table 5.9).[10] The results can be compared with data on average annual hours of work compiled by EUROSTAT on a common basis for each country (see Annex 5.A).[11] An additional source of data is provided by surveys carried out under the auspices of the International Social Science Programme (ISSP) in 1989.

Countries in which average annual hours of work per person are already relatively low tend to be those in which the average preference for fewer hours is relatively strong, and that for higher earnings weak. In 1994, the correlation between the level of average hours and the desire for fewer hours was –0.69: with the desire for higher earnings, the correlation was 0.73. Results for 1985 are similar. Figures (not shown here) from the ISSP survey of 1989, covering Austria, Germany, Ireland, Italy, the Netherlands, Norway, the United Kingdom and the

United States, confirm this finding.[12] The correlations between reported average hours of work and the proportion of respondents replying that they would prefer "less hours and less pay" are –0.41 for all workers and –0.58 for full-time workers, again showing a tendency for workers in countries where hours of work are relatively low to display a stronger preference for reductions in hours.[13]

Both the data in Table 5.9 and the ISSP data show that many more people expressed a preference for increased earnings than for a reduction in hours. The same is true for Canada [Drolet and Morissette (1997)]. However, the direction of change in the European data is generally towards a preference for reduced hours. In 1985, on average, 62 per cent of people in the European Union said they would prefer "more earnings" as opposed to 31 per cent opting for "fewer hours". By 1994, only 56 per cent mentioned more earnings and 38 per cent mentioned fewer hours. An increased preference for a reduction in hours was apparent in all countries except Greece, Italy and Spain. It is interesting to note that the correlation between preferences in 1985 and the change in actual hours between 1985 and 1994 was relatively small (–0.35), although the sign is what might have been expected – on average, countries where the preference for hours reduction was stronger saw larger reductions in actual hours.

Bell and Freeman (1994) show that, over the longer term, employee preferences can undergo striking changes. On the basis of the ISSP data set, they note that United States employees showed a relatively strong preference for "more hours and more pay" (32.7 per cent of the workers responding) as against "less hours and less pay" (5.5 per cent).[14] German workers, on the other hand, had the lowest desire for "more hours and more pay" (13.5 per cent) and a relatively high preference for "less hours and less pay" (10.1 per cent). Comparing these ISSP results with others derived from roughly similar surveys in the early 1970s, the authors conclude that, over the period, the position of the two countries had reversed – in the earlier period, employees in Germany both worked longer hours than their US counterparts and indicated a greater desire for longer hours. The causes of these changes in preferences remain unclear, though changes in real earnings are likely to be relevant, as are patterns of taxation [Liebfritz et al. (1997)].[15]

The importance of collective bargaining is illustrated by the correlations between figures for the reduction of annual working hours per employee over the most recent cycle, shown in Table 5.1, and the indicators of collective bargaining developed in OECD (1997b). Of the twelve countries for which both sets of data are available, Sweden is distin-

Table 5.9. **Working hours and earnings preferences of workers, European Union, 1985 and 1994**[a]

| | Percentage of employees preferring: | | | | | | Average annual hours per employee | | |
| | More earnings | | | Fewer hours | | | | | |
	1985	1994	Ratio 1994/85	1985	1994	Ratio 1994/85	1985	1994	Ratio 1994/85
Belgium	58	48	0.83	36	40	1.11	1 643	1 603	0.98
Denmark	38	32	0.84	51	66	1.29	1 586	1 568	0.99
France	62	53	0.85	34	40	1.18	1 696	1 670	0.99
Germany	56	54	0.96	30	34	1.13	1 674	1 590	0.95
Greece	68	84	1.24	26	14	0.54	1 803	1 803	1.00
Ireland	78	59	0.76	19	37	1.95	1 815	1 747	0.96
Italy	55	54	0.98	39	39	1.00	1 710	1 682	0.98
Netherlands	46	43	0.93	47	52	1.11	1 654	1 447	0.87
Portugal	82	58	0.71	11	35	3.18	1 871[b]	1 847	0.99
Spain	64	70	1.09	31	24	0.77	. .	1 741	. .
United Kingdom	77	62	0.81	19	32	1.68	1 684	1 683	1.00
Unweighted average	62	56	0.90	31	38	1.20	1 696	1 671	0.99

. . Data not available.
a) Figures exclude people unable to choose between more earnings and fewer hours, and non-respondents.
b) Data refer to 1986.
Sources: Data on preferences are from the European Commission (1986, 1995a). Data on annual hours worked were calculated by EUROSTAT using a common method for each country and supplied to the Secretariat.

guished by the fact that reductions in working hours have not been an major aim of the trade union movement there [Campbell (1989). For the 11 remaining countries, there are negative correlations between changes in hours, on the one hand, and trade union density, coverage of collective bargaining and centralisation, on the other hand (the figures are –0.43, –0.68 and –0.65, respectively).[16] This reflects a tendency for those countries where collective bargaining is more developed to have shown a faster decline in working hours.

Overall, these data are consistent with the proposition that employee preferences do explain part of the differences between hours of work across countries, and that collective bargaining arrangements are also important. In addition, while there may be a threshold beneath which the desire for fewer hours becomes weaker, the available data give no indication that it has been reached in European countries.

F. GOVERNMENT POLICIES ON WORKING TIME: WHAT ROLE HAVE THEY PLAYED?

This section surveys the main directions of recent policies on working time. It covers initiatives designed to: regulate the duration of working time; allow for greater flexibility in working arrangements; modify incentives for adopting different forms of working arrangements, *via* the tax and social security

system; and provide incentives for a reduction in working time coupled with increases in employment. In each of these areas there have been significant changes in a number of countries.[17]

1. Regulations on the duration of normal and maximum working hours, and on overtime

While regulations on working hours are often extremely complex, they generally contain the following elements: normal hours of work, beyond which overtime premia become payable; maximum permitted overtime hours; maximum total hours (generally equal to normal hours plus the maximum permitted overtime hours); and the overtime premium or premia to be paid. Table 5.10 shows that these regulations differ widely across countries. For example, in a few countries, there are no legislative limits on the maximum number of weekly hours of work (except, perhaps, through regulations on minimum rest periods, not included in the table). It should be noted that, in many countries, national legislation is modified by collective agreements.

Over recent years, there have been only a small number of instances of nation-wide changes in the legislation on the duration of working hours, though others may be forthcoming. In Japan, a "Five-year Plan for Improvement of Living Standards" was approved by the Cabinet in July 1992. This advocated an early shift to a 40-hour week through a revision of the Labour Standards Law: statutory

Table 5.10. **Legislative limits on normal weekly hours of work and overtime work**

	Legal maxima			Premium for overtime hours	Normal weekly hours set by collective agreements
	Normal weekly hours	Weekly overtime hours	Maximum weekly hours		
Australia	38-40	none	none	50% for first 4 hours, 100% thereafter	35-40
Austria	40	5 (10 during 12 weeks per year)	50 (60 in some circumstances)	50%	36-40
Belgium	40	10	50	50% for hours worked during the week 100% for hours worked during the weekend	38
Canada	40-48	none	none	generally 50%	35-40
Czech Republic	40.5	8	51	25%	
Denmark	37	none	48	50% for 1 hour; rising to 100%	37
Finland	40	5	45	50% for 2 hours, then 100%	37.5-40
France	39	9	48	25% for first 8 hours, then 50%	39
Germany	48	12	60	25%	35-39
Greece	40	8	48	25% for the first 60 hours per year 50% for the second 60 hours per year	40
Hungary	40	12 (typically 8 hours)	52	50%	
Ireland	48	12	60	25%	38-40
Italy	48	12	60	10% plus 15% for unemployment fund	36-40
Japan	40	none	none	25%	40-44
Korea	44	12	56	50%	
Luxembourg	40	8	48	25% for blue-collar, 50% for white-collar	40
Mexico	48	9	57	100%	
Netherlands	45	15	60 (maximum average over 13 weeks is 48)	no legislation on premium	36-40
New Zealand	40	none	none	no legislation on premium	40
Norway	40	10	50	40%	37.5
Portugal	40	12	54	50% for first hour, then 75%	35-44
Spain	40	2 (average 80 hours per year)	47		38-40
Sweden	40	12 (maximum 200 hours per year)	48 or 52	no legislation on premium	40
Switzerland	45 or 50	16	61 or 66	25%	40-42
Turkey	45	3 hours per day, 90 days per year (i.e. 270 hours per year)		50%	
United Kingdom	none	none	none	collectively-bargained	34-40
United States	40	none	none	50%	35-40

Australia: Working-time is generally regulated by industrial awards. The maximum number of normal hours can also be prescribed in State legislation (which generally provides that normal hours of work shall not exceed an average of 40 hours per week).
Austria: Collective agreements may permit up to 10 additional overtime hours (e.g. in hotels and restaurants or transport services). Work agreements may permit hours of overtime during 12 weeks up to a weekly working time of 60 hours to prevent severe economic detriments, if other measures are not feasible. The Labour Inspectorate may permit a larger number of overtime hours. There are many exceptions to the maximum weekly hours rule, which allow 60 hours and more. The average maximum weekly working time must not exceed 48 hours over a reference period of 4 months, which may be extended by collective agreement up to 1 year.
Belgium: Normal weekly hours (or less where there is a collective agreement) must be maintained, on average, over the specified reference period. The reference period is legally one quarter, but may be up to one year under a collective agreement. The maximum permitted overtime is 65 hours over a quarter.
Canada: Normal weekly hours vary from 40 hours in some provinces to 48 hours in others.
Denmark: Normal weekly hours of 37 and overtime premiums have been established through collective bargaining.
Finland: Maximum weekly overtime hours are based on an averaging of permitted maxima of 250 hours of overtime annually.
Germany: Weekly hours limits are based on a six-day week. Overtime is limited to 2 hours per day.
Hungary: Legislation specifies an 8 hours per day threshold before overtime hours. A five-day week is assumed. Maximum overtime hours are 8 per four working days; 144 hours per year if no collective agreement; 200 hours per year by general collective agreement; and 300 hours per year by collective agreement at branch level.
Italy: Weekly hours limits are based on a six-day week. Overtime hours are limited to 2 hours per day.
Luxembourg: The weekly overtime limit is based on a daily limit of 2 hours applied over a five-day week.
Mexico: Beyond 9 hours, the premium for overtime rises from double to triple time and sanctions can be imposed on the employer.
Portugal: Weekly overtime hours are based on a maximum of 2 hours daily over a six-day week. The maximum overtime hours per year is 200.
Sweden: The weekly limit on overtime hours is a weekly average of the limit on overtime hours of 48 hours in 4 weeks. The 48 hour weekly maximum is by collective agreement.
Switzerland: Normal weekly hours are 45 for those employed in industrial enterprises and white-collar workers and 50 for individuals employed in crafts or construction. The limit on overtime hours is based on a maximum of 61 or 66 hours per week.
Turkey: Overtime hours are limited to 3 hours per day over a maximum of 90 days. Normal weekly hours are often worked over fewer than 6 days, so that overtime hours are usually limited to 15 hours per week.
United States: Figures refer only to those workers considered to be paid hourly.
Sources: Data were supplied by national authorities on the basis of a questionnaire sent to all OECD Member countries, and were taken from European Commission (1996) and Blanpain (1990).

working hours were reduced to 40 hours during the period 1 April 1994 to 1 April 1997, depending on the type of activity. In the Netherlands, legislation adopted in the Spring of 1996 involved a reduction in normal weekly hours from 48 to 45. In Portugal, normal weekly hours for office workers were reduced from 42 to 40 hours in December 1996, with a reduction to 40 hours for other groups of workers in December 1997. At the international level, in November 1993 the Council of Ministers of the European Union adopted a directive according to which the average working time for each seven-day period, including overtime, is limited to 48 hours. However, only the changes in Japan were designed to have a major effect on actual working hours.

Recently, the French government has introduced legislation to reduce normal weekly hours to 35 by the year 2000 for firms with 20 or more employees, two years later for the remainder, partly with the aim of increasing levels of employment (see the Box for further details). In October 1997, the Italian government announced its intention to reduce hours of work to 35 hours by 2001, again giving special treatment to smaller firms, and also with increases in employment as one of the aims. However, no legislation has yet been introduced in Italy. A discussion of the possible effects of this type of policy is reserved for the next section.

Apart from national legislation, working hours have been reduced through collective agreements, either at the branch or enterprise level. In general, these have been accompanied by provisions to enhance working-time flexibility. A particularly significant example is the 35-hour week operated by the metal-working industry of western Germany from October 1995 onwards. Since 1984, consecutive bargaining rounds in this branch have resulted in reductions in working-time combined with

---

Legislation in favour of reduced working hours in France

The law *d'orientation et d'incitation relative à la réduction du temps de travail*, enacted in May 1998, includes the following provisions:

- the normal working week (*durée légale du travail*) falls from 39 to 35 hours on 1 January 2000 for enterprises with more than 20 employees, and on 1 January 2002 for the remainder;
- any consequent effects on earnings are left for negotiation between the social partners (special arrangements may be made for firms which have no union representatives);
- financial incentives are granted to firms whose hours of work, for part or all of their workforce, are reduced to 35 hours, or a lower figure, before 1 January 2000 (1 January 2002 for firms with 20 employees or less), through an agreement negotiated at enterprise or establishment level. A number of conditions apply. The reduction in working hours must be at least 10 per cent, and must be combined with net hiring of 6 per cent of the number of people whose hours are reduced or, alternatively, the preservation of the same number of jobs previously scheduled to be lost through a redundancy plan. The total number of jobs must be maintained for at least two years. The agreements are to lay down the scale and scheduling of the reduction in hours and the creation or preservation of jobs, as well as any changes in working arrangements. Special arrangements may be negotiated for managers (*cadres*), part-time and shift workers. The financial incentive is a flat-rate deduction of employer social security charges, ranging between FF 5 000 and FF 9 000 per year for each employee whose hours have been reduced and lasting for up to five years, at a reducing rate each year. A higher system of incentives applies to firms making further cuts in hours (at least 15 per cent in total) coupled with higher levels of job creation (at least 9 per cent in total) before 1 January 2003. Incentives may also be higher for firms which undertake to make more than the minimum number of hirings (especially in the case of small firms) or if the hirings are done entirely on the basis of indefinite contracts, for firms whose employees contain a high proportion of blue-collar workers or workers whose pay is close to the minimum wage, and for firms making an engagement to hire young people, handicapped people or the long-term unemployed. The public sector, and certain private sector firms with strong links to the public sector, are excluded from the current legislation.
- A report on the workings of the new provisions will be presented to the Parliament by September 1999. This report will draw on this information to propose ways in which certain provisions of the law will be implemented, notably the overtime rates applying to hours worked above 35 but below 39 per week, the regulations relating to the organisation and "modulation" of working time, ways of encouraging voluntary part-time working, the place of professional training in the negotiations, and special arrangements applying to managers.

provisions for greater flexibility, including the annualisation of working hours. Agreements to reach the
35-hour week by 1995 were also reached in a number of other industries, including steel and printing.
The paper industry reached the 35-hour level in
1997 and several other industries were scheduled to
do likewise in 1998, including the timber and news-
paper industries. At least a quarter of the workforce
of western Germany now enjoys a normal working
week of 35 hours [EIRR (1995)].

Many recent agreements for reductions in normal hours at branch or enterprise levels have been
associated with earnings reduction or moderation,
and increases in the flexibility of working hours, with
the aim of avoiding lay-offs. One example is the
agreement reached in the German metal-working
industry in 1994 to permit employees and employers, in such cases, to reduce working-time to a minimum of 30 hours a week.

2. Regulations on the flexibility of working-time

Over recent years, the main thrust of policy has
been to accommodate greater flexibility in working-
time arrangements. Part of the reason for this has
been to enable firms to match labour inputs more
closely with requirements, and to allow the extension of operating and opening hours. In a number of
countries, the treatment of weekend, evening, night
and overtime working has been the subject of legislation and/or collective bargaining at the branch
level. For example, in Italy, several sectoral agreements in 1994 permitted greater recourse to Saturday and Sunday working. In Germany, the Working-
time Act of 1994 reduced some of the restrictions on
Sunday working and, following legislation passed in
other countries since the mid-1980s, lifted restrictions on night working by women.

Another facet of recent policy developments
has been measures to facilitate reductions in labour
costs through the averaging and annualisation of
working time. Under annualisation, employers may
set normal weekly hours at varying levels over the
year, subject to a fixed annual total. Only when
these limits are exceeded do overtime premia
become payable. The "modulation" of hours over
the year may be organised in different ways. The full
schedule of hours may be fixed in advance, or there
may be a "working-time corridor" of minimum and
maximum hours of work, with overtime payments
being paid when the average level of weekly or
daily hours, taken over the year, exceeds an agreed
limit. Annualisation may be thought of as a special
case of "averaging" in which the reference period is
a year. In general, three key elements in the averaging of working hours are the "unit" of worktime
employed as the basis of the averaging procedure,

the "reference period" over which the averaging is
done, and the "limitations" that apply.

Table 5.11 shows conditions under which hours
averaging may be applied. In most cases, the possibility of such arrangements has been established
through amendments to legislation, in others
through collective bargaining at the national
(Denmark) or branch level (Germany and Italy). The
working-time unit is generally a week of normal
working hours, though sometimes it is a day. In
some countries, no working-time unit is prescribed
at the national level and branches enjoy considerable freedom in its determination (Germany, Italy,
and the United Kingdom). The reference period is
one year in Belgium, France, Italy, Japan, Norway,
Spain and Switzerland. In other countries it is generally, though not always, less than a year, ranging
from 2 to 3 weeks in Finland and Luxembourg, to
6 months in Germany and Denmark.

Data on the incidence of annualisation are
available from Cranfield School of Management (1996). In response to a 1995 survey of a number of large firms in 15 European countries,
10 per cent said they had increased their use of
annualisation over the previous three years, as
against 3 per cent who said their use had decreased.
Around 60 per cent of firms said that the practice
was not used. Comparatively large increases in the
number of firms reporting the use of annualisation
were reported in Finland, Germany, the Netherlands
and the United Kingdom.

3. Social security thresholds

The distribution of working hours may be influenced by earnings or hours thresholds that apply to
the liability for contributions to social security
schemes and the eligibility for benefits. Where such
thresholds apply to the lower part of the hours distribution, they may affect the rate of part-time working. Other things being equal, a threshold on
employers' social security contributions is likely to
give an incentive to create disproportionate numbers of jobs with hours (or earnings levels) just
under the threshold. A threshold on employee benefits may give an incentive to work longer hours than
otherwise desired. It may also cause opposition to
cuts in working hours likely to bring hours below the
threshold (though this will also depend on whether
the cuts also remove the liability to contributions).

Currently, only a small number of countries set
thresholds on the payment of employers' social
security contributions. In Germany, no contributions
are payable for work of less than 15 hours a week,
or under DM 620 monthly earnings. In the
United Kingdom, no contributions are payable on
account of employees earning under £64 per week.

Table 5.11. **Provisions for averaged/annualised hours of work**[a]

	Date of legislation	Working time unit used in averaging	Reference period[b]	Limitations
Austria	1997	Legal week (40 hours) or any shorter normal weekly working time which is provided for under a collective agreement	Unlimited; averaging schemes have to be permitted by collective agreement; if the reference period is more than one year, time off in lieu has to be granted in blocks of several consecutive weeks	9 hours per day; 10 hours if time off in lieu can be taken in blocks of several consecutive days or, in case of reference periods of more than one year, in blocks of several consecutive weeks; 48 hours per week or 50 hours per week if the reference period does not exceed 8 weeks
Belgium	1985	Legal week (40 hours) or shorter week provided under a collective agreement	1 quarter[c]	11 hours per day, 50 hours per week, maximum of 65 hours of overtime, at any moment
Czech Republic	1962 amendments 1991	Legal week (42.5 hours)	4 weeks[d]	9.5-12 hours per day, 120 overtime hours per year
Denmark	1990	Collective agreement Legal week (37 hours)	6 months	Must be agreed by employees on each occasion
Finland	1965 and 1996	Legal week (40 hours)	4 weeks	9 hours per day
France	1982, 1993	Legal week (39 hours)[e]	At least 1 year	44 hours per week or 464 hours over 12 consecutive weeks, or 10 hours per day and 48 hours per week
Germany	1994	Legal working day (8 hours) Agreed weekly hours by branch	6 months Unlimited[f]	10 hours per day, 60 hours per week
Hungary	1995	Legal working day (8 hours)	2 months	12 hours per day
Ireland	1997	Legal week (48 hours)	3 weeks[f]	56 hours per week
Italy	1923	Agreed weekly hours by branch	1 year	48 hours per week, 96 extra hours per year
Korea	1997	Legal week (44 hours)	1 month	12 hours per day, 56 hours per week
Luxembourg		Legal week (40 hours)	4 weeks for white-collar[g]/variable for blue-collar	10 hours per day
Netherlands	1996	40-hour week	13 weeks or 4 weeks	10 hours per day, 50 hours per week over 4 weeks; 9 hours per day, 45 hours per week over 13 weeks[h]
Norway	1977	Legal week (40 hours)	1 year	9 hours per day and 48 hours per week[i]
Portugal	1997	Legal week (40 hours)	4 months	Maximum of 2 additional hours per day; 50 hours per week[j]
Spain	1994	Legal week (40 hours)	1 year	9 hours per day, 45 hours per week; restrictions on rest periods
Sweden	1983	Legal week (40 hours)	4 weeks	No maximum specified
Switzerland	1966	Agreed weekly hours by branch (45 or 50 hours)	1 year[j]	61 or 66 hours per week, depending upon branch
Turkey	1971, 1983	Legal week (45 hours)	1 week	Five-day week: 9 hours per day or 45 hours per week / Six-day week: 7.5 hours per day or 45 hours per week
United Kingdom	No special regulation	Agreed weekly hours	Unlimited[k]	None

a) Maxima as laid down by labour legislation and by collective agreements at the national level.
b) The maximum period of reference may be lower in certain branches.
c) The period for averaging is normally a quarter, but it can be extended to 1 year by Arrêté royal (AR) or Convention collective de travail (CCT).
d) For some jobs with "an uneven intensity of work", the period of annualisation may be as long as 1 year.
e) Part-time hours may also be annualised.
f) Flexibilisation is only possible when associated with shift-work.
g) The Minister of Labour may specify the period for averaging, which can be extended up to one year in certain industries.
h) The basic legislated limit is that no more than 520 hours may be worked over 13 weeks. Under discretionary requirements, which require an agreement between the parties, a maximum of 200 hours can be worked per four-week period and 585 hours per 13-week period.
i) In certain situations the maximum daily hours can be extended to 10 and maximum weekly hours to 54.
j) Up to 40 hours may be carried over from one year to another.
k) Often 1 year.

Sources: Data were supplied by national authorities on the basis of a questionnaire sent to all OECD Member countries. Data were also obtained from the European Commission (1996); *European Industrial Relations Review*, various issues, 1994 and 1995; and other sources of information on collective agreements.

In France, as part of the system of measures to support low-paid employment, contributions in respect of family allocations are not payable under the threshold of 110 per cent of the minimum wage. For similar reasons, a reduction in the rate of contributions in Ireland is made at levels under Ir£173 per week.

Thresholds also often apply in respect of eligibility for three different types of benefits: health, old-age pensions and unemployment (Table 5.12).[18] The table reveals wide cross-country differences. Overall, Germany and Japan stand out as having the highest thresholds. The social protection systems of Greece, Hungary, the Netherlands, New Zealand, Norway and Spain, on the other hand, have very low thresholds or none at all.

The trend appears to be towards modifying thresholds so as to reduce their influence on the distribution of hours. Canada and Finland have both altered their arrangements for employer social security contributions, so that payments are now proportional to hours. The United Kingdom has moved to reduce the potential effect of employer social security contributions on the distribution of hours worked, by levying contributions above the bottom limit of £64 per week along a stepped scale, at the rate of 2 per cent of £64 plus 10 per cent of additional earnings between £64 and £440.[19] In 1994, Japan reduced the minimum number of hours necessary for eligibility for social benefits from 30 to 20 hours per week. In Canada, as of 1997, there is no longer a minimum threshold for unemployment

Table 5.12. **Thresholds for social security coverage**

	Public health benefits	Old-age pension benefits	Unemployment benefits
Austria	Sch 3 830/month	Sch 3 830/month	Sch 3 830/month (earnings above this level for at least 52 weeks over preceding 2 years)
Belgium	400 hours in preceding 6 months or 3 hours/day	4 hours/day	–
Canada	–	C$ 67/week or C$ 3 500/year	No weekly minimum as of January 1997
Czech Republic	–	–	22 hours/week
Denmark	–	9 hours/week for Supplementary Pensions and 15 hours/week for labour market pension schemes in certain sectors	37 hours/week for at least 52 weeks over preceding 3 years
Finland	–	–	18 hours/week
France	200 hours in last 3 months	–	4 months contributions in last 8 months
Germany	15hours/week (45hours/month for blue-collars)	15 hours/week	18 hours/week
Greece	–	–	–
Hungary	–	–	–
Ireland	earnings over Ir£ 9 256	earnings over Ir£ 2 600	earnings over Ir£ 2 600
Italy	24 hours/week	–	–
Japan	20 hours/week	20 hours/week	20 hours/week
Netherlands	–	–	26 weeks work during previous 39 for basic benefit (52 days/year in 4 out of 5 previous calendar years for wage-related benefits)
New Zealand	–	–	–
Norway	–	–	–
Portugal	12 days in last 4 months	–	–
Spain	–	–	–
Sweden	SKr 6 000/year	SKr 6 000/year	17 hours/week
United Kingdom	–	£61/week	£61/week
United States	–	–	Depends on the State

Note: "–" means that there are no thresholds.
Sources: Data were supplied by national authorities on the basis of a questionnaire sent to all OECD Member countries; and taken from the OECD Taxes and Benefits database.

benefits (prior to that it was C$ 150, or 15 hours of work per week).

4. Subsidies and reductions in social security contributions targeted on lower working hours

A new policy orientation has emerged in several countries in the shape of incentives, paid either to employees or to employers, and occasionally to both, to encourage the reduction of working hours, with the primary aim of increasing employment and reducing unemployment. These innovations include: subsidies to encourage reductions of working-time at the enterprise level; voluntary reductions of individuals' weekly working-time; and long-term leave with replacement (Table 5.13).

Subsidies to encourage reductions in hours of work at the enterprise level in order to increase employment generally take the form of a reduction in payroll taxes, such as employer social security contributions. If paid at a flat rate (rather than as a proportion of earnings), as in the case of the subsidies recently announced by the French government in connection with the reduction of normal working hours from 39 to 35, they also have the effect of subsiding the employment of lower paid employees. As with marginal employment subsidies in general, they are likely to suffer from dead-weight and displacement effects [OECD (1996b)]. Dead-weight effects occur when firms benefiting from the subsidy intended to reduce hours and increase employment in any case. Displacement effects follow if the same firms are able to use the subsidy to reduce prices and take market share from competitors. There is also the danger that the extra jobs will be maintained only as long as the subsidies last. Owing to these possible effects, overall net employment gains may be significantly smaller than the gross rise in employment in participating firms. The net budgetary cost would then be correspondingly higher [Cette and Taddéi (1997)].

Empirical evidence about the performance of such schemes in practice is not extensive. In particular, estimates of their dead-weight and displacement effects are not yet available. The take-up rates for the schemes introduced in Belgium and France have generally been low, although a relatively high rate of take-up (2 per cent of eligible employees) has been achieved by the French Loi de Robien programme, introduced in 1996 [Table 5.13; Freyssinet (1997); DARES (1998a)], and a recent acceleration can be seen in the rate of take-up of some of the Belgian schemes. A preliminary evaluation of the Loi de Robien programme was undertaken for the Commission des Finances de l'Assemblée nationale (1997), on the basis of detailed studies of six large enterprises and a series of macro-economic simulations. The conclusion of the case studies was that the financial incentives had, in several cases, facilitated the introduction or extension of valuable modifications in working practices, or investments in skills. However, a much larger-scale employer survey involving both participating and non-participating firms would be required to assess the extent of the dead-weight and displacement effects. In addition, the question of the longevity of the jobs created or saved by the subsidy is raised by the fact that the subsidy is payable for seven years, but the jobs need only last for two. While the macro-economic simulations mentioned above suggested that the bulk of these jobs would be durable, the results of such simulations must be regarded as particularly uncertain. The actual situation remains to be assessed by means of follow-up studies.[20]

At least one of the schemes to encourage part-time working by means of subsidies to enterprises, introduced in France in 1992, has had a high rate of take-up, at just over 200 000 contracts a year (and 400 000 beneficiaries). This programme mainly involves low-paid workers in the service sector, for whom employers may receive a rebate representing up to 16 per cent of labour costs.[21] The substantial take-up no doubt also reflects the potential for further growth in this type of employment. The proportion of subsidised workers coming directly from the unemployment rolls is currently around a quarter of the total, and just under a quarter were previously out of the labour force [DARES (1997)]. As noted above, programmes of this kind are generally subject to substantial dead-weight and displacement effects. However, no empirical evidence on the size of these effects is available.

Recent years have seen a variety of innovative programmes designed to facilitate voluntary reductions in individual working hours, either through shorter working weeks or some form of career break (Table 5.13). These generally involve subsidies paid to both employees and employers (except when the employer is the State). Results so far, for example with respect to the Danish training, sabbatical and parental leave programmes, all of which involve the obligation to hire an unemployed person as a replacement, appear to indicate that the potential take-up of such schemes may be quite high. However, in a time of tightening labour markets, both the Danish sabbatical leave entitlement and the child-care leave programme have recently been made less generous, in terms of replacement income. Again, few if any evaluations of such schemes appear to have been carried out.

Table 5.13. **Government measures designed to foster working-time redistribution**

		Incentives		Results/Take up
		to employees	to employers	
A. Collective working-time reductions				
Belgium	*Plans d'entreprises de redistribution du travail* (since 1994). Firms create new jobs to compensate for reductions in individual working hours.	None.	Reduction of social security contributions by a maximum of BF 37 500 per extra employee, for 13 quarters.	637 enterprise plans approved by 30 April 1997, in which enterprises agreed to hire 5 654 extra employees.
	Accords pour l'emploi (Employment agreements). Reductions in working time are combined with at least one other measure designed to hire extra workers, without reduction in the overall volume of work.	None.	Reduction of social security contributions by BF37 500 per quarter per extra employee, for duration of agreement.	100 agreements in the private sector, agreed by joint committees at sectoral level, 220 in total at enterprise level.
Canada	In the province of Quebec, the duration of the standard work week is being progressively reduced from 44 to 40 hours, at a rate of one hour every year from October 1st, 1997 to the year 2000.	None.	None.	Not yet available.
France	*Aménagement et réduction du temps de travail: loi "de Robien".* [Organisation and reduction of working time (since 1996)]. Firms reduce the working hours of part, or all of their employees by at least 10% and create jobs in the same proportion for at least two years, or avoid job losses (in some proportion) already programmed for economic reasons.	None.	For a 10-15% hours reduction, a reduction in social security contributions of 40-50% for the first year and 30-40% for the following 6 years.	At 30 Sept 1997, 1 144 agreements (795 "offensif", involving job creation; 349 "defensif", involving job retention), reducing working time of 121 137 employees and creating or preserving around 12 000 jobs (gross of deadweight and displacement effects).
B. Voluntary reductions in individual working-time				
Austria	*Solidaritätsprämienmodell.* From 1998, collective or works agreements may permit reduction of normal working hours in order to recruit registered unemployed persons. Reductions have to be agreed between the employer and each employee.	Employees working less than normal hours receive a proportion of unemployment benefit; employment rights are maintained.	None.	Not yet available.
Belgium	*Interruption de carrière à temps partiel* (part-time career break). A full-time worker reduces his working time by between 80 and 50%, being replaced by a previously unemployed person.	Monthly, flat-rate benefit between BF 2 413 and BF 6 033, depending on the size of the reduction.	Temporary reduction in employers' social security contributions for hiring unemployed person.	At December 1996, 32 470 workers had reduced their working time in this way.

Table 5.13. **Government measures designed to foster working-time redistribution** *(cont.)*

		Incentives		Results/Take up
		to employees	to employers	
	Prépension à mi-temps (early pension at half-time working). Employees aged 55 and over may reduce their working time to half-time, the other half being worked by a previously unemployed person.	Unemployment benefits and a complementary payment from the employer.	Reductions in employers' social security payments for hiring unemployed person.	In 1996, there were 190 beneficiaries of the programme, on average.
	Redistribution du travail dans le secteur public (Redistribution of work in the public sector) (since 1995). Employees in the public sector are allowed to work 4 days a week at 80 per cent of previous earnings, provided that the remaining time in worked by a previously unemployed person. Those with permanent status may work half-time for up to five years before their normal retirement date, provided the time is replaced by a additional employee, with similar status.	Monthly allowance of BF 3 250, in addition to pay for hours worked. Monthly allowance of BF 11 940, in addition to pay for hours worked.	Not applicable.	7 000 employees (approximately 8 per cent of federal public sector employees) participated in the scheme at end 1995.

C. Part-time working

		Incentives		Results/Take up
		to employees	to employers	
Austria	From 1998, employers over 50 with family care responsibilities may reduce working time while maintaining employment rights, subject to employer's agreement. This must be given if there are more than 10 employees and the employee is entitled to a part-time pension (*Gleitpension*).	Employment rights are maintained.	None.	Not available.
Belgium	*Plans d'entreprises de redistribution du travail* (Enterprise plans to redistribute employment) (since 1994). Firms create new jobs to compensate for reductions in individual working hours (see *a)* above).	See *a)* above.	See *a)* above.	See *a)* above.
	Accords pour l'emploi (Employment agreements). Firms introduce part-time working, on a voluntary basis together with another measure designed to encourage hiring (see *a)* above).	See *a)* above.	See *a)* above.	See *a)* above.
	Promotion de la remise au travail de chômeurs à l'aide de la redistribution du travail. (Promotion of vocational reintegration for the unemployed through the re-distribution of employment). Workers who opt for part-time work receive an incentive (Flemish region only, up to end 1995).	3 000 to BF 5 000 per month for two years maximum, depending on the extent of hours reduction.	Unemployed workers receiving full benefits may be hired to make up lost hours.	6 048 persons during first quarter of 1997 (including the beneficiaries of the career break scheme).

Table 5.13. **Government measures designed to foster working-time redistribution** *(cont.)*

	Incentives		Results/Take up
	to employees	to employers	
Finland	*Part-time supplement* (since 1994). Employees reduce their working-time from 40 per cent to 60 per cent, with the agreement of the employer, for one year. An unemployed person must be recruited to the same position. The government pays half of lost wages, up to 1.7 times the unemployment benefit.	None.	3 500 unemployed people hired in 1995, mainly in the public sector.
France	*Abattement de cotisations sociales patronales pour les emplois à temps partiel* [Reduction of employers' social security contributions for part-time employment) (since 1992). Employers transform positions from full-time to part-time or hire part-time workers (with hours between 16 and 32). The volume of employment in hours must be maintained. None.	The reduction of social security contributions was 30 per cent as of April 1994, for jobs with duration between 16 and 32 % of normal hours. Since Septembre 1995, it can be combined with the abatement for low-paid workers.	More than 200 000 contracts have been signed each year.
Netherlands	The general principle of equal treatment, regardless of working time, was introduced in Labour Law in November 1996. None.	None.	Not available.

D. Long-term leaves with job rotation

	to employees	to employers	
Austria	*Bildungskarenz* (Training leave) and *Freistellung gegen Entfall des Arbeitsengelts* (career breaks), from 1998. Employees can take leave for a period between 6 months and one year, subject to the employer's agreement. Unemployment benefits. Employment rights are maintained.	None.	Not available.
Belgium	*Interruption complète de la carrière* (full-time career breaks) of between 3 months to a year, with replacement by previously unemployed workers. A special scheme applies in Flanders. BF 12 066 per month.	Partial exoneration of unemployment benefits on account of hiring of unemployed person.	At December 1996, 19 973 employees.
	Plans d'entreprises (Enterprise plans) (since 1994). Firms create job openings through promotion of career breaks. See *a)* above.	See *a)* above.	See *a)* above.
Denmark	*Orlov til uddannelse* (Education leave); *Sabbatorlov* (Sabbatical leave); *Orlov til bornepasning* (Parental leave) (since 1994). Workers can take leaves over a period of up to one year subject to agreement by the employer. Persons unemployed one year or more must be recruited in the case of sabbatical leave. Allowances of 100 per cent (educational leave) or 60 per cent (parental and sabbatical leave) of the maximum unemployment benefit which is 2 625 Dkr per week.	None.	1996: 121 000 (parental 47 000; educational 72 500; sabbatical 1 500) 1997 (Jan.-Oct.): 99 000 (parental 31 000; educational 67 100; sabbatical 900).

Table 5.13. **Government measures designed to foster working-time redistribution** *(cont.)*

		Incentives		Results/Take up
		to employees	to employers	
Finland	*Laki vuorotteluvapaa-kokeilusta* (Job rotation pilot scheme act) (since 1996). Full-time workers taking leave for between 3 months and one year receive an allowance if an unemployed person is hired.	Allowances of 60 per cent of unemployment benefits with a ceiling of 4 500 Mk per month.	None.	Not available.
Netherlands	*Wetsvoorstel financiering loopbaanonderbreking* (Cabinet proposal for an Act on the Financement of Career breaks, 1997). Workers taking a career break (between 2 and 6 months for reasons of care and/or training) will receive financial support on condition that the employer hires an unemployed worker (who received a benefit).	Financial support up to a maximum Gld 960 gross per month. Allowance depending upon the actual reduction of the number of hours worked.	None.	Not available (still a Cabinet proposal).
Norway	Job rotation scheme. Temporary employment as substitute for employee on leave, including further education for regular employees. Designed to aid unemployed people and those needing updating of skills.	Receipt of standard wages.	13 000 Nkr per month in respect of unemployed person taken on as substitute.	2 539 participants on average in 1996.
	Job rotation schemes in connection with care leave. Temporary employment to replace employees on care leave. Designed to help unemployed people, as well as parents.	Receipt of standard wages.	10 000 Nkr per month.	Not available.

Sources: *Austria*: Information supplied by the Austrian Ministry for Employment, Health and Social Affairs.
Belgium: Information supplied by the Ministère de l'emploi et du travail.
Denmark: Documents issued by the Ministry of Labour; *European Industrial Relations Review*, No. 246, July 1994, and *Employment Observatory, Denmark. Institutions, Procedures and Measures*, 1995.
Finland: Documents issued by the Ministry of Labour; and *European Industrial Relations Review*, No. 244, May 1994.
France: "Durée et aménagement du temps de travail", *Liaisons sociales*, No. 6959, 23 February 1994; "Loi quinquennale relative à l'emploi et à la formation professionnelle, texte intégral commenté", *Liaisons sociales*, No. 6959, 27 December 1993; and *Employment Observatory, Basic information report, France, Institutions, Procedures and Measures*, 1996.
Netherlands: Tweede Kamer der Staten Generaal, 1996-1997, 25477, 1-2. Bepalingen inzake de financiering van de loopbaanonderbreking (Wet financiering loopbaanonderbreking).
Norway: *Norwegian labour market policy, 1998*, Royal Ministry of Local Government and Labour, October, 1997.

G. THE EFFECTS OF REDUCTIONS IN NORMAL HOURS OF WORK ON EMPLOYMENT

This section concentrates on the question of the possible effects on employment of a reduction in normal hours, laid down either by legislation or collective bargaining. It begins by considering the effects at the level of the firm.

1. Theoretical considerations

Standard economic theory gives relatively few predictions about the balance between numbers of workers employed and the average hours they work. It is widely accepted that, at a given level of normal hours, an increase in the proportion of total labour costs represented by fixed costs (in terms of the costs of recruitment, accommodation and initial training, and any social security and welfare benefits paid on a *per capita* basis) will give an employer a financial incentive to increase hours worked per worker and to decrease the numbers of workers involved. The reason is that the marginal costs of each extra hour of work will be reduced relative to the costs of employing an extra worker. The same logic implies that increases in the overtime premium will give an incentive to reduce hours of work. However, these propositions alone are insufficient to make unambiguous predictions about the effects of a reduction in normal hours.

Hamermesh (1993) sets out three reasons to expect that, *ceteris paribus*, a firm will decrease its level of employment consequent upon a reduction in normal hours. First, at constant hours and wage rates, the reduction in the standard work-week will have the result of increasing wage costs, because the firm will pay extra overtime premia. This will tend to lead the firm to reduce the level of its activities (the "scale" effect), and so reduce employment. Second, the same increase in labour costs may cause the firm to substitute capital for labour over the medium-term. Third, provided the firm regularly uses overtime working, the extra overtime premia that become payable – on account of those hours of work which are below the old standard but above the new one – act as an incentive for the firm to reduce employment and increase hours, in the same way as an addition to fixed costs.

However, when a number of other factors are taken into account, the result becomes indeterminate. Instead of maintaining hours at the previous level and paying out more in the form of overtime premia, the firm may choose to reduce actual hours per employee. In this case, the effect on costs and employment will depend on the combined effects of at least four other factors: the degree of "wage compensation" – the extent to which hourly wage rates

are increased, possibly over a period of time, to make up for any shortfall in employee earnings resulting from the decrease in hours; any gains in productivity stemming directly from the reduction in hours, tending to reduce unit wage costs; the fixed costs involved in recruiting extra employees to make up the required number of hours of labour input; and, any government subsidies which might be provided to ease the transition to the new working hours regime.

There are also theoretical reasons for thinking that a reduction in actual hours of work may lead to an increase in hourly productivity. Employees working fewer hours may be able to work more intensively and productively during the hours that they are working, and may be willing to agree to shorter breaks, or "bell-to-bell" working. A reduction in working hours may pave the way for a reorganisation of working arrangements in more productive ways. Employees may work in such a way as to be on hand only when needed for the production process or, in service industries, so that they are present in the greatest numbers at times of peak demand. In addition, a cut in working time may lead to gains in capital productivity. Shift working may be used to secure increases in capital operating time, lowering unit capital costs, and allowing a faster amortisation of capital. This is of particular advantage in those cases, perhaps the majority, where capital normally becomes obsolete before it wears out. Finally, a re-organisation of working time may lead to savings in the cost of each hour of labour through, for example, greater recourse to part-time working and to the annualisation of hours of work.

2. Circumstances favourable to a gain in employment at the level of the firm[22]

Leaving aside the question of government subsidies for the moment, the theory outlined above suggests that, following a reduction in normal working hours, gains in employment are more likely (and losses less likely) when the following conditions hold:

– **the firm is used to working at or just under normal hours.** As noted above, if firms are routinely working substantial amounts of overtime, a reduction in normal hours will tend to increase the amount of overtime worked and reduce employment. On the other hand, if firms are already working well below normal hours, their labour costs might not be affected by the reduction;

– **there are possibilities for a substantial gain in hourly productivity**. Here, it may be objected that, if the gains are high enough to compensate for the reduction in hours, there will be no need to hire additional workers. However, in this case, the firm may be able to lower prices. Depending on the elasticity of product demand, this may allow an increase in output and, in turn, an increase in employment over the medium-term;

- **any wage compensation for reductions in actual hours is low**, avoiding large increases in hourly wage costs;
- **the decrease in normal hours is calculated in terms of annual hours**, rather than weekly or monthly hours. This will give employers flexibility in scheduling working hours over the year, reducing the need for overtime payments, and limiting the effect on wage costs; and
- **fixed costs of employment are low**. If the firm is to increase employment, it must be able to find suitable, well-qualified applicants, and be willing to accept the costs of recruitment, initial training, and other fixed employment costs.

In addition, the industrial relations system may play a role. It is most efficient to make decisions about working arrangements at enterprise level, in order to take account of the specific features of each enterprise. However, Bastian (1994), Bosch *et al.* (1993), Campbell (1989) and Freyssinet (1997), *inter alia*, have concluded that the effects on employment of a reduction in normal hours are likely to be more favourable when collective bargaining takes place not only at the enterprise level, but also at the branch or sector level. One argument is that, in negotiations at the firm level, in cases where their jobs are not in danger, existing workers will be more likely to press for higher wages, rather than a reduction in actual hours of work, even if the latter is more conducive to the recruitment of additional employees. Negotiations at a higher level are seen as better able to take account of the interests of other employees, including those at risk of losing their jobs, who would welcome an extension of the numbers employed. Cette and Taddéi (1994) suggest that higher-level negotiations may be important to set limits on the range of flexible working practices that are allowed in each branch or industry.

3. Empirical evidence

Granted that the predictions from theory are uncertain, it is important to draw on empirical evidence. However, while there is a considerable amount of evidence about cases where reductions in working hours have been negotiated as a package with wages, to answer the question posed here it is necessary to restrict attention to the much smaller number of cases where the reduction in working time may be considered to have been imposed on the firm.

Estimations of the possible effects of such reductions in normal hours of work have been based on a number of different types of analysis. They include:

- **regression analyses** of trends in employment levels against hours of work and other variables;
- **component calculations** based on an *ex post* division of changes in production at industry or branch level into its components: hourly productivity, employment and hours of work;
- **macro-economic simulations** applied either retrospectively, for example to estimate the effect of a reduction in normal hours in the past, or prospectively, to project the effects of a change into the future;
- **cross-sectional studies** of firms in circumstances where some firms have introduced reductions in hours while other, similar, firms have not; and
- **surveys of firms and case studies** which ask managers or personnel representatives for their opinion as to the likely effects of changes in normal hours of work on employment levels.

The discussion below draws on analyses using the last two methods. Both are subject to methodological problems. In cross-sectional studies, it is hard to be sure about the direction of causality. Interview methods depend upon the ability of managers to isolate the employment effects of changes in working time from those due to other factors. However, these two methods appear to have decisive advantages over the other three approaches for answering the question posed. Regression analyses of the type described incorporate no behavioural content and are concerned with correlations rather than causes. The results of component calculations are a mechanical consequence of the assumptions they incorporate, in particular about employment outcomes if hours of work had not been reduced. Macro-economic simulations, which often tend to suggest much higher employment effects than other methods, depend critically on the assumptions they embody about the reactions of firms, including the use that is made of overtime working, the effects on productivity, and the degree of wage compensation. They also tend to ignore the effects of fixed costs on hiring, as well as the costs of making changes in working arrangements necessary to achieve large gains in productivity [Hart (1987, 1989)].

Over the past two decades, there have been at least four cases where reductions in normal hours of work were imposed on firms in an important part of the economy. Normal hours of work in the UK engineering industry were reduced from 40 to 39 hours following the settlement of a protracted dispute in 1979, and then, following a further campaign over the period 1989-1991, to 37 hours. Detailed analyses at the firm level are reported in White and Ghobadian (1984) and Rubin and Richardson (1997), respectively. In the German metal-working industry, a reduction from 40 to 38¹/₂ hours followed the strike of early 1984, and a review of the results of a large number of analyses of this reduction, using a range of different methods, is provided by Bosch (1993). Hunt (forthcoming) provides further micro-economic evidence from cross-sectional data. Finally, normal hours of work were reduced from 40 to 39 hours for a substantial part of the French economy by government decree in 1982, at the same time as an extra week of holiday entitlement was granted. The effects on firms were studied by Marchand *et al.* (1983).

In all cases, actual hours were judged to have fallen substantially in response to the reduction in normal hours. Only in the case of the UK engineering industry in 1979 did White and Ghobadian (1984) find signs of a more than transient increase in overtime. Hunt (forthcoming) estimates the change in actual hours in Germany to have been 88 to 100 per cent of the reduction in normal hours, while Marchand *et al.* (1983) report that the effect in France was close to 100 per cent. In none of the cases was there much evidence of a loss in earnings. Hourly productivity is considered to have risen, substantially in the cases of France and Germany, and in the United Kingdom in 1979. In the last case, the rise was estimated to have been large enough to completely outweigh the reduction in hours. It may be noted that, in the engineering industry with its relatively high proportion of larger, capital-intensive firms, it may have been relatively easy to achieve hourly productivity gains.

Conclusions about the changes in employment need to take into account both the number of jobs created, and the number of jobs that were saved. For France, Marchand *et al.* (1983) estimate that the first-round effects of the reduction in hours involved the creation of between 14 000 and 28 000 net new jobs, while avoiding the loss of three times as many jobs, bringing the total of jobs created or saved into the 50 000 to 100 000 range (the higher figure representing around 0.5 per cent of total employment).[23] For Germany, Bosch (1993) notes a consensus that the reduction in hours led to positive effects on employment. In particular, a company survey by the German Engineering Employer's Association found a figure of 0.2 per cent for the employment effect, plus a further 1.4 per cent extra overtime, which was later

reduced, and which may, in part, have led to jobs being saved.[24] However, the results of Hunt (forthcoming) for the period 1984-1994 do not support this: while not always statistically significant, they tend to suggest that the change in hours led to falls in employment. For the UK engineering industry in 1979, White and Ghobadian (1984) found some reductions in employment, which they attribute to the particularly rapid gain in hourly productivity. Rubin and Richardson (1997), on the other hand, find evidence of positive employment effects following the later UK engineering industry strike, but make no numerical estimates of their magnitude.

None of the studies quoted have been able to consider the question of the permanence of the jobs that are created, or the length of time during which endangered jobs are preserved. Where extra jobs are created, they may be on a temporary contract basis, which allows the firm the option of restoring employment levels to the previous level, without loss of output, as soon as productivity gains allow. It is frequently argued that reductions in normal hours of work will be more easily accommodated by larger firms and will tend to favour the more highly-skilled workers. However, there seems to be little empirical evidence in support of either proposition.

4. Issues at the national level

The discussion above has been primarily concerned with the impact of reductions in normal hours at the level of the firm. At the national level, a number of other important issues present themselves. The first follows from the observation that past large-scale reductions in working hours have been accompanied by complete, or very substantial wage compensation, implying an increase in wage costs and possible inflationary pressures

Reductions in unemployment are likely to be smaller than any gains in employment, for a number of reasons. The first is the general observation that the labour force may tend to increase for demographic reasons and perhaps also through overall increases in participation rates which would occur in any case. However, hours reductions may cause additional growth in the labour supply, because jobs of shorter hours may be more attractive to a number of potential labour force entrants. In addition, as noted above, reductions in hours might perhaps result in a bias in favour of more highly-skilled workers, reducing the chances of employment for the unskilled unemployed.

The question of public finances comes to the fore when a system of subsidies is used to ease the transition to the new-working hours regime. In principle, a subsidy paid to firms at a flat rate for each employee whose hours are reduced may both facilitate wage moderation and reduce any bias against low-skilled workers. For the effects to be large, and extended to all firms, the impact on public finances will be considerable. However, provided the reduction in hours led to sufficient extra, permanent employment to make substantial inroads into unemployment, it might be possible for the costs of the subsidies to be defrayed by reductions in the costs of unemployment benefits, under certain circumstances.[25] A series of recent macro-economic simulations carried out for the French economy have sought to establish the most favourable conditions for this result to occur [DARES (1998); Cornilleau et al. (1998)]. It appears that success is most likely when there is a favourable response by both employers and employees. Firms have to be prepared to hire extra workers and reorganise their production methods, and to absorb part of the extra costs that will be entailed. Employees have to be prepared to accept somewhat lower wages, on average, than they would have otherwise received. Negotiations at enterprise level are highly desirable to achieve such compromises and are also needed to facilitate the reorganisations of working arrangements needed to secure sufficiently high gains in hourly productivity.

H.   CONCLUSIONS

Since the beginning of the 1980s, the rate of decline in average annual hours of work of employees has slowed. Currently, the level of average annual hours appears to have stabilised in some countries, while a few have recorded increases. The early 1980s saw a wave of statutory, or collectively agreed, working-time reductions in Europe. However, in most countries, with the notable exception of Germany, the momentum was not sustained, and further reductions in hours tended to take place only at enterprise or plant level, often with the aim of avoiding lay-offs. Until recently, Japan was the only country having measures designed to produce major reductions in working hours. However, France has now introduced provisions in favour of substantial reductions in normal hours of work, in the context of measures designed to raise employment levels, and the Italian government has announced its intention to follow suit.

An important factor underlying the falling rate of decline of average hours of work appears to be the long-term slowing of the growth rate of hourly productivity. This limits the extent to which hours reductions are possible in the context of continued increases in average real earnings. Employee preferences, while relevant to developments in working hours, appear to have played only a limited role. In the United States, the recent increases in aver-

age hours have paralleled changes in employee preferences, which have moved strongly in favour of increased earnings rather than reduced hours. However, in Europe, the slowdown in the trend has occurred despite signs of an increased preference for reductions in hours, though the balance is still in favour of increased earnings. It is noticeable that recent declines in hours have generally been strongest in countries, such as Germany and the Netherlands, where collective bargaining activity remains at high levels.

While policies designed to produce large reductions in actual working hours have been rare, there has been widespread policy action to increase the flexibility of working hours from the point of view of the enterprise, in the sense of working arrangements which allow hours to vary outside the range of the standard working day, or which allow for a variation of labour input within it. Governments have taken a number of steps to increase such kinds of flexibility. These have included the introduction of measures to allow greater use of "averaging" procedures such as the annualisation of working time, and the removal, or attenuation, of social security thresholds which impinge on the choice of working hours. Management has tended to insist on increases in flexibility as a counterpart to reductions in working time, when the latter issue has been on the negotiating agenda.

However, the statistical evidence available on specific types of flexible working practices suggests that, from a long-term perspective, comparatively little change has actually occurred. There is, for example, little evidence of large increases in shift-working outside the manufacturing sector, where there are special opportunities for increases in capital operating time, and where jobs are declining in number. The only type of flexible working for which there is evidence of a large-scale increase in the majority of OECD countries over the past twenty-five years is part-time working. While there are many forms of part-time working which provide no more, or even less, flexibility to employers than full-time working, it seems reasonable to conclude that many forms of part-time working do represent an increase in flexibility.

A few countries have introduced measures designed to raise employment levels through incentives to firms to reduce the working hours of full-time workers, or to hire part-time workers. While experience with these measures is still being accumulated, it appears that it has not yet been possible to devise a measure which will encourage large numbers of firms to reduce hours of full-time workers, without incurring a heavy cost to the public purse. Schemes to encourage part-time working have been more successful, in terms of take-up.

However, the cost-effectiveness of these schemes will not be settled until thorough evaluations of the likely "dead-weight" and "displacement" effects have been carried out. In general, the dearth of evaluations is a severe problem in assessing the impact of most working-time policy developments.

Finally, the question of the effects on employment of national, across-the-board cuts in normal working hours appears to rest largely where it did at the time of the OECD *Jobs Study* [OECD (1994)]. That study concluded, mainly on theoretical grounds, that a reduction in normal hours would not necessarily lead to any increases in employment, largely because of the likely, associated increases in labour costs. The effect is likely to vary according to the circumstances of each individual firm and the extent to which it is able and willing to reorganise its work-

ing practices to achieve productivity gains. Employment gains will ensue only if suitable workers are available to be hired, and firms are willing to accept the extra fixed costs (in terms of the costs of recruitment, accommodation and initial training, and any social security and welfare benefits paid on a *per capita* basis) associated with a larger workforce. Recent analyses confirm the importance of negotiating wage moderation and reorganisation of working practices, concurrently with the implementation of hours reductions. Overall, taking into account the most recent evidence, it appears that reductions in normal hours may lead to some overall job creation, and to some job losses being avoided or delayed. However, there is no reason to believe the number of extra jobs will be large, and the risk of job losses cannot be ruled out.

Notes

1. A somewhat different picture may result from figures based on an alternative method of calculating average hours of work per employee, in which the denominator is the number of people in work at any time during the year. According to results provided by the US Bureau of Labor Statistics, the increase in average annual hours of work per person in employment between 1983 and 1993 would then average 11.3 hours per year, as opposed to the figure of 7.3 hours shown in Table 5.2. The difference is largely due to the increasing propensity of women in the United States to work full-time and full-year.

2. Differences between the figures in Tables 5.1 and 5.2 may arise partly from the differences in the sources, and partly from the fact that the self-employed are included only in Table 5.1.

3. Nevertheless, all labour force data on hours of work must be treated with some caution. For the United States, Robinson and Bostrom (1994) conclude that, on average, they produce slight overestimates of the numbers working very short and very long hours, compared with the results obtained from a time-diary approach (in which respondents are asked to give details of their use of time throughout the day). In addition, both for actual and usual hours, there may be a tendency for respondents to cite either the standard contract hours, or a "round-number" figure.

4. Part-time working covers different types of situations in different countries. This is reflected in the fact that the hours worked by part-time workers are by no means the same. In general, where part-time working is relatively common, a substantial proportion of people identifying themselves as part-time workers have usual hours of 30 or more. When part-time working is less common, a substantial proportion of self-assessed full-time workers tend to have usual hours of under 30 hours [Van Bastelaar *et al.* (1997)]. In the Southern European countries, part-time work contracts are relatively unfamiliar, and a substantial proportion of employees usually working short hours fail to report themselves as "part-time" workers.

5. Part of the recent decline in overtime working in Australia may be the result of "rolling in" or "cashing out" of overtime into regular time, as part of enterprise agreements negotiated at a growing number of workplaces.

6. Household survey data are particularly sensitive to the precise form of the question that is asked. Establishment surveys tend to produce overestimates of the incidence of shift-working, because they are usually restricted to larger firms (10 or even 50 employees and over), and sometimes to the manufacturing sector and/or blue-collar workers and/or full-time workers and/or men. Each of these restrictions tends to result in successively higher estimates.

7. France is an exception.

8. The fact that shift-working tends to increase in recoveries should be borne in mind when interpreting the Cranet-E results.

9. The data in Table 5.8 suffer from the deficiency that the compensation data refer to employees, while the hours data cover all in employment. This will make little difference to the results where the rate of change of dependent employment and self-employment are similar. However, if self-employment is growing more rapidly, there will be a bias owing to the fact that average hours of work of the self-employed are higher. For example, in the case of the United Kingdom over the 1980s, where self-employment grew particularly rapidly, the figures shown in the third and fourth columns of each panel of the table are likely to be underestimates – the change in annual hours per dependent employee is likely to have been higher than shown (*i.e.* the reduction would not have been so pronounced) while real wage gains would have been somewhat higher.

10. The European Commission (1986, 1995*a*) question was: "If the choice were offered in the next pay round between an increase in pay for the same hours of work and shorter working time for the same pay you get now, which would you prefer?" Respondents were asked to respond, "increase in pay" or "shorter working time". A certain number said they were undecided, or declined to answer.

11. See Annex 5.A for a brief description of these data. They are available only between 1983 and 1994 and so are not suitable for studying long-term trends.

12. The ISSP survey used the following, more elaborate question than the European Commission surveys: "Think of the number of hours you work and the money you earn in your main job, including regular overtime. If you only had one of these three choices, which of the following would you prefer? (Please tick one box only):

   1. Work longer hours and earn more money
   2. Work the same number of hours and earn the same money
   3. Work fewer hours and earn less money.

   Other possible responses included "Can't choose".

13. Among the possible reasons for these findings are differences in real GDP per capita. For 1989, the correlation between data on GDP per capita on a PPP basis, taken from OECD *National Accounts* and average annual hours of work per employee, taken from EUROSTAT (1995*a*), is –0.60, while the correlation between the same GDP per capita figures and the

proportion of employees expressing a desire for reductions in hours of work, taken from European Commission (1991), is 0.80.

14. This does not mean that US workers are happy to work long hours. When no reference is made to the trade-off with earnings, the ISSP data indicate that a some what higher percentage of US workers than European workers wished to reduce their hours of work.

15. Bell and Freeman (1994) suggest that one cause may be the increase in wage inequality in the United States, as opposed to the decline in Germany. However, at least over the period 1985-1994, it is notable that, according to the data in Table 5.9, the proportion of employees in Ireland and the United Kingdom expressing a preference for reduced hours rose, despite the increase in wage inequality in both countries over the period.

16. The last two correlations are statistically significant at the 5 per cent level. Corresponding figures including Sweden are –0.15, –0.59 and –0.53, and only the second is statistically significant.

17. Another area of government intervention in the field of working hours is short-time working, As this is primarily intended as a cyclical measure, it is not covered here. See Van Audenrode (1994), Mosley et al. (1995), and Mosley and Kruppe (1996) for recent reviews.

18. In some countries maternity benefits and employment security legislation are also subject to minimum requirements, in terms of either hours worked per week or earnings.

19. The 1998 Budget announced plans to raise the lower limit to £81 over the period April 1999 to April 2000, with a rate of 12.2 per cent applying to additional payments.

20. According to information provided by the *Direction de l'animation de la recherche, des études et des statistiques* of the French *Ministère de l'Emploi et de la Solidarité*, initial results from an analysis of a thousand agreements signed before December 1997 indicate that the reduction in working time was very often undertaken in the context of a re-organisation of working arrangements, including *modulation* or annualisation of working hours.

21. This figure applies at the level of the minimum wage, or SMIC (see Chapter 2) and results from the cumulation of the provisions for subsidising low-paid employment in general with those applying to part-time working.

22. The discussion in this sub-section draws on Bosch and Lehndorff (1998).

23. Gilbert Cette has carried out a macro-economic simulation designed to capture the longer-term effects of the reduction of normal hours from 40 to 39. His figures for net job creation over the first, second and third years after the reduction in normal hours are 85 000, 130 000 and 145 000, respectively [Cette and Taddéi (1997)]. However, macro-economic simulations are typically found to give higher figures than employer surveys [Hart (1989), Whitley and Wilson (1988)] and are subject to the limitations noted in the text.

24. Most of the other results reviewed by Bosch (1993) are higher, often significantly so.

25. For example, Lehmann (1997) arrives at a favourable, long-term result for the impact of a reduction of normal working hours, combined with lower social security contributions by employers, in simulations based on models of the bargaining process, in which unemployment benefits are endogenous.

ANNEX 5.A

International data on annual hours of work

This Annex provides summary information about the methods used for constructing estimates of average annual hours of work per person in employment, including in those in Tables 5.1, 5.2 and 5.9 of this chapter, and in Table F of the Statistical Annex.

The wide range of existing methods may be divided, roughly, into two main types: the "component" method and the "direct" method.

In the "component" method, information on hours worked, according to a particular definition, such as usual or normal hours, is taken from a source considered to be particularly appropriate for the purpose, and then supplemented by available information on the missing components of working time, so as to arrive at an estimate of annual hours actually worked for the whole economy. The method may either yield average hours per person employed, or the total number of hours worked in the economy over the year, which is then divided by an estimate of the average number of people in employment over the year to give the average. (This is not the only way to obtain such an average – see endnote 1 to the main text.) For example, in Germany, the basic information refers to negotiated weekly working hours of full-time workers in their main job for a particular week. This is supplemented by information, from a range of sources, on inter alia, absences due to public holidays, holidays, sickness, accidents, maternity and paternity leave, leave for family reasons, short-time working, overtime working, part-time working and the hours of self-employed workers. Germany is the only country for which it is currently possible to obtain regular information on almost all components of working time. For some countries using this method, information on several important components appears to be omitted, so that the concept is not strictly that of annual hours actually worked per person in employment.

The "direct" method is only possible on the basis of monthly, or continuous, labour force surveys, which allow a direct measure of the actual hours worked during 12 weeks of the year, or every week of the year, respectively. In the first case, supplementary information on the distribution of public holidays over the year is also required. Information from establishment surveys may be used for particular sectors, where they are considered to provide more accurate information.

Countries employing the "component" method may be categorised according to the primary data source that is used, whether a labour force survey or one of the range of possible types of establishment surveys, or a combination of the two (for example, an establishment survey for the manufacturing sector and a labour force survey for other sectors, and for the self-employed). Both types of survey have their characteristic strengths and weaknesses. Establishment surveys tend to measure hours paid rather than hours actually worked. Thus, for example, they are generally unable to measure unpaid overtime working, which this chapter suggests is likely to be increasing in several countries.

In sum, it is not possible to say that any one method is certain to give better results than any other especially as supplementary information may be used to compensate for at least some of the deficiencies of the primary source.

Countries which may be said to use a "component" method based primarily or wholly on a labour force survey include Finland, Switzerland and the United States. Those using a "component" method based primarily on an establishment survey include France, Germany, and the Netherlands. Norway and Sweden use a combination of both types of source, without giving primacy to either. Canada, New Zealand, Portugal, Spain and the United Kingdom use the "direct" method.

EUROSTAT (1995a) provides a set of figures for the EU12 countries on the basis of the same, simplified "component" method, applied to each country on a uniform basis with the intention of providing a basis for international comparisons. The approach uses information from the European Union Labour Force Surveys, available from 1983 onwards, supplemented by a certain amount of national information, including data on public holidays and vacations. No account was taken of extra hours due to overtime working (other than regular overtime included in 'usual' working hours) and second jobs; nor of the effects of hours lost due to labour disputes and to complete absences in the reference week (apart from those due to vacations). It is possible that, to some extent, these omissions cancel out.

Table 5.A.1 compares 1994 estimates for annual hours of employees, taken from the national data shown in Table F of the Statistical Annex, with corresponding figures calculated by EUROSTAT. The countries included, France, Germany (western Germany only), the Netherlands and Spain, are the only ones for which corresponding data are available from both sources.

With the exception of Spain, the estimates are different, especially so in the case of France. The choice of one or other source may make an considerable difference to international comparisons.

Table 5.A.1. **Estimates of average annual hours worked per person employed, 1994**

	National (1)	EUROSTAT (2)	Ratio (1)/(2)
France	1520	1670	0.91
western Germany	1530	1590	0.96
Netherlands	1388	1447	0.96
Spain	1746	1741	1.00

Sources: Table F of the Statistical Annex and EUROSTAT (1995a).

Bibliography

ANXO, D. (1995), "Working-time Policy in Sweden", in Hoffmann, R. and Lapeyre, J. (eds.), A Time for Working, A Time for Living, Documentation of the December 1994 Joint Conference, European Trade Union Confederation (ETUC) and European Trade Union Institute (ETUI).

ANXO, D. and STERNER, T. (1995), "Shiftworking and Capital Operating Time in Swedish Manufacturing", in Anxo et al. (eds.), Work Patterns and Capital Utilisation – An International Comparative Study, Kluwer Academic Publishers, Dordrecht, the Netherlands, pp. 1-20.

ANXO, D. and TADDEI, D. (1995), "Shiftwork and Capital Operating Time in Industry: A Comparative International Survey", in Anxo et al. (eds.), Work Patterns and Capital Utilisation – An International Comparative Study, Kluwer Academic Publishers, Dordrecht, the Netherlands, pp. 121-148.

ANXO, D., BOSCH, G., BOSWORTH, D., CETTE, G., STERNER, G. and TADDEI, D. (1995), Work Patterns and Capital Utilisation – An International Comparative Study, Kluwer Academic Publishers, Dordrecht, the Netherlands.

Australian Bureau of Statistics (ABS) (1988), Alternative Working Arrangements, September and November 1986, Catalogue No. 6341.0, Commonwealth of Australia.

Australian Bureau of Statistics (ABS)(1994), Alternative Working Arrangements, August 1993, Catalogue No. 6342.0, Commonwealth of Australia.

BASTIAN, J. (1994), A Matter of Time, Avebury, Aldershot.

BELL, L. and FREEMAN, R. (1994), "Why do Americans and Germans Work Different Hours?", National Bureau of Economic Research, Working Paper No. 4808.

BETCHERMAN, G. (1997), Changing Workplace Strategies: Achieving Better Outcomes for Enterprises, Workers, and Society, Human Resources Development Canada and OECD.

BIELENSKI, H. (1994), New Forms of Work and Activity – Survey of Experience at Establishment Level in Eight European Countries, European Foundation for the Improvement of Living and Working Conditions, Dublin.

BLANPAIN, R. (general editor) (1990), Comparative Labour Law and Industrial Relations in Industrialised Market Economies, Kluwer Law and Taxation Publishers, Deventer, the Netherlands.

BLS (US Bureau of Labor Statistics) (1991), "Workers on Flexible and Shift Schedules", Press Notice USDL 92-491, August.

BOSCH, G. (1993), "Federal Republic of Germany", in Bosch, G., Dawkins, P. and Michon, F. (eds.) (1993), Times are Changing: Working-time in 14 Industrialised Countries, International Institute for Labour Studies, Geneva, pp. 127-152.

BOSCH, G. (1996), "Working Hours", Report on a meeting of trade union experts held under the OECD Labour Management Programme, OCDE/GD(96)140.

BOSCH, G. and LEHNDORFF, S. (1998), "Réduction de temps de travail et emploi", Travail et Emploi, No. 2, pp. 1-74.

BOSCH, G. and STILLE, F. (1995), "Duration of Utilisation of Plant and Machinery in Germany", in Anxo et al. (eds.), Work Patterns and Capital Utilisation – An International Comparative Study, Kluwer Academic Publishers, Dordrecht, the Netherlands, pp. 177-200.

BOSCH, G., DAWKINS, P. and MICHON, F. (eds.) (1993), Times are Changing: Working-time in 14 Industrialised Countries, International Institute for Labour Studies, Geneva.

BOSWORTH, D. (1995), "Shiftworking and Capital Utilisation in the U.K.", in Anxo et al. (eds.), Work Patterns and Capital Utilisation – An International Comparative Study, Kluwer Academic Publishers, Dordrecht, the Netherlands, pp. 247-280.

CAMPBELL, D.C. (1989), "Worksharing and Labour Market Flexibility: A Comparative Institutional Analysis", in Gladstone, A. (ed.), Current Issues in Labour Relations: An International Perspective, Walter de Gruyter, Berlin, pp. 175-192.

CETTE, G. (1995), "Capital Operating Time and Shiftworking in France", in Anxo et al. (eds.), Work Patterns and Capital Utilisation – An International Comparative Study, Kluwer Academic Publishers, Dordrecht, the Netherlands, pp. 149-176.

CETTE, G. and TADDÉI, D. (1994), Temps de travail, modes d'emploi, Editions La Découverte, Paris.

CETTE, G. and TADDÉI, D. (1997), Réduire la durée du travail: de la théorie à la pratique, Livres de Poche, Paris.

COMMISSION DES FINANCES DE L'ASSEMBLÉE NATIONALE (1997), "La Loi Robien : une première évaluation", Information Report No. 3506, Paris.

CORNILLEAU, G., HEYER, E. and TIMBEAU, X. (1998), "Le temps et l'argent : les 35 heures en douceur", Revue de l'OFCE, January, pp. 17-68.

CRANFIELD SCHOOL OF MANAGEMENT (1996), Working Time and Contract Flexibility in the EU, Cranfield, UK.

DARES (Direction de l'animation de la recherche, des études et des statistiques) (1997), "Les incitations financières en faveur du travail à temps partiel en 1996", Premières informations et premières synthèses, No. 49.1, December.

DARES (Direction de l'animation de la recherche, des études et des statistiques) (1998a), "La réduction de la durée du travail dans le cadre de la Loi Robien", Premières informations et premières synthèses, No. 03.1, January.

DARES (Direction de l'animation de la recherche, des études et des statistiques) (1998b), "L'impact macroéconomique d'une politique de réduction de la durée du travail", Premières informations et premières synthèses, No. 05.2, February.

DROLET, M. and MORISSETTE, R. (1997), "Working More? Less? What do Workers Prefer?", Perspectives on Labour and Income, No. 4, pp. 32-38.

DUCHESNE, D. (1997), "Working Overtime in Today's Labour Market", Perspectives on Labour and Income, No. 4, pp. 9-24.

EUROPEAN COMMISSION (1986), European Economy, No. 27, Brussels, March.

EUROPEAN COMMISSION (1991), European Economy, No. 47, Brussels, March.

EUROPEAN COMMISSION (1995a), European Economy, Reports and Studies No. 3, Brussels.

EUROPEAN COMMISSION (1995b), Employment in Europe, Brussels.

EUROPEAN COMMISSION (1996), Tableau de bord, Observatoire de l'emploi, Brussels.

European Industrial Relations Review (EIRR) (1995), "Germany: Quarter of Workforce now on 35-hour Week", November.

EUROSTAT (1995a), "Le temps de travail dans l'Union européenne : estimation de la durée effective annuelle (1983-1993)", Statistiques en bref, No. 4, Luxembourg.

EUROSTAT (1995b), "Le travail atypique dans l'Union européenne (1992-1993), Partie I", Statistiques en bref, No. 7, Luxembourg.

EUROSTAT (1995c), "La durée hebdomadaire du travail pour les non-salariés et certains salariés atypiques (1983-1994)", Statistiques en bref, No. 13, Luxembourg.

EUROSTAT (1995d), Labour Force Survey: Results 1993, Luxembourg.

EUROSTAT (1997), Labour Force Survey: Results 1995, Luxembourg.

FREYSSINET, J. (1997), Le temps de travail en miettes, Les Éditions de l'Atelier, Paris.

GOLOMBEK, R. and NYMOEN, R. (1995), "Capital Operating Time and Shift Work in Norway", in Anxo et al. (eds.), Work Patterns and Capital Utilisation – An International Comparative Study, Kluwer Academic Publishers, Dordrecht, the Netherlands, pp. 201-214.

GREEN, F. and POTEPAN, M.J. (1988), "Vacation Time and Unionism in the US and Europe", Industrial Relations, No. 2, pp. 180-194.

GREGG, P. (1994), "Share and Share Alike", New Economy, No. 1, pp. 13-19.

HAMERMESH, D.S. (1993), Labour Demand, Princeton University Press, Princeton.

HART, R.A. (1987), Working Time and Employment, Allen and Unwin, Winchester, MA.

HART, R.A. (1989), "Working-time Reductions and Employment: the Discrepancy between Microeconomic and Macroeconomic Research Findings", in Gladstone, A.

(ed.), Current Issues in Labour Relations: An International Perspective, Walter de Gruyter, Berlin, pp. 219-228.

HUNT, J. (forthcoming), "Has Work-sharing Worked in Germany?", Quarterly Journal of Economics.

LEHMANN, E. (1997), "Réduction de la durée du travail. Emploi et croissance dans un modèle de négociations salariales avec détermination centralisée des allocations de chômage", in Cahuc, P. and Granier, P. (eds.), La réduction du temps de travail. Une solution pour l'emploi?, Economica, Paris, pp. 311-330.

LIEBFRITZ, W., THORNTON, J. and BIBBEE, A. (1997), "Taxation and Economic Performance", OECD Economics Department Working Paper No. 176.

MADDISON, A. (1995), Monitoring the World Economy, 1820-1992, OECD, Paris.

MARCHAND, O., RAULT, D. and TURPIN, E. (1983), "Des 40 heures aux 39 heures : processus et réactions des entreprises", Économie et Statistique, April, pp. 3-16.

MELLOR, E.F. (1986), "Shift Work and Flexitime: How Prevalent Are They?", Monthly Labor Review, November, pp. 14-21

MOSLEY, H. and KRUPPE, T. (1996), "Employment Stabilisation through Short-time Work", in Schmid, G., O'Reilly, J. and Schömann, K. (eds.), International Handbook of Labour Market Policy and Evaluation, Edward Elgar, Cheltenham, UK, pp. 594-622.

MOSLEY, H., KRUPPE, T. and SPECKESSER, S. (1995), "Flexible Adjustment through Short-time Work: A Comparison of France, Germany, Italy and Spain", Wissenshaftszentrum Berlin Discussion Paper No. 205.

NÄTTI, J. (1995), "Working-time Policy in Finland: Flexibilisation and Work-Sharing", paper presented at the International Symposium on Working-time, Blankenberge, Belgium, 4-6 December.

OECD (1994), The OECD Jobs Study, Evidence and Explanations, Part II, Paris.

OECD (1995), Flexible Working-time: Collective Bargaining and Government Intervention, Paris.

OECD (1996a), Technology, Productivity and Job Creation: Vol. 2 Analytical Report, Paris.

OECD (1996b), The OECD Jobs Strategy: Enhancing the Effectiveness of Labour Market Policies, Paris.

OECD (1997a), Implementing the Jobs Strategy: Member Countries Experience, Paris.

OECD (1997b), Employment Outlook 1997, Paris.

ROBINSON, J.P. and BOSTROM, A. (1994), "The Overestimated Workweek? What Time-diary Measures Suggest", Monthly Labor Review, August, pp. 11-23.

RUBERY, J., FAGAN, C. and SMITH, M. (1994), Changing Patterns of Work and Working-time in the European Union and the Impact on Gender Divisions, Report for the Commission of the European Communities, Brussels.

RUBIN, M. and RICHARDSON, R. (1997), The Microeconomics of the Shorter Working Week, Avebury, Aldershot.

TADDEI, D. (1995), "Capital Operating Time (COT) In Macroeconomic Modelling", in Anxo et al. (eds.), Work Patterns and Capital Utilisation – An International Compara-

live Study, Kluwer Academic Publishers, Dordrecht, the Netherlands, pp. 61-88.

VAN AUDENRODE, M. (1994), "Short-Time Compensation, Job Security, and Employment Contracts: Evidence from Selected OECD Countries", *Journal of Political Economy*, February, pp. 45-52.

VAN BASTELAER, A., LEMAÎTRE, G. and MARIANNA, P. (1997), "The Definition of Part-time Work for the Purpose of International Comparisons", OECD Labour Market and Social Policy Occasional Papers No. 22, Paris.

WALWEI, U. (1995), "The Growth in Part-time Employment: Institutional versus Economic Explanations", paper presented to the Sixth International Symposium on Working Time, Blankenberge, Belgium, December.

WHITE, M. (1987), *Working hours: Assessing the Potential for Reduction*, ILO, Geneva.

WHITE, M. and GHOBADIAN, A. (1984), *Shorter Working Hours in Practice*, Policy Studies Institute, London.

WHITLEY, J.D. and WILSON, R.A. (1988), "Hours reductions within Large-Scale Macroeconomic Models: Conflict between Theory and Empirical Application", in Hart, R.A. (ed.), *Employment, Unemployment and Labor Utilization*, Unwin Hyman, Inc., Winchester MA, pp. 90-106.

Statistical Annex

Sources and definitions

An important source for the statistics in these tables is Part III of OECD, *Labour Force Statistics, 1977-1997*.

The data on employment, unemployment and the labour force are not always the same as the series used for policy analysis and forecasting by the OECD Economics Department, reproduced in Tables 1.2 and 1.3.

Conventional signs

.. Data not available
| Break in series
– Nil or less than half of the last digit used

Note on statistical treatment of Germany

In this publication, data up to end-1990 are for western Germany only; unless otherwise indicated, they are for the whole of Germany from 1991 onwards.

Table A. **Standardized unemployment rates in 21 OECD countries**

As a percentage of total labour force

	1990	1991	1992	1993	1994	1995	1996	1997
Australia	7.0	9.5	10.8	11.0	9.8	8.6	8.6	8.7
Austria	..	..	..	4.0	3.8	3.9	4.3	4.4
Belgium	6.7	6.6	7.3	8.9	10.0	9.9	9.7	9.2
Canada	8.1	10.4	11.3	11.2	10.4	9.5	9.7	9.2
Denmark	7.7	8.5	9.2	10.1	8.2	7.2	6.9	6.1
Finland	3.2	7.2	12.4	17.0	17.4	16.2	15.3	14.0
France	9.0	9.5	10.4	11.7	12.3	11.7	12.4	12.4
Germany[a]	4.8 I	5.6	6.6	7.9	8.4	8.2	8.9	9.7
Ireland	13.4	14.8	15.4	15.6	14.3	12.3	11.6	10.2
Italy	9.1	8.8	9.0	10.3	11.4	11.9	12.0	..
Japan	2.1	2.1	2.2	2.5	2.9	3.1	3.4	3.4
Luxembourg	1.7	1.7	2.1	2.7	3.2	2.9	3.3	3.7
Netherlands	6.2	5.8	5.6	6.6	7.1	6.9	6.3	5.2
New Zealand	7.8	10.3	10.3	9.5	8.1	6.3	6.1	6.7
Norway	5.3	5.6	6.0	6.1	5.5	5.0	4.9	4.1
Portugal	4.6	4.0	4.2	5.7	7.0	7.3	7.3	6.8
Spain	16.2	16.4	18.5	22.8	24.1	22.9	22.1	20.8
Sweden	1.8	3.3	5.9	9.5	9.8	9.2	10.0	10.2
Switzerland	..	2.0	3.1	4.0	3.8	3.5	3.9	..
United Kingdom	7.1	8.8	10.1	10.5	9.6	8.8	8.2	7.1
United States	5.6	6.8	7.5	6.9 I	6.1	5.6	5.4 I	4.9
European Union[b]	..	8.2	9.2	10.7	11.1	10.8	10.9	10.6
OECD Europe[b]	..	8.0	9.1	10.5	10.9	10.5	10.6	10.4
Total OECD[b]	..	6.8	7.5	8.0 I	7.9	7.5	7.6 I	7.3

a)   Up to and including 1990, western Germany; subsequent data concern the whole of Germany.

b)   Unemployment rates for the years 1991, 1992 and 1997 are estimates.

Note: In so far as possible, the data have been adjusted to ensure comparability over time and to conform to the guidelines of the International Labour Office. All series are benchmarked to labour-force-survey-based estimates. In countries with annual surveys, monthly estimates are obtained by interpolation/extrapolation and by incorporating trends in administrative data, where available. The annual figures are then calculated by averaging the monthly estimates (for both unemployed and the labour force). For countries with monthly or quarterly surveys, the annual estimates are obtained by averaging the monthly or quarterly estimates, respectively. For several countries, the adjustment procedure used is similar to that of the *Bureau of Labor Statistics, US Department of Labor.* For EU countries, the procedures are similar to those used in deriving the Comparable Unemployment Rates (CURs) of the Statistical Office of the European Communities. Minor differences may appear mainly because of various methods of calculating and applying adjustment factors, and because EU estimates are based on the civilian labour force.

Source: OECD (1998), *Quarterly Labour Force Statistics*, No. 1.

Table B. **Employment/population ratios, activity rates and unemployment rates by sex for persons aged 15-64 years**[a]

Percentages

	Both sexes																	
	Employment/population ratio						Labour force participation rate						Unemployment rate					
	1990	1993	1994	1995	1996	1997	1990	1993	1994	1995	1996	1997	1990	1993	1994	1995	1996	1997
Australia	67.9	64.1	65.7	67.5	67.3	66.3	73.0	71.9	72.4	73.5	73.7	72.5	7.0	10.9	9.3	8.2	8.6	8.5
Austria	..	..	..	68.4	67.3	67.2	..	..	..	71.5	71.1	70.9	..	..	..	4.4	5.3	5.2
Belgium	54.4 I	56.0	55.7	56.3	56.3	57.0	58.7 I	60.9	61.7	62.1	62.2	62.6	7.3 I	8.1	9.7	9.4	9.5	9.0
Canada	70.5	66.7	67.1	67.5	67.5	67.9	76.8	75.2	75.0	74.7	74.8	74.9	8.2	11.3	10.5	9.6	9.8	9.3
Czech Republic	..	71.3	71.5	69.6	69.4	68.7	..	74.2	74.3	72.5	72.2	72.1	..	3.9	3.8	4.1	3.8	4.7
Denmark	75.4 I	72.4	72.4	73.9	74.0	75.4	82.4 I	81.2	78.8	79.5	79.5	79.8	8.5 I 10.9		8.1	7.0	6.9	5.4
Finland	73.7	60.5	59.7	61.0	61.8	63.6	76.3	73.6	73.1	73.6	73.7	74.3	3.4	17.7	18.3	17.1	16.2	14.5
France	59.9	59.0	58.3	59.0	59.2	58.8	66.0	66.5	66.6	66.8	67.4	67.1	9.2	11.2	12.5	11.7	12.2	12.4
Germany	64.1	65.2	64.8	64.9	64.5	63.5	68.4	70.8	70.8	70.6	70.8	70.4	6.3	7.9	8.4	8.2	8.8	9.8
Greece	54.8 I	53.5	54.1	54.5	54.9	54.8	59.1 I	59.2	59.5	60.1	61.0	60.8	7.2 I	9.6	9.1	9.3	9.9	9.8
Hungary[b]	..	49.3	48.2 I	52.9	53.0	52.7	..	56.0	54.0 I	58.9	58.8	57.8	..	11.9	10.7 I 10.2		9.8	8.7
Iceland[c, d]	79.9	78.2	78.5	80.5	80.4	80.0	82.1	82.6	83.1	84.7	83.5	83.2	2.7	5.3	5.4	4.9	3.8	3.8
Ireland	52.3	51.0	52.3	53.8	54.8	56.1	60.2	60.8	61.4	61.5	62.3	62.7	13.2	16.0	14.9	12.4	12.0	10.5
Italy	53.9 I	51.8	50.9	50.5	50.6	50.5	59.8 I	57.9	57.5	57.3	57.7	57.7	9.9 I 10.5		11.5	11.9	12.3	12.5
Japan	68.6	69.5	69.3	69.2	69.5	70.0	70.1	71.3	71.4	71.5	72.0	72.6	2.2	2.6	3.0	3.3	3.5	3.5
Korea	61.2	62.3	63.2	63.7	63.8	63.5	62.8	64.1	64.8	65.1	65.1	65.3	2.5	2.9	2.5	2.1	2.1	2.7
Luxembourg	59.1 I	60.9	60.2	58.5	59.1	..	60.1 I	62.4	62.3	60.3	61.1	..	1.6 I	2.3	3.5	2.9	3.3	..
Mexico[d]	58.0	59.3	58.7	58.2	59.1	60.8	59.9	61.4	61.4	61.8	61.9	63.1	3.1	3.3	4.4	5.8	4.5	3.6
Netherlands	61.1	63.5	63.8	64.2	65.4	67.5	66.2	67.8	68.7	69.2	69.9	71.5	7.7	6.3	7.2	7.2	6.5	5.6
New Zealand	67.3	66.0	67.8	70.0	71.1	65.4	73.0	73.0	73.9	74.7	75.7	70.5	7.8	9.6	8.2	6.4	6.2	7.2
Norway[c]	73.1	71.3	72.2	67.5 I	75.3	77.3	77.1	75.9	76.4	70.9 I	79.2	80.6	5.3	6.1	5.4	4.8 I	4.9	4.1
Poland	..	58.9	58.3	58.1	58.4	58.8	..	68.8	68.4	67.4	66.9	66.4	..	14.4	14.8	13.7	12.7	11.5
Portugal	65.5	64.3	62.9	62.5	62.3	63.4	68.8	68.1	67.6	67.4	67.5	68.2	4.8	5.5	7.0	7.4	7.7	6.9
Spain[c]	50.2	46.2	46.5	46.7	47.6	49.0	60.0	59.9	61.3	60.8	61.3	61.9	16.4	22.9	24.1	23.1	22.4	20.9
Sweden	83.1 I	72.6	71.5	72.2	71.6	70.7	84.5 I	79.1	77.6	78.2	77.8	76.8	1.7 I	8.2	8.0	7.7	8.1	8.0
Switzerland[d]	78.1	75.6	74.2	75.3	73.4	78.1	79.6	78.6	77.4	78.1	76.4	81.5	1.9	3.9	4.2	3.5	3.9	4.2
Turkey	54.5	52.2	52.0	52.7	52.5	50.2	59.4	56.7	56.7	56.8	56.0	53.7	8.2	7.9	8.3	7.1	6.3	6.6
United Kingdom[c]	72.4	68.3	68.8	69.3	69.8	70.8	77.8	76.3	76.2	75.9	76.1	76.2	6.8	10.4	9.7	8.7	8.2	7.1
United States[c]	72.2	71.2 I	72.0	72.5	72.9 I 73.5		76.5	76.6 I	76.7	76.9	77.1 I 77.4		5.7	7.0 I	6.2	5.6	5.5 I	5.0
European Union[e]	61.5 I	59.9	59.6	60.1	60.2	60.4	67.1 I	67.2	67.2	67.3	67.6	67.7	8.4 I	10.8	11.4	10.7	10.9	10.8
OECD Europe[e]	61.0	59.3	58.9 I	59.4 I	59.6	59.5	66.5 I	66.3	66.2 I	66.2 I	66.4	66.1	8.2 I	10.5	11.0 I 10.3 I 10.2			10.0
Total OECD[e]	65.2 I	63.9 I	63.9 I	64.3 I	64.5 I 64.8		69.3 I	69.3 I	69.3 I	69.4 I	69.6 I 69.7		6.0 I	7.8 I	7.8 I	7.5 I	7.3 I	7.0

a) Ratios refer to persons aged 15 to 64 years who are in employment or in the labour force divided by the working age population, or in unemployment divided by the labour force.
b) For years prior to 1995, data cover persons aged 15 and over.
c) Refers to persons ages 16 to 64.
d) The year 1990 refers to 1991.
e) Above countries only.
Sources: OECD, *Labour Force Statistics, 1977-1997*, Part III, forthcoming.
       For Austria, Belgium, Denmark, Greece, Italy, Luxembourg, Netherlands and Portugal, data are from the European Labour Force Survey.

Table B. **Employment/population ratios, activity rates and unemployment rates by sex for persons aged 15-64 years**[a] *(cont.)*

Percentages

	Men																	
	Employment/population ratio						Labour force participation rate						Unemployment rate					
	1990	1993	1994	1995	1996	1997	1990	1993	1994	1995	1996	1997	1990	1993	1994	1995	1996	1997
Australia	78.5	73.1	74.8	76.1	75.9	74.7	84.4	82.7	82.7	83.2	83.4	81.9	6.9	11.6	9.6	8.6	9.0	8.8
Austria	..	..	..	77.6	76.1	75.9	..	..	..	80.8	80.4	80.0	..	..	..	4.0	5.4	5.1
Belgium	68.1	67.0	66.5	66.9	66.8	67.1	71.3	71.4	72.0	72.3	72.2	72.2	4.6	6.2	7.7	7.4	7.4	7.1
Canada	77.9	72.6	73.2	73.5	73.4	74.1	84.9	82.4	82.2	81.5	81.5	81.8	8.3	11.9	10.9	9.9	10.0	9.4
Czech Republic	..	76.8	76.8	77.6	78.1	77.4	..	79.4	79.4	80.4	80.7	80.5	..	3.3	3.3	3.5	3.2	3.8
Denmark	80.1	75.9	77.6	80.7	80.5	81.3	87.1	84.9	83.7	85.6	85.3	85.2	8.0	10.6	7.3	5.7	5.6	4.6
Finland	76.9	62.1	61.5	63.6	64.8	66.7	80.0	77.2	76.6	77.0	77.1	77.5	3.9	19.6	19.7	17.4	15.9	13.9
France	69.7	67.1	65.9	66.6	66.7	51.5	75.0	74.1	74.0	73.9	74.5	60.1	7.0	9.5	10.9	9.8	10.5	14.2
Germany	75.7	75.0	74.3	74.0	73.3	72.1	80.1	80.3	80.1	79.7	79.7	79.3	5.4	6.7	7.3	7.2	8.1	9.0
Greece	73.4	71.7	72.2	72.2	72.6	71.9	76.8	76.5	77.0	77.2	77.4	76.9	4.4	6.3	6.2	6.4	6.2	6.4
Hungary[b]	..	55.6	55.1	60.2	60.2	60.3	..	64.0	62.4	67.9	67.4	66.6	..	13.2	11.8	11.4	10.7	9.5
Iceland[c, d]	85.1	82.3	82.5	84.0	84.5	84.2	87.2	86.7	86.9	88.4	87.4	87.2	2.4	5.1	5.0	4.9	3.4	3.3
Ireland	67.8	63.7	64.4	66.3	66.6	67.6	77.7	75.9	75.9	75.8	75.8	75.6	12.8	16.1	15.0	12.5	12.1	10.6
Italy	72.0	68.1	66.5	65.7	65.3	65.0	77.0	74.0	73.1	72.4	72.3	72.2	6.5	7.9	9.0	9.3	9.7	9.8
Japan	81.3	82.3	81.9	81.9	82.1	82.4	83.0	84.4	84.4	84.5	85.0	85.4	2.1	2.5	2.9	3.1	3.5	3.5
Korea	73.9	75.8	76.6	77.2	76.7	75.9	76.2	78.3	78.8	79.0	78.6	78.1	3.0	3.3	2.8	2.3	2.4	2.9
Luxembourg	76.4	76.6	74.9	74.3	74.4	..	77.4	78.1	77.3	75.9	76.3	..	1.3	1.9	3.0	2.1	2.5	..
Mexico[d]	84.1	84.3	82.9	81.5	82.7	84.4	86.4	86.9	86.4	86.4	86.4	87.0	2.6	3.0	4.1	5.7	4.3	3.0
Netherlands	75.2	75.1	74.5	75.0	75.7	77.9	79.7	79.3	79.8	79.9	80.0	81.4	5.7	5.4	6.6	6.2	5.3	4.4
New Zealand	76.1	74.2	76.0	78.5	79.0	72.8	83.0	82.6	83.2	83.8	84.2	78.5	8.3	10.1	8.6	6.3	6.2	7.2
Norway[c]	78.6	75.8	76.8	78.1	80.0	82.0	83.4	81.3	81.6	82.4	84.1	85.4	5.8	6.7	6.0	5.2	4.8	4.0
Poland	..	65.9	64.9	64.7	65.2	66.1	..	75.7	75.0	73.9	73.5	73.2	..	13.0	13.4	12.5	11.3	9.8
Portugal	78.6	74.6	72.5	71.2	71.0	71.9	81.4	78.3	77.2	76.4	76.1	76.7	3.4	4.7	6.1	6.8	6.7	6.2
Spain[c]	69.1	61.3	62.2	61.7	62.4	63.7	78.6	75.8	77.4	75.5	75.8	76.0	12.1	19.1	19.6	18.3	17.7	16.2
Sweden	85.2	73.1	72.3	73.5	73.2	72.4	86.6	80.9	79.5	80.2	80.0	79.1	1.7	9.7	9.1	8.5	8.5	8.5
Switzerland[d]	88.8	85.4	83.3	84.7	83.5	85.9	90.0	88.2	86.6	87.4	86.6	89.8	1.3	3.2	3.8	3.0	3.6	4.4
Turkey	76.9	73.9	73.8	74.6	74.5	74.0	83.6	80.5	80.8	80.5	79.8	78.8	8.0	8.2	8.6	7.3	6.6	6.2
United Kingdom[c]	82.1	74.8	75.4	76.1	76.3	77.4	88.3	85.5	85.2	84.7	84.6	84.4	7.1	12.5	11.5	10.2	9.8	8.2
United States[c]	80.7	78.7	79.0	79.5	79.7	80.1	85.6	84.9	84.3	84.3	84.3	84.2	5.7	7.3	6.2	5.6	5.4	4.9
European Union[e]	74.4	70.6	70.1	70.3	70.2	70.2	79.8	78.2	78.1	77.7	77.8	77.6	6.7	9.8	10.3	9.5	9.7	9.5
OECD Europe[e]	75.0	70.6	70.2	70.6	70.6	70.6	80.5	78.2	78.0	77.8	77.7	77.5	6.8	9.6	10.0	9.2	9.2	8.9
Total OECD[e]	78.1	75.3	75.2	75.4	75.5	75.8	82.6	81.4	81.2	81.1	81.1	81.0	5.4	7.4	7.4	7.0	6.9	6.5

a)   Ratios refer to persons aged 15 to 64 years who are in employment or in the labour force divided by the working age population, or in unemployment divided by the labour force.
b)   For years prior to 1995, data cover persons aged 15 and over.
c)   Refers to persons ages 16 to 64.
d)   The year 1990 refers to 1991.
e)   Above countries only.
Sources: OECD, *Labour Force Statistics, 1977-1997*, Part III, forthcoming.
          For Austria, Belgium, Denmark, Greece, Italy, Luxembourg, Netherlands and Portugal, data are from the European Labour Force Survey.

Table B. **Employment/population ratios, activity rates and unemployment rates by sex for persons aged 15-64 years**[a] *(cont.)*

Percentages

	Women																	
	Employment/population ratio						Labour force participation rate						Unemployment rate					
	1990	1993	1994	1995	1996	1997	1990	1993	1994	1995	1996	1997	1990	1993	1994	1995	1996	1997
Australia	57.1	55.1	56.4	58.9	58.7	57.8	61.5	61.1	61.9	63.7	63.8	63.0	7.2	9.9	8.9	7.6	8.0	8.2
Austria	..	..	..	59.2	58.6	58.5	..	..	..	62.3	61.8	61.8	..	..	..	4.9	5.3	5.3
Belgium	40.8	44.8	44.8	45.4	45.6	46.7	46.1	50.3	51.2	51.7	52.0	52.9	11.5	10.9	12.5	12.3	12.4	11.6
Canada	63.0	60.8	61.1	61.5	61.6	61.7	68.6	68.0	67.8	67.8	68.0	68.0	8.2	10.6	9.9	9.3	9.5	9.2
Czech Republic	..	65.8	66.2	61.6	60.7	60.0	..	69.1	69.3	64.7	63.6	63.7	..	4.7	4.5	4.8	4.6	5.8
Denmark	70.6	68.7	67.1	67.0	67.4	69.4	77.6	77.4	73.8	73.3	73.6	74.2	9.0	11.2	9.0	8.6	8.4	6.5
Finland	70.4	58.9	57.9	58.3	58.7	60.4	72.5	69.9	69.6	70.1	70.4	71.1	2.8	15.7	16.8	16.8	16.6	15.1
France	50.3	51.0	50.7	51.5	51.7	66.2	57.2	58.9	59.2	59.8	60.3	74.3	12.1	13.4	14.4	13.9	14.3	10.9
Germany	52.2	55.1	54.9	55.5	55.5	54.6	56.4	61.0	61.1	61.3	61.5	61.4	7.5	9.6	10.0	9.5	9.8	11.0
Greece	37.5	36.4	37.1	38.0	38.5	39.1	42.6	43.0	43.2	44.3	45.8	46.0	12.0	15.3	14.0	14.1	15.8	15.1
Hungary[b]	..	43.5	41.9	45.9	46.1	45.4	..	48.5	46.3	50.3	50.6	49.2	..	10.4	9.4	8.7	8.7	7.7
Iceland[c, d]	74.3	73.9	74.6	76.9	76.3	75.5	76.7	78.4	79.1	80.9	79.7	79.0	3.1	5.7	5.7	4.9	4.3	4.4
Ireland	36.6	38.1	39.9	41.2	43.0	44.6	42.6	45.4	46.9	47.0	48.8	49.7	14.0	15.9	14.8	12.3	11.9	10.4
Italy	36.4	36.0	35.6	35.6	36.1	36.2	43.2	42.2	42.2	42.5	43.3	43.6	15.8	14.8	15.7	16.3	16.6	16.8
Japan	55.8	56.6	56.5	56.4	56.8	57.6	57.1	58.2	58.3	58.4	58.9	59.7	2.3	2.8	3.1	3.4	3.6	3.6
Korea	49.0	49.2	50.1	50.6	51.1	51.4	49.9	50.3	51.1	51.5	51.9	52.7	1.8	2.3	2.0	1.7	1.6	2.4
Luxembourg	41.4	44.7	44.9	42.2	43.6	..	42.5	46.1	47.0	44.1	45.7	..	2.5	3.1	4.3	4.4	4.7	..
Mexico[d]	34.2	36.0	36.2	36.5	37.4	39.4	35.7	37.5	38.1	38.9	39.3	41.4	4.3	4.0	4.9	6.1	4.9	4.9
Netherlands	46.7	51.7	52.7	53.2	54.8	56.9	52.4	56.0	57.4	58.3	59.6	61.3	10.9	7.7	8.1	8.7	8.1	7.2
New Zealand	58.5	57.8	59.7	61.5	63.3	58.0	63.2	63.5	64.7	65.7	67.4	62.6	7.3	8.9	7.8	6.4	6.2	7.3
Norway[c]	67.2	66.6	67.5	78.1	70.4	72.3	70.7	70.4	70.9	82.4	74.1	75.6	4.9	5.3	4.8	5.2	4.9	4.3
Poland	..	52.1	51.9	51.8	51.8	51.8	..	62.1	62.1	61.0	60.5	59.9	..	16.1	16.4	15.1	14.3	13.5
Portugal	53.3	54.9	54.1	54.3	54.2	55.5	57.1	58.7	58.8	59.1	59.5	60.3	6.7	6.5	8.0	8.1	8.8	7.9
Spain[c]	31.6	31.1	31.0	32.0	33.0	34.3	41.8	44.1	45.4	46.2	47.0	48.0	24.4	29.5	31.6	30.8	29.8	28.4
Sweden	81.0	72.1	70.6	70.8	69.9	68.9	82.3	77.2	75.7	76.1	75.6	74.5	1.6	6.6	6.7	6.9	7.5	7.5
Switzerland[d]	66.9	65.2	64.6	65.4	63.2	69.8	68.7	68.6	67.8	68.3	66.1	72.7	2.7	5.0	4.7	4.2	4.4	3.9
Turkey	32.9	31.1	30.6	31.5	31.0	27.2	36.0	33.5	33.2	33.7	32.8	29.4	8.7	7.3	7.8	6.7	5.5	7.7
United Kingdom[c]	62.8	61.8	62.1	62.5	63.3	64.0	67.2	67.0	67.1	67.1	67.5	68.0	6.5	7.7	7.4	6.9	6.3	5.8
United States[c]	64.0	64.0	65.2	65.8	66.3	67.1	67.8	68.6	69.4	69.7	70.1	70.7	5.6	6.7	6.1	5.7	5.5	5.1
European Union[e]	48.6	49.3	49.1	49.8	50.2	50.5	54.5	56.2	56.4	56.9	57.4	57.7	10.8	12.3	12.9	12.4	12.5	12.4
OECD Europe[e]	47.1	48.0	47.8	48.5	48.6	48.3	52.6	54.5	54.5	55.0	55.0	54.7	10.3	11.8	12.3	11.7	11.7	11.7
Total OECD[e]	52.4	52.6	52.9	53.4	53.7	54.0	56.3	57.4	57.7	58.1	58.3	58.5	6.9	8.3	8.4	8.1	8.0	7.8

a)   Ratios refer to persons aged 15 to 64 years who are in employment or in the labour force divided by the working age population, or in unemployment divided by the labour force.
b)   For years prior to 1995, data cover persons aged 15 and over.
c)   Refers to persons ages 16 to 64.
d)   The year 1990 refers to 1991.
e)   Above countries only.
Sources: OECD, *Labour Force Statistics, 1977-1997*, Part III, forthcoming.
For Austria, Belgium, Denmark, Greece, Italy, Luxembourg, Netherlands and Portugal, data are from the European Labour Force Survey.

Table C. **Unemployment, labour force participation rates and employment/population ratios by age and sex**

Both sexes

Percentages

		1990			1994			1995			1996			1997		
		15 to 24	25 to 54	55 to 64	15 to 24	25 to 54	55 to 64	15 to 24	25 to 54	55 to 64	15 to 24	25 to 54	55 to 64	15 to 24	25 to 54	55 to 64
Australia	Unemployment rates	13.2	5.1	5.4	16.3	7.2	8.6	14.4	6.4	7.4	14.8	6.8	7.8	15.9	6.6	7.2
	Labour force participation rates	70.4	79.9	44.1	68.4	79.4	43.7	69.7	80.4	44.9	70.3	80.1	45.9	66.9	79.6	45.3
	Employment/population ratios	61.1	75.8	41.8	57.3	73.6	40.0	59.7	75.3	41.5	59.9	74.7	42.4	56.3	74.4	42.0
Austria	Unemployment rates	:	:	:	:	:	:	5.9	4.1	3.9	6.9	5.1	4.6	7.6	4.8	5.2
	Labour force participation rates	:	:	:	:	:	:	61.7	83.3	30.2	59.6	83.5	30.8	58.4	83.9	30.0
	Employment/population ratios	:	:	:	:	:	:	58.1	79.9	29.0	55.5	79.3	29.4	54.0	79.9	28.5
Belgium	Unemployment rates	14.5	6.5	3.5	21.8	8.4	4.9	21.5	8.3	4.0	20.5	8.6	4.5	21.3	7.9	4.7
	Labour force participation rates	35.5	76.7	22.2	35.2	79.9	23.5	33.9	80.4	24.2	32.8	80.8	22.8	32.0	81.0	23.1
	Employment/population ratios	30.4	71.7	21.4	27.5	73.1	22.4	26.6	73.8	23.3	26.1	73.9	21.8	25.2	74.6	22.0
Canada	Unemployment rates	12.7	7.3	6.0	16.5	9.3	9.0	15.6	8.4	8.2	16.1	8.6	7.7	16.7	7.9	7.6
	Labour force participation rates	69.2	84.5	50.0	62.9	83.6	48.7	62.2	83.4	47.4	61.5	83.7	47.9	61.2	83.8	48.4
	Employment/population ratios	60.4	78.4	47.0	52.5	75.8	44.3	52.5	76.4	43.6	51.6	76.5	44.2	51.0	77.2	44.7
Czech Republic	Unemployment rates	:	:	:	7.7	3.0	3.0	7.9	3.3	3.0	7.1	3.2	3.5	8.4	4.0	3.6
	Labour force participation rates	:	:	:	54.0	91.8	33.1	50.6	89.6	35.6	49.5	88.7	38.5	48.3	88.7	39.7
	Employment/population ratios	:	:	:	49.9	89.1	32.1	46.6	86.6	34.5	45.9	85.9	37.1	44.3	85.1	38.3
Denmark	Unemployment rates	11.5	7.9	6.1	10.2	7.8	6.5	9.9	6.2	8.0	10.6	6.0	6.1	8.1	4.8	5.1
	Labour force participation rates	73.5	91.2	57.1	69.1	87.2	53.7	73.2	87.1	53.6	73.8	87.5	50.6	74.2	87.0	54.1
	Employment/population ratios	65.0	84.0	53.6	62.1	80.5	50.2	65.9	81.7	49.3	66.0	82.2	47.5	68.2	82.8	51.4
Finland	Unemployment rates	6.4	2.9	3.3	30.9	16.0	23.3	27.2	14.9	24.1	24.7	13.9	25.0	24.8	12.2	20.1
	Labour force participation rates	58.1	89.5	42.4	44.6	87.8	42.9	44.9	88.2	44.4	44.6	88.1	46.4	49.3	88.3	44.7
	Employment/population ratios	54.4	86.9	41.0	30.9	73.8	32.9	32.7	75.1	33.7	33.6	75.8	34.8	37.1	77.5	35.7
France	Unemployment rates	19.1	8.0	6.7	27.5	11.2	7.0	25.9	10.5	7.2	26.3	11.0	8.4	28.1	11.1	8.5
	Labour force participation rates	36.4	84.1	38.1	30.7	85.9	35.9	29.8	86.0	36.1	29.2	86.4	36.6	28.0	86.0	36.7
	Employment/population ratios	29.5	77.4	35.6	22.3	76.2	33.4	22.0	77.0	33.5	21.5	76.9	33.5	20.1	76.4	33.6
Germany	Unemployment rates	5.6	5.7	11.6	8.2	8.0	11.7	8.2	7.6	11.7	9.0	8.1	13.1	10.0	9.1	14.5
	Labour force participation rates	59.8	78.0	41.6	56.2	83.2	40.7	53.7	83.4	42.5	52.4	83.7	43.6	52.1	83.3	43.7
	Employment/population ratios	56.4	73.6	36.8	51.6	76.5	36.0	49.3	77.0	37.5	47.6	76.9	37.9	46.9	75.7	37.3
Greece	Unemployment rates	23.3	5.1	1.6	27.7	7.0	3.1	27.9	7.3	3.4	31.2	7.7	3.0	31.0	7.7	3.2
	Labour force participation rates	39.4	72.2	41.5	36.9	73.7	40.7	36.7	74.2	41.9	36.9	75.3	41.9	35.5	75.5	42.1
	Employment/population ratios	30.3	68.5	40.8	26.7	68.6	39.5	26.5	68.8	40.5	25.4	69.5	40.7	24.5	69.7	40.7
Hungary[a]	Unemployment rates	:	:	:	19.4	9.3	8.0	18.6	8.9	5.4	18.0	8.7	5.1	15.9	7.5	5.7
	Labour force participation rates	:	:	:	40.8	79.1	12.5	38.4	77.6	18.1	37.1	77.1	20.4	37.2	75.9	18.3
	Employment/population ratios	:	:	:	32.9	71.8	11.5	31.3	70.7	17.1	30.4	70.4	19.4	31.3	70.2	17.3
Iceland[b, c]	Unemployment rates	5.0	2.2	2.2	11.5	4.2	3.9	11.0	2.6	3.9	8.4	2.6	4.0	7.9	3.0	2.9
	Labour force participation rates	59.6	90.1	87.3	58.5	91.3	88.1	59.8	92.4	88.6	59.8	91.7	87.0	60.3	91.0	86.6
	Employment/population ratios	56.6	88.1	85.4	51.8	87.5	84.7	54.8	89.2	85.1	54.8	89.2	83.5	55.6	88.2	84.1

Table C. **Unemployment, labour force participation rates and employment/population ratios by age and sex** (cont.)

Both sexes

Percentages

		1990			1994			1995			1996			1997		
		15 to 24	25 to 54	55 to 64	15 to 24	25 to 54	55 to 64	15 to 24	25 to 54	55 to 64	15 to 24	25 to 54	55 to 64	15 to 24	25 to 54	55 to 64
Ireland	Unemployment rates	17.6	12.4	8.4	23.3	13.3	8.5	19.1	11.1	7.8	18.2	11.0	6.8	16.1	9.5	6.0
	Labour force participation rates	50.4	68.7	42.2	45.4	72.6	43.0	45.5	72.6	42.5	43.9	74.5	43.2	45.5	74.4	42.6
	Employment/population ratios	41.5	60.2	38.6	34.8	62.9	39.4	36.8	64.5	39.2	35.9	66.3	40.3	38.1	67.3	40.1
Italy	Unemployment rates	28.9	6.6	1.8	31.6	8.6	3.6	32.8	8.9	4.3	34.1	9.3	4.3	33.6	9.6	4.4
	Labour force participation rates	46.8	72.8	32.5	39.1	71.6	29.4	38.8	71.6	28.3	38.5	72.2	28.5	38.0	72.4	28.6
	Employment/population ratios	33.3	68.0	32.0	26.8	65.4	28.3	26.1	65.2	27.0	25.4	65.5	27.3	25.2	65.5	27.3
Japan	Unemployment rates	4.3	1.6	2.7	5.5	2.4	3.5	6.1	2.6	3.7	6.7	2.7	4.1	5.6	2.8	3.9
	Labour force participation rates	44.1	80.9	64.7	47.6	81.4	66.1	47.6	81.4	66.2	48.3	81.8	66.3	48.6	82.2	66.9
	Employment/population ratios	42.2	79.6	62.9	45.0	79.5	63.7	44.7	79.3	63.7	45.0	79.6	63.6	45.3	79.9	64.2
Korea	Unemployment rates	7.0	1.9	0.8	7.2	1.9	0.6	6.3	1.6	0.8	6.1	1.6	0.7	7.7	2.1	1.3
	Labour force participation rates	35.0	74.6	62.5	37.1	75.3	63.9	36.5	75.6	64.1	35.4	76.1	63.6	34.4	76.6	63.4
	Employment/population ratios	32.5	73.2	62.0	34.4	73.9	63.5	34.2	74.4	63.6	33.2	74.9	63.2	31.8	75.0	62.6
Luxembourg	Unemployment rates	3.7	1.4	0.8	7.9	3.0	0.7	7.2	2.5	0.3	9.2	2.7	0.0	..	..	..
	Labour force participation rates	44.7	72.8	28.4	46.5	75.8	23.3	41.2	73.8	24.0	40.7	75.2	22.6	..	..	..
	Employment/population ratios	43.1	71.8	28.2	42.8	73.5	23.2	38.2	71.9	24.0	36.9	73.2	22.6	..	..	..
Mexico[c]	Unemployment rates	5.4	2.2	1.0	7.1	3.3	2.0	9.3	4.4	3.3	7.7	3.3	2.1	6.6	2.6	1.4
	Labour force participation rates	52.2	65.9	54.6	54.1	67.2	53.5	54.1	67.8	52.9	53.1	68.4	53.2	53.2	69.9	55.8
	Employment/population ratios	49.3	64.4	54.1	50.3	65.0	52.4	49.1	64.8	51.2	49.0	66.2	52.1	49.7	68.1	55.0
Netherlands	Unemployment rates	11.1	7.2	3.8	11.3	6.6	3.3	12.1	6.4	3.5	11.4	5.6	4.0	9.7	4.8	3.9
	Labour force participation rates	59.6	76.0	30.9	60.6	79.1	30.2	62.0	79.4	29.9	61.1	80.3	31.2	63.1	81.8	32.7
	Employment/population ratios	53.0	70.6	29.7	53.7	73.9	29.2	54.5	74.4	28.8	54.1	75.8	30.0	56.9	77.8	31.4
New Zealand	Unemployment rates	14.1	6.0	4.6	15.0	6.6	4.8	11.9	5.1	3.3	11.7	4.9	3.7	15.0	5.6	4.1
	Labour force participation rates	67.9	81.2	43.8	66.0	81.5	49.8	67.4	81.7	52.1	67.5	82.4	55.8	58.2	77.7	54.5
	Employment/population ratios	58.3	76.3	41.8	56.1	76.1	47.4	59.4	77.5	50.4	59.6	78.4	53.8	49.5	73.3	52.2
Norway[b]	Unemployment rates	11.8	4.2	2.1	12.6	4.5	2.6	11.9	4.1	2.6	12.4	3.9	2.2	10.9	3.2	2.0
	Labour force participation rates	60.5	85.9	63.1	55.4	85.1	63.3	55.9	85.9	64.8	59.7	87.1	66.0	61.9	88.1	67.7
	Employment/population ratios	53.4	82.3	61.8	48.4	81.3	61.6	49.2	82.4	63.1	52.3	83.7	64.6	55.2	85.3	66.4
Poland	Unemployment rates				32.6	12.8	7.0	31.2	11.7	5.9	28.5	10.8	5.9	24.7	10.0	5.3
	Labour force participation rates				41.5	84.7	37.0	39.7	84.0	35.9	39.0	83.6	35.0	38.3	82.9	35.5
	Employment/population ratios				28.0	73.8	34.4	27.3	74.2	33.8	27.9	74.6	33.0	28.9	74.7	33.6
Portugal	Unemployment rates	10.4	3.7	1.7	14.5	5.8	3.7	16.0	6.1	4.0	17.0	6.2	5.0	14.1	5.7	5.2
	Labour force participation rates	58.4	79.8	47.6	45.2	83.0	47.6	43.1	83.4	47.4	42.3	83.4	48.7	44.2	83.4	49.4
	Employment/population ratios	52.4	76.9	46.8	38.7	78.3	45.8	36.2	78.3	45.5	35.1	78.2	46.3	37.9	78.6	46.8
Spain[b]	Unemployment rates	32.3	13.1	8.1	42.8	20.9	12.3	42.5	20.0	12.2	42.0	19.3	11.6	39.0	18.2	11.3
	Labour force participation rates	51.2	70.2	40.0	49.1	73.5	36.8	45.1	73.9	36.5	44.4	74.6	37.3	44.3	75.2	37.8
	Employment/population ratios	34.7	61.0	36.8	28.1	58.1	32.3	25.9	59.1	32.1	25.7	60.2	33.0	27.0	61.5	33.5

EMPLOYMENT OUTLOOK

Table C. **Unemployment, labour force participation rates and employment/population ratios by age and sex** (cont.)

Both sexes

Percentages

		1990			1994			1995			1996			1997		
		15 to 24	25 to 54	55 to 64	15 to 24	25 to 54	55 to 64	15 to 24	25 to 54	55 to 64	15 to 24	25 to 54	55 to 64	15 to 24	25 to 54	55 to 64
Sweden[b]	Unemployment rates	3.7	1.2	1.5	16.7	6.9	6.5	15.4	6.6	7.4	15.7	7.0	7.6	15.4	7.1	7.3
	Labour force participation rates	68.5	92.8	70.5	49.7	88.0	66.2	50.0	88.4	66.9	47.8	87.9	68.6	46.8	86.8	67.6
	Employment/population ratios	66.0	91.6	69.4	41.4	81.9	61.9	42.3	82.6	61.9	40.3	81.8	63.4	39.6	80.6	62.7
Switzerland[c]	Unemployment rates	3.3	1.7	1.2	6.3	3.7	4.3	5.8	3.1	3.3	4.9	3.8	3.5	5.9	4.0	2.9
	Labour force participation rates	69.3	84.5	71.1	64.1	82.7	69.2	62.5	83.9	69.8	64.2	83.3	59.5	66.9	86.9	72.7
	Employment/population ratios	67.1	83.1	70.3	60.4	79.7	66.2	58.8	81.3	67.5	61.1	80.1	57.5	62.9	83.4	70.6
Turkey	Unemployment rates	16.0	5.4	3.1	15.7	6.0	2.2	14.7	4.9	2.3	12.9	4.4	1.7	14.4	4.4	1.4
	Labour force participation rates	54.7	65.1	44.1	49.4	63.6	41.6	47.9	64.0	43.4	47.1	63.0	42.5	44.5	60.9	40.3
	Employment/population ratios	45.9	61.6	42.7	41.7	59.8	40.6	40.9	60.9	42.4	41.0	60.2	41.8	38.1	58.2	39.7
United Kingdom[b]	Unemployment rates	10.1	5.8	7.2	16.2	8.3	9.1	15.3	7.4	7.5	14.7	7.0	7.1	13.5	5.9	6.3
	Labour force participation rates	78.0	83.9	53.0	70.2	83.5	52.1	69.8	83.4	51.4	70.7	83.3	51.4	70.5	83.3	51.7
	Employment/population ratios	70.1	79.0	49.2	58.9	76.6	47.4	59.1	77.2	47.6	60.3	77.5	47.7	61.0	78.4	48.5
United States[b]	Unemployment rates	11.2	4.6	3.3	12.5	5.0	4.1	12.1	4.5	3.6	12.0	4.3	3.4	11.3	3.9	2.9
	Labour force participation rates	67.3	83.5	55.9	66.4	83.4	56.8	66.3	83.5	57.2	65.5	83.8	57.9	65.4	84.1	58.9
	Employment/population ratios	59.8	79.7	54.0	58.1	79.2	54.4	58.3	79.7	55.1	57.6	80.2	55.9	58.0	80.9	57.2
European Union[d]	Unemployment rates	15.9	6.8	6.4	21.2	9.8	8.6	20.6	9.3	8.5	21.0	9.4	9.0	20.4	9.3	9.2
	Labour force participation rates	54.3	78.7	41.0	48.6	80.5	39.4	47.5	80.7	39.5	46.9	81.1	40.2	46.6	81.1	40.4
	Employment/population ratios	45.7	73.3	38.4	38.2	72.6	36.0	37.7	73.2	36.2	37.0	73.4	36.5	37.1	73.5	36.7
OECD Europe[d]	Unemployment rates	15.6	6.6	5.9	20.3	9.4	7.7	19.6	8.8	7.5	19.4	8.8	7.8	19.0	8.6	7.9
	Labour force participation rates	54.7	77.3	41.9	48.4	79.3	39.8	47.1	79.4	39.6	46.4	79.5	40.0	45.8	79.2	40.2
	Employment/population ratios	46.1	72.3	39.4	38.6	71.9	36.8	37.9	72.4	36.7	37.4	72.5	36.9	37.1	72.4	37.0
Total OECD[d]	Unemployment rates	11.6	4.8	4.1	14.3	6.6	5.4	14.1	6.3	5.3	13.9	6.2	5.3	13.4	5.9	5.2
	Labour force participation rates	55.6	78.9	50.4	53.1	79.8	49.2	52.4	79.9	49.1	51.9	80.1	49.6	51.5	80.2	50.2
	Employment/population ratios	49.1	75.1	48.3	45.5	74.5	46.6	45.0	74.9	46.5	44.7	75.1	46.9	44.6	75.4	47.6

a)   For 1994, data cover persons aged 55 and over.
b)   Age group 15 to 24 refers to 16 to 24.
c)   The year 1990 refers to 1991.
d)   Above countries only.

Sources: OECD, *Labour Force Statistics, 1977-1997,* Part III, forthcoming.
For Austria, Belgium, Denmark, Greece, Italy, Luxembourg, Netherlands and Portugal, data are from the European Labour Force Survey.

Table C. **Unemployment, labour force participation rates and employment/population ratios by age and sex** (cont.)

Men
Percentages

		1990			1994			1995			1996			1997		
		15 to 24	25 to 54	55 to 64	15 to 24	25 to 54	55 to 64	15 to 24	25 to 54	55 to 64	15 to 24	25 to 54	55 to 64	15 to 24	25 to 54	55 to 64
Australia	Unemployment rates	13.9	4.9	6.3	16.7	7.5	10.3	14.8	6.9	9.0	15.4	7.2	9.8	17.2	6.6	8.7
	Labour force participation rates	73.0	93.1	63.2	70.7	91.4	60.7	71.8	91.6	60.9	72.9	91.5	60.3	68.9	90.6	59.6
	Employment/population ratios	62.8	88.5	59.2	58.9	84.5	54.4	61.1	85.4	55.4	61.6	84.9	54.6	57.1	84.6	54.4
Austria	Unemployment rates	..	..	..	..	..	..	5.7	3.6	4.4	7.1	5.1	5.1	7.8	4.5	6.0
	Labour force participation rates	..	..	..	..	..	..	64.6	93.2	42.6	62.9	93.0	44.7	61.4	93.3	43.0
	Employment/population ratios	..	..	..	..	..	..	60.9	89.8	40.8	58.4	88.2	42.4	56.6	89.1	40.5
Belgium	Unemployment rates	10.1	4.0	3.1	20.5	6.4	4.5	19.7	6.2	3.8	17.3	6.6	4.7	17.6	6.2	4.8
	Labour force participation rates	37.0	92.2	35.4	37.3	92.1	34.5	36.0	92.3	35.9	35.6	92.4	33.8	34.7	92.1	33.9
	Employment/population ratios	33.3	88.5	34.3	29.7	86.2	33.0	28.9	86.5	34.5	29.4	86.3	32.2	28.5	86.4	32.2
Canada	Unemployment rates	13.9	7.1	6.2	18.5	9.5	9.5	17.0	8.6	8.3	17.5	8.7	7.8	17.6	7.9	7.5
	Labour force participation rates	71.4	93.3	64.9	65.2	91.4	60.3	63.9	91.0	58.9	63.5	91.0	59.3	63.4	91.1	60.6
	Employment/population ratios	61.5	86.6	60.9	53.2	82.7	54.6	53.1	83.2	54.0	52.4	83.1	54.7	52.2	83.9	56.1
Czech Republic	Unemployment rates	..	..	..	7.8	2.3	2.8	7.5	2.6	2.6	6.4	2.5	3.2	7.3	3.1	3.2
	Labour force participation rates	..	..	..	56.3	95.2	48.5	58.0	95.4	52.0	57.8	95.2	55.8	56.1	95.2	56.4
	Employment/population ratios	..	..	..	51.9	93.1	47.2	53.7	92.9	50.6	54.1	92.8	54.0	52.0	92.3	54.7
Denmark	Unemployment rates	11.4	7.5	5.2	10.2	6.7	6.3	7.8	5.0	6.9	9.0	4.7	6.0	6.6	4.1	4.4
	Labour force participation rates	76.5	94.5	69.2	72.1	91.9	63.8	77.0	91.8	67.9	76.6	92.8	62.1	77.7	92.5	63.8
	Employment/population ratios	67.8	87.4	65.6	64.8	85.7	59.8	71.0	87.3	63.2	69.7	88.5	58.4	72.5	88.7	61.0
Finland	Unemployment rates	7.3	3.4	2.8	26.5	15.1	25.4	41.3	14.6	16.3	24.5	13.5	24.6	23.3	11.7	19.3
	Labour force participation rates	61.9	92.8	45.4	50.3	91.1	46.0	51.1	88.3	41.6	50.5	90.6	48.8	53.8	91.0	46.9
	Employment/population ratios	57.4	89.7	44.2	37.0	77.3	34.3	30.0	75.4	34.9	38.1	78.4	36.8	41.3	80.3	37.8
France	Unemployment rates	15.3	5.9	6.0	24.2	9.7	7.3	21.0	8.8	7.7	22.1	9.3	8.6	25.4	9.9	8.5
	Labour force participation rates	39.6	95.4	45.8	33.5	95.1	42.1	32.8	94.9	41.5	32.4	95.2	42.3	32.8	94.9	31.6
	Employment/population ratios	33.6	89.8	43.0	25.4	85.9	39.1	25.9	86.6	38.4	25.3	86.3	38.6	24.5	85.5	28.9
Germany	Unemployment rates	5.3	4.7	9.9	8.3	6.6	10.6	8.3	6.4	10.7	9.3	7.2	12.2	10.3	8.0	13.4
	Labour force participation rates	62.0	91.2	57.7	59.0	93.3	53.3	57.0	93.1	54.1	56.4	93.2	54.7	56.1	92.5	54.6
	Employment/population ratios	58.7	86.9	52.0	54.2	87.1	47.6	52.3	87.1	48.3	51.2	86.5	48.0	50.3	85.1	47.3
Greece	Unemployment rates	15.1	3.2	1.8	19.8	4.8	3.3	19.4	5.1	3.6	21.5	4.8	2.9	22.2	4.9	3.3
	Labour force participation rates	44.1	94.3	59.5	41.8	94.5	60.1	41.3	94.5	61.1	40.1	94.9	61.0	38.7	94.6	61.0
	Employment/population ratios	37.4	91.3	58.4	33.5	90.0	58.1	33.3	89.7	58.9	31.5	90.3	59.2	30.1	89.9	59.0
Hungary[a]	Unemployment rates	..	..	..	21.5	10.2	7.1	20.7	9.9	5.4	19.0	9.4	5.7	16.9	8.2	6.3
	Labour force participation rates	..	..	..	46.0	86.9	19.4	44.6	86.5	28.6	43.7	85.9	28.0	43.6	85.0	27.8
	Employment/population ratios	..	..	..	36.1	78.1	18.0	35.3	77.9	27.1	35.4	77.8	26.4	36.2	78.0	26.1
Iceland[b, c]	Unemployment rates	5.6	1.8	1.1	12.6	3.5	4.2	13.1	3.0	4.3	8.9	2.1	3.3	8.1	2.3	3.3
	Labour force participation rates	59.9	97.1	93.1	58.0	96.1	96.0	64.0	96.7	92.9	60.3	96.4	93.9	59.4	96.7	91.9
	Employment/population ratios	56.5	95.3	92.2	50.7	92.8	91.9	55.7	93.8	88.9	54.9	94.3	90.8	54.6	94.6	88.9

Table C. **Unemployment, labour force participation rates and employment/population ratios by age and sex** (cont.)

Men

Percentages

Country	Indicator	1990 15 to 24	1990 25 to 54	1990 55 to 64	1994 15 to 24	1994 25 to 54	1994 55 to 64	1995 15 to 24	1995 25 to 54	1995 55 to 64	1996 15 to 24	1996 25 to 54	1996 55 to 64	1997 15 to 24	1997 25 to 54	1997 55 to 64
Ireland	Unemployment rates	18.9	11.8	8.5	25.4	13.4	8.6	20.5	11.2	7.5	19.2	11.2	6.9	16.9	9.7	6.4
	Labour force participation rates	53.4	91.9	65.1	48.2	91.1	64.7	49.0	90.6	63.9	47.1	91.5	63.0	48.9	90.5	61.7
	Employment/population ratios	43.3	81.1	59.6	35.9	78.8	59.1	38.9	80.5	59.1	38.0	81.3	58.7	40.6	81.7	57.8
Italy	Unemployment rates	23.4	3.9	1.7	28.7	6.4	3.8	29.0	6.7	4.1	30.0	7.1	4.3	28.7	7.5	4.6
	Labour force participation rates	50.7	94.0	51.7	44.1	90.1	46.5	43.8	89.5	44.1	43.0	89.7	44.0	42.2	89.8	43.5
	Employment/population ratios	38.8	90.2	50.9	31.4	84.3	44.8	31.1	83.5	42.3	30.1	83.4	42.1	30.1	83.0	41.5
Japan	Unemployment rates	4.5	1.4	3.4	5.6	2.0	4.5	6.1	2.2	4.7	6.8	2.5	5.1	6.9	2.5	5.0
	Labour force participation rates	43.4	97.5	83.3	48.0	97.5	85.0	48.0	97.5	84.8	48.9	97.7	84.9	49.4	97.6	85.1
	Employment/population ratios	41.4	96.2	80.4	45.4	95.5	81.2	45.1	95.3	80.8	45.6	95.3	80.6	46.0	95.1	80.9
Korea	Unemployment rates	9.5	2.5	1.2	9.3	2.4	0.9	8.0	1.9	1.1	8.3	2.0	0.9	9.4	2.4	1.7
	Labour force participation rates	28.4	94.6	77.2	31.0	94.6	79.7	30.1	94.6	79.7	29.5	94.4	79.2	28.2	94.0	79.1
	Employment/population ratios	25.7	92.2	76.3	28.1	92.3	79.0	27.7	92.8	78.8	27.1	92.5	78.5	25.6	91.8	77.7
Luxembourg	Unemployment rates	2.7	1.1	1.1	8.5	2.5	0.4	6.7	1.7	0.0	10.1	1.8	0.0	..	..	..
	Labour force participation rates	45.7	95.1	43.2	47.9	94.9	33.6	42.4	93.9	35.1	42.8	93.8	35.6	..	..	..
	Employment/population ratios	44.5	94.0	42.7	43.8	92.6	33.5	39.6	92.2	35.1	38.5	92.1	35.6	..	..	..
Mexico[c]	Unemployment rates	5.2	1.5	1.0	6.5	3.2	2.1	8.6	4.6	3.5	7.1	3.2	2.6	5.6	2.1	1.1
	Labour force participation rates	71.2	96.8	85.9	72.6	96.1	82.4	72.5	96.2	80.7	71.8	96.5	80.2	71.5	96.8	83.2
	Employment/population ratios	67.5	95.4	85.1	67.9	93.0	80.7	66.3	91.8	77.9	66.7	93.4	78.2	67.6	94.8	82.3
Netherlands	Unemployment rates	10.3	5.0	2.8	13.6	5.6	2.6	11.5	5.4	3.6	11.3	4.3	3.5	9.2	3.6	3.2
	Labour force participation rates	60.0	93.4	45.8	61.6	92.6	42.3	62.2	92.6	41.4	61.3	92.7	42.2	64.3	93.5	44.4
	Employment/population ratios	53.8	88.8	44.5	53.2	87.4	41.2	55.0	87.7	39.9	54.4	88.7	40.7	58.4	90.1	43.0
New Zealand	Unemployment rates	14.9	6.6	4.9	15.6	7.0	5.4	11.9	5.1	3.6	12.3	4.7	4.3	15.1	5.6	4.9
	Labour force participation rates	71.4	93.4	56.8	69.8	92.3	63.0	71.4	92.1	65.4	70.9	92.0	69.0	60.6	87.3	66.1
	Employment/population ratios	60.7	87.2	54.0	58.9	85.9	59.6	62.8	87.4	63.0	62.1	87.7	66.1	51.4	82.4	62.9
Norway[b]	Unemployment rates	12.4	4.7	3.0	13.1	5.0	3.1	11.9	4.3	3.2	12.1	3.8	2.5	10.1	3.2	2.2
	Labour force participation rates	63.9	92.3	72.8	57.8	90.6	71.5	58.0	91.2	72.3	62.0	92.1	73.2	65.4	92.6	75.1
	Employment/population ratios	56.0	88.0	70.7	50.2	86.0	69.3	51.1	87.3	70.0	54.5	88.6	71.4	58.8	89.7	73.5
Poland	Unemployment rates	..	..	..	30.8	11.3	7.5	29.0	10.4	6.7	26.3	9.3	6.3	22.0	8.2	5.6
	Labour force participation rates	..	..	..	45.2	90.9	46.7	43.9	90.1	45.5	43.4	89.7	44.5	42.3	89.4	45.3
	Employment/population ratios	..	..	..	31.3	80.6	43.2	31.1	80.8	42.5	32.0	81.4	41.7	33.0	82.1	42.7
Portugal	Unemployment rates	7.9	2.4	1.9	12.5	4.8	4.6	15.1	5.3	4.9	14.6	5.2	5.9	11.0	5.0	6.4
	Labour force participation rates	63.8	94.0	65.9	48.9	93.7	63.6	47.2	93.6	61.9	46.2	93.4	62.2	48.5	92.7	62.2
	Employment/population ratios	58.7	91.7	64.6	42.8	89.2	60.6	40.1	88.6	58.9	39.4	88.5	58.5	43.1	88.0	58.2
Spain[b]	Unemployment rates	26.2	9.3	8.4	37.4	16.4	13.3	37.0	15.3	12.6	36.3	14.9	11.4	33.1	13.6	10.8
	Labour force participation rates	54.6	94.1	62.4	54.7	92.9	56.1	47.7	92.5	54.9	47.1	92.6	56.3	47.2	92.4	56.6
	Employment/population ratios	40.3	85.4	57.2	34.3	77.6	48.6	30.1	78.3	48.0	30.0	78.8	49.9	31.6	79.9	50.5

Table C. **Unemployment, labour force participation rates and employment/population ratios by age and sex** (cont.)

Men

Percentages

		1990			1994			1995			1996			1997		
		15 to 24	25 to 54	55 to 64	15 to 24	25 to 54	55 to 64	15 to 24	25 to 54	55 to 64	15 to 24	25 to 54	55 to 64	15 to 24	25 to 54	55 to 64
Sweden[b]	Unemployment rates	3.8	1.3	1.3	19.0	7.8	7.8	16.7	7.2	8.5	16.7	7.4	8.6	16.3	7.3	8.5
	Labour force participation rates	68.7	94.7	75.3	49.4	89.8	69.9	50.1	90.6	70.4	48.9	90.0	72.2	48.2	89.1	70.7
	Employment/population ratios	66.1	93.5	74.4	40.0	82.8	64.5	41.8	84.0	64.4	40.7	83.4	66.0	40.3	82.6	64.7
Switzerland[c]	Unemployment rates	3.0	0.9	1.4	5.6	3.2	4.9	5.8	2.3	4.0	5.4	3.3	3.3	7.9	3.9	3.1
	Labour force participation rates	70.8	97.0	85.2	64.5	94.4	78.5	64.2	95.5	78.8	65.4	94.0	77.9	69.0	97.0	81.9
	Employment/population ratios	68.7	96.1	84.0	60.9	91.4	74.7	60.5	93.2	75.7	61.9	90.9	75.3	63.5	93.2	79.3
Turkey	Unemployment rates	16.6	5.2	4.0	17.3	6.2	2.9	16.3	4.9	3.1	14.6	4.6	2.3	14.0	4.3	1.8
	Labour force participation rates	71.8	94.2	61.3	64.8	93.4	58.3	61.9	93.4	60.9	60.9	92.6	57.4	59.4	92.1	56.5
	Employment/population ratios	59.9	89.3	58.8	53.5	87.6	56.6	51.8	88.8	59.1	52.0	88.3	56.1	51.1	88.1	55.4
United Kingdom[b]	Unemployment rates	11.1	5.6	8.4	19.1	9.8	11.6	17.9	8.5	10.1	17.8	8.0	9.5	15.6	6.7	7.8
	Labour force participation rates	83.5	94.8	68.1	75.1	93.0	64.1	74.4	92.7	62.4	75.3	91.9	62.9	74.6	91.6	63.6
	Employment/population ratios	74.2	89.5	62.4	60.8	83.9	56.6	61.1	84.8	56.1	61.9	84.6	57.0	63.0	85.4	58.6
United States[b]	Unemployment rates	11.6	4.6	3.8	13.2	4.9	4.4	12.5	4.4	3.6	12.6	4.2	3.3	11.8	3.7	3.1
	Labour force participation rates	71.8	93.4	67.8	70.3	91.7	65.5	70.2	91.6	66.0	68.8	91.8	67.0	68.2	91.8	67.6
	Employment/population ratios	63.5	89.1	65.2	61.0	87.2	62.6	61.5	87.6	63.6	60.1	87.9	64.7	60.1	88.4	65.5
European Union[d]	Unemployment rates	13.8	5.3	6.2	20.5	8.6	8.9	19.2	8.0	8.7	19.7	8.2	9.0	18.8	8.1	9.0
	Labour force participation rates	57.8	93.7	56.6	52.5	92.8	52.5	51.1	92.6	51.8	50.6	92.6	52.3	50.3	92.3	52.4
	Employment/population ratios	49.8	84.8	53.1	41.7	84.8	47.8	41.3	85.2	47.3	40.6	85.0	47.6	40.8	84.9	47.6
OECD Europe[d]	Unemployment rates	14.1	5.2	5.8	19.9	8.3	8.0	18.7	7.6	7.7	18.5	7.7	7.9	17.5	7.4	7.8
	Labour force participation rates	60.2	93.8	57.7	54.0	92.6	53.0	52.4	92.4	52.3	51.9	92.4	52.3	51.4	92.0	52.5
	Employment/population ratios	51.7	89.0	54.3	43.2	84.9	48.8	42.6	85.4	48.2	42.3	85.2	48.2	42.4	85.2	48.4
Total OECD[d]	Unemployment rates	11.2	4.2	4.4	14.4	6.1	5.9	13.9	5.7	5.7	13.7	5.6	5.7	12.9	5.3	5.5
	Labour force participation rates	61.0	94.4	66.4	58.6	93.3	63.2	57.8	93.1	62.6	57.3	93.1	63.0	56.8	93.0	63.5
	Employment/population ratios	54.1	90.5	63.5	50.1	87.6	59.5	49.8	87.8	59.0	49.4	87.9	59.4	49.5	88.1	60.1

a) For 1994, data cover persons aged 55 and over.
b) Age group 15 to 24 refers to 16 to 24.
c) The year 1990 refers to 1991.
d) Above countries only.
Sources: OECD, *Labour Force Statistics, 1977-1997*, Part III, forthcoming.
For Austria, Belgium, Denmark, Greece, Italy, Luxembourg, Netherlands and Portugal, data are from the European Labour Force Survey.

Table C. **Unemployment, labour force participation rates and employment/population ratios by age and sex** (cont.)

Women

Percentages

		1990			1994			1995			1996			1997		
		15 to 24	25 to 54	55 to 64	15 to 24	25 to 54	55 to 64	15 to 24	25 to 54	55 to 64	15 to 24	25 to 54	55 to 64	15 to 24	25 to 54	55 to 64
Australia	Unemployment rates	12.4	5.5	3.0	15.7	6.9	4.7	14.0	5.7	4.0	14.1	6.4	4.3	14.6	6.6	4.2
	Labour force participation rates	67.7	66.6	24.9	65.9	67.4	26.5	67.6	69.2	28.6	67.6	68.8	31.3	64.8	68.6	30.6
	Employment/population ratios	59.3	63.0	24.2	55.6	62.7	25.3	58.2	65.2	27.5	58.0	64.4	30.0	55.4	64.1	29.3
Austria	Unemployment rates	:	:	:	:	:	:	6.2	4.8	2.9	6.5	5.1	3.5	7.3	5.0	3.3
	Labour force participation rates	:	:	:	:	:	:	58.9	73.3	18.8	56.4	73.9	17.9	55.4	74.4	17.9
	Employment/population ratios	:	:	:	:	:	:	55.2	69.8	18.3	52.7	70.1	17.3	51.4	70.7	17.3
Belgium	Unemployment rates	19.2	10.3	4.9	23.4	11.2	5.9	23.7	11.1	4.4	24.4	11.3	4.0	25.7	10.2	4.3
	Labour force participation rates	34.1	60.8	9.9	33.0	67.2	13.2	31.7	68.2	13.3	29.9	69.0	12.5	29.3	69.7	13.0
	Employment/population ratios	27.5	54.5	9.4	25.3	59.7	12.4	24.2	60.6	12.7	22.6	61.2	12.0	21.8	62.6	12.4
Canada	Unemployment rates	11.3	7.5	5.6	14.3	9.0	8.3	14.0	8.3	8.0	14.6	8.5	7.6	15.7	7.9	7.8
	Labour force participation rates	67.0	75.7	35.5	60.6	75.7	37.4	60.4	75.9	36.3	59.5	76.4	36.9	59.0	76.6	36.5
	Employment/population ratios	59.4	70.0	33.5	51.9	68.9	34.3	51.9	69.6	33.4	50.8	69.9	34.1	49.7	70.5	33.6
Czech Republic	Unemployment rates	:	:	:	7.6	3.8	3.4	8.5	4.2	3.8	8.3	4.0	4.1	9.9	5.1	4.5
	Labour force participation rates	:	:	:	51.7	88.4	19.7	42.9	83.7	21.3	40.8	82.1	23.2	40.2	82.0	25.0
	Employment/population ratios	:	:	:	47.8	85.0	19.1	39.2	80.3	20.5	37.4	78.9	22.3	36.2	77.9	23.8
Denmark	Unemployment rates	11.6	8.4	7.5	10.2	9.0	6.7	12.3	7.6	9.8	12.4	7.6	6.3	9.9	5.7	6.0
	Labour force participation rates	70.4	87.7	45.8	65.9	82.7	43.1	69.4	82.1	40.1	70.8	82.1	39.5	70.4	81.7	43.9
	Employment/population ratios	62.2	80.3	42.4	59.1	75.2	40.2	60.9	75.9	36.1	62.0	75.8	37.0	63.4	77.0	41.2
Finland	Unemployment rates	5.2	2.3	3.8	30.1	14.5	22.2	28.1	14.6	22.8	25.0	14.3	26.3	26.6	12.7	20.9
	Labour force participation rates	54.1	86.0	39.7	39.8	84.7	40.8	39.3	85.1	42.9	38.7	85.4	44.2	44.6	85.5	42.6
	Employment/population ratios	51.3	84.0	38.2	27.8	72.5	31.7	28.2	72.7	33.1	29.0	73.2	32.6	32.7	74.6	33.7
France	Unemployment rates	23.9	10.7	7.6	31.6	13.1	6.7	32.2	12.6	6.6	31.9	13.0	8.2	24.6	9.7	8.6
	Labour force participation rates	33.1	72.9	31.1	27.8	76.7	30.1	26.7	77.3	30.9	25.9	77.8	31.3	31.4	94.8	42.0
	Employment/population ratios	25.2	65.1	28.8	19.0	66.6	28.1	18.1	67.5	28.9	17.7	67.6	28.8	23.7	85.6	38.4
Germany	Unemployment rates	6.0	7.1	15.2	8.2	10.0	13.5	8.0	9.2	13.5	8.7	9.3	14.7	9.6	10.4	16.5
	Labour force participation rates	57.4	64.1	26.4	53.1	72.8	28.4	50.1	73.3	31.1	48.0	73.9	32.9	47.8	73.7	33.0
	Employment/population ratios	54.0	59.6	22.4	48.8	65.5	24.6	46.1	66.6	26.9	43.9	67.1	28.0	43.2	66.0	27.5
Greece	Unemployment rates	32.6	8.6	1.2	36.9	10.7	2.6	37.7	10.9	2.9	41.3	12.3	3.0	40.6	11.9	3.1
	Labour force participation rates	35.3	51.5	24.3	32.6	53.9	23.0	32.5	55.0	24.5	34.1	56.9	24.5	32.6	57.5	25.1
	Employment/population ratios	23.8	47.1	24.0	20.6	48.1	22.4	20.3	49.0	23.8	20.0	49.9	23.8	19.4	50.7	24.4
Hungary[a]	Unemployment rates	:	:	:	16.6	8.1	9.6	15.6	7.7	5.3	16.4	7.8	4.0	14.5	6.7	4.4
	Labour force participation rates	:	:	:	35.3	71.5	7.3	31.9	68.9	9.7	30.2	68.5	14.4	30.6	67.2	10.8
	Employment/population ratios	:	:	:	29.5	65.7	6.6	27.0	63.6	9.2	25.2	63.2	13.8	26.1	62.7	10.3
Iceland[b, c]	Unemployment rates	4.3	2.7	3.6	10.4	4.9	3.6	8.6	4.3	3.5	7.8	3.3	4.9	6.7	3.9	3.6
	Labour force participation rates	58.7	83.0	80.8	59.0	86.4	80.6	59.8	88.1	84.3	59.6	86.8	81.2	61.3	85.1	80.6
	Employment/population ratios	56.1	80.8	77.9	52.8	82.1	77.7	54.6	84.3	81.4	54.9	84.0	77.2	57.2	81.8	77.7

Table C. **Unemployment, labour force participation rates and employment/population ratios by age and sex** (cont.)

Women

Percentages

		1990			1994			1995			1996			1997		
		15 to 24	25 to 54	55 to 64	15 to 24	25 to 54	55 to 64	15 to 24	25 to 54	55 to 64	15 to 24	25 to 54	55 to 64	15 to 24	25 to 54	55 to 64
Ireland	Unemployment rates	16.1	13.5	8.3	20.8	13.2	8.2	17.4	10.9	8.5	17.0	10.7	6.7	15.2	9.3	4.9
	Labour force participation rates	47.3	45.5	19.9	42.5	54.1	21.4	42.0	54.6	21.2	40.6	57.5	23.4	41.9	58.4	23.3
	Employment/population ratios	39.6	39.3	18.2	33.7	47.0	19.7	34.7	48.6	19.4	33.7	51.4	21.8	35.6	53.0	22.2
Italy	Unemployment rates	35.4	11.3	2.0	35.4	12.3	3.0	37.6	12.6	4.9	39.2	12.9	4.3	39.9	13.1	3.8
	Labour force participation rates	43.0	52.1	15.0	34.3	53.2	13.7	33.8	53.7	13.8	33.9	54.8	14.4	33.8	55.1	15.0
	Employment/population ratios	27.8	46.2	14.7	22.1	46.6	13.3	21.1	47.0	13.1	20.6	47.7	13.8	20.3	47.9	14.4
Japan	Unemployment rates	4.1	2.1	1.4	5.3	2.8	1.9	6.1	3.1	2.1	6.7	3.2	2.3	6.3	3.2	2.2
	Labour force participation rates	44.8	64.2	47.2	47.1	65.3	48.1	47.2	65.2	48.5	47.6	65.8	48.8	47.7	66.7	49.5
	Employment/population ratios	43.0	62.9	46.5	44.6	63.4	47.2	44.4	63.2	47.5	44.4	63.7	47.6	44.7	64.6	48.4
Korea	Unemployment rates	5.5	0.9	0.1	6.0	1.0	0.2	5.3	0.9	0.4	4.8	1.0	0.4	6.6	1.7	.6
	Labour force participation rates	40.7	54.2	49.6	42.3	50.1	50.1	41.9	55.6	50.4	40.5	56.9	49.6	39.8	58.4	49.2
	Employment/population ratios	38.5	53.7	49.5	39.7	49.9	49.9	39.7	55.1	50.2	38.5	56.4	49.4	37.:	57.5	48.9
Luxembourg	Unemployment rates	4.7	2.2	0.0	7.2	3.9	1.2	7.8	3.9	1.0	8.3	4.2	0.0	:	:	:
	Labour force participation rates	44.0	49.7	13.8	45.0	55.7	13.4	40.0	52.7	13.3	38.5	55.9	10.2	:	:	:
	Employment/population ratios	42.0	48.6	13.8	41.8	53.5	13.2	36.8	50.6	13.2	35.3	53.6	10.2	:	:	:
Mexico[c]	Unemployment rates	5.8	3.8	1.0	8.3	3.5	1.7	10.8	4.1	2.6	8.8	3.5	1.0	8.4	3.6	2.2
	Labour force participation rates	34.5	38.2	24.4	35.8	41.3	25.8	36.0	42.3	26.9	35.2	43.4	27.8	36.2	46.1	30.1
	Employment/population ratios	32.5	36.8	24.2	32.8	39.8	25.4	32.1	40.6	26.2	32.1	41.9	27.5	33.2	44.4	29.4
Netherlands	Unemployment rates	11.9	10.9	6.3	9.0	8.0	4.9	12.7	7.9	3.2	11.6	7.5	5.1	10.3	6.5	5.5
	Labour force participation rates	59.2	57.9	16.9	59.6	65.0	18.4	61.8	65.7	18.6	60.9	67.5	20.5	61.8	69.6	21.0
	Employment/population ratios	52.2	51.6	15.8	54.3	59.8	17.5	53.9	60.5	18.0	53.9	62.5	19.4	55.4	65.1	19.8
New Zealand	Unemployment rates	13.2	5.4	4.0	14.3	6.1	3.5	11.7	5.1	2.7	11.0	5.1	2.7	14.8	5.7	3.1
	Labour force participation rates	64.3	69.3	30.7	62.2	71.0	36.7	63.3	71.6	38.9	64.0	73.2	42.8	55.7	68.5	43.0
	Employment/population ratios	55.8	65.6	29.5	53.3	66.6	35.4	55.9	68.0	37.9	56.9	69.5	41.7	47.4	64.6	41.7
Norway[b]	Unemployment rates	11.0	3.9	1.9	12.1	3.8	1.9	11.8	3.7	1.9	12.7	3.9	1.8	11.1	3.5	1.7
	Labour force participation rates	56.9	79.2	53.9	53.0	79.4	55.4	53.7	80.4	57.4	57.3	81.7	59.2	58.1	83.3	60.6
	Employment/population ratios	50.7	76.1	52.8	46.6	76.4	54.3	47.3	77.4	56.4	50.0	78.5	58.1	51.6	80.4	59.6
Poland	Unemployment rates	:	:	:	34.7	14.5	6.4	33.8	13.2	4.9	31.2	12.5	5.2	28.0	12.0	4.9
	Labour force participation rates	:	:	:	37.9	78.6	28.7	35.6	78.0	27.6	34.6	77.5	26.9	34.3	76.5	27.1
	Employment/population ratios	:	:	:	24.8	67.2	26.8	23.5	67.7	26.3	23.8	67.8	25.5	24.7	67.3	25.7
Portugal	Unemployment rates	13.3	5.4	1.4	16.9	6.8	2.1	17.1	7.0	2.6	20.0	7.4	3.6	18.0	6.5	3.4
	Labour force participation rates	53.0	67.0	31.5	41.6	73.4	33.8	38.9	74.1	34.5	38.3	74.3	36.8	39.8	74.8	38.3
	Employment/population ratios	46.0	63.4	31.1	34.5	68.4	33.1	32.3	68.9	33.6	30.6	68.8	35.4	32.6	69.9	37.0
Spain[b]	Unemployment rates	39.7	20.6	7.2	50.1	28.4	9.8	49.1	27.5	11.4	48.8	26.3	12.1	46.1	25.4	12.7
	Labour force participation rates	47.5	46.9	19.5	43.1	54.3	19.3	42.4	55.5	19.9	41.4	56.8	20.2	41.2	58.1	20.6
	Employment/population ratios	28.7	37.2	18.1	21.5	38.9	17.4	21.6	40.2	17.6	21.2	41.9	17.8	22.2	43.4	18.0

EMPLOYMENT OUTLOOK

Table C. **Unemployment, labour force participation rates and employment/population ratios by age and sex** *(cont.)*

Women

Percentages

		1990			1994			1995			1996			1997		
		15 to 24	25 to 54	55 to 64	15 to 24	25 to 54	55 to 64	15 to 24	25 to 54	55 to 64	15 to 24	25 to 54	55 to 64	15 to 24	25 to 54	55 to 64
Sweden[b]	Unemployment rates	3.6	1.2	1.6	14.3	5.8	5.0	14.0	5.9	6.3	14.5	6.7	6.5	14.3	6.9	6.0
	Labour force participation rates	68.3	90.8	65.8	49.9	86.0	62.5	49.9	86.2	63.4	46.7	85.8	65.0	45.4	84.4	64.6
	Employment/population ratios	65.9	89.7	64.7	42.8	81.0	59.4	42.9	81.1	59.5	39.9	80.1	60.7	38.9	78.6	60.7
Switzerland[c]	Unemployment rates	3.5	2.7	0.7	7.0	4.3	3.4	5.9	4.1	2.0	4.3	4.6	3.8	3.8	4.2	2.5
	Labour force participation rates	67.8	71.7	53.1	63.6	70.8	56.9	60.7	72.1	57.9	63.0	72.5	42.1	64.8	76.7	60.7
	Employment/population ratios	65.4	69.8	52.7	59.1	67.7	55.0	57.1	69.1	56.7	60.3	69.2	40.5	62.3	73.5	59.2
Turkey	Unemployment rates	15.0	5.9	1.0	13.1	5.7	0.4	12.1	4.7	0.4	10.4	3.7	0.3	15.0	4.8	0.5
	Labour force participation rates	39.4	36.0	26.6	35.7	33.5	24.3	35.3	34.4	26.1	34.7	32.8	27.9	31.2	29.5	24.3
	Employment/population ratios	33.5	33.9	26.4	31.0	31.6	24.2	31.0	32.8	26.0	31.1	31.6	27.8	26.5	28.1	24.2
United Kingdom[b]	Unemployment rates	9.0	5.9	5.0	12.6	6.4	5.4	12.2	6.0	3.7	11.1	5.6	3.4	11.0	4.9	3.9
	Labour force participation rates	72.4	72.9	38.7	65.1	74.0	40.7	64.9	74.0	40.8	65.8	74.5	40.2	66.1	75.0	40.3
	Employment/population ratios	65.9	68.6	36.7	56.9	69.3	38.5	57.0	69.5	39.3	58.6	70.3	38.8	58.8	71.3	38.7
United States[b]	Unemployment rates	10.7	4.6	2.8	11.6	5.0	3.9	11.6	4.5	3.6	11.3	4.4	3.4	10.7	4.1	2.7
	Labour force participation rates	62.9	74.0	45.2	62.5	75.3	48.9	62.3	75.6	49.2	62.2	76.1	49.6	62.6	76.7	50.9
	Employment/population ratios	56.1	70.6	44.0	55.3	71.5	47.0	55.1	72.2	47.5	55.2	72.8	47.9	55.9	73.5	49.5
European Union[d]	Unemployment rates	18.3	9.2	6.9	22.1	11.5	8.0	22.2	11.0	8.2	22.6	11.0	8.9	22.4	11.0	9.4
	Labour force participation rates	50.7	63.7	26.5	44.5	68.1	27.1	43.8	68.7	27.9	43.0	69.5	28.7	42.8	69.8	29.1
	Employment/population ratios	41.5	57.9	24.7	34.7	60.3	24.9	34.0	61.2	25.7	33.3	61.8	26.1	33.2	62.1	26.3
OECD Europe[d]	Unemployment rates	17.5	8.7	6.2	20.7	11.0	7.1	20.7	10.4	7.0	20.5	10.3	7.7	20.9	10.3	8.1
	Labour force participation rates	49.1	60.8	27.1	42.8	66.0	27.4	41.7	66.3	27.7	40.9	66.5	28.5	40.1	66.3	28.6
	Employment/population ratios	40.5	55.5	25.4	33.9	58.7	25.4	33.1	59.4	25.8	32.6	59.7	26.3	31.7	59.4	26.3
Total OECD[d]	Unemployment rates	12.1	5.8	3.6	14.2	7.4	4.6	14.4	7.0	4.6	14.0	7.0	4.7	14.0	6.8	4.7
	Labour force participation rates	50.3	63.6	35.5	47.6	66.4	36.2	47.0	66.8	36.4	46.5	67.2	37.0	46.2	67.5	37.7
	Employment/population ratios	44.2	59.9	34.2	40.8	61.5	34.5	40.3	62.1	34.8	39.9	62.5	35.3	39.7	62.9	35.9

a) For 1994, data cover persons aged 55 and over.
b) Age group 15 to 24 refers to 16 to 24.
c) The year 1990 refers to 1991.
d) Above countries only.
Sources: OECD, *Labour Force Statistics, 1977-1997,* Part III, forthcoming.
For Austria, Belgium, Denmark, Greece, Italy, Luxembourg, Netherlands and Portugal, data are from the European Labour Force Survey.

Table D. **Unemployment, labour force participation rates and employment/population ratios by educational attainment for persons aged 25-64, 1995**

Percentages

		Both sexes			Men			Women		
		Less than upper secondary education	Upper secondary education	Tertiary level education	Less than upper secondary education	Upper secondary education	Tertiary level education	Less than upper secondary education	Upper secondary education	Tertiary level education
Australia	Unemployment rates	8.5	6.2	4.0	11.0	6.2	4.0	6.2	6.3	4.0
	Labour force participation rates	66.4	80.8	86.7	82.4	89.6	92.7	56.4	63.5	80.0
	Employment/population ratios	60.8	75.8	83.2	73.4	84.1	88.9	52.9	59.5	76.8
Austria	Unemployment rates	5.7	2.9	2.0	5.3	2.5	1.7	6.1	3.4	2.3
	Labour force participation rates	59.2	78.9	90.1	73.9	87.0	93.2	50.2	68.7	85.9
	Employment/population ratios	55.8	76.7	88.3	70.0	84.8	91.6	47.1	66.4	84.0
Belgium	Unemployment rates	13.4	7.5	3.6	10.3	4.6	3.0	18.8	11.6	4.2
	Labour force participation rates	54.6	77.9	86.8	70.3	88.5	91.6	39.4	66.5	82.0
	Employment/population ratios	47.3	72.1	83.7	63.0	84.4	88.9	32.0	58.7	78.5
Canada	Unemployment rates	13.0	8.6	6.5	13.2	8.6	6.5	12.7	8.6	6.4
	Labour force participation rates	60.6	79.1	86.1	74.0	88.2	91.1	47.0	71.2	80.8
	Employment/population ratios	52.7	72.3	80.6	64.2	80.6	85.1	41.1	65.1	75.6
Czech Republic	Unemployment rates	7.7	2.1	0.7	8.9	1.7	0.5	7.1	2.7	1.0
	Labour force participation rates	60.2	84.3	92.5	73.7	88.7	93.9	54.6	79.4	90.3
	Employment/population ratios	55.6	82.4	91.9	67.1	87.2	93.4	50.8	77.2	89.4
Denmark	Unemployment rates	14.6	8.3	4.6	12.5	7.4	5.1	16.6	9.5	4.1
	Labour force participation rates	72.0	87.8	92.9	79.0	90.1	94.4	66.3	84.8	91.4
	Employment/population ratios	61.5	80.5	88.6	69.1	83.4	89.6	55.3	76.7	87.7
Finland	Unemployment rates	21.6	16.1	7.6	21.7	16.6	8.1	21.5	15.6	7.1
	Labour force participation rates	69.0	84.7	88.9	72.4	88.2	90.9	65.4	81.3	86.5
	Employment/population ratios	54.1	71.0	82.1	56.6	73.6	83.6	51.4	68.6	80.4
France	Unemployment rates	14.0	8.9	6.5	12.8	7.9	6.3	15.3	12.8	6.7
	Labour force participation rates	60.3	82.8	87.7	70.9	89.7	92.5	52.5	74.7	83.2
	Employment/population ratios	51.9	75.4	82.0	61.8	82.6	86.7	44.5	65.2	77.6
Germany	Unemployment rates	13.3	7.9	4.9	13.5	6.5	4.3	13.2	9.8	6.2
	Labour force participation rates	56.8	77.1	88.5	79.1	85.2	91.7	46.2	68.7	82.8
	Employment/population ratios	49.2	71.0	84.2	68.4	79.6	87.8	40.1	62.0	77.6
Greece	Unemployment rates	6.3	9.0	8.1	4.8	6.0	5.7	9.2	14.2	11.4
	Labour force participation rates	60.0	68.2	86.2	84.3	88.4	91.1	39.2	49.2	80.2
	Employment/population ratios	56.2	62.0	79.2	80.3	83.1	85.9	35.6	42.2	71.1
Ireland	Unemployment rates	16.4	7.6	4.2	15.4	7.0	4.0	19.3	8.3	4.4
	Labour force participation rates	58.1	72.1	86.7	80.8	92.6	94.4	32.2	57.1	78.5
	Employment/population ratios	48.6	66.6	83.0	68.4	86.1	90.6	26.0	52.3	75.0

Table D. **Unemployment, labour force participation rates and employment/population ratios by educational attainment for persons aged 25-64, 1995** (cont.)

Percentages

		Both sexes			Men			Women		
		Less than upper secondary education	Upper secondary education	Tertiary level education	Less than upper secondary education	Upper secondary education	Tertiary level education	Less than upper secondary education	Upper secondary education	Tertiary level education
Italy	Unemployment rates	9.1	7.9	7.3	7.1	5.5	5.0	13.5	11.2	10.6
	Labour force participation rates	53.8	76.5	87.4	76.3	86.8	91.8	33.0	65.7	81.9
	Employment/population ratios	48.9	70.4	80.9	70.9	82.1	87.2	28.5	58.3	73.3
Korea	Unemployment rates	1.0	1.6	2.0	1.5	1.8	2.1	0.5	1.1	1.4
	Labour force participation rates	71.8	72.4	81.8	89.2	93.1	95.8	61.0	46.8	53.9
	Employment/population ratios	71.1	71.2	80.2	87.9	91.4	93.7	60.7	46.3	53.1
Luxembourg[a]	Unemployment rates	3.8	2.1	0.6	2.5	2.1	0.4	6.3	2.1	1.3
	Labour force participation rates	58.8	77.4	89.1	80.3	87.7	93.3	39.4	65.6	81.2
	Employment/population ratios	56.6	75.8	88.5	78.4	85.9	93.0	36.9	64.2	80.2
Netherlands	Unemployment rates	7.9	4.8	4.1	6.7	3.6	3.6	9.5	6.6	4.9
	Labour force participation rates	56.5	77.7	86.4	76.4	87.0	90.7	41.3	66.8	80.6
	Employment/population ratios	52.1	74.0	82.8	71.3	83.9	87.4	37.4	62.4	76.7
New Zealand	Unemployment rates	6.7	3.3	3.2	7.4	3.1	3.3	6.0	3.7	3.0
	Labour force participation rates	67.8	84.5	84.2	80.9	91.7	93.2	57.8	73.1	77.2
	Employment/population ratios	63.2	81.8	81.5	74.9	88.9	90.1	54.4	70.4	74.9
Norway	Unemployment rates	6.5	4.0	2.4	6.6	4.3	2.7	6.3	3.6	2.0
	Labour force participation rates	65.5	83.8	91.0	76.0	89.3	93.9	55.1	78.2	88.0
	Employment/population ratios	61.2	80.5	88.9	70.9	85.4	91.4	51.6	75.4	86.2
Poland	Unemployment rates	13.9	11.4	3.8	14.2	9.6	3.5	13.6	13.7	4.1
	Labour force participation rates	58.1	78.5	87.0	69.4	84.6	90.2	49.1	71.9	84.7
	Employment/population ratios	50.0	69.6	83.7	59.5	76.4	87.1	42.5	62.0	81.2
Portugal	Unemployment rates	6.2	6.4	3.2	5.5	4.7	3.5	7.2	8.4	3.0
	Labour force participation rates	71.6	82.3	92.0	84.6	87.2	93.9	59.7	77.2	90.5
	Employment/population ratios	67.2	77.0	89.0	80.0	83.0	90.6	55.4	70.8	87.8
Spain	Unemployment rates	20.6	18.5	14.5	16.6	13.0	10.4	28.5	26.7	19.8
	Labour force participation rates	58.3	79.9	87.4	81.3	91.2	91.7	37.4	67.3	82.5
	Employment/population ratios	46.3	65.1	74.7	67.8	79.3	82.1	26.7	49.3	66.1
Sweden	Unemployment rates	10.1	8.7	4.5	10.6	9.6	5.2	9.4	7.7	3.8
	Labour force participation rates	86.4	91.4	93.2	91.3	93.6	93.7	80.5	89.2	92.7
	Employment/population ratios	77.7	83.5	89.0	81.6	84.7	88.8	72.9	82.3	89.2
Switzerland	Unemployment rates	5.8	2.8	1.9	6.3	2.3	1.8	5.4	3.3	2.6
	Labour force participation rates	71.5	81.9	92.0	90.4	94.9	96.3	62.7	70.5	79.5
	Employment/population ratios	67.4	79.7	90.2	84.7	92.7	94.6	59.3	68.2	77.5

Table D. **Unemployment, labour force participation rates and employment/population ratios by educational attainment for persons aged 25-64, 1995** (cont.)

Percentages

		Both sexes			Men			Women		
		Less than upper secondary education	Upper secondary education	Tertiary level education	Less than upper secondary education	Upper secondary education	Tertiary level education	Less than upper secondary education	Upper secondary education	Tertiary level education
Turkey	Unemployment rates	4.8	6.9	3.3	4.9	5.3	3.0	4.6	13.6	4.1
	Labour force participation rates	67.2	67.9	76.6	97.7	89.1	84.0	30.4	33.4	62.5
	Employment/population ratios	64.0	63.2	74.1	92.9	84.4	81.5	29.0	28.9	59.9
United Kingdom	Unemployment rates	12.2	7.4	3.7	17.2	8.4	4.1	8.0	6.1	3.2
	Labour force participation rates	61.8	82.1	88.8	73.2	89.2	92.7	54.6	74.1	84.2
	Employment/population ratios	54.3	76.0	85.5	60.7	81.7	88.9	50.3	69.6	81.5
United States	Unemployment rates	10.0	5.0	2.7	10.9	5.2	2.9	8.6	4.8	2.6
	Labour force participation rates	59.8	79.1	88.2	72.0	87.9	93.6	47.2	71.2	82.4
	Employment/population ratios	53.9	75.1	85.8	64.2	83.3	91.0	43.2	67.8	80.3
European Union	Unemployment rates	13.7	8.2	5.8	12.8	7.4	5.1	14.8	9.8	6.7
	Labour force participation rates	60.7	80.1	88.4	77.9	87.9	92.1	47.4	71.5	83.7
	Employment/population ratios	52.4	73.5	83.3	67.9	81.4	87.4	40.4	64.5	78.1
OECD Europe	Unemployment rates	13.4	7.7	5.5	12.6	6.9	4.9	14.4	9.1	6.5
	Labour force participation rates	60.8	80.4	88.6	78.0	88.1	92.3	47.8	71.9	83.8
	Employment/population ratios	52.7	74.2	83.7	68.1	82.0	87.8	40.9	65.3	78.4
Total OECD	Unemployment rates	12.3	6.5	4.2	12.1	6.2	4.0	12.6	7.1	4.4
	Labour force participation rates	60.9	79.8	88.1	76.5	88.1	92.9	48.2	71.5	82.7
	Employment/population ratios	53.4	74.6	84.4	67.2	82.6	89.2	42.2	66.4	79.1

a) Data are for the year 1996.
Source: OECD (1997). Education at a Glance – OECD Indicators.

Table E.　**Incidence and composition of part-time employment,**[a] **1990-1997**

Percentages

Part-time employment as a proportion of employment

	Men					Women				
	1990	1994	1995	1996	1997	1990	1994	1995	1996	1997
Australia[b]	12.2	13.9	14.2	14.9	..	39.4	40.7	40.9	41.3	..
Austria	..	..	2.3	1.9	2.1	..	..	21.6	22.2	22.0
Belgium	5.1	5.2	5.0	5.0	5.0	32.8	33.4	33.5	34.0	34.3
Canada	9.1	10.7	10.6	10.7	10.5	26.8	28.6	28.2	28.9	29.4
Czech Republic	..	..	1.8	2.0	1.9	..	..	5.7	5.3	5.5
Denmark	10.6	10.2	10.0	10.6	11.9	29.9	26.7	25.8	24.4	24.7
Finland	..	..	5.0	5.2	4.8	..	..	11.2	10.5	10.2
France	4.7	5.5	5.8	6.0	6.3	22.0	24.5	24.7	24.6	25.6
Germany	1.8	2.7	3.0	3.3	..	29.6	27.9	29.0	29.8	..
Greece	5.0	5.5	5.2	5.3	5.3	12.8	13.5	13.3	13.9	14.2
Hungary	..	..	1.9	1.8	1.8	..	..	4.6	4.6	5.0
Iceland[c, d]	7.6	8.2	8.3	6.7	..	40.3	37.4	37.7	33.0	..
Ireland	4.6	6.9	7.4	7.1	8.0	19.8	24.7	26.5	26.5	27.1
Italy	4.0	4.2	4.6	4.6	5.1	19.7	22.3	22.8	22.6	24.0
Japan[b, e]	9.5	11.7	10.1	11.7	..	33.4	35.8	34.9	36.6	..
Korea[b, f]	..	3.0	2.9	2.7	3.3	..	6.9	6.7	6.9	7.8
Luxembourg	1.5	1.9	1.9	2.1	..	19.3	26.4	29.2	25.3	..
Mexico	..	..	9.6	8.0	8.6	..	..	31.3	25.3	29.9
Netherlands	13.3	10.7	10.9	10.8	10.6	50.8	53.5	54.2	55.2	54.6
New Zealand	8.4	9.7	10.0	10.4	10.9	35.0	36.6	36.1	37.3	37.4
Norway	6.7	7.6	7.5	8.0	7.9	39.1	37.6	37.4	37.3	36.8
Portugal	2.1	3.0	2.2	2.5	2.7	12.5	13.1	13.2	13.5	14.1
Spain	0.9	2.0	2.0	2.4	2.8	10.8	14.4	15.8	15.8	16.6
Sweden	5.3	7.1	6.8	6.7	6.5	24.5	24.9	24.9	24.1	22.6
Switzerland[c]	8.5	8.5	7.8	9.4	7.9	45.9	48.7	48.5	49.1	47.8
Turkey	..	5.0	5.2	4.0	2.9	..	20.4	19.4	13.9	12.7
United Kingdom	4.8	6.3	6.7	7.2	7.6	39.3	40.4	39.8	40.6	40.1
United States[d]	8.3	8.0	7.8	7.7	..	20.0	19.5	19.3	19.1	..
European Union[g]	4.1	4.6	4.9	5.2	6.1	28.4	29.3	29.1	29.4	29.6
OECD Europe[g]	4.4	4.9	4.7	4.8	5.9	28.3	29.0	27.0	27.2	28.5
Total OECD[g]	6.4	6.5	6.6	6.4	6.6	25.1	24.3	24.1	23.8	26.5

	Part-time employment as a proportion of total employment					Women's share in part-time employment				
	1990	1994	1995	1996	1997	1990	1994	1995	1996	1997
Australia[b]	23.5	25.2	25.6	26.2	..	69.4	68.2	68.3	67.4	..
Austria	..	..	10.6	10.7	10.8	..	..	87.9	89.9	89.1
Belgium	15.8	16.9	16.7	17.1	17.4	80.0	82.0	82.5	83.1	83.2
Canada	17.0	18.8	18.6	18.9	19.0	70.1	68.8	68.8	69.1	69.7
Czech Republic	..	..	3.5	3.4	3.4	..	..	70.5	67.4	68.9
Denmark	19.9	18.0	17.3	17.0	17.9	72.4	70.1	68.9	66.7	64.8
Finland	..	..	8.4	8.0	7.5	..	..	72.6	69.5	68.6
France	12.6	14.5	14.8	14.8	15.5	79.6	79.9	79.1	78.8	78.8
Germany	13.2	13.5	14.2	15.0	..	91.7	88.7	88.2	87.6	..
Greece	7.7	8.4	8.2	8.5	8.7	57.8	58.3	60.6	61.3	62.9
Hungary	..	..	3.2	3.1	3.3	..	..	67.7	69.4	71.3
Iceland[c, d]	24.1	23.3	23.5	20.0	..	84.0	82.1	82.9	82.8	..
Ireland	10.7	14.8	15.9	15.7	16.7	74.1	74.0	74.4	74.9	74.0
Italy	9.6	11.0	11.5	11.6	12.4	73.7	76.1	75.3	75.4	74.7
Japan[b, e]	19.2	21.4	20.1	21.8	..	70.7	67.6	70.1	68.0	..
Korea[b, f]	..	4.6	4.4	4.4	5.1	..	60.6	61.2	63.5	62.4
Luxembourg	7.6	10.9	11.8	10.7	..	87.5	88.9	89.4	87.8	..
Mexico	..	..	16.6	14.8	15.8	..	..	60.8	62.4	63.7
Netherlands	27.3	28.4	28.8	29.4	29.1	69.4	77.9	77.6	78.5	78.9
New Zealand	20.0	21.5	21.5	22.4	22.7	76.4	75.1	74.0	74.3	73.4
Norway	21.3	21.2	21.2	21.4	21.2	82.9	81.2	80.9	80.1	80.0
Portugal	6.4	7.6	7.3	7.6	7.9	81.2	78.4	83.6	81.9	81.3
Spain	4.1	6.3	6.9	7.2	7.9	84.7	79.4	81.1	78.6	77.1
Sweden	14.5	15.8	15.1	14.8	14.2	81.1	76.8	76.8	76.5	76.3
Switzerland[c]	24.4	25.7	25.2	26.7	25.4	80.1	81.3	82.1	80.1	82.5
Turkey	..	9.5	9.3	6.9	5.8	..	62.6	60.3	59.2	63.7
United Kingdom	20.8	22.6	22.5	23.2	23.1	87.6	85.5	84.4	83.7	82.8
United States[d]	13.8	13.5	13.3	13.2	..	68.2	69.0	69.3	69.8	..
European Union[g]	14.1	15.3	15.5	15.9	16.5	83.0	82.7	82.2	81.8	79.3
OECD Europe[g]	13.9	14.8	14.0	14.2	15.9	80.9	80.7	80.5	80.6	79.4
Total OECD[g]	14.4	14.3	14.1	14.0	14.9	74.6	74.5	73.3	73.7	74.3

a)　Part-time employment refers to persons who usually work less than 30 hours per week.
b)　Data refer to actual hours worked.
c)　1990 refers to 1991.
d)　Employees.
e)　Less than 35 hours per week.
f)　Civilian employment.
g)　Above countries only.
Notes, sources and definitions: See OECD Labour Market and Social Policy, Occasional Paper No. 22, «The Definition of Part-time Work for the Purpose of International Comparisons», which is available on Internet (http://www.oecd.org/els/papers/papers.htm).

Table F. **Average annual hours actually worked per person in employment**[a]

	1979	1983	1990	1993	1994	1995	1996	1997
Total employment								
Australia	1 904	1 852	1 869	1 874	1 879	1 876	1 867	1 866
Canada	1 802	1 731	1 738	1 718	1 735	1 737	1 732	..
Czech Republic	..	..	..	..	..	2 065	2 072	2 062
Finland[b]	..	1 809	1 764	1 744	1 780	1 775	1 790	1 779
Finland[c]	1 868	1 821	1 764	1 754	1 768	1 773	1 773	1 763
France	1 813	1 711	1 668	1 639	1 635	1 638	1 666	1 656
Germany	..	..	1 625	1 610	1 604	1 581	1 577	1 574
Western Germany	1 764	1 724	1 611	1 582	1 581	1 561	1 558	1 558
Iceland[d]	..	..	1 777	1 828	1 813	1 832	1 860	1 839
Italy	1 788	1 764	..	..	..	..	..	..
Japan	2 126	2 095	2 031	1 905	1 898	1 889	..	..
Mexico	..	..	..	1 804	..	1 834	1 955	1 909
New Zealand	..	..	1 820	1 844	1 851	1 843	1 838	..
Norway	1 514	1 485	1 432	1 434	1 431	1 414	1 407	1 399
Portugal	..	..	..	2 000	2 009	..	..	..
Spain	2 022	1 912	1 824	1 815	1 815	1 814	1 810	1 809
Sweden	1 451	1 453	1 480	1 501	1 537	1 544	1 554	1 552
Switzerland	..	..	..	1 633	1 639	1 643	..	..
United Kingdom	1 821	1 719	1 773	1 715	1 728	1 735	1 732	1 731
United States	1 905	1 882	1 943	1 946	1 945	1 952	1 951	1 966
Dependent employment								
Canada	1 757	1 708	1 718	1 704	1 720	1 726	1 721	..
Czech Republic	..	..	..	..	..	1 984	1 990	1 981
Finland[b]	..	..	1 668	1 635	1 674	1 673	1 692	1 687
France	1 667	1 558	1 539	1 521	1 520	1 523	1 547	1 539
Germany	..	..	1 583	1 558	1 552	1 529	1 522	1 519
Western Germany	1 699	1 686	1 557	1 527	1 527	1 506	1 502	1 503
Iceland[d]	..	..	1 843	1 790	1 774	1 776	1 799	1 790
Italy	1 748	1 724	1 694	1 687	1 682	..	..	..
Japan[e]	2 114	2 098	2 052	1 913	1 904	1 909	1 919	1 990
Japan[f]	..	..	2 064	1 920	1 910	1 910	1 919	1 891
Korea	..	2 736	2 512	2 475	2 470	2 486	2 465	2 434
Mexico	..	..	..	1 921	..	1 933	2 006	1 955
Netherlands	1 591	1 530	1 433	1 404	1 395	1 397	..	..
Spain	1 936	1 837	1 762	1 748	1 746	1 749	1 747	1 745
United States	1 884	1 866	1 936	1 939	1 947	1 953	1 951	1 967

a) The concept used is the total number of hours worked over the year divided by the average numbers of people in employment. The data are intended for comparisons of trends over time; they are unsuitable for comparisons of the level of average annual hours of work for a given year, because of differences in their sources. Part-time workers are covered as well as full-time.
b) Data estimated from the Labour Force Survey.
c) Data estimated from National Accounts; total employment figure for 1997 is preliminary.
d) Data for 1990 refer to 1991.
e) Data refer to establishments with 30 or more regular employees.
f) Data refer to establishments with 5 or more regular employees.

Sources and definitions:
Australia: Data supplied by the Australian Bureau of Statistics from the Labour Force Survey. Annual hours worked are adjusted to take account of public holidays occuring during the reporting period. The method of estimation is consistent with the National Accounts.
Canada: Series supplied by Statistics Canada, based mainly on the monthly Labour Force Survey supplemented by the Survey of Employment Payrolls and Hours, the annual Survey of Manufacturers and the Census of Mining.
Czech Republic: Data supplied by the Czech Statistical Office and based on the quarterly Labour Force Sample Survey. Main meal breaks (one half hour a day) are included.
Finland: Data supplied by Statistics Finland, National Accounts series based on an establishment survey for manufacturing, and the Labour Force Survey for other sectors and for the self-employed. Alternative series based solely on the Labour Force Survey.
France: Data supplied by Institut National de la Statistique et des Études Économiques, produced within the framework of the National Accounts. Data for 1992 to 1994 have been revised slightly.
Iceland: Data are provided by Statistics Iceland and are based on the Icelandic Labour Force Survey. Annual actual hours worked per person in employment are computed by multiplying daily actual hours worked by annual actual working days net of public holidays and anual vacations. The latter are for a typical work contract by sector of activity.
Germany: Data supplied by the Institut für Arbeitsmarkt- und Berufsforschung, calculated within a comprehensive accounting structure, based on establishment survey estimates of weekly hours worked by full-time workers whose hours are not affected by absence, and extended to annual estimates of actual hours by adjusting for a wide range of factors, including public holidays, sickness, overtime working, short-time working, bad weather, strikes, part-time working and parental leave.
Italy: Data for total employment based on a special establishment survey discontinued in the mid 1980s. For dependent employment, data for 1983 to 1994 supplied by Eurostat and from 1960 to 1982 trend in data is taken from the total employment series.
Japan: Data for total employment are Secretariat estimates based on data from the monthly Labour Survey of Establishments, extended to agricultural and government sectors and to the self-employed by means of the Labour Force Survey. Data for dependent employment supplied by Statistics Bureau, Management and Coordination Agency, from the Monthly Labour Survey, referring to all industries excluding agriculture, forest, fisheries and government services.
Korea: Data supplied by the Ministry of Labour from the Report on Monthly Labour Survey.
Mexico: Data supplied by STPS-INEGI from the bi-annual National Survey of Employment, based on the assumption of 44 working weeks per year.
Netherlands: From 1977 onwards, figures are "Annual Contractual Hours" per job, supplied by Statistics Netherlands, compiled within the framework of the Labour Accounts. Overtime hours are excluded. For 1970 to 1976, the trend has been derived from data supplied by the Economisch Instituut voor het Midden en Kleinbedrijf, referring to persons employed in the private sector, excluding agriculture and fishing.
New Zealand: Data supplied by Statistics New Zealand and derived from the quarterly Labour Force Survey, whose continuous sample design avoids the need for adjustments for public holidays and other days lost. Total employment figures revised slightly.
Norway: Data supplied by Statistics Norway, based on National Accounts and estimated from a number of different data sources, the most important being establishment surveys, the Labour Force Surveys and the public sector accounts. For 1978 to 1995, data revised due to major revision of National Accounts, for earlier years, trend in data taken from old series.
Portugal: Data derived from the quarterly Labour Force Survey, whose continuous sample design avoids the need for adjustments for public holidays and other days lost, supplied by Ministério do Emprego e da Segurança Social.
Spain: Series supplied by Instituto Nacional de Estadística and derived from the quarterly Labour Force Survey. Series break at 1986/87 due to changes in the Survey.
Sweden: Series supplied by Statistics Sweden derived from National Accounts data, based on both the Labour Force Survey and establishment surveys. Figures for 1993 to 1994 revised slightly.
Switzerland: Data supplied by Office fédéral de la statistique. The basis of the calculation is the Swiss Labour Force Survey which provides information on weekly hours of work during one quarter of the year. The estimates of annual hours are based also on supplementary annual information on vacations, public holidays and overtime working and have been extended to correspond to National Accounts concepts.
United Kingdom: Figures refer to Great Britain. Break in series 1994/95 due to small change in the way estimates of employment are derived. For 1992 to 1995, the levels are derived directly from the continuous Labour Force Survey. For 1984 to 1991, the trend in the data is taken from the annual Labour Force Survey. From 1970 to 1983, the trend corresponds to estimates by Professor Angus Maddison.
United States: Data supplied by the Bureau of Labor Statistics and are based on the Current Population Survey. Series breaks at 1975/76 and 1989/90 due to changes in population controls and at 1993/94 due to redesigned CPS questionaire. Data beginning in 1997 are not strictly comparable with data for 1996 and earlier years due to the introduction of revised population controls.

Table G. **Incidence of long-term unemployment from survey-based data in selected OECD countries**[a, b, c, d, e]

As a percentage of total unemployment

	1990		1994		1995		1996		1997	
	6 months and over	12 months and over	6 months and over	12 months and over	6 months and over	12 months and over	6 months and over	12 months and over	6 months and over	12 months and over
Australia	41.1	21.6	56.9	36.3	51.4	30.8	48.7	28.4	51.5	30.8
Austria	..	..	..	..	42.8	27.5	42.5	25.6	47.7	28.7
Belgium	81.4	68.7	75.2	58.3	77.7	62.4	77.3	61.3	77.2	60.5
Canada	18.8	5.7	30.9	15.2	27.8	14.1	27.7	13.9	25.7	12.5
Czech Republic	..	..	40.9	21.6	52.5	30.6	52.4	31.6	53.0	30.5
Denmark	53.2	29.9	54.0	32.1	46.6	27.9	44.4	26.5	45.7	27.2
Finland[f]	32.6	9.2	52.8	30.6	54.3	37.0	58.6	39.3	50.4	31.1
France	55.5	38.0	61.7	38.3	64.0	42.3	61.5	39.5	63.7	41.2
Germany	64.7	46.8	63.8	44.3	65.9	48.7	65.3	47.8	..	..
Greece	71.9	49.8	72.8	50.5	72.7	51.4	74.7	56.7	76.5	55.7
Hungary	..	..	62.6	41.3	73.0	50.6	75.2	54.4	73.5	51.3
Iceland	..	..	32.9	15.7	33.3	17.5	31.4	19.6	26.0	16.0
Ireland	81.0	66.0	80.7	64.3	77.9	61.4	75.7	59.5	73.6	57.0
Italy	85.2	69.8	79.5	61.5	80.2	63.6	80.8	65.6	81.8	66.3
Japan	39.0	19.1	36.1	17.5	37.7	18.1	40.4	20.2	41.3	21.8
Korea	14.3	3.3	20.7	5.5	17.7	4.3	15.8	3.8	15.7	2.5
Luxembourg[g]	(66.7)	(42.9)	(54.7)	(29.6)	(49.5)	(23.8)	(44.6)	(27.6)	..	..
Mexico	..	..	..	..	7.9	1.5	9.8	2.2	5.3	2.3
Netherlands	63.6	49.3	77.5	49.4	80.4	46.8	81.8	50.0	80.4	49.1
New Zealand	39.5	20.9	50.0	32.3	43.3	25.5	36.5	20.7	36.5	19.5
Norway	40.4	19.2	43.3	28.0	43.3	26.5	29.9	14.0	26.6	12.8
Poland	..	..	65.2	40.4	63.1	40.0	62.8	39.0	62.2	38.0
Portugal	62.4	44.8	57.2	43.4	65.1	50.9	66.7	53.1	66.7	55.6
Spain	70.2	54.0	73.4	56.1	72.8	56.9	72.2	55.7	71.8	55.5
Sweden	15.9	4.7	38.5	17.3	35.6	15.8	38.4	17.1	46.7	29.6
Switzerland	..	..	50.3	28.9	50.4	33.6	52.1	25.0	49.4	28.5
Turkey	72.6	47.0	68.5	45.4	60.3	36.3	65.9	43.5	62.7	41.6
United Kingdom	50.3	34.4	63.4	45.4	60.8	43.6	58.1	39.8	54.8	38.6
United States	10.0	5.5	20.3	12.2	17.3	9.7	17.5	9.5	15.9	8.7
European Union[h]	65.3	48.6	67.5	48.1	68.1	50.1	67.4	49.3	68.2	50.2
OECD Europe[h]	65.9	48.2	66.8	46.5	66.8	47.7	66.6	47.5	66.7	47.6
Total OECD[h]	44.6	30.8	52.4	35.2	49.7	33.8	50.1	34.0	48.3	32.7

a) While data from labour force surveys make international comparisons easier, compared to a mixture of survey and registration data, they are not perfect. Questionnaire wording and design, survey timing, differences across countries in the age groups covered, and other reasons mean that care is required in interpreting cross-country differences in levels.

b) The duration of unemployment data base maintained by the Secretariat is composed of detailed duration categories disaggregated by age and sex. All totals are derived by adding each component. Thus, the total for men is derived by adding the number of unemployed men by each duration and age group category. Since published data are usually rounded to the nearest thousand, this method sometimes results in slight differences between the percentages shown here and those that would be obtained using the available published figures.

c) Data are averages of monthly figures for the Canada, Sweden and the United States, averages of quarterly figures for the Czech Republic, Hungary, Norway, New Zealand, Poland and Spain, and averages of semi-annual figures for Turkey. The reference period for the remaining countries is as follows (among EU countries it occasionally varies from year to year): Australia, August; Austria, April; Belgium, April; Denmark, April-May; Finland, autumn; France, March; Germany, April; Greece, March-July; Iceland, April; Ireland, May; Italy, April; Japan, February; Luxembourg, April; Mexico, April; the Netherlands, March-May; Portugal, February-April; Switzerland, second quarter; and the United Kingdom, March-May.

d) Data refer to persons aged 15 and over in Australia, Austria, Belgium, Canada, Czech Republic, Denmark, France, Germany, Greece, Ireland, Italy, Japan, Luxembourg, Mexico, the Netherlands, New Zealand, Poland, Portugal, Switzerland and Turkey; and aged 16 and over in Iceland, Spain, the United Kingdom and the United States. Data for Finland refer to persons aged 15-64 (excluding unemployment pensioners). Data for Hungary refer to persons aged 15-74, data for Norway refer to persons aged 16-74 and data for Sweden refer to persons aged 16-64.

e) Persons for whom no duration of unemployment was specified are excluded.

f) Data for 1990 refer to 1991 and data for 1994 refer to 1993.

g) Data in brackets are based on small sample sizes and, therefore, must be treated with care.

h) For above countries only.

Sources:
Data for *Austria, Belgium, Denmark, Germany, Greece, Ireland, Italy, Luxembourg, the Netherlands, Portugal and the United Kingdom* are based on the European Labour Force Survey and were supplied by Eurostat.
Australia: Australian Bureau of Statistics, *The Labour Force Australia*.
Canada: Unpublished data from the Labour Force Survey supplied by Statistics Canada.
Czech Republic: Data from the Labour Force Sample Survey supplied by the Czech Statistical office.
Finland: Unpublished data from the *Supplementary Labour Force Survey* (biennial since 1989) supplied by the Central Statistical Office. From 1995 onwards, data supplied by Eurostat and based on the European Labour Force Survey.
France: Institut National de la Statistique et des Études Économiques, *Enquête sur l'Emploi*.
Hungary: Data from the Labour Force Survey supplied by the Central Statistical Office.
Iceland: Data from the Labour Force Survey supplied by Statistics Iceland.
Japan: Statistics Bureau, Managment and Coordination Agency, *Report on the Special survey of the Labour Force Survey*.
Korea: National Statistical Office (NSO), *Annual report on the Economically Active Population Survey*.
Mexico: Statistics Bureau, Management and Coordination Agency, *Report on the Special Survey of the Labour Force Survey*.
New Zealand: Unpublished data from the Household Labour Force Survey supplied by the Department of Statistics.
Norway: Unpublished data from the Labour Force Survey supplied by the Central Statistical Office.
Poland: Data from the Labour Force Survey supplied by the Central Statistical Office.
Spain: Unpublished data from the Labour Force Survey supplied by the Ministry of Employment and Social Security.
Sweden: Statistics Sweden, AKU.
Switzerland: Data from the Labour Force Survey supplied by the Swiss Federal Statistical Office.
Turkey: Data from the Household Labour Force Survey supplied by the State Institute of Statistics.
United States: Bureau of Labor Statistics, *Employment and Earnings*.

Table H. **Incidence of long-term unemployment from survey-based data among men**[a, b, c, d, e]

As a percentage of male unemployment

	1990		1994		1995		1996		1997	
	6 months and over	12 months and over	6 months and over	12 months and over	6 months and over	12 months and over	6 months and over	12 months and over	6 months and over	12 months and over
Australia	42.7	24.4	59.4	38.6	54.1	34.2	50.8	30.9	54.7	33.1
Austria	..	..	..	..	36.5	24.6	38.2	23.2	42.1	28.9
Belgium	79.5	66.1	72.4	53.4	76.4	61.4	75.2	58.9	76.6	59.4
Canada	19.1	6.6	32.7	17.1	29.1	15.9	28.4	15.3	27.2	14.5
Czech Republic	..	..	38.9	20.8	51.5	30.2	50.9	31.0	53.0	31.3
Denmark	48.9	27.8	52.1	31.9	51.9	31.9	44.2	28.1	44.5	26.3
Finland[f]	36.8	9.7	53.7	34.0	58.6	42.0	60.7	43.6	50.8	33.9
France	53.1	35.4	60.2	37.3	62.1	41.4	58.6	37.1	61.7	39.1
Germany	65.2	49.1	60.4	41.2	63.3	45.9	61.8	44.5	..	..
Greece	61.8	39.9	65.8	41.3	64.3	42.3	66.7	47.3	69.1	45.8
Hungary	..	..	65.0	43.6	74.0	52.0	76.8	57.0	74.2	52.6
Iceland	..	..	29.7	13.5	32.4	17.6	34.6	23.1	28.0	20.0
Ireland	84.3	71.1	83.0	68.5	80.7	66.8	79.2	64.6	77.9	63.3
Italy	84.1	68.6	77.4	59.6	78.9	62.7	78.7	64.1	81.2	66.5
Japan	47.6	26.2	40.2	21.4	43.7	23.5	46.2	23.8	49.2	28.8
Korea	16.6	4.1	22.8	6.6	19.0	4.7	17.9	4.1	18.5	3.5
Luxembourg[g]	(80.0)	(60.0)	(59.6)	(33.8)	(50.6)	(26.0)	(49.0)	(30.1)	..	..
Mexico	..	..	..	..	7.4	1.3	9.7	2.1	6.0	2.1
Netherlands	65.6	55.2	74.3	50.0	78.7	51.6	81.4	54.3	76.6	49.9
New Zealand	44.1	24.5	55.1	36.7	48.2	29.6	40.2	23.8	40.4	22.2
Norway	39.7	19.0	43.5	28.1	44.4	28.6	31.0	15.5	28.0	14.0
Poland	..	..	61.8	36.8	59.4	36.2	59.3	35.2	57.8	33.5
Portugal	56.3	38.2	54.2	42.3	63.0	48.4	64.1	51.7	64.8	53.4
Spain	63.3	45.8	68.6	49.6	67.7	51.1	67.4	49.8	67.2	49.9
Sweden	16.2	5.4	40.5	19.4	37.6	17.4	40.3	18.5	48.5	31.8
Switzerland	..	..	47.4	22.4	46.8	30.6	50.0	20.8	47.9	25.5
Turkey	71.2	44.9	66.2	43.2	56.1	32.2	63.7	39.9	59.3	38.1
United Kingdom	56.8	41.8	68.6	51.2	66.2	49.6	63.5	45.9	60.2	44.9
United States	12.1	7.0	22.2	13.9	18.7	11.0	18.5	10.3	16.7	9.4
European Union[h]	63.5	47.0	66.0	46.7	66.7	49.0	65.2	47.4	66.6	48.9
OECD Europe[h]	64.4	46.5	65.1	44.9	64.8	45.9	64.4	45.5	64.6	45.8
Total OECD[h]	43.7	29.7	51.8	34.6	48.4	32.7	48.9	32.7	47.7	32.1

Notes and sources: See Table G.

Table I. **Incidence of long-term unemployment from survey-based data among women**[a, b, c, d, e]

As a percentage of female unemployment

	1990		1994		1995		1996		1997	
	6 months and over	12 months and over	6 months and over	12 months and over	6 months and over	12 months and over	6 months and over	12 months and over	6 months and over	12 months and over
Australia	38.8	17.8	53.1	33.0	47.4	25.6	45.4	24.8	47.1	27.5
Austria	..	..	..	..	49.4	30.6	48.1	28.8	54.5	28.4
Belgium	82.5	70.0	77.7	62.6	78.7	63.2	79.1	63.3	77.8	61.5
Canada	18.4	4.5	28.3	12.5	26.1	11.9	26.8	12.2	23.9	10.2
Czech Republic	..	..	42.6	22.2	53.3	30.9	53.7	32.1	53.0	29.9
Denmark	57.7	32.0	55.8	32.4	42.5	24.9	44.6	25.3	46.7	27.9
Finland[f]	26.3	8.4	51.3	25.7	49.6	31.5	55.5	34.1	50.0	28.2
France	57.3	40.0	63.0	39.3	65.7	43.2	64.0	41.6	65.6	43.3
Germany	64.2	44.5	67.1	47.2	68.4	51.3	69.4	51.7	..	..
Greece	78.2	55.9	78.0	57.2	78.9	58.3	79.7	62.5	81.4	62.2
Hungary	..	..	58.9	37.6	71.3	48.3	72.7	50.4	72.3	49.2
Iceland	..	..	32.4	14.7	34.5	17.2	28.0	16.0	28.0	12.0
Ireland	75.0	56.8	76.8	57.4	74.0	52.9	70.1	51.2	66.6	46.9
Italy	86.0	70.7	81.5	63.3	81.5	64.4	82.8	67.1	82.5	66.2
Japan	26.3	8.8	30.5	12.2	28.8	10.0	30.7	12.5	30.1	11.8
Korea	9.0	0.8	16.1	3.2	15.1	3.6	11.2	3.0	11.0	0.9
Luxembourg[g]	(55.6)	(33.3)	(48.9)	(24.6)	(48.0)	(21.0)	(40.6)	(25.3)	..	..
Mexico	..	..	..	..	9.0	1.7	10.0	2.4	4.4	2.6
Netherlands	62.0	44.6	80.9	48.7	82.1	42.0	82.1	46.1	83.4	48.5
New Zealand	32.7	15.5	42.7	26.0	37.1	20.2	31.9	16.9	31.6	16.1
Norway	42.5	20.0	43.9	29.8	31.4	17.3	28.6	12.2	24.4	11.1
Poland	..	..	68.4	43.8	66.6	43.7	66.1	42.5	66.0	41.9
Portugal	66.4	49.4	60.1	44.3	67.2	53.4	69.2	54.4	68.5	57.7
Spain	76.5	61.5	78.4	62.9	77.5	62.6	76.7	61.3	75.9	60.4
Sweden	15.0	3.9	35.3	14.1	33.0	13.8	35.9	15.4	44.4	26.9
Switzerland	..	..	53.4	35.6	54.0	36.5	54.4	29.4	51.6	32.8
Turkey	75.6	51.2	74.3	51.0	71.1	46.9	72.3	53.6	69.7	49.0
United Kingdom	40.8	23.7	53.3	33.9	50.6	32.3	47.7	28.0	45.3	27.8
United States	7.3	3.7	18.0	10.2	15.6	8.1	16.2	8.4	14.9	8.0
European Union[h]	66.9	50.1	69.3	49.7	69.6	51.2	69.7	51.2	69.9	51.5
OECD Europe[h]	67.4	50.0	68.7	48.4	69.0	49.7	69.0	49.8	68.9	49.5
Total OECD[h]	45.7	32.1	53.1	35.8	51.2	35.1	51.5	35.4	49.1	33.5

Notes and sources: See Table G.

Table J. **Public expenditures and participant inflows in labour market programmes in OECD countries**

	Australia[a]								Austria				Belgium							
	Public expenditures as a percentage of GDP				Participant inflows as a percentage of the labour force				Public expenditures as a percentage of GDP				Public expenditures as a percentage of GDP				Participant inflows as a percentage of the labour force			
Programme categories	1993-94	1994-95	1995-96	1996-97	1993-94	1994-95	1995-96	1996-97	1994	1995	1996	1997	1993	1994	1995	1996	1993	1994	1995	1996
1. **Public employment services and administration**	0.23	0.20	0.24	0.24					0.13	0.13	0.14	0.13	0.21	0.23	0.22	0.22				
2. **Labour market training**	0.16	0.17	0.15	0.09	3.8	4.2	4.8	2.1	0.11	0.12	0.15	0.17	0.27	0.28	0.28	0.28	8.7	9.2	8.9	9.1
a) Training for unemployed adults and those at risk	0.14	0.16	0.14	0.08	3.4	3.7	4.2	1.8	0.11	0.12	0.15	0.17	0.16	0.18	0.17	0.17	2.5	3.1	2.7	2.9
b) Training for employed adults	0.01	0.01	0.01	0.01	0.4	0.5	0.6	0.4	–	–	–	–	0.11	0.11	0.12	0.12	6.2	6.1	6.2	6.2
3. **Youth measures**	0.08	0.07	0.06	0.06	1.2	1.2	1.3	1.2	0.01	0.01	0.01	0.02	–	0.08	0.07	0.03	–	0.8	0.7	0.5
a) Measures for unemployed and disadvantaged youth	0.04	0.04	0.03	0.01	0.5	0.5	0.4	0.2	0.01	0.01	0.01	0.02	–	–	–	–	–	–	–	–
b) Support of apprenticeship and related forms of general youth training	0.05	0.03	0.03	0.05	0.8	0.7	0.9	1.1	–	–	–	–	–	0.08	0.07	0.03	–	0.8	0.7	0.5
4. **Subsidised employment**	0.22	0.21	0.31	0.21	2.3	2.0	2.5	1.5	0.04	0.05	0.05	0.07	0.61	0.62	0.68	0.84	3.5	3.5	4.6	7.4
a) Subsidies to regular employment in the private sector	0.11	0.06	0.06	0.07	1.8	1.2	1.2	1.0	0.01	0.02	0.02	0.03	0.06	0.05	0.12	0.27	0.6	0.6	1.8	4.5
b) Support of unemployed persons starting enterprises	0.02	0.03	0.03	0.03	0.1	0.1	0.1	0.1	–	–	–	–	–	–	–	–	–	–	–	–
c) Direct job creation (public or non-profit)	0.09	0.13	0.22	0.11	0.4	0.7	1.1	0.4	0.03	0.03	0.03	0.04	0.55	0.57	0.57	0.56	2.9	2.9	2.9	2.8
5. **Measures for the disabled**	0.07	0.07	0.07	0.06	0.6	0.6	0.7	0.7	0.06	0.06	0.05	0.05	0.15	0.14	0.14	0.14	..	..	..	..
a) Vocational rehabilitation	0.03	0.03	0.03	0.02	0.3	0.3	0.3	0.3	0.03	0.03	0.03	0.02	0.04	0.04	0.04	0.04	..	..	..	..
b) Work for the disabled	0.04	0.04	0.04	0.04	0.3	0.3	0.4	0.4	0.03	0.03	0.02	0.03	0.10	0.10	0.10	0.10	..	..	..	..
6. **Unemployment compensation**	1.88	1.62	1.29	1.30					1.42	1.30	1.29	1.22	2.30	2.20	2.11	2.12				
7. **Early retirement for labour market reasons**	–	–	–	–					0.13	0.13	0.13	0.07	0.71	0.68	0.66	0.64				
TOTAL	2.62	2.34	2.12	1.97	7.9	8.0	9.2	5.6	1.91	1.80	1.81	1.73	4.25	4.23	4.17	4.27	12.3	13.5	14.3	17.0
Active measures (1-5)	0.75	0.72	0.84	0.66					0.36	0.36	0.39	0.44	1.24	1.36	1.40	1.50				
Passive measures (6 and 7)	1.88	1.62	1.29	1.30					1.55	1.43	1.41	1.29	3.01	2.88	2.77	2.77				
For reference:																				
GDP (national currency, at current prices, 10^9)	429.7	457.3	487.6	509.8					2 239.6	2 334.4	2 421.6	2 508.1	7 409.6	7 762.3	8 055.6	8 305.0				
Labour Force (10^3)					8 733	8 917	9 114	9 222									4 273	4 280	4 297	4 290

a) Fiscal year starts on July 1 in Australia

Table J. **Public expenditures and participant inflows in labour market programmes in OECD countries** (cont.)

Programme categories	Canada[a] Public expenditures as a percentage of GDP				Participant inflows as a percentage of the labour force			Czech Republic Public expenditures as a percentage of GDP				Participant inflows as a percentage of the labour force				Denmark Public expenditures as a percentage of GDP				Participant inflows as a percentage of the labour force		
	1993-94	1994-95	1995-96	1996-97	1993-94	1994-95	1995-96	1994	1995	1996	1997	1994	1995	1996	1997	1994	1995	1996	1997	1994	1995	1996
1. Public employment services and administration	0.23	0.22	0.21	0.20				0.10	0.10	0.09	0.08					0.12	0.12	0.12	0.13			
2. Labour market training	0.31	0.28	0.25	0.17	2.7	2.3	1.9	0.01	0.01	0.01	0.01	0.3	0.3	0.2	0.2	0.72	1.02	1.12	0.97	12.2	13.7	..
a) Training for unemployed adults and those at risk	0.30	0.27	0.24	0.16	2.6	2.3	1.9	0.01	0.01	0.01	0.01	0.3	0.3	0.2	0.2	0.49	0.71	0.82	0.67	2.8	4.6	4.3
b) Training for employed adults	0.01	0.01	0.01	–	0.2	–	–	–	–	–	–	–	–	–	–	0.23	0.31	0.30	0.30	9.3	9.2	–
3. Youth measures	0.02	0.02	0.02	0.02	0.4	0.5	0.5	0.01	0.01	0.01	0.01	0.1	0.1	0.1	0.1	0.19	0.15	0.09	0.10	1.8	1.7	1.9
a) Measures for unemployed and disadvantaged youth	0.01	0.01	0.01	0.01	0.1	–	0.2	0.01	0.01	0.01	0.01	0.1	0.1	0.1	0.1	0.19	0.15	0.09	0.10	1.8	1.7	1.9
b) Support of apprenticeship and related forms of general youth training	0.01	0.02	0.01	0.01	0.4	0.5	0.3	–	–	–	–	–	–	–	–	–	–	–	–	–	–	–
4. Subsidised employment	0.08	0.07	0.06	0.06	0.4	0.4	0.3	0.04	0.03	0.02	0.02	0.4	0.3	0.3	0.3	0.44	0.36	0.32	0.31	1.6	1.2	1.1
a) Subsidies to regular employment in the private sector	0.01	0.01	0.01	0.01	0.1	0.1	–	0.02	0.01	–	–	0.2	0.1	0.1	0.1	0.06	0.04	0.03	0.02	0.4	0.3	0.4
b) Support of unemployed persons starting enterprises	0.02	0.02	0.02	0.02	–	0.1	0.1	–	–	–	–	–	–	–	–	0.10	0.08	0.08	0.06	0.2	0.1	0.1
c) Direct job creation (public or non-profit)	0.05	0.04	0.03	0.02	0.2	0.2	0.2	0.02	0.01	0.01	0.01	0.2	0.2	0.2	0.2	0.29	0.24	0.21	0.23	1.1	0.8	0.6
5. Measures for the disabled	0.03	0.03	0.02	0.03	–	–	–	0.01	–	–	–	0.01	–	–	–	0.34	0.31	0.29	0.28	2.8	2.8	..
a) Vocational rehabilitation	0.03	0.03	0.02	0.01	–	–	–	–	–	–	–	–	–	–	–	0.34	0.31	0.28	0.27	2.8	2.8	..
b) Work for the disabled	–	–	–	–	–	–	–	0.01	–	–	–	0.01	–	–	–	–	–	–	–	–	–	–
6. Unemployment compensation	1.93	1.50	1.29	1.17				0.16	0.13	0.14	0.20					3.75	3.06	2.54	2.22			
7. Early retirement for labour market reasons	0.01	0.01	0.01	0.01				–	–	–	–					1.39	1.55	1.80	1.79			
TOTAL	**2.60**	**2.13**	**1.87**	**1.65**	3.5	3.2	2.7	**0.32**	**0.28**	**0.26**	**0.32**	0.9	0.7	0.6	0.6	**6.97**	**6.57**	**6.27**	**5.80**	18.4	19.4	..
Active measures (1-5)	0.66	0.61	0.57	0.48				0.16	0.14	0.13	0.12					1.82	1.97	1.93	1.79			
Passive measures (6 and 7)	1.94	1.52	1.30	1.18				0.16	0.13	0.14	0.20					5.15	4.61	4.35	4.01			
For reference:																						
GDP (national currency, at current prices, 10^9)	733.0	774.1	803.1	829.4				1 143.0	1 338.9	1 524.7	1 670.9					925.7	969.1	1 013.9	1 066.2			
Labour Force (10^3)					14 780	14 946	15 038	5 179	5 173	5 175	5 191									2 777	2 798	2 822

a) Fiscal year starts on April 1 in Canada

Table J. **Public expenditures and participant inflows in labour market programmes in OECD countries** (cont.)

Programme categories	Finland — Public expenditures as a percentage of GDP				Finland — Participant inflows as a percentage of the labour force				France — Public expenditures as a percentage of GDP				France — Participant inflows as a percentage of the labour force				Germany — Public expenditures as a percentage of GDP				Germany — Participant inflows as a percentage of the labour force			
	1994	1995	1996	1997	1994	1995	1996	1997	1993	1994	1995	1996	1993	1994	1995	1996	1994	1995	1996	1997	1994	1995	1996	1997
1. Public employment services and administration	**0.17**	**0.16**	**0.16**	**0.14**					**0.15**	**0.16**	**0.15**	**0.16**					**0.24**	**0.23**	**0.24**	**0.21**				
2. Labour market training	**0.47**	**0.45**	**0.57**	**0.55**	**3.3**	**3.7**	**4.7**	**5.2**	**0.45**	**0.42**	**0.38**	**0.36**	**3.9**	**3.9**	**3.5**	..	**0.42**	**0.38**	**0.45**	**0.36**	**1.8**	**2.0**	**1.9**	**1.3**
a) Training for unemployed adults and those at risk	0.47	0.44	0.55	0.53	3.3	3.7	4.7	5.2	0.40	0.37	0.34	0.32	3.2	3.1	2.8	..	0.40	0.38	0.45	0.36	1.7	1.9	1.9	1.3
b) Training for employed adults	–	–	0.01	0.02	–	–	–	–	0.05	0.05	0.04	0.04	0.7	0.8	0.7	..	0.02	–	–	–	0.1	–	–	–
3. Youth measures	**0.12**	**0.16**	**0.22**	**0.22**	**1.8**	**2.0**	**2.5**	**2.6**	**0.30**	**0.30**	**0.27**	**0.24**	**2.9**	**3.1**	**2.8**	..	**0.06**	**0.06**	**0.07**	**0.07**	**0.6**	**0.7**	**0.7**	**0.7**
a) Measures for unemployed and disadvantaged youth	0.06	0.08	0.12	0.11	1.2	1.2	1.6	1.6	0.11	0.10	0.10	0.08	1.0	1.0	1.0	..	0.06	0.05	0.06	0.06	0.4	0.4	0.4	0.4
b) Support of apprenticeship and related forms of general youth training	0.06	0.08	0.10	0.11	0.6	0.8	0.9	1.0	0.19	0.20	0.17	0.16	1.9	2.1	1.9	..	0.01	0.01	0.01	0.01	0.2	0.2	0.3	0.3
4. Subsidised employment	**0.77**	**0.68**	**0.66**	**0.53**	**6.2**	**5.1**	**4.8**	**4.4**	**0.29**	**0.33**	**0.40**	**0.48**	**3.4**	**4.2**	**4.5**	..	**0.39**	**0.44**	**0.42**	**0.34**	**1.4**	**1.4**	**1.4**	**1.2**
a) Subsidies to regular employment in the private sector	0.15	0.11	0.09	0.09	1.9	1.2	1.2	1.3	0.09	0.12	0.16	0.25	1.5	2.0	2.3	..	0.06	0.07	0.07	0.05	0.1	0.3	0.2	0.2
b) Support of unemployed persons starting enterprises	0.06	0.04	0.03	0.03	0.5	0.3	0.2	0.2	0.02	0.03	0.04	0.02	0.2	0.3	0.3	..	0.01	0.02	0.03	0.03	0.1	0.2	0.2	0.2
c) Direct job creation (public or non-profit)	0.56	0.53	0.54	0.41	3.8	3.6	3.4	2.9	0.17	0.18	0.21	0.22	1.6	1.9	1.8	..	0.32	0.34	0.32	0.26	1.1	0.9	1.0	0.8
5. Measures for the disabled	**0.15**	**0.14**	**0.13**	**0.12**	**0.8**	**0.7**	**0.8**	**0.8**	**0.09**	**0.09**	**0.10**	**0.08**	**0.3**	**0.4**	**0.4**	..	**0.26**	**0.26**	**0.27**	**0.28**	**0.2**	**0.3**	**0.3**	**0.3**
a) Vocational rehabilitation	0.08	0.07	0.06	0.07	0.8	0.7	0.8	0.8	0.02	0.03	0.03	0.02	0.3	0.4	0.4	..	0.14	0.13	0.14	0.13	0.2	0.3	0.3	0.3
b) Work for the disabled	0.08	0.07	0.06	0.06	–	–	–	–	0.06	0.06	0.06	0.06	..	..	..	..	0.12	0.13	0.14	0.14	–	–	–	–
6. Unemployment compensation	**4.22**	**3.57**	**3.27**	**2.79**					**1.73**	**1.57**	**1.43**	**1.44**					**2.03**	**2.08**	**2.37**	**2.49**				
7. Early retirement for labour market reasons	**0.46**	**0.44**	**0.42**	**0.43**					**0.39**	**0.38**	**0.36**	**0.36**					**0.49**	**0.29**	**0.15**	**0.05**				
TOTAL	**6.36**	**5.59**	**5.41**	**4.79**	**12.0**	**11.5**	**12.8**	**13.1**	**3.39**	**3.24**	**3.09**	**3.13**	**10.5**	**11.5**	**11.3**	..	**3.88**	**3.73**	**3.96**	**3.79**	**4.0**	**4.3**	**4.2**	**3.6**
Active measures (1-5)	1.68	1.58	1.73	1.57					1.28	1.29	1.31	1.32					1.37	1.36	1.45	1.25				
Passive measures (6 and 7)	4.69	4.01	3.68	3.23					2.11	1.95	1.79	1.81					2.51	2.37	2.52	2.54				
For reference:																								
GDP (national currency, at current prices, 10³)	511.0	549.9	574.8	618.0					7 077.1	7 389.7	7 662.4	7 860.5					3 328.2	3 459.6	3 541.5	3 641.8				
Labour Force (10³)	2 502	2 522	2 531	2 562					25 202	25 324	25 378	25 613					39 628	39 394	39 294	39 257				

Table J. **Public expenditures and participant inflows in labour market programmes in OECD countries** *(cont.)*

Programme categories	Greece – Public expenditures as a percentage of GDP				Greece – Participant inflows as a percentage of the labour force				Hungary – Public expenditures as a percentage of GDP				Hungary – Participant inflows as a percentage of the labour force				Ireland – Public expenditures as a percentage of GDP			Ireland – Participant inflows as a percentage of the labour force			Italy[a] – Public expenditures as a percentage of GDP			
	1993	1994	1995	1996	1993	1994	1995	1996	1993	1994	1995	1996	1993	1994	1995	1996	1994	1995	1996	1994	1995	1996	1993	1994	1995	1996
1. Public employment services and administration	0.14	0.12	0.13	0.11					0.15	0.15	0.13	0.11					0.28	0.27	0.24				0.04	0.04	0.04	0.04
2. Labour market training	0.08	0.06	0.11	0.07	1.3	1.2	2.0	2.1	0.23	0.19	0.13	0.08	1.3	1.2	0.8	1.2	0.23	0.22	0.21	4.7	4.8	4.1	0.01	0.01	0.01	0.01
a) Training for unemployed adults and those at risk	0.01	0.01	0.01	0.02	0.2	0.2	0.1	0.2	0.23	0.19	0.12	0.08	1.3	1.2	0.7	1.1	0.16	0.15	0.14	1.7	1.8	1.6	0.01	0.01	–	–
b) Training for employed adults	0.07	0.04	0.10	0.05	1.2	1.0	1.9	1.9	–	–	–	–	–	0.1	0.1	0.1	0.07	0.06	0.08	3.0	2.9	2.5	–	0.01	0.01	0.01
3. Youth measures	0.02	0.03	0.03	0.03	0.3	0.3	0.3	0.4	–	–	–	–	–	–	–	–	0.27	0.25	0.24	1.4	1.4	1.3	0.94	0.46	0.39	0.42
a) Measures for unemployed and disadvantaged youth	–	–	–	–	–	–	–	–	–	–	–	–	–	–	–	–	0.13	0.11	0.11	0.8	0.7	0.7	0.04	0.06	0.03	0.04
b) Support of apprenticeship and related forms of general youth training	0.02	0.03	0.03	0.03	0.3	0.3	0.3	0.4	–	–	–	–	–	–	–	–	0.15	0.14	0.13	0.7	0.6	0.6	0.89	0.40	0.36	0.38
4. Subsidised employment	0.07	0.10	0.09	0.05	0.6	0.9	0.9	0.5	0.28	0.27	0.17	0.18	2.3	3.0	2.7	4.4	0.68	0.86	0.88	5.2	5.6	5.7	0.89	0.86	0.69	0.61
a) Subsidies to regular employment in the private sector	0.06	0.07	0.06	0.04	0.5	0.7	0.7	0.4	0.10	0.12	0.06	0.06	1.1	1.6	0.8	1.1	0.11	0.17	0.24	1.4	1.8	1.9	0.89	0.86	0.68	0.56
b) Support of unemployed persons starting enterprises	0.01	0.03	0.02	0.01	0.1	0.2	0.2	0.1	0.05	0.02	–	–	0.3	0.2	0.1	0.1	0.02	0.01	0.02	0.1	0.1	0.1	–	–	–	–
c) Direct job creation (public or non-profit)	–	–	–	–	–	–	–	–	0.14	0.14	0.10	0.12	0.9	1.2	1.9	3.2	0.55	0.67	0.63	3.6	3.8	3.7	–	–	0.01	0.04
5. Measures for the disabled	0.01	–	–	0.01	–	–	–	–	–	–	–	–	–	–	–	–	0.12	0.09	0.08	0.2	0.1	0.1	–	–	–	–
a) Vocational rehabilitation	–	–	–	–	–	–	–	–	–	–	–	–	–	–	–	–	0.12	0.09	0.08	0.2	0.1	0.1	–	–	–	–
b) Work for the disabled	–	–	–	–	–	–	–	–	–	–	–	–	–	–	–	–	–	–	–	–	–	–	–	–	–	–
6. Unemployment compensation	0.41	0.43	0.44	0.45					2.02	1.07	0.71	0.60					2.77	2.57	2.29				0.90	0.92	0.68	0.68
7. Early retirement for labour market reasons	–	–	–	–					0.11	0.15	0.19	0.16					0.16	0.14	0.13				0.26	0.20	0.19	0.20
TOTAL	**0.72**	**0.73**	**0.80**	**0.71**	**2.2**	**2.5**	**3.3**	**3.0**	**2.79**	**1.83**	**1.32**	**1.13**	**3.6**	**4.2**	**3.5**	**5.7**	**4.51**	**4.39**	**4.07**	**11.5**	**11.9**	**11.3**	**3.04**	**2.48**	**2.00**	**1.96**
Active measures (1-5)	0.31	0.30	0.36	0.27					0.66	0.61	0.42	0.37					1.58	1.68	1.66				1.88	1.36	1.13	1.08
Passive measures (6 and 7)	0.41	0.43	0.44	0.45					2.13	1.22	0.90	0.76					2.93	2.71	2.42				1.16	1.12	0.87	0.88
For reference:																										
GDP (national currency, at current prices, 10⁹)	21 106.2	23 755.8	26 486.1	29 474.0					3 548.3	4 364.8	5 613.5	6 843.0					36.1	40.3	44.2				1 550.3	1 638.7	1 771.0	1 873.5
Labour Force (10³)	4 118	4 193	4 249	4 318					4 346	4 203	4 095	4 048					1 425	1 449	1 494							

a) National currency at current prices 10¹² for Italy

Table J. **Public expenditures and participant inflows in labour market programmes in OECD countries** (cont.)

Programme categories	Japan[a] — Public expenditures as a percentage of GDP				Korea — Public expenditures as a percentage of GDP				Korea — Participant inflows as a percentage of the labour force				Luxembourg — Public expenditures as a percentage of GDP				Netherlands — Public expenditures as a percentage of GDP				Netherlands — Participant inflows as a percentage of the labour force			
	1993-94	1994-95	1995-96	1996-97	1993	1994	1995	1996	1993	1994	1995	1996	1993	1994	1995	1996	1994	1995	1996	1997	1994	1995	1996	1997
1. Public employment services and administration	0.03	0.03	0.03	0.03	0.03	0.03	0.03	0.04	–	–	–	–	0.03	0.03	0.03	0.03	0.42	0.37	0.34	0.35	–	–	–	–
2. Labour market training	0.03	0.03	0.03	0.03	0.02	0.01	0.02	0.03	0.4	0.4	0.3	0.4	0.03	0.02	0.02	0.01	0.22	0.17	0.13	0.13	1.2	1.0	0.6	0.6
a) Training for unemployed adults and those at risk	0.03	0.03	0.03	0.03	0.01	0.01	0.01	0.01	0.4	0.3	0.3	0.3	0.03	0.01	0.02	0.01	0.22	0.17	0.13	0.13	1.2	1.0	0.6	0.6
b) Training for employed adults	–	–	–	–	0.01	0.01	0.01	0.02	–	–	–	0.1	–	–	–	–	–	–	–	–	–	–	–	–
3. Youth measures	–	–	–	–	0.03	0.02	0.02	0.02	0.1	0.1	0.1	0.1	0.07	0.09	0.07	0.14	0.09	0.09	0.11	0.10	0.3	0.8	0.8	0.8
a) Measures for unemployed and disadvantaged youth	–				0.03	0.02	0.02	0.02	0.1	0.1	0.1	0.1	0.04	0.05	0.05	0.06	0.05	0.06	0.07	0.06	0.3	0.3	0.3	0.3
b) Support of apprenticeship and related forms of general youth training	–				–				–				0.03	0.04	0.02	0.07	0.04	0.02	0.05	0.04	0.5	0.5	0.5	0.5
4. Subsidised employment	0.03	0.04	0.06	0.04	–	–	–	–	–	–	0.1	0.4	0.01	0.01	0.03	0.06	0.09	0.10	0.27	0.42	0.3	0.4	11.2	12.7
a) Subsidies to regular employment in the private sector	0.03	0.04	0.06	0.04	–				–	–	0.1	0.4	0.01	0.01	0.03	0.05	0.01	0.02	0.14	0.23	0.2	0.2	11.0	12.4
b) Support of unemployed persons starting enterprises	–				–				–				–	–	–	–	–				–			
c) Direct job creation (public or non-profit)	–				–				–				–	–	–	–	0.07	0.08	0.12	0.19	0.1	0.2	0.2	0.2
5. Measures for the disabled	–	–	–	–	0.01	–	–	–	0.1	0.1	0.1	0.2	0.04	0.04	0.05	0.04	0.58	0.55	0.54	0.54	0.1	0.1	0.2	0.2
a) Vocational rehabilitation	–				0.01				–	0.1	0.1	0.1	0.01	0.01	–	–	–	–	–	–	0.1	0.1	0.2	0.2
b) Work for the disabled	–				–				0.1	0.1	0.1	0.1	0.03	0.03	0.04	0.04	0.58	0.55	0.54	0.54				
6. Unemployment compensation	0.30	0.35	0.39	0.40	–	–	–	–					0.28	0.35	0.36	0.41	3.29	3.14	4.06	3.33				
7. Early retirement for labour market reasons	–	–	–	–	–	–	–	–					0.42	0.24	0.24	0.26	–	–	–	–				
TOTAL	**0.39**	**0.45**	**0.52**	**0.50**	**0.08**	**0.06**	**0.08**	**0.09**					**0.88**	**0.78**	**0.80**	**0.95**	**4.69**	**4.42**	**5.44**	**4.86**				
Active measures (1-5)	0.09	0.10	0.13	0.10	0.08	0.06	0.08	0.09					0.19	0.19	0.20	0.27	1.40	1.28	1.38	1.53				
Passive measures (6 and 7)	0.30	0.35	0.39	0.40	–	–	–	–					0.69	0.59	0.60	0.67	3.29	3.14	4.06	3.33				
For reference:																								
GDP (national currency, at current prices, 10^9)	476.7	479.0	488.9	503.7	267 146.0	305 970.2	351 974.7	389 979.2					444.3	487.7	509.7	525.4	614.3	638.4	667.6	705.1				
Labour Force (10^3)					19 803	20 326	20 797	21 188									7 184	7 410	7 517	7 618				

a) Fiscal year starts on April 1; and national currency at current prices 10^12 in Japan.

Table J. **Public expenditures and participant inflows in labour market programmes in OECD countries** (cont.)

Programme categories	New Zealand[a] Public expenditures as a percentage of GDP				New Zealand[a] Participant inflows as a percentage of the labour force				Norway Public expenditures as a percentage of GDP				Norway Participant inflows as a percentage of the labour force				Poland Public expenditures as a percentage of GDP				Poland Participant inflows as a percentage of the labour force			
	1993-94	1994-95	1995-96	1996-97	1993-94	1994-95	1995-96	1996-97	1994	1995	1996	1997	1994	1995	1996	1997	1993	1994	1995	1996	1993	1994	1995	1996
1. Public employment services and administration	0.11	0.11	0.13	0.15					0.18	0.18	0.16	0.16					0.02	0.01	0.01	0.02				
2. Labour market training	0.39	0.36	0.32	0.31	5.2	5.5	5.5	5.3	0.28	0.23	0.18	0.17	3.6	2.8	2.1	1.6	0.03	0.03	0.02	0.02	0.4	0.5	0.5	0.5
a) Training for unemployed adults and those at risk	0.39	0.36	0.32	0.31	5.2	5.5	5.5	5.3	0.28	0.23	0.18	0.17	3.6	2.8	2.1	1.6	0.03	0.03	0.02	0.02	0.4	0.5	0.5	0.5
b) Training for employed adults	–	–	–	–	–	–	–	–	–	–	–	–	–	–	–	–	–	–	–	–	–	–	–	–
3. Youth measures	0.07	0.08	0.09	0.10	0.3	..	2.0	..	0.11	0.08	0.06	0.04	..	..	1.1	0.8	0.09	0.07	0.08	0.10	1.9	1.5	1.9	1.9
a) Measures for unemployed and disadvantaged youth	0.03	0.01	0.02	0.02	0.1	0.2	0.2	..	0.11	0.08	0.06	0.04	..	..	1.1	0.8	–	0.01	0.02	0.03	–	–	0.1	0.2
b) Support of apprenticeship and related forms of general youth training	0.04	0.07	0.08	0.08	0.3	..	1.8	1.8	–	–	–	–	–	–	–	–	0.08	0.06	0.06	0.06	1.8	1.5	1.7	1.7
4. Subsidised employment	0.19	0.15	0.14	0.14	2.7	2.5	2.2	2.2	0.28	0.22	0.15	0.07	0.6	..	1.0	0.5	0.20	0.24	0.21	0.16	1.2	1.8	2.0	1.6
a) Subsidies to regular employment in the private sector	0.09	0.10	0.09	0.09	1.4	1.5	1.3	1.2	0.09	0.08	0.06	0.04	0.1	..	0.3	0.3	0.10	0.13	0.12	0.08	0.8	1.2	1.2	0.8
b) Support of unemployed persons starting enterprises	0.05	0.02	0.01	0.02	0.2	–	–	–	–	–	–	–	–	–	0.4	0.1	0.02	0.02	0.02	0.02	–	–	–	–
c) Direct job creation (public or non-profit)	0.05	0.04	0.03	0.04	1.2	0.9	0.9	1.0	0.19	0.14	0.09	0.03	0.6	..	0.2	0.1	0.08	0.10	0.08	0.07	0.4	0.6	0.7	0.7
5. Measures for the disabled	0.05	0.03	0.03	0.03	1.5	..	1.7	..	0.48	0.63	0.61	0.47	..	..	..	..	0.05	0.04	0.01	0.01	0.2	0.8	0.1	0.1
a) Vocational rehabilitation	0.01	0.01	0.01	0.02	1.5	–	0.7	..	0.19	0.29	0.29	0.22	..	..	..	..	0.01	0.01	0.01	–	0.2	0.3	0.1	0.1
b) Work for the disabled	0.04	0.01	0.01	0.02	–	–	1.1	–	0.29	0.34	0.31	0.26	..	..	..	..	0.04	0.04	0.01	0.01	–	0.4	–	0.1
6. Unemployment compensation	1.59	1.26	1.14	1.17					1.32	1.10	0.90	0.70					1.72	1.77	1.88	1.77				
7. Early retirement for labour market reasons	–	–	–	–					–	–	–	–					0.15	0.10	0.05	0.05				
TOTAL	**2.39**	**2.00**	**1.85**	**1.91**	9.8	..	11.5	..	**2.66**	**2.44**	**2.06**	**1.60**	..	..	4.1	3.0	**2.25**	**2.27**	**2.27**	**2.14**	3.7	4.7	4.4	4.1
Active measures (1-5)	0.80	0.74	0.71	0.73					1.34	1.34	1.16	0.91					0.38	0.39	0.34	0.32				
Passive measures (6 and 7)	1.59	1.26	1.14	1.17					1.32	1.10	0.90	0.70					1.87	1.87	1.93	1.82				
For reference: GDP (national currency, at current prices, 10^9)	82.3	88.1	92.1	95.8					867.6	929.0	1 017.8	1 085.1					155.8	210.4	286.0	362.2				
Labour Force (10^3)	1 684	1 728	1 782	1 816					2 151	2 186	2 246	2 292					17 321	17 132	17 068	17 034				

a) Fiscal year starts on July 1 in New Zealand

Table J. **Public expenditures and participant inflows in labour market programmes in OECD countries** (cont.)

Programme categories	Portugal — Public expenditures as a percentage of GDP				Portugal — Participant inflows as a percentage of the labour force				Spain — Public expenditures as a percentage of GDP				Spain — Participant inflows as a percentage of the labour force				Sweden[a] — Public expenditures as a percentage of GDP				Sweden[a] — Participant inflows as a percentage of the labour force			
	1993	1994	1995	1996	1993	1994	1995	1996	1994	1995	1996	1997	1994	1995	1996	1997	1993-94	1994-95	1995-96	1997	1993-94	1994-95	1995-96	1997
1. **Public employment services and administration**	0.10	0.11	0.11	0.11					0.10	0.09	0.09	0.08					0.25	0.27	0.26	0.26				
2. **Labour market training**	0.26	0.21	0.24	0.31	1.3	2.0	4.2	4.2	0.22	0.32	0.35	0.14	0.7	0.8	0.8	0.8	0.76	0.77	0.55	0.43	4.3	4.4	4.6	4.2
a) Training for unemployed adults and those at risk	0.04	0.05	0.05	0.05	0.2	0.4	0.2	0.3	0.17	0.24	0.26	0.11	0.4	0.5	0.5	0.6	0.73	0.75	0.54	0.43	3.4	3.7	3.9	3.7
b) Training for employed adults	0.22	0.16	0.19	0.25	1.1	1.5	4.0	3.9	0.06	0.08	0.09	0.04	0.2	0.3	0.3	0.3	0.03	0.02	0.02	0.01	0.9	0.7	0.6	0.5
3. **Youth measures**	0.35	0.28	0.35	0.34	2.6	2.0	2.0	2.7	0.09	0.09	0.08	0.07	0.3	0.3	0.3	0.3	0.31	0.23	0.02	0.02	3.4	2.5	0.7	0.7
a) Measures for unemployed and disadvantaged youth	0.22	0.15	0.15	0.16	1.5	1.1	1.1	1.3	0.09	0.09	0.08	0.07	0.3	0.3	0.3	0.3	0.31	0.23	0.02	0.02	3.4	2.5	0.7	0.7
b) Support of apprenticeship and related forms of general youth training	0.13	0.14	0.19	0.18	1.1	0.9	0.9	1.4	–	–	–	–	–	–	–	–	–	–	–	–	–	–	–	–
4. **Subsidised employment**	0.10	0.05	0.09	0.12	0.4	0.6	0.7	0.9	0.17	0.31	0.14	0.20	1.2	1.2	1.5	1.6	0.87	0.90	0.82	0.70	6.6	6.1	7.7	7.5
a) Subsidies to regular employment in the private sector	–	–	0.03	0.07	–	–	0.1	0.4	0.11	0.24	0.08	0.11	0.1	–	–	–	0.22	0.27	0.32	0.20	2.1	2.1	3.6	3.2
b) Support of unemployed persons starting enterprises	0.08	0.04	0.03	0.01	0.2	0.2	0.2	0.1	0.02	0.01	0.01	0.03	0.2	0.1	0.1	0.1	0.06	0.09	0.07	0.08	0.4	0.5	0.4	0.5
c) Direct job creation (public or non-profit)	0.02	0.01	0.03	0.03	0.1	0.5	0.4	0.5	0.04	0.05	0.05	0.06	1.0	1.0	1.3	1.5	0.58	0.54	0.43	0.42	4.1	3.6	3.6	3.8
5. **Measures for the disabled**	0.05	0.06	0.05	0.07	0.2	0.1	0.1	0.1	0.01	0.01	0.01	0.02	0.1	0.1	0.1	0.2	0.79	0.82	0.70	0.67	1.2	1.4	0.9	1.0
a) Vocational rehabilitation	0.05	0.05	0.04	0.05	0.1	0.1	0.1	0.1	–	–	–	–	–	–	–	–	0.09	0.10	0.08	0.08	0.7	0.8	0.6	0.6
b) Work for the disabled	–	0.01	0.01	0.03	–	–	–	–	0.01	0.01	0.01	0.02	0.1	0.1	0.1	0.2	0.70	0.72	0.62	0.59	0.6	0.6	0.3	0.4
6. **Unemployment compensation**	0.82	0.97	0.88	0.89					3.09	2.46	2.12	1.87					2.71	2.51	2.26	2.16				
7. **Early retirement for labour market reasons**	0.11	0.15 l	0.08	0.13					–	–	–	–					0.05	0.02	–	–				
TOTAL	1.80	1.83	1.79	1.97	4.4	4.7	7.1	8.0	3.68	3.27	2.79	2.37	2.2	2.4	2.8	2.9	5.73	5.52	4.62	4.25	15.5	14.4	13.8	13.5
Active measures (1-5)	0.87	0.71	0.83	0.95					0.59	0.81	0.67	0.50					2.97	2.99	2.36	2.09				
Passive measures (6 and 7)	0.94	1.12	0.96	1.02					3.09	2.46	2.12	1.87					2.76	2.53	2.26	2.16				
For reference:																								
GDP (national currency, at current prices, 10^9)	13 209.6	14 082.6	15 073.2	15 975.7					65 271.1	70 233.0	74 081.8	78 325.5					1 482.8	1 592.9	2 517.4	1 738.9				
Labour Force (10^3)	4 722	4 820	4 802	4 885					15 701	15 849	16 159	16 332					4 275	4 296	4 325	4 257				

a) Fiscal year used to start on July 1 in Sweden. From 1997, it starts on January 1. The 1995-96 fiscal year lasts 18 months, from July 1, 1995 to December 31, 1996. The 1995-96 GDP is for 18 months, the 1995-96 labour force is an average of the 6 quarters concerned

Table J. **Public expenditures and participant inflows in labour market programmes in OECD countries** *(cont.)*

Programme categories	Switzerland — Public expenditures as a percentage of GDP 1994	1995	1996	1997	Participant inflows as a percentage of the labour force 1994	1995	United Kingdom[a] — Public expenditures as a percentage of GDP 1993-94	1994-95	1995-96	1996-97	Participant inflows as a percentage of the labour force 1993-94	1994-95	1995-96	1996-97	United States[b] — Public expenditures as a percentage of GDP 1993-94	1994-95	1995-96	1996-97	Participant inflows as a percentage of the labour force 1995-96	1996-97
1. Public employment services and administration	**0.11**	**0.11**	**0.12**	**0.15**			**0.24**	**0.22**	**0.20**	**0.18**					**0.08**	**0.07**	**0.08**	**0.06**		
2. Labour market training	**0.08**	**0.09**	**0.06**	**0.23**	**1.3**	**1.5**	**0.15**	**0.14**	**0.10**	**0.09**	**1.3**	**1.3**	**1.0**	**1.0**	**0.04**	**0.04**	**0.04**	**0.04**	**0.7**	**0.8**
a) Training for unemployed adults and those at risk	0.08	0.08	0.06	0.23	1.2	1.5	0.14	0.13	0.09	0.08	1.2	1.2	0.9	0.9	0.04	0.04	0.04	0.04	0.7	0.8
b) Training for employed adults	–	–	–	–	0.1	–	0.01	0.01	0.01	0.01	0.1	0.1	–	–	–	–	–	–	–	–
3. Youth measures	–	–	–	–	–	–	**0.14**	**0.14**	**0.12**	**0.13**	**0.8**	**0.9**	**1.0**	**1.2**	**0.04**	**0.03**	**0.03**	**0.03**	..	**0.6**
a) Measures for unemployed and disadvantaged youth	–	–	–	–	–	–	–	–	–	–	–	–	–	–	0.04	0.03	0.03	0.03	0.4	0.5
b) Support of apprenticeship and related forms of general youth training	–	–	–	–	–	–	0.14	0.14	0.12	0.12	0.8	0.8	1.0	1.1	–	–	–	–	..	0.1
4. Subsidised employment	**0.05**	**0.09**	**0.16**	**0.23**	**0.6**	**0.7**	**0.02**	**0.03**	**0.02**	–	**0.2**	**0.3**	**0.1**	–	**0.01**	**0.01**	**0.01**	**0.01**	..	..
a) Subsidies to regular employment in the private sector	0.01	0.01	0.01	0.01	0.1	0.1	–	–	–	–	–	–	–	–	–	0.01	–	–	..	..
b) Support of unemployed persons starting enterprises	–	–	–	–	–	–	–	0.01	–	–	0.1	0.1	–	–	–	–	–	–	..	..
c) Direct job creation (public or non-profit)	0.04	0.08	0.16	0.22	0.5	0.5	0.02	0.01	0.01	–	0.1	0.2	0.1	–	0.01	0.01	–	0.01	0.1	..
5. Measures for the disabled	**0.20**	**0.19**	**0.19**	**0.15**	**0.3**	**0.3**	**0.03**	**0.03**	**0.03**	**0.02**	**0.1**	**0.2**	**0.2**	**0.2**	**0.04**	**0.04**	**0.04**	**0.03**	..	..
a) Vocational rehabilitation	0.14	0.15	0.15	0.15	0.3	0.3	–	–	–	–	0.1	0.1	0.1	0.1	0.04	0.04	0.04	0.03	..	..
b) Work for the disabled	0.05	0.05	0.04	–	–	–	0.02	0.02	0.02	0.02	0.1	0.1	0.1	0.1	–	–	–	–	–	–
6. Unemployment compensation	**1.41**	**1.15**	**1.28**	**1.42**			**1.60**	**1.41**	**1.26**	**1.05**					**0.43**	**0.35**	**0.34**	**0.26**		
7. Early retirement for labour market reasons	–	–	–	–			–	–	–	–					–	–	–	–		
TOTAL	**1.85**	**1.63**	**1.81**	**2.18**	**2.1**	**2.5**	**2.18**	**1.95**	**1.72**	**1.47**	**2.5**	**2.6**	**2.3**	**2.4**	**0.65**	**0.55**	**0.53**	**0.43**		
Active measures (1-5)	0.44	0.48	0.53	0.76			0.57	0.54	0.46	0.42					0.21	0.20	0.19	0.17		
Passive measures (6 and 7)	1.41	1.15	1.28	1.42			1.60	1.41	1.26	1.05					0.43	0.35	0.34	0.26		
For reference: GDP (national currency, at current prices, 10^9)	357.2	364.6	363.8	366.7			625.6	663.1	697.0	735.0					6 849.1	7 193.9	7 533.3	7 971.3		
Labour Force (10^3)					3 941	3 937					27 516	27 416	27 352	27 475					134 652	137 075

a) Excluding Northern Ireland; fiscal year starts on April 1 in the United Kingdom.
b) Fiscal year starts on October 1 in the United States.
Source: OECD Database on labour market programmes.

LABOUR MARKET AND SOCIAL POLICY OCCASIONAL PAPERS

Already available, free of charge

Most recent releases are:

No. 18 ENHANCING THE EFFECTIVENESS OF ACTIVE LABOUR MARKET POLICIES: EVIDENCE FROM PROGRAMME EVALUATIONS IN OECD COUNTRIES (1996) (Robert G. Fay)

No. 19 NET PUBLIC SOCIAL EXPENDITURE (1996)
(Willem Adema, Marcel Einerhand, Bengt Eklind, Jórgen Lotz and Mark Pearson)

No. 20 OCCUPATIONAL CLASSIFICATION (ISCO-88): CONCEPTS, METHODS, RELIABILITY, VALIDITY AND CROSS-NATIONAL COMPARABILITY (1997) (Peter Elias) *Available in French*

No. 21 PRIVATE PENSIONS IN OECD COUNTRIES – THE UNITED KINGDOM (1997)
(E. Philip Davis) *Available in French*

No. 22 THE DEFINITION OF PART-TIME WORK FOR THE PURPOSE OF INTERNATIONAL COMPARISONS (1997) (Alois van Bastelaer, Eurostat; Georges Lemaître, Pascal Marianna) *Available in French*

No. 23 PRIVATE PENSIONS IN OECD COUNTRIES – AUSTRALIA (1997)
(Hazel Bateman and John Piggott)

No. 24 TRENDS IN SECRETARIAL OCCUPATIONS IN SELECTED COUNTRIES (1980-95)
(Hilary Steedman) (1997)

No. 25 MAKING THE PUBLIC EMPLOYMENT SERVICE MORE EFFECTIVE THROUGH THE INTRODUCTION OF MARKET SIGNALS (1997) (Robert G. Fay)

No. 26 THE CONCENTRATION OF WOMEN'S EMPLOYMENT AND RELATIVE OCCUPATIONAL PAY:
A STATISTICAL FRAMEWORK FOR COMPARATIVE ANALYSIS (1997)
(Damian Grimshaw and Jill Rubery)

No. 27 CHILDCARE AND ELDERLY CARE: WHAT OCCUPATIONAL OPPORTUNITIES FOR WOMEN? (1997)
(Susan Christopherson)

No. 28 OECD SUBMISSION TO THE IRISH NATIONAL MINIMUM WAGE COMMISSION (1997)

No. 29 OECD SUBMISSION TO THE UK LOW PAY MISSION (1997)

No. 30 PRIVATE PENSIONS IN OECD COUNTRIES – FRANCE (1997)
(Emmanuel Reynaud) *Available in French*

No. 31 KEY EMPLOYMENT POLICY CHALLENGES FACED BY OECD COUNTRIES (1998) OECD SUBMISSION TO THE G8 GROWTH, EMPLOYABILITY AND INCLUSION CONFERENCE
– London, 21-22 February 1998

No. 32 THE GROWING ROLE OF PRIVATE SOCIAL BENEFITS (1998)
(Willem Adema and Marcel Einerhand)

Mailing List for Labour Market and Social Policy Occasional Papers

Please include the following name on the mailing list:
(write in capitals)

Name . . . .
Organisation . . . .
Address . . . .
Country . . . .

This form should be returned to:
Labour Market and Social Policy Occasional Papers
Directorate for Education, Employment, Labour and Social Affairs, Office 110
OECD, 2, rue André-Pascal, 75775 Paris Cedex 16, France

Information also available on Internet: http://www.oecd.org/els/papers/papers.htm

ALSO AVAILABLE

Flexible Working Time: Collective Bargaining and Government Intervention (1995)
(81 19 95 011 P 1) ISBN 92-64-14316-5   FF 195   US$38   DM 59

Human Capital Investment: An International Comparison (1998)
(96 19 98 021 P 1) ISBN 92-64-16067-1   FF 150   US$25   DM 45

Making Work Pay: Taxation, Benefits, Employment and Unemployment (1997)
(21 19 97 091 P 1) ISBN 92-64-15666-6   FF 95   US$19   DM 28

Pathways and Participation in Vocational and Technical Education and Training (1998)
(91 19 98 011 P 1) ISBN 92-64-15368-3   FF 240   US$47   DM 70

Education Policy Analysis (1997)
(96 19 97 051 P 1) ISBN 92-64-15682-8   FF 50   US$8   DM 15

Literacy Skills for the Knowledge Society: Further Results from the International Adult Literacy survey (1997)
(81 19 97 071 P 1) ISBN 92-64-15624-0   FF 180   US$30   DM 53

Labour Market Policies: New Challenges Policies for Low-Paid Workers and Unskilled Job Seekers (1997)
General distribution document   Free of charge

Prices charged at the OECD Bookshop.
The OECD CATALOGUE OF PUBLICATIONS and supplements will be sent free of charge
on request addressed either to OECD Publications Service,
or to the OECD Distributor in your country.

OECD PUBLICATIONS, 2, rue André-Pascal, 75775 PARIS CEDEX 16
PRINTED IN FRANCE
(81 98 06 1 P) ISBN 92-64-16077-9 – No. 50073 1998